MY HERO ACADEMIA

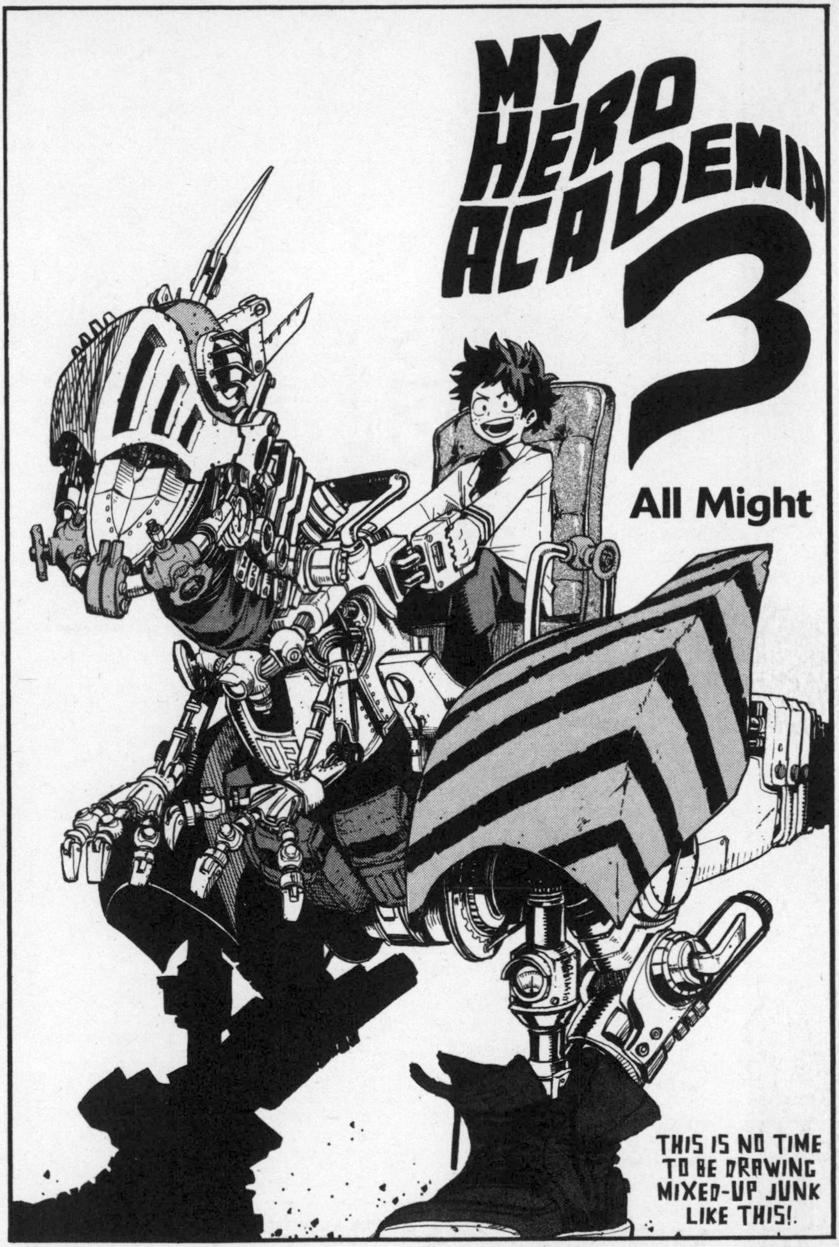
MY HERO ACADEMIA
3
All Might
THIS IS NO TIME TO BE DRAWING MIXED-UP JUNK LIKE THIS!.

KOHEI HORIKOSHI

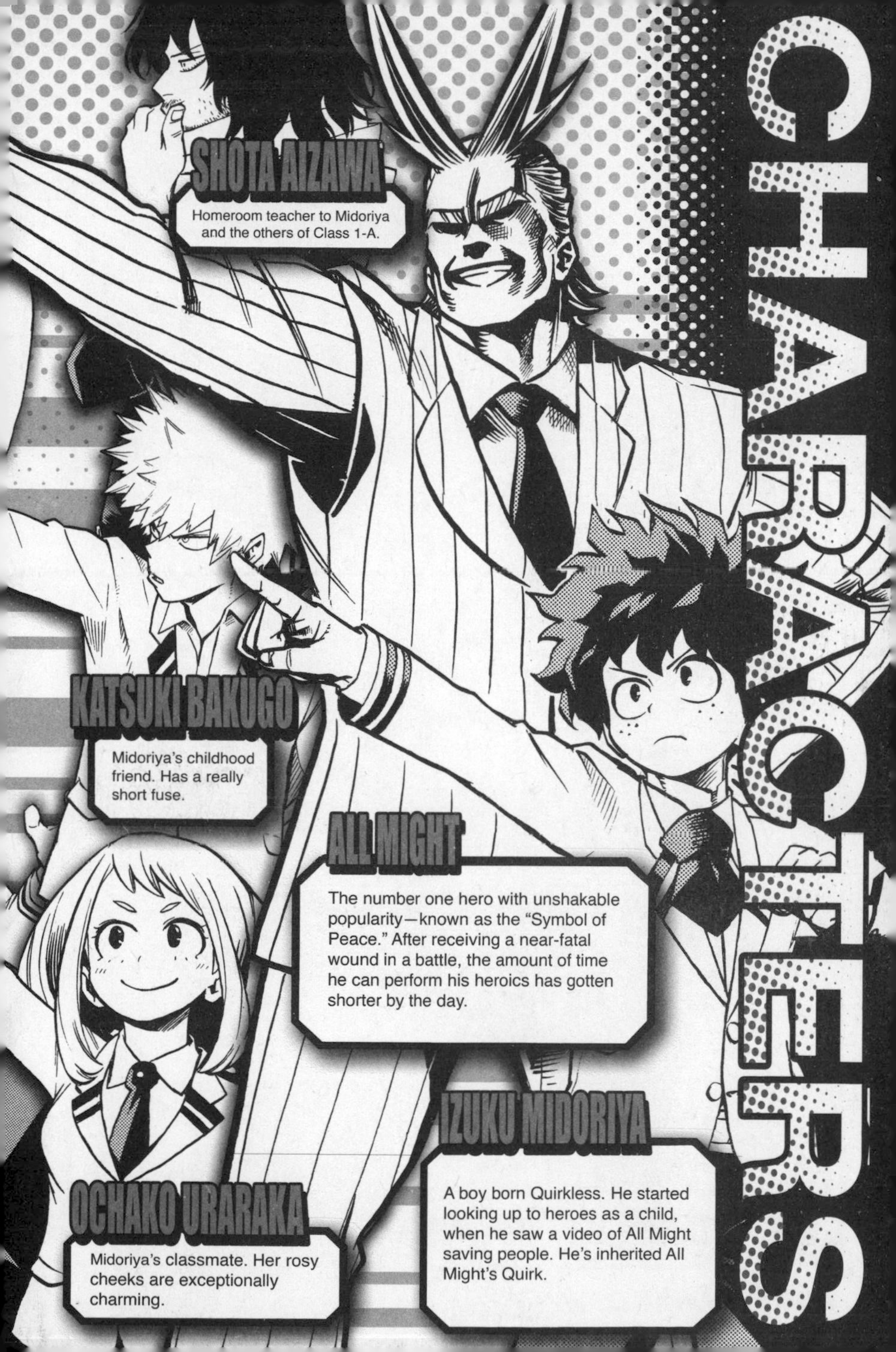
CHARACTERS
SHOTA AIZAWA
Homeroom teacher to Midoriya and the others of Class 1-A.
KATSUKI BAKUGO
Midoriya's childhood friend. Has a really short fuse.
ALL MIGHT
The number one hero with unshakable popularity—known as the "Symbol of Peace." After receiving a near-fatal wound in a battle, the amount of time he can perform his heroics has gotten shorter by the day.
IZUKU MIDORIYA
A boy born Quirkless. He started looking up to heroes as a child, when he saw a video of All Might saving people. He's inherited All Might's Quirk.
OCHAKO URARAKA
Midoriya's classmate. Her rosy cheeks are exceptionally charming.

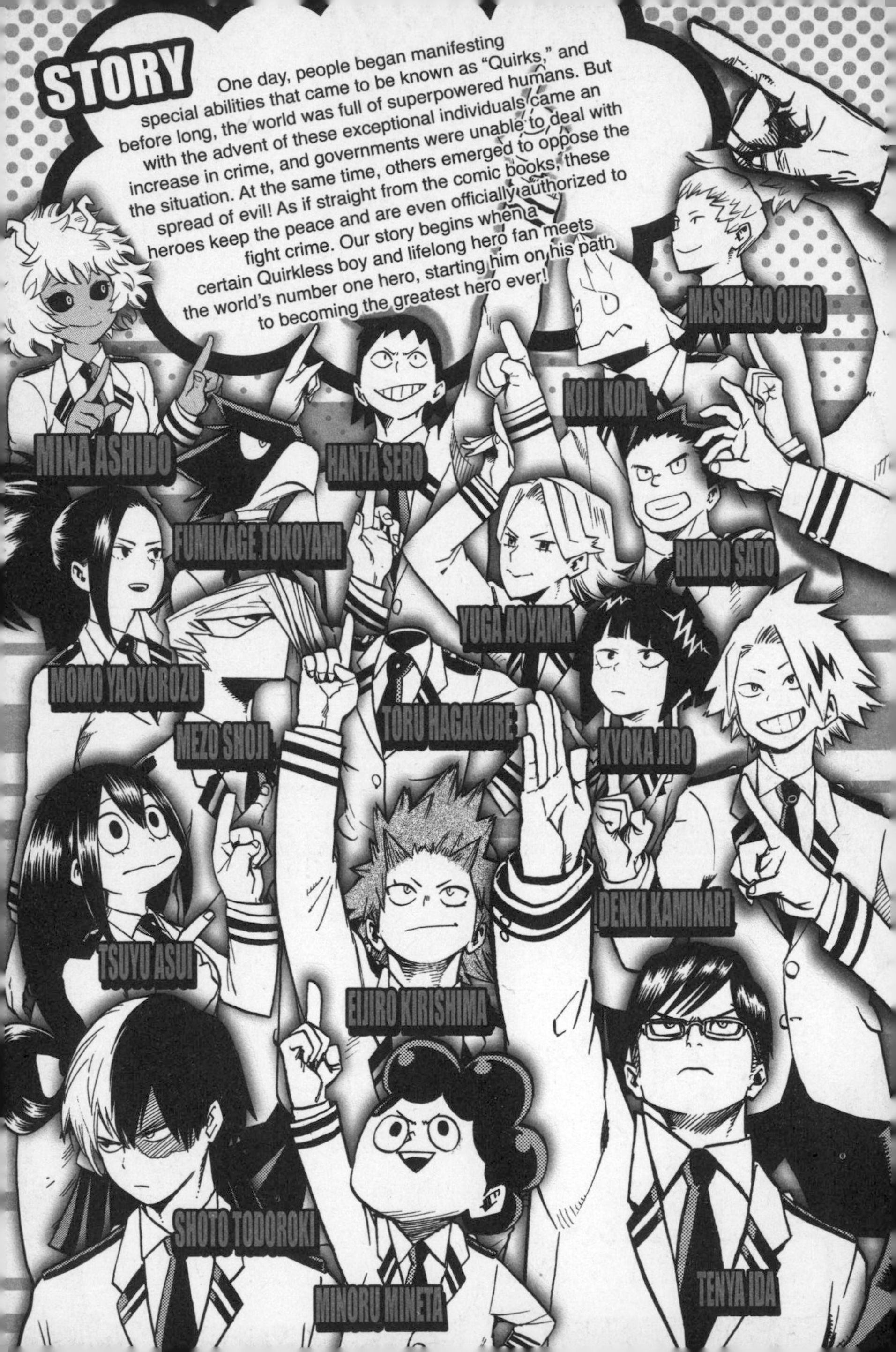
STORY
One day, people began manifesting special abilities that came to be known as "Quirks," and before long, the world was full of superpowered humans. But with the advent of these exceptional individuals came an increase in crime, and governments were unable to deal with the situation. At the same time, others emerged to oppose the spread of evil! As if straight from the comic books, these heroes keep the peace and are even officially authorized to fight crime. Our story begins when a certain Quirkless boy and lifelong hero fan meets the world's number one hero, starting him on his path to becoming the greatest hero ever!
MASHIRAO OJIRO
KOJI KODA
HANTA SERO
MINA ASHIDO
RIKIDO SATO
FUMIKAGE TOKOYAMI
YUGA AOYAMA
MOMO YAOYOROZU
KYOKA JIRO
TORU HAGAKURE
MEZO SHOJI
DENKI KAMINARI
TSUYU ASUI
EIJIRO KIRISHIMA
SHOTO TODOROKI
TENYA IDA
MINORU MINETA

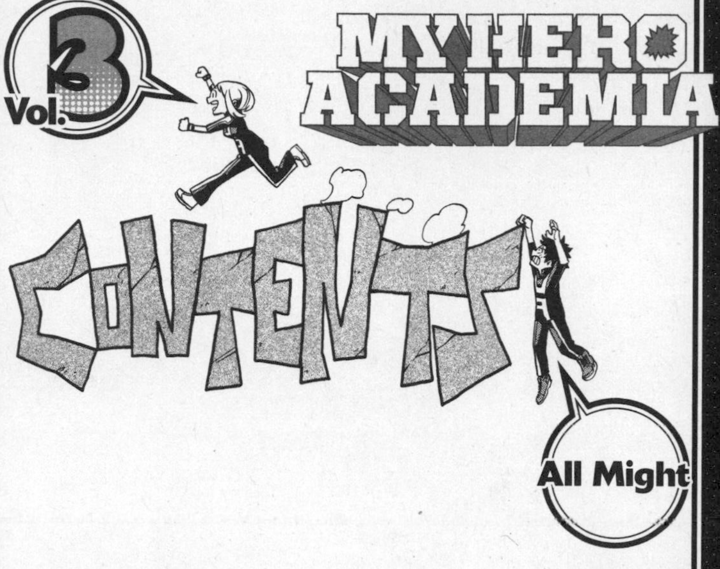
Vol. 3
MY HERO ACADEMIA
CONTENTS
All Might

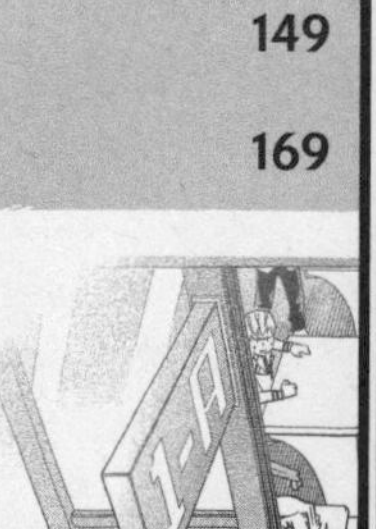
1-A

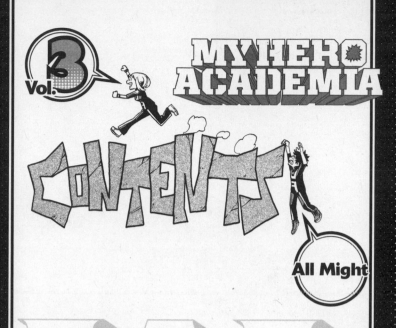

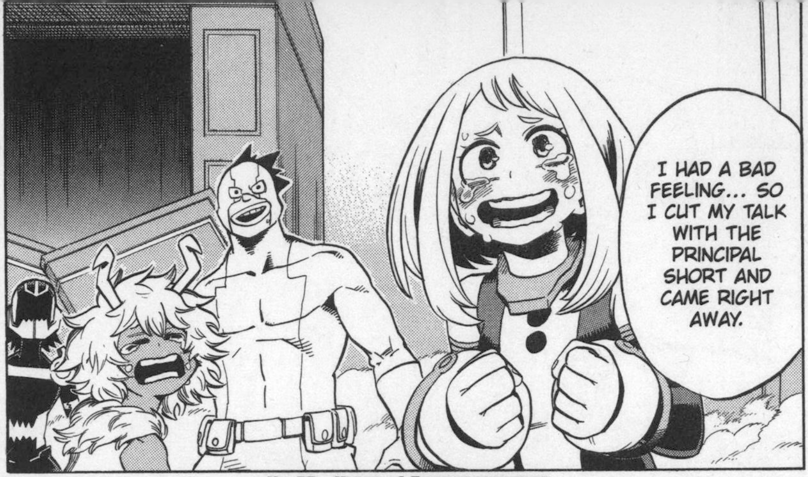
I HAD A BAD FEELING... SO I CUT MY TALK WITH THE PRINCIPAL SHORT AND CAME RIGHT AWAY.

No.18 - Heroes' Counterattack

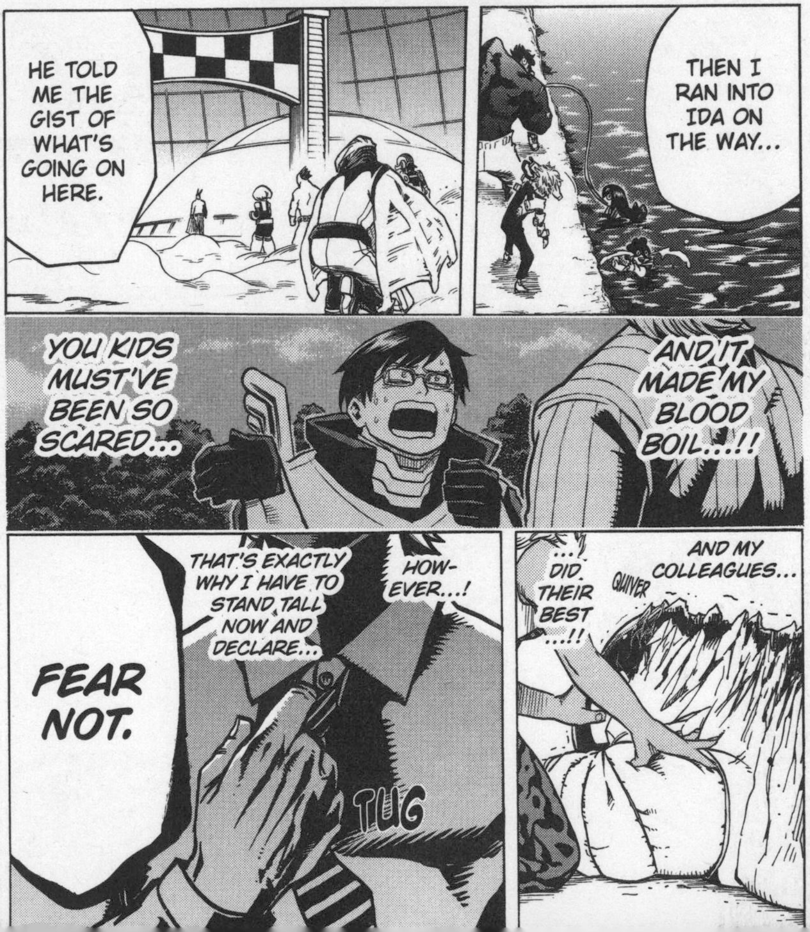
THEN I RAN INTO IDA ON THE WAY...
HE TOLD ME THE GIST OF WHAT'S GOING ON HERE.
AND IT MADE MY BLOOD BOIL...!!
YOU KIDS MUST'VE BEEN SO SCARED...
AND MY COLLEAGUES...
QUIVER
...DID THEIR BEST ...!!
HOW-EVER...!
THAT'S EXACTLY WHY I HAVE TO STAND TALL NOW AND DECLARE...
TUG
FEAR NOT.

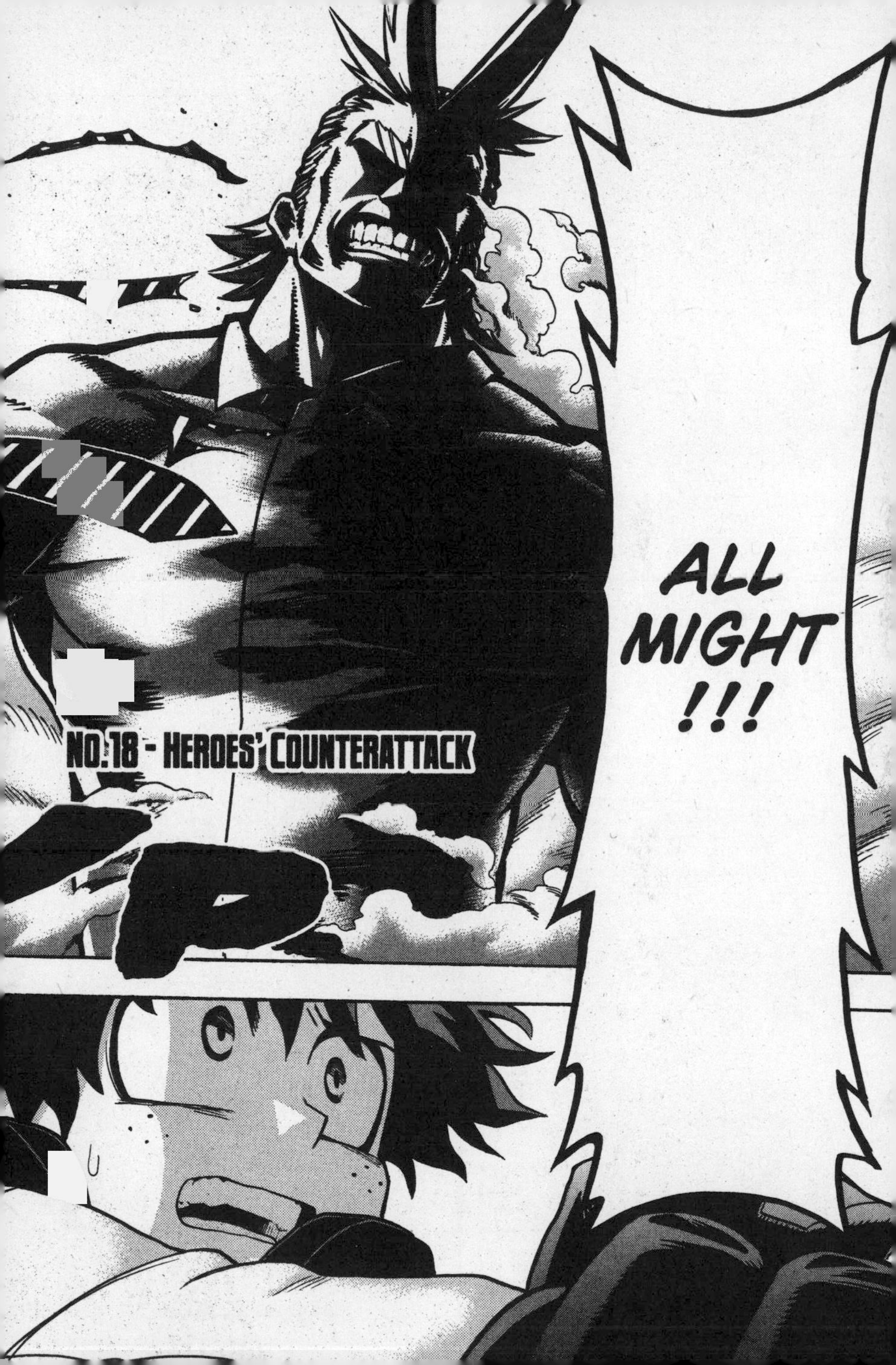
ALL MIGHT !!!
No.18 - Heroes' Counterattack

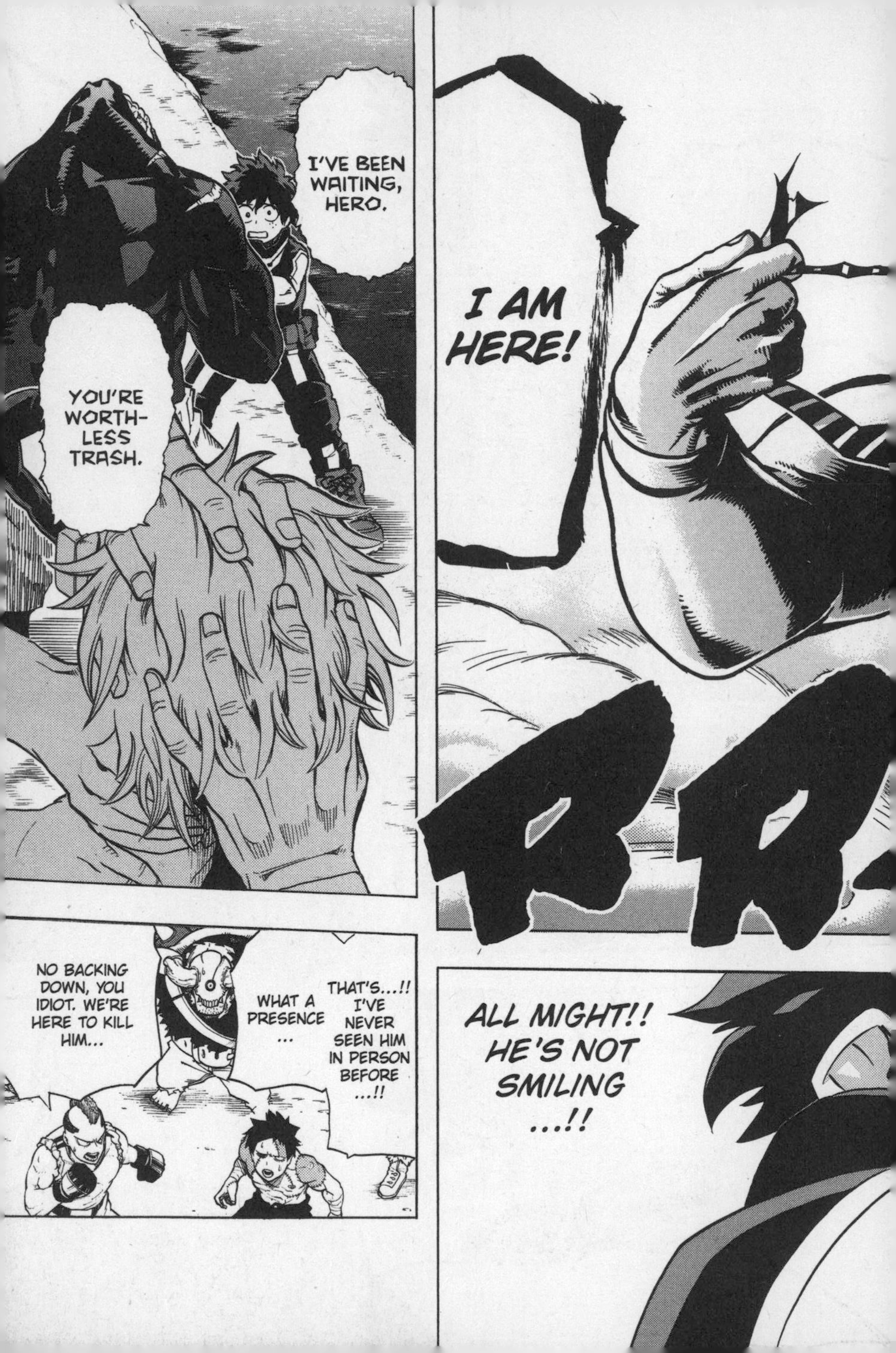
I AM HERE!
I'VE BEEN WAITING, HERO.
YOU'RE WORTHLESS TRASH.
THAT'S...!! I'VE NEVER SEEN HIM IN PERSON BEFORE ...!!
WHAT A PRESENCE ...
NO BACKING DOWN, YOU IDIOT. WE'RE HERE TO KILL HIM...
ALL MIGHT!! HE'S NOT SMILING ...!!

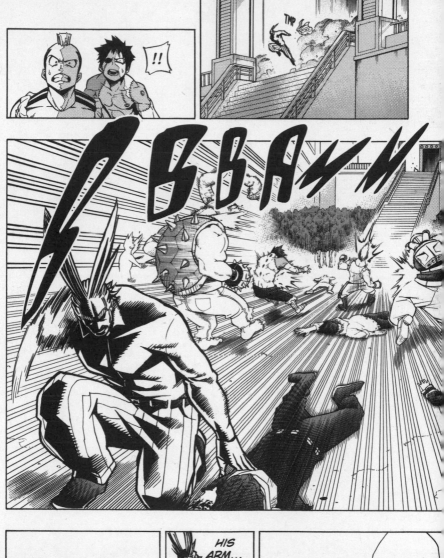

!!

SBBAWW

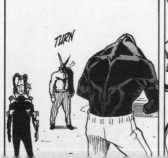

TURN

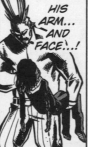

HIS ARM... AND FACE...!

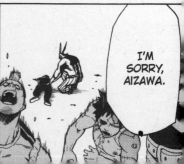

I'M SORRY, AIZAWA.

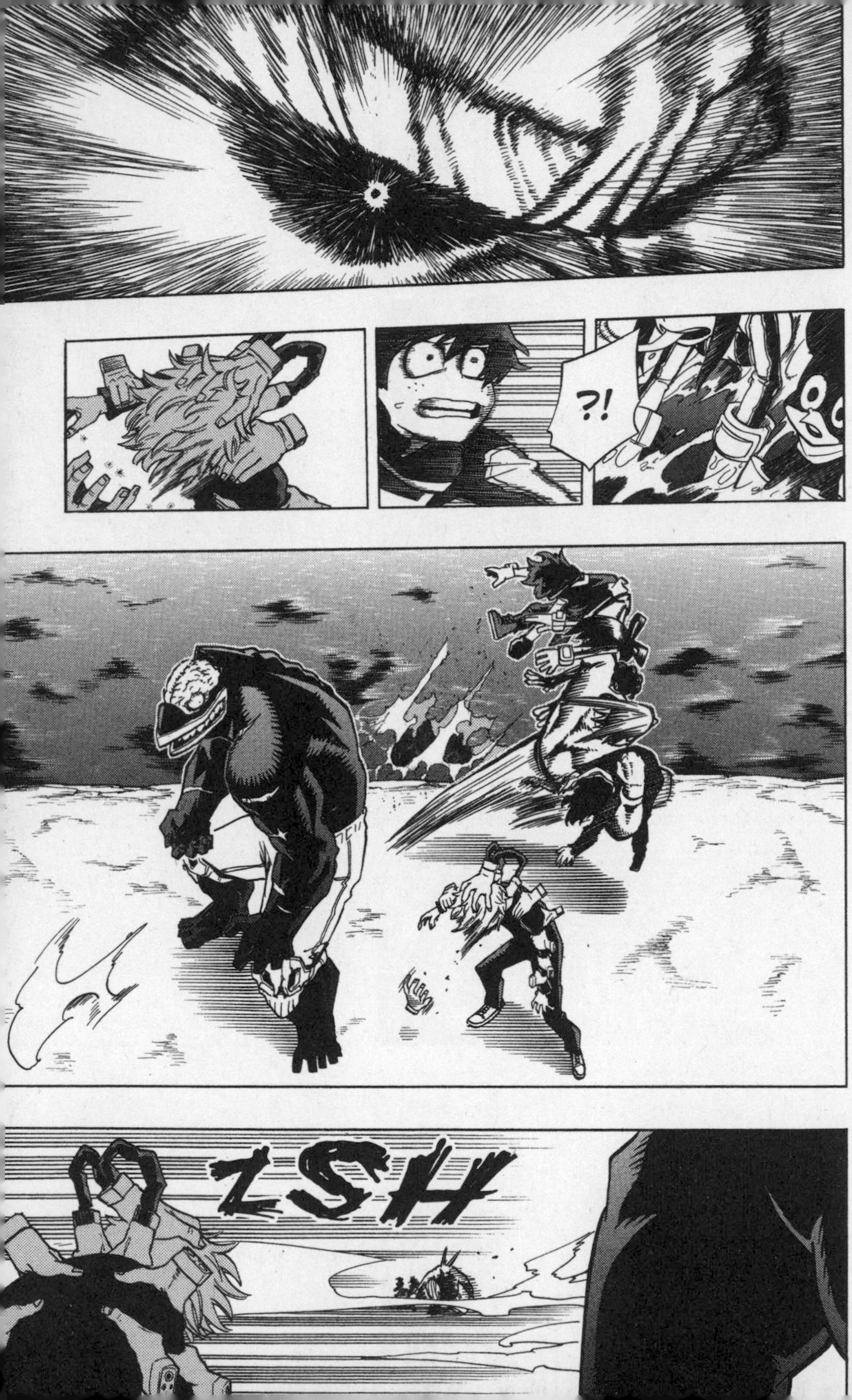
?!
ZSH

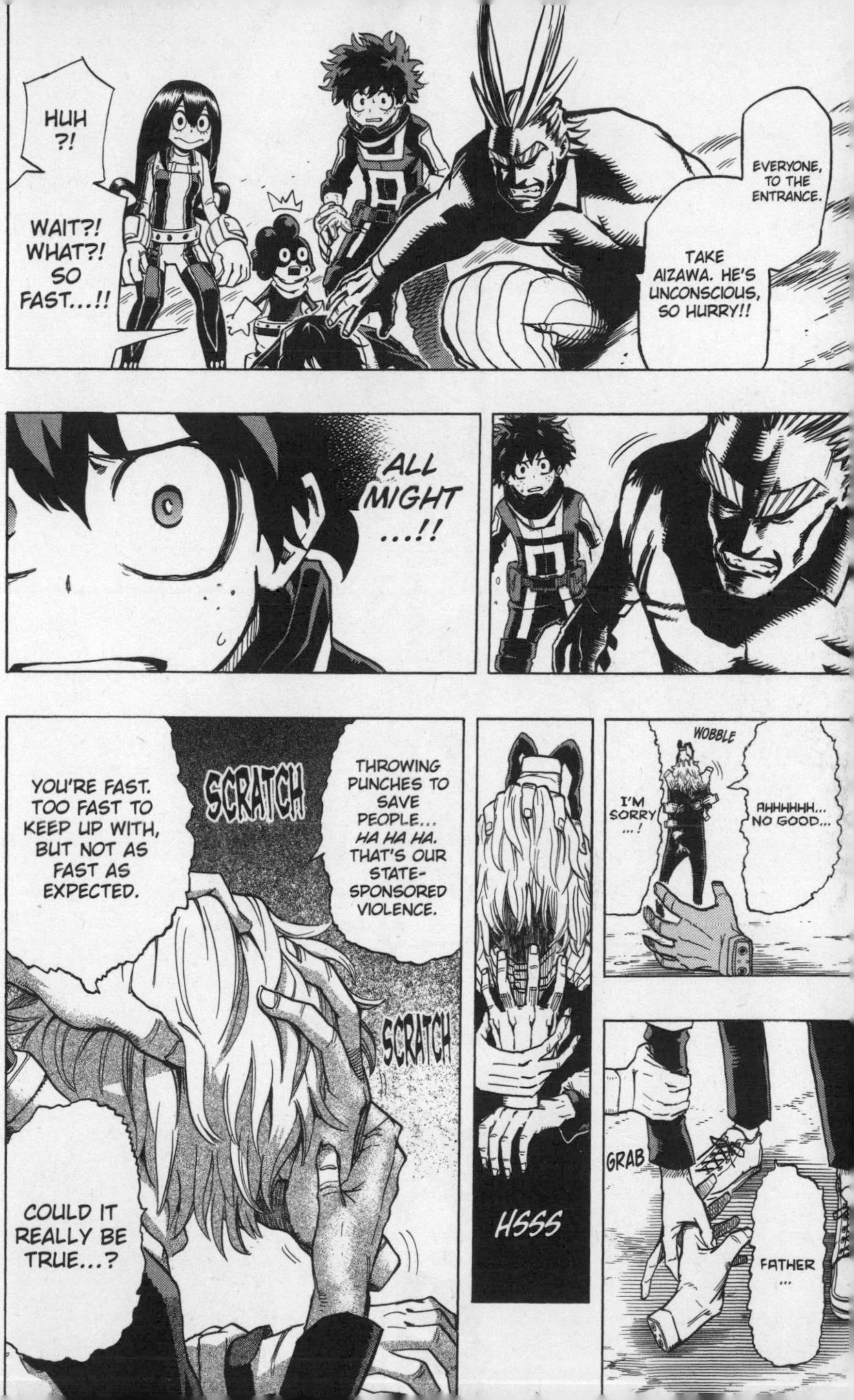
EVERYONE, TO THE ENTRANCE.
TAKE AIZAWA. HE'S UNCONSCIOUS, SO HURRY!!
HUH ?!
WAIT?! WHAT?! SO FAST...!!
ALL MIGHT ...!!
WOBBLE
AHHHHHH... NO GOOD...
I'M SORRY ...!
GRAB
FATHER ...
HSSS
THROWING PUNCHES TO SAVE PEOPLE... *HA HA HA.* THAT'S OUR STATE-SPONSORED VIOLENCE.
SCRATCH
YOU'RE FAST. TOO FAST TO KEEP UP WITH, BUT NOT AS FAST AS EXPECTED.
SCRATCH
COULD IT REALLY BE TRUE...?

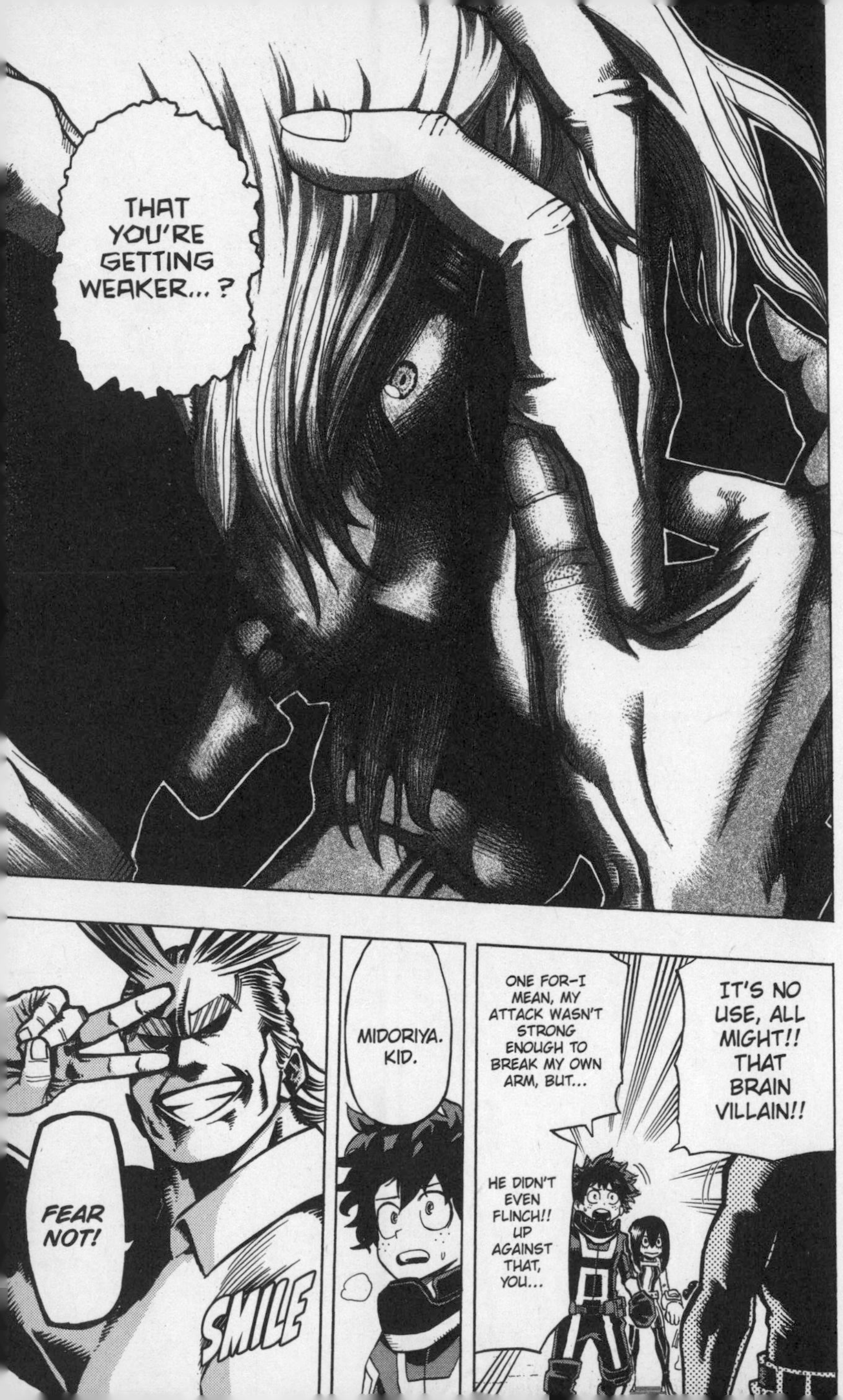
THAT YOU'RE GETTING WEAKER...?
IT'S NO USE, ALL MIGHT!! THAT BRAIN VILLAIN!!
ONE FOR—I MEAN, MY ATTACK WASN'T STRONG ENOUGH TO BREAK MY OWN ARM, BUT...
HE DIDN'T EVEN FLINCH!! UP AGAINST THAT, YOU...
MIDORIYA. KID.
FEAR NOT!
SMILE

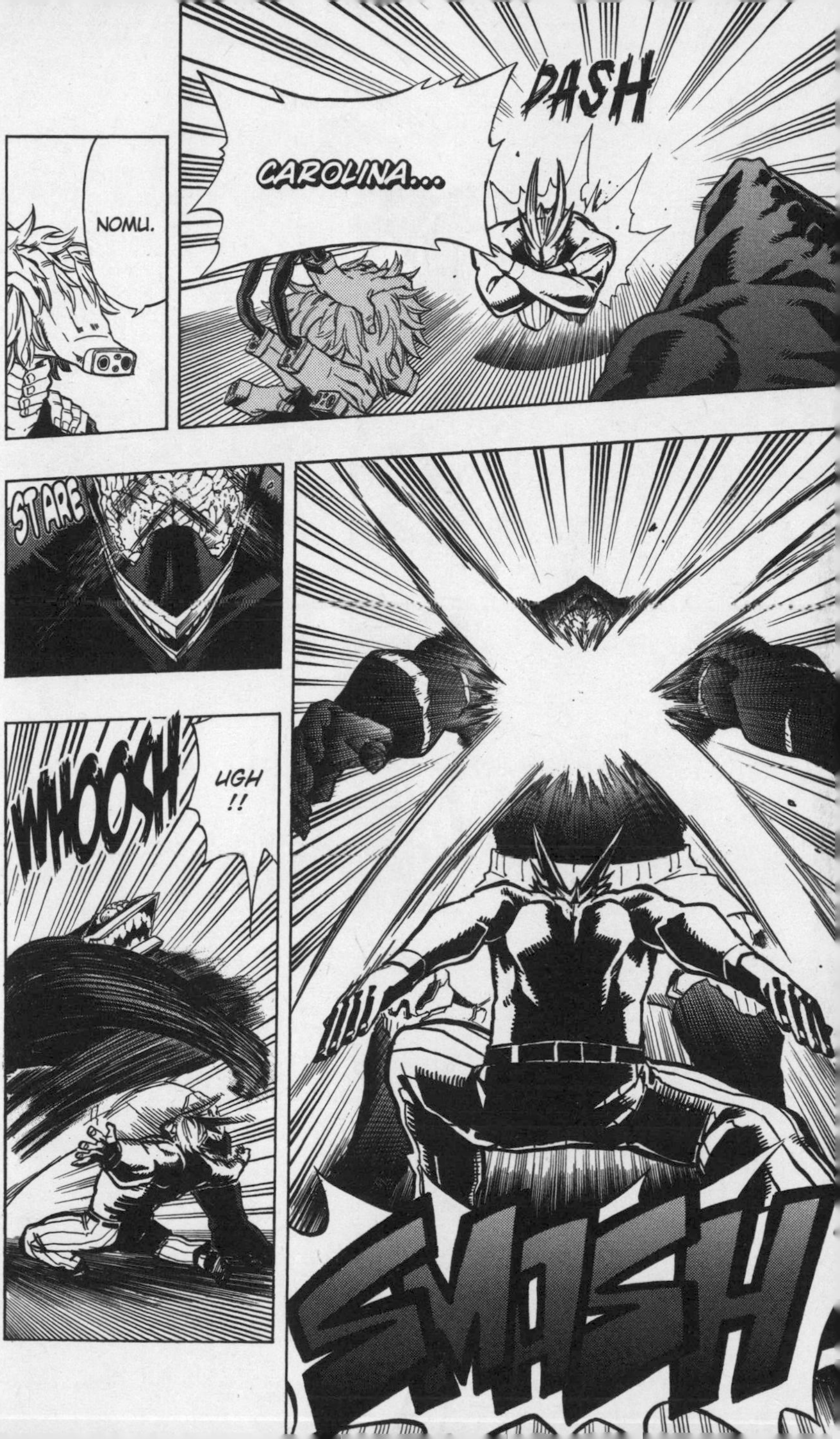
DASH
CAROLINA...
NOMU.
SMASH
STARE
WHOOSH
UGH!!

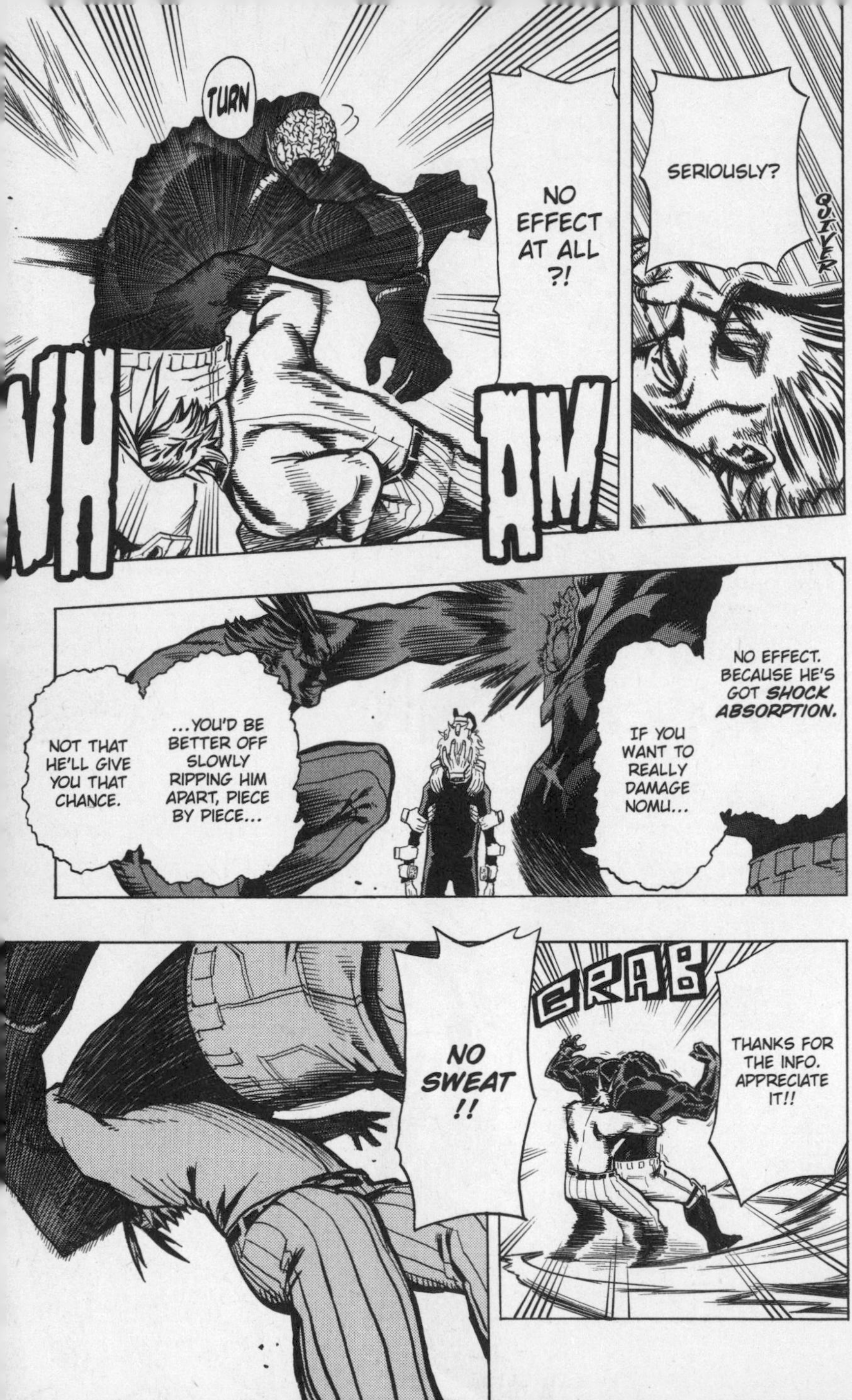
SERIOUSLY?
QUIVER
NO EFFECT AT ALL ?!
TURN
WHAM
NO EFFECT. BECAUSE HE'S GOT **SHOCK ABSORPTION.**
IF YOU WANT TO REALLY DAMAGE NOMU...
...YOU'D BE BETTER OFF SLOWLY RIPPING HIM APART, PIECE BY PIECE...
NOT THAT HE'LL GIVE YOU THAT CHANCE.
GRAB
THANKS FOR THE INFO. APPRECIATE IT!!
NO SWEAT !!

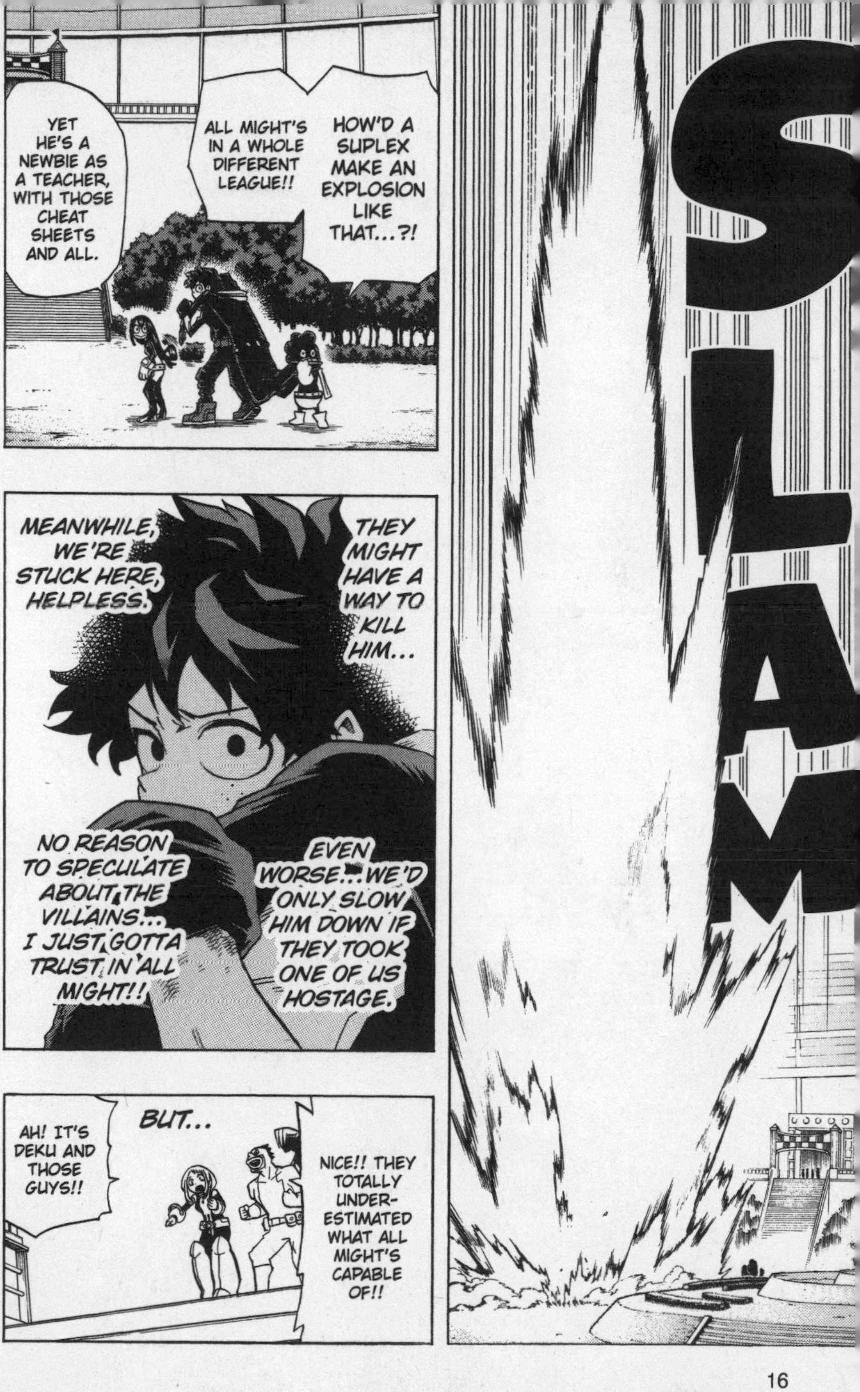
SLAM
HOW'D A SUPLEX MAKE AN EXPLOSION LIKE THAT...?!
ALL MIGHT'S IN A WHOLE DIFFERENT LEAGUE!!
YET HE'S A NEWBIE AS A TEACHER, WITH THOSE CHEAT SHEETS AND ALL.
THEY MIGHT HAVE A WAY TO KILL HIM...
MEANWHILE, WE'RE STUCK HERE, HELPLESS.
EVEN WORSE... WE'D ONLY SLOW HIM DOWN IF THEY TOOK ONE OF US HOSTAGE.
NO REASON TO SPECULATE ABOUT THE VILLAINS... I JUST GOTTA TRUST IN ALL MIGHT!!
NICE!! THEY TOTALLY UNDER-ESTIMATED WHAT ALL MIGHT'S CAPABLE OF!!
BUT...
AH! IT'S DEKU AND THOSE GUYS!!

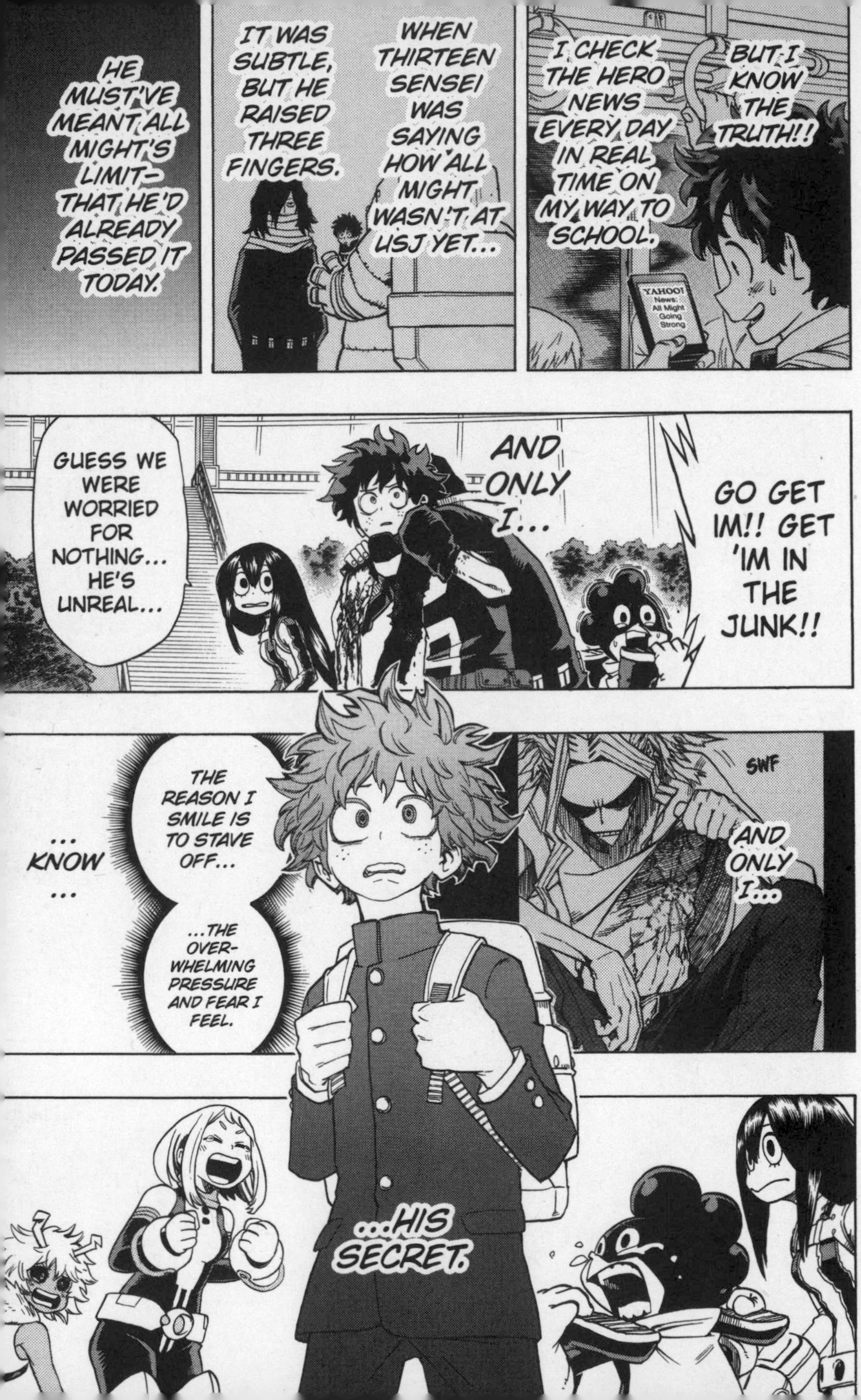
I CHECK THE HERO NEWS EVERY DAY IN REAL TIME ON MY WAY TO SCHOOL.
BUT I KNOW THE TRUTH!!
YAHOO! News: All Might Going Strong
WHEN THIRTEEN SENSEI WAS SAYING HOW ALL MIGHT WASN'T AT USJ YET...
IT WAS SUBTLE, BUT HE RAISED THREE FINGERS.
HE MUST'VE MEANT ALL MIGHT'S LIMIT—THAT HE'D ALREADY PASSED IT TODAY.
GO GET IM!! GET 'IM IN THE JUNK!!
AND ONLY I...
GUESS WE WERE WORRIED FOR NOTHING... HE'S UNREAL...
SWF
AND ONLY I...
THE REASON I SMILE IS TO STAVE OFF...
...THE OVER-WHELMING PRESSURE AND FEAR I FEEL.
... KNOW ...
...HIS SECRET.

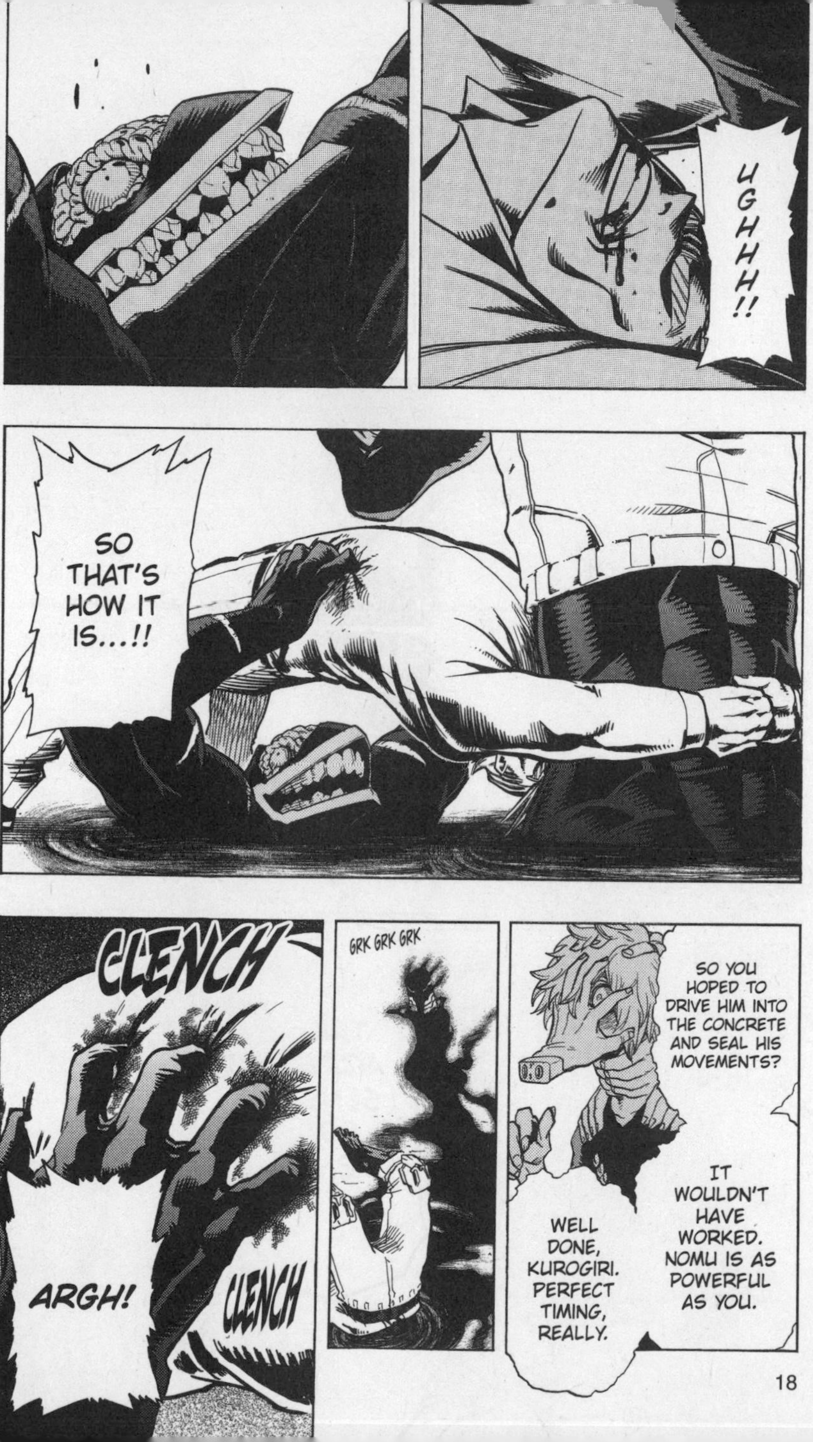
UGHHHH!!
SO THAT'S HOW IT IS...!!
SO YOU HOPED TO DRIVE HIM INTO THE CONCRETE AND SEAL HIS MOVEMENTS?
IT WOULDN'T HAVE WORKED. NOMU IS AS POWERFUL AS YOU.
WELL DONE, KUROGIRI. PERFECT TIMING, REALLY.
GRK GRK GRK
CLENCH
ARGH!
CLENCH

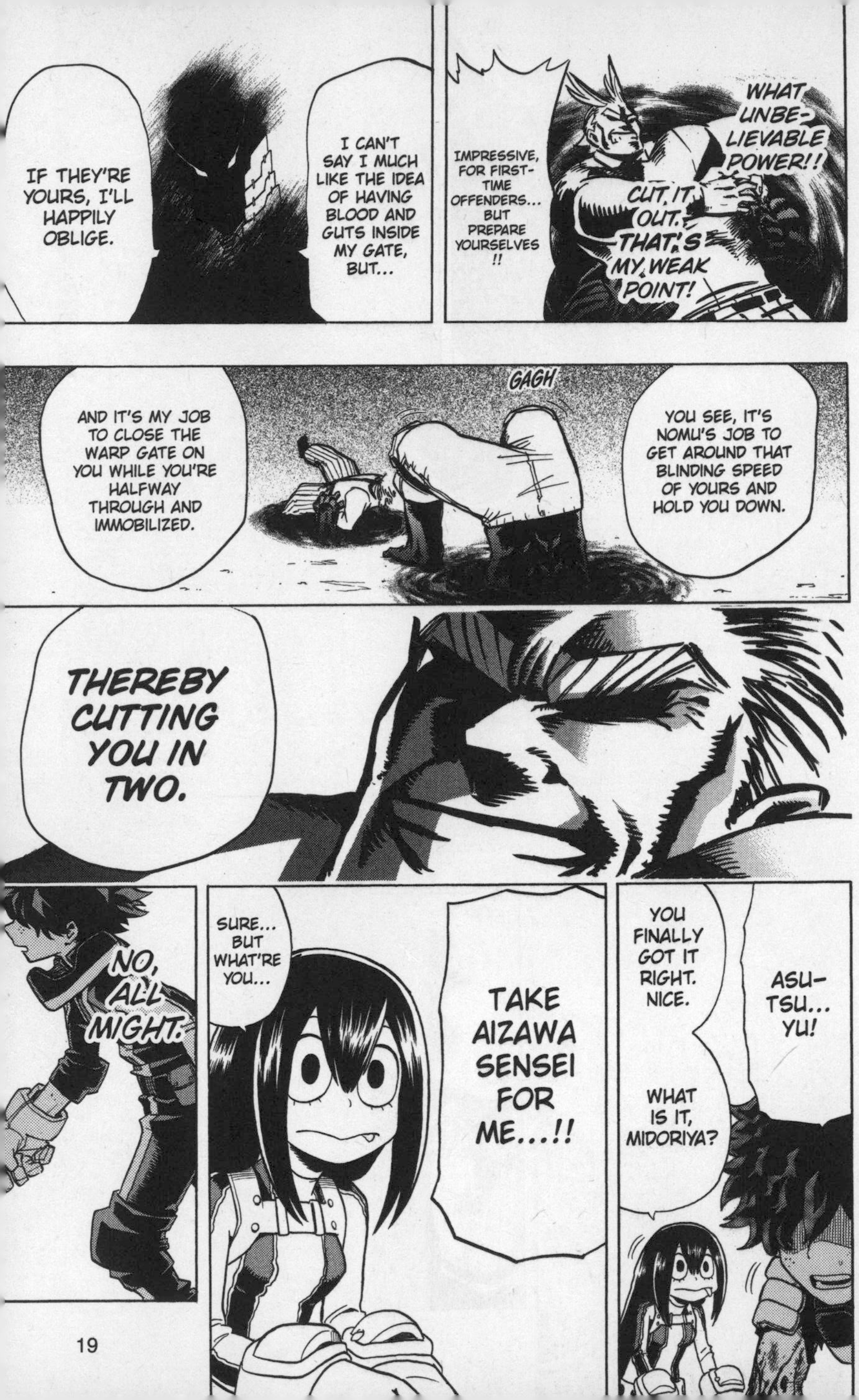
WHAT UNBE-LIEVABLE POWER!!
CUT IT OUT. THAT'S MY WEAK POINT!
IMPRESSIVE, FOR FIRST-TIME OFFENDERS... BUT PREPARE YOURSELVES!!
I CAN'T SAY I MUCH LIKE THE IDEA OF HAVING BLOOD AND GUTS INSIDE MY GATE, BUT...
IF THEY'RE YOURS, I'LL HAPPILY OBLIGE.
YOU SEE, IT'S NOMU'S JOB TO GET AROUND THAT BLINDING SPEED OF YOURS AND HOLD YOU DOWN.
GAGH
AND IT'S MY JOB TO CLOSE THE WARP GATE ON YOU WHILE YOU'RE HALFWAY THROUGH AND IMMOBILIZED.
THEREBY CUTTING YOU IN TWO.
ASU-TSU... YU!
YOU FINALLY GOT IT RIGHT. NICE.
WHAT IS IT, MIDORIYA?
TAKE AIZAWA SENSEI FOR ME...!!
SURE... BUT WHAT'RE YOU...
NO, ALL MIGHT.

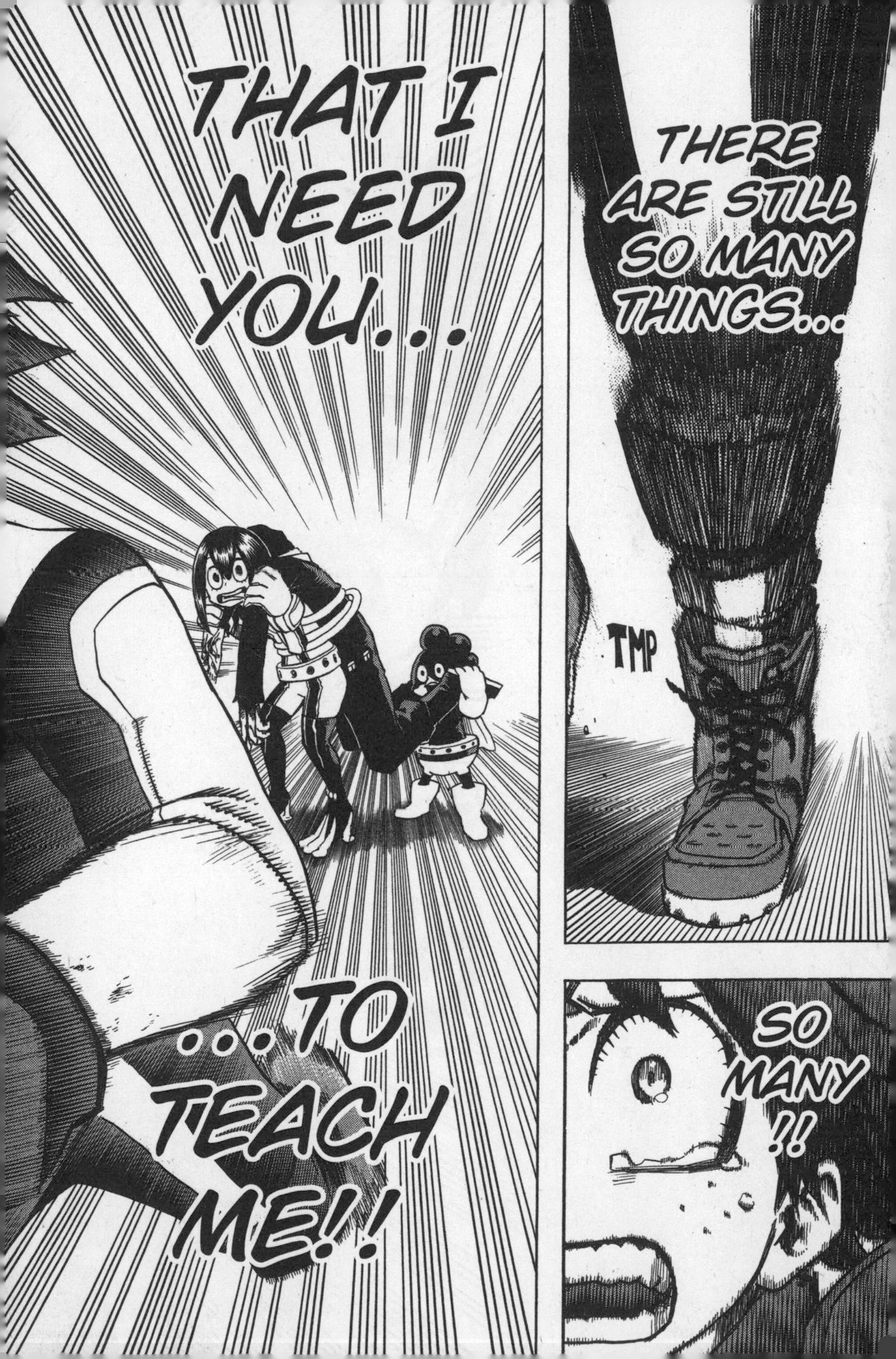
THERE ARE STILL SO MANY THINGS...
TMP
SO MANY!!
THAT I NEED YOU...
...TO TEACH ME!!

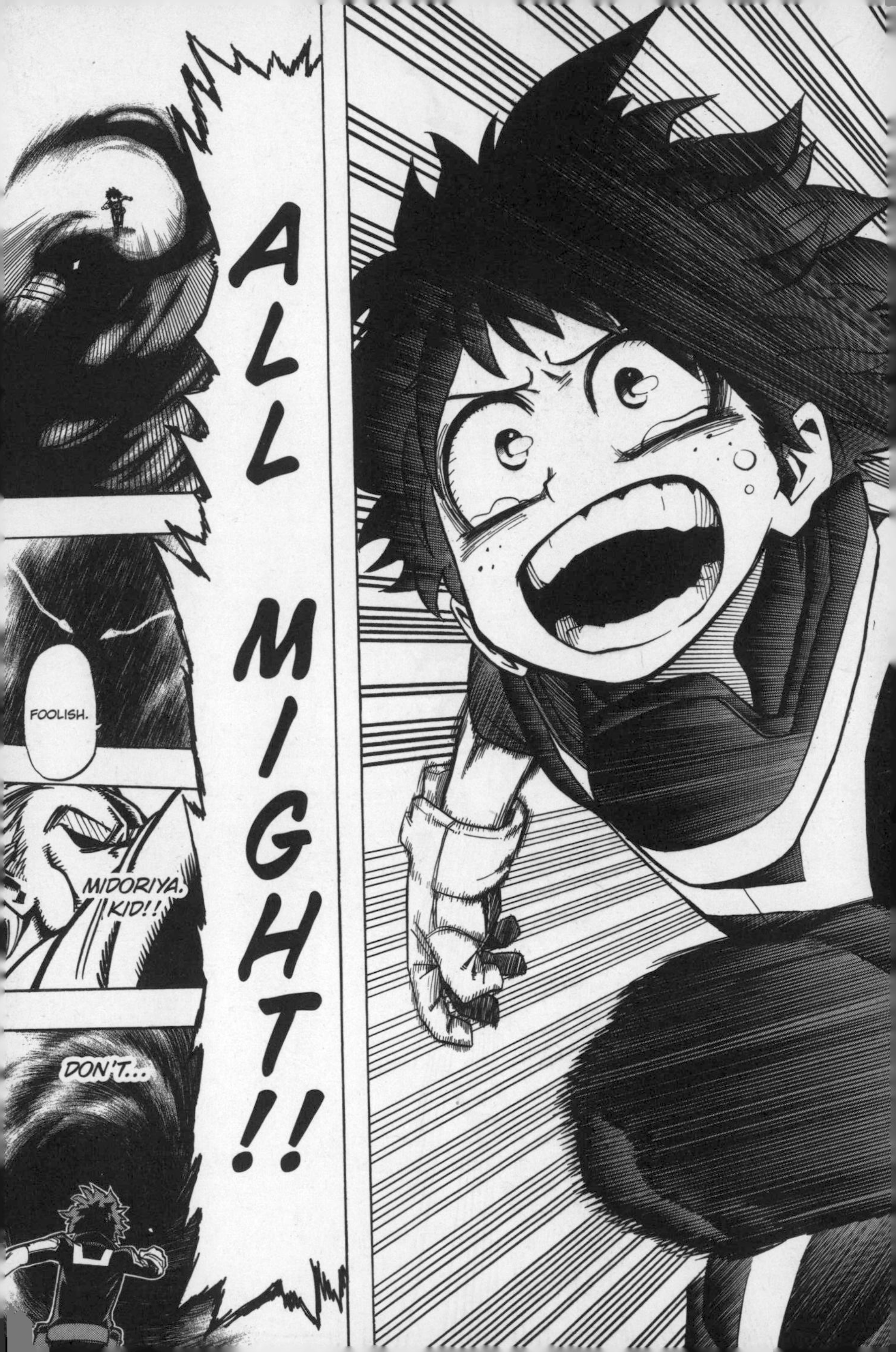
ALL MIGHT!!
FOOLISH.
MIDORIYA. KID!!
DON'T...

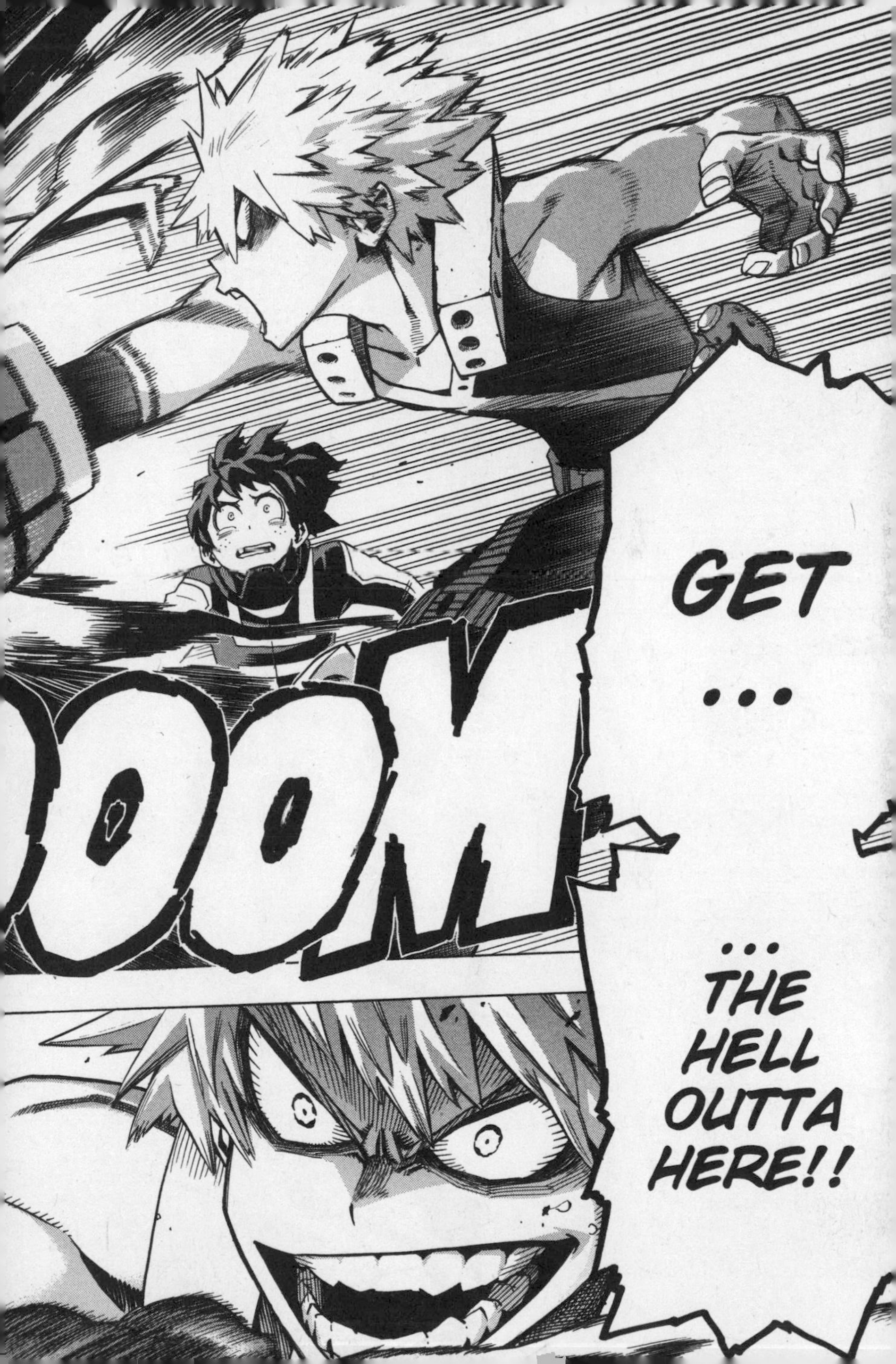
GET ... ... THE HELL OUTTA HERE!!
OOM

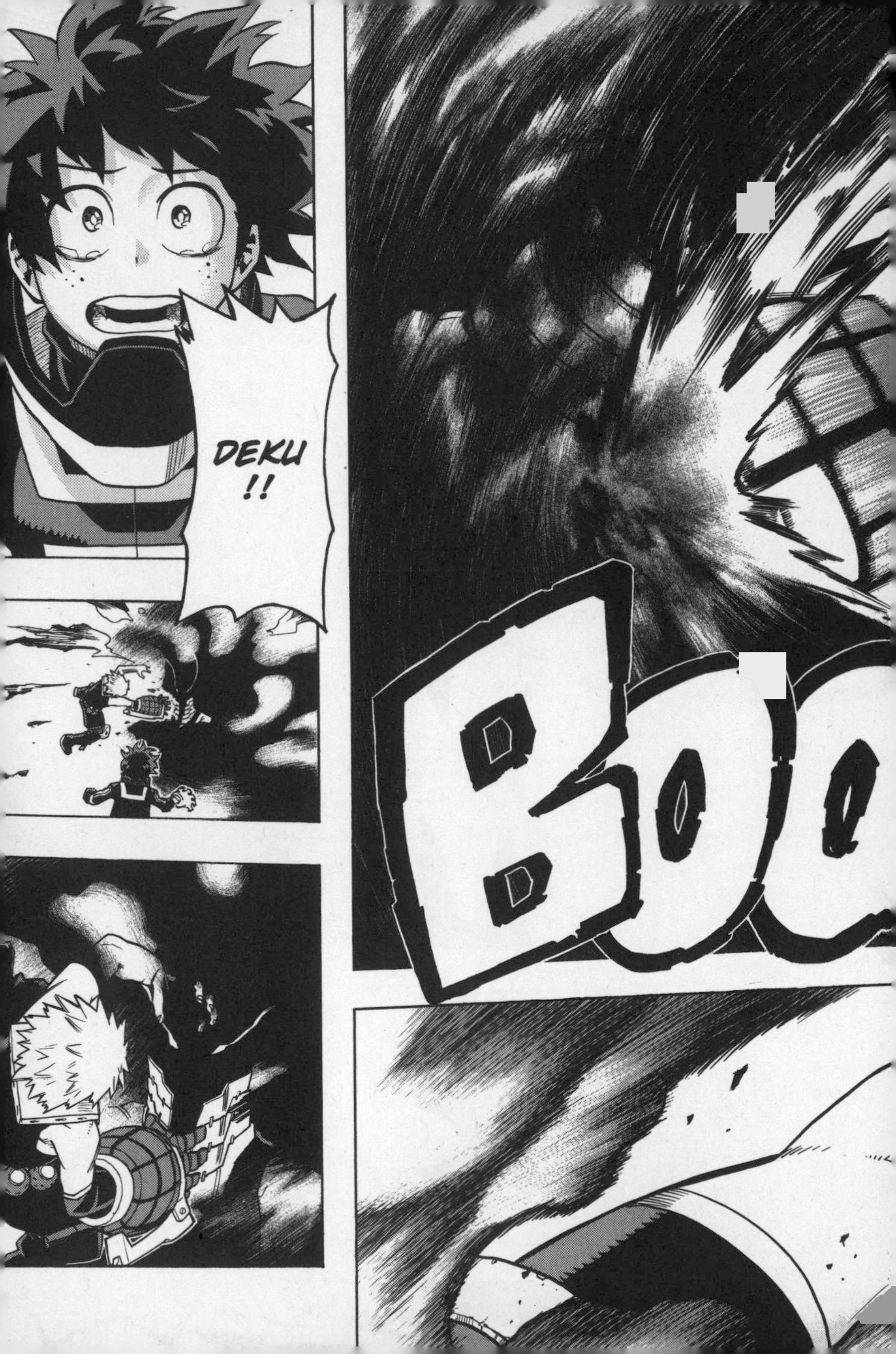
BOO
DEKU !!

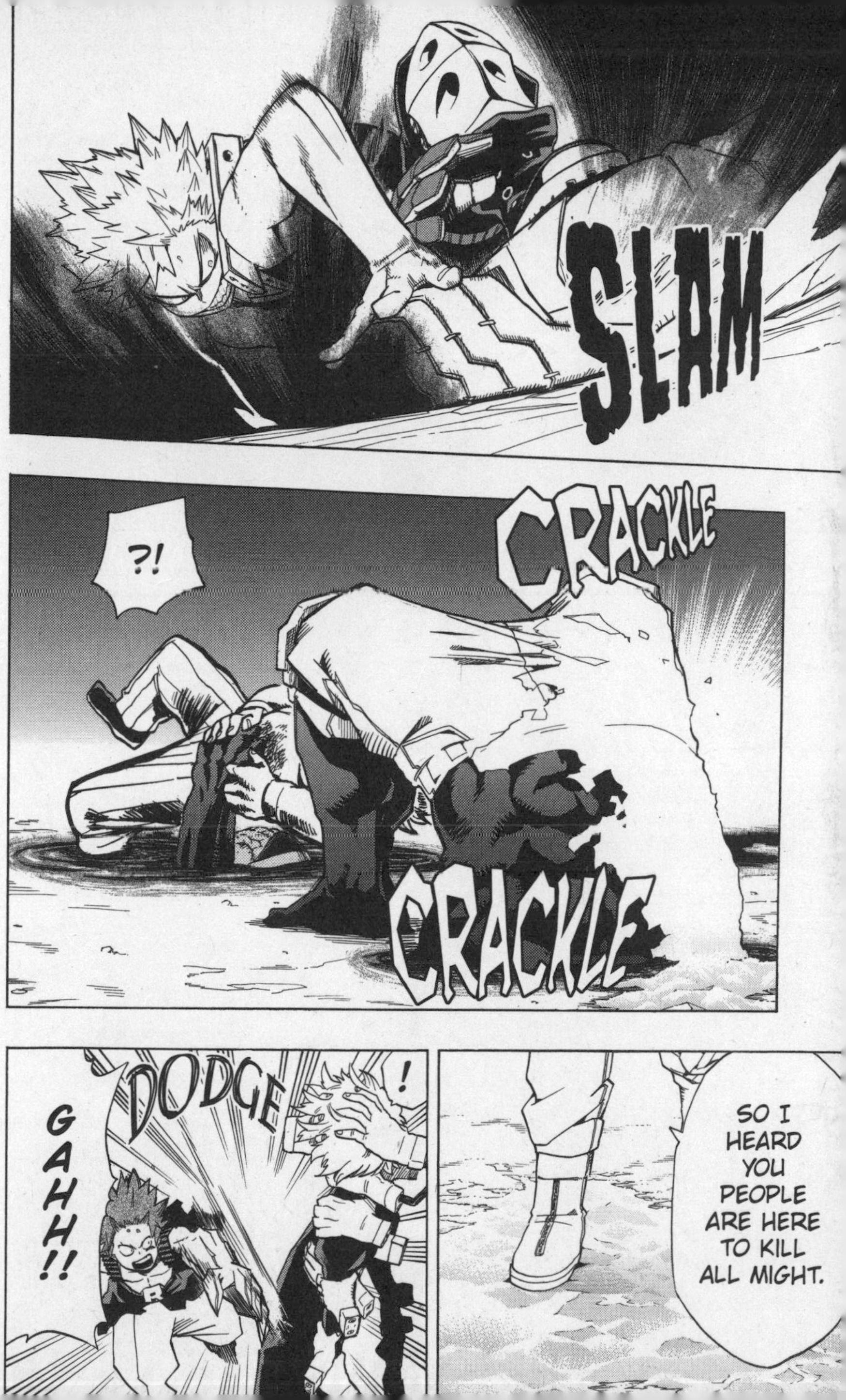
SLAM
CRACKLE
?!
CRACKLE
SO I HEARD YOU PEOPLE ARE HERE TO KILL ALL MIGHT.
!
DODGE
GAHH!!

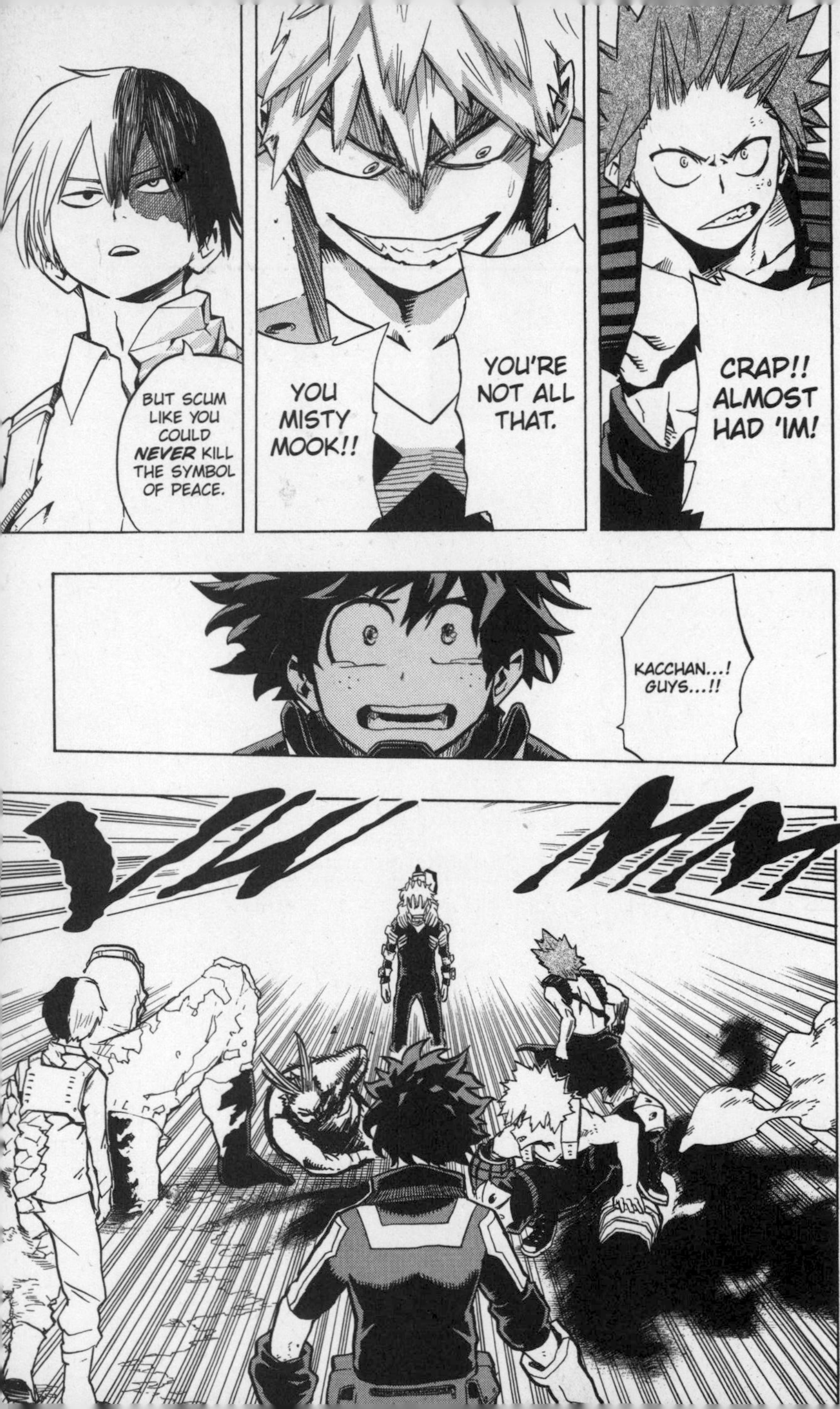
CRAP!! ALMOST HAD 'IM!
YOU'RE NOT ALL THAT.
YOU MISTY MOOK!!
BUT SCUM LIKE YOU COULD **NEVER** KILL THE SYMBOL OF PEACE.
KACCHAN...! GUYS...!!
VWUMM

STREET CLOTHES

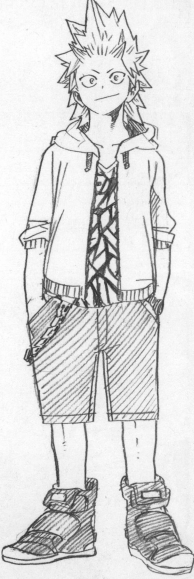

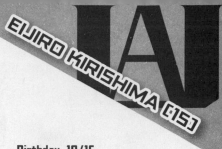

Birthday: 10/16
Height: 170 cm
Favorite Things: Hard-liners,
tough guys

BEHIND THE SCENES

This guy was born from a need to have someone who could bring the different members of the class together and bridge gaps.

He's a cheery and all-around decent guy.

When I'm working on storyboards he often helps me out in subtle ways.

The scar over his right eye happened when he was three years old. One night, he woke up with the urge to pee. Still half-asleep, he started rubbing his eyes, but that was the exact moment his Quirk manifested, so he ended up scarring himself.

He actually hasn't appeared much since his debut in chapter three.

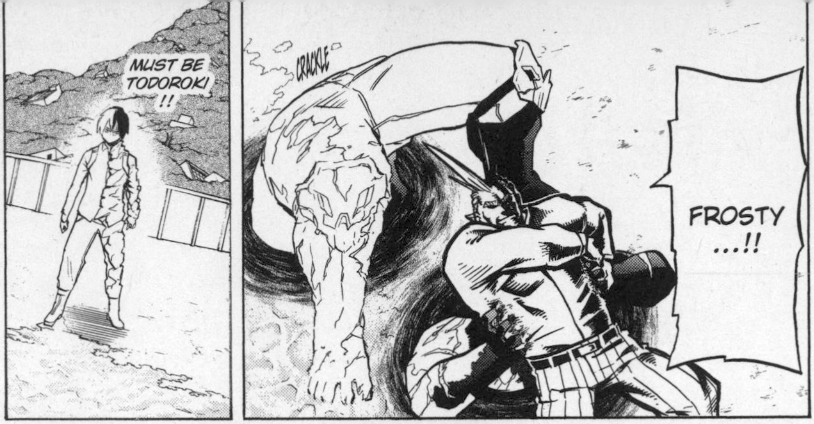
FROSTY ...!!
CRACKLE
MUST BE TODOROKI !!

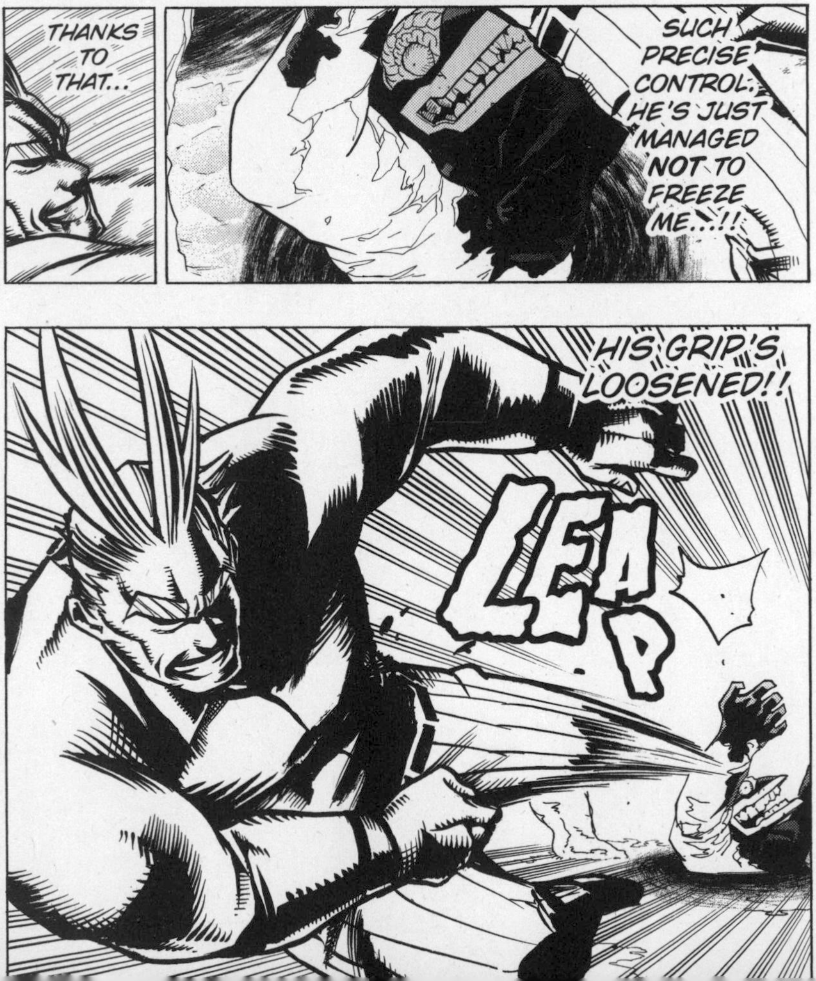
SUCH PRECISE CONTROL. HE'S JUST MANAGED NOT TO FREEZE ME...!!
THANKS TO THAT...
HIS GRIP'S LOOSENED!!
LEAP

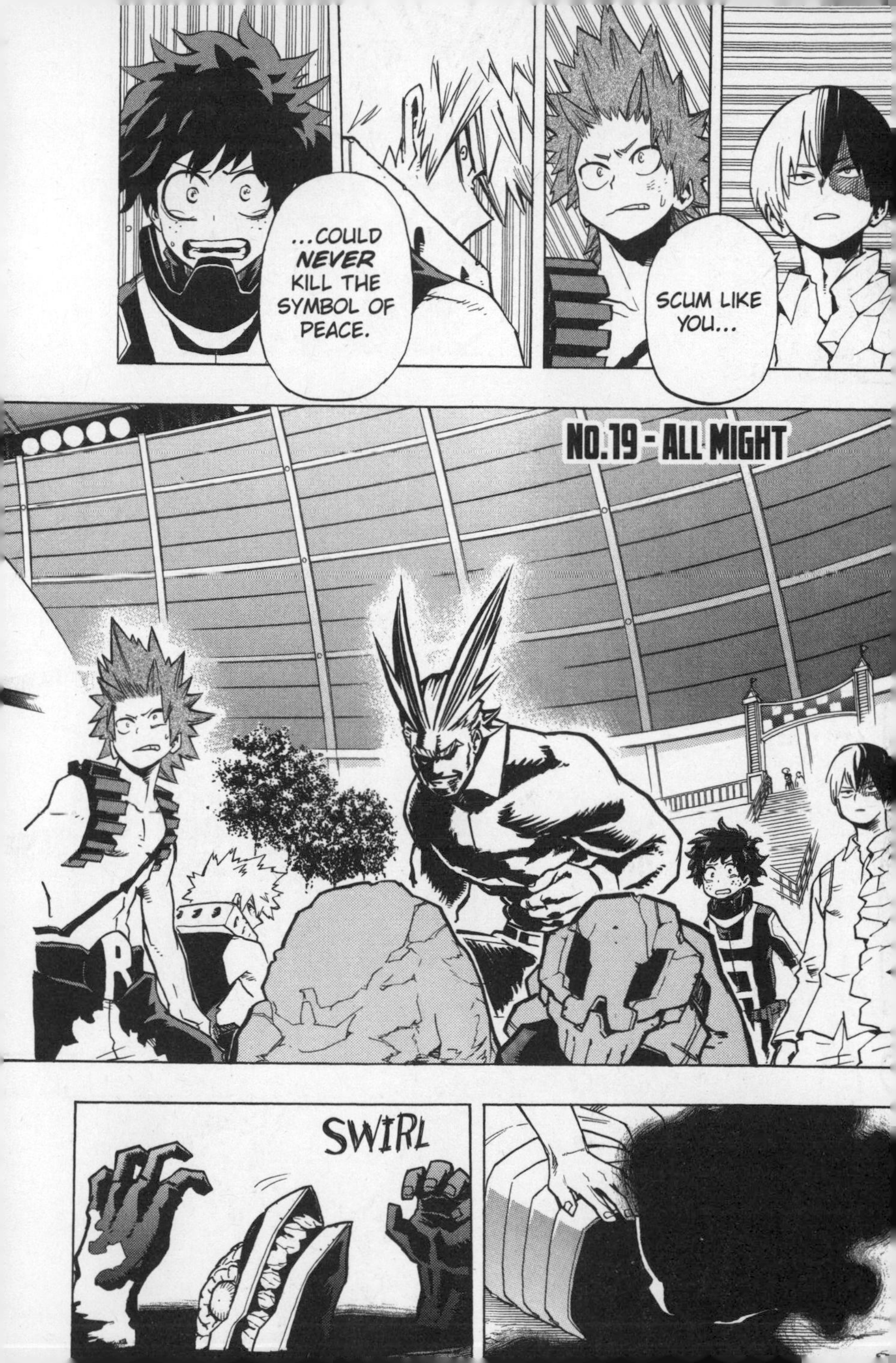
SCUM LIKE YOU...
...COULD NEVER KILL THE SYMBOL OF PEACE.
NO.19 - ALL MIGHT
SWIRL

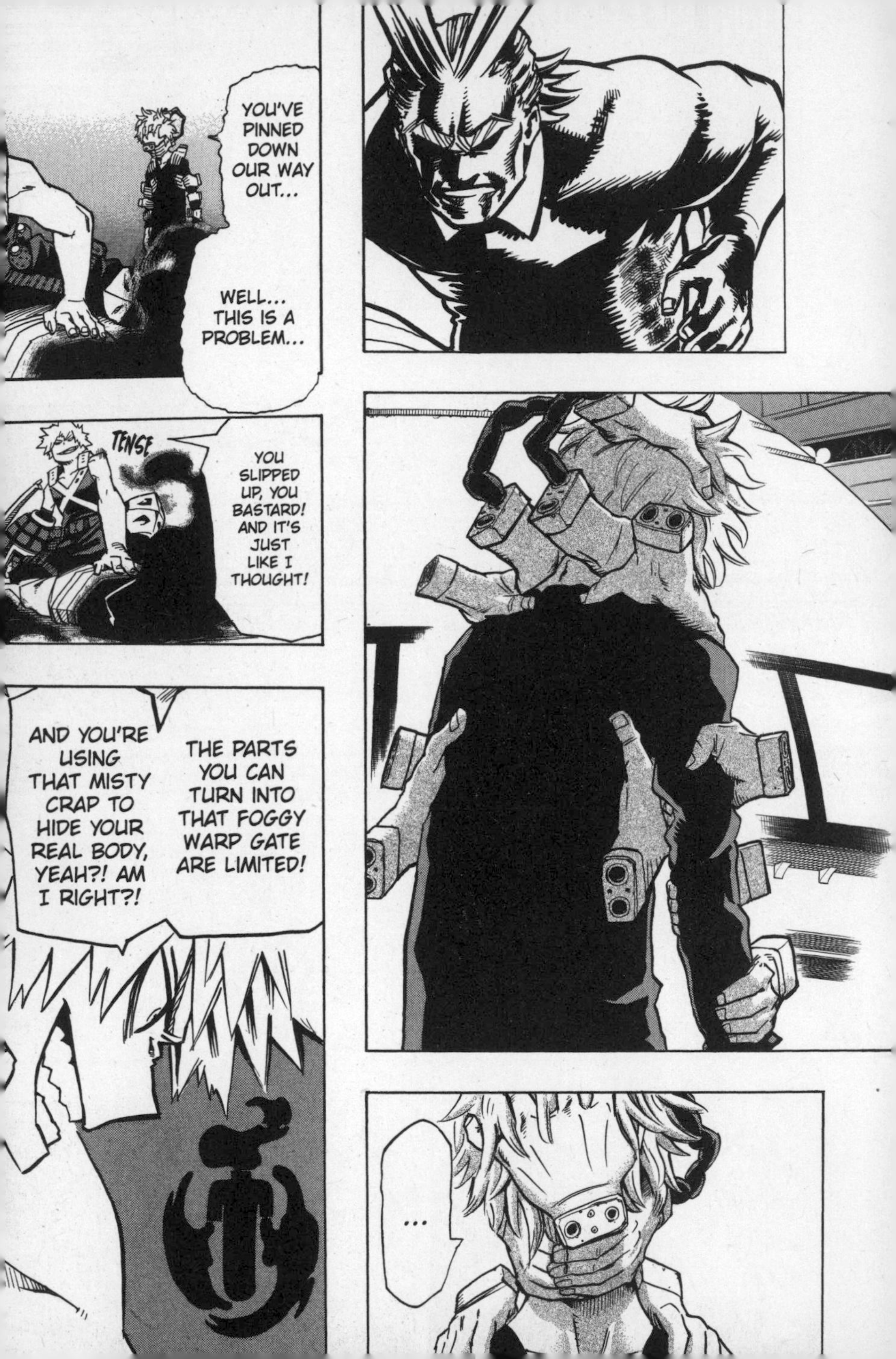
YOU'VE PINNED DOWN OUR WAY OUT...
WELL... THIS IS A PROBLEM...
TENSE
YOU SLIPPED UP, YOU BASTARD! AND IT'S JUST LIKE I THOUGHT!
THE PARTS YOU CAN TURN INTO THAT FOGGY WARP GATE ARE LIMITED!
AND YOU'RE USING THAT MISTY CRAP TO HIDE YOUR REAL BODY, YEAH?! AM I RIGHT?!
...

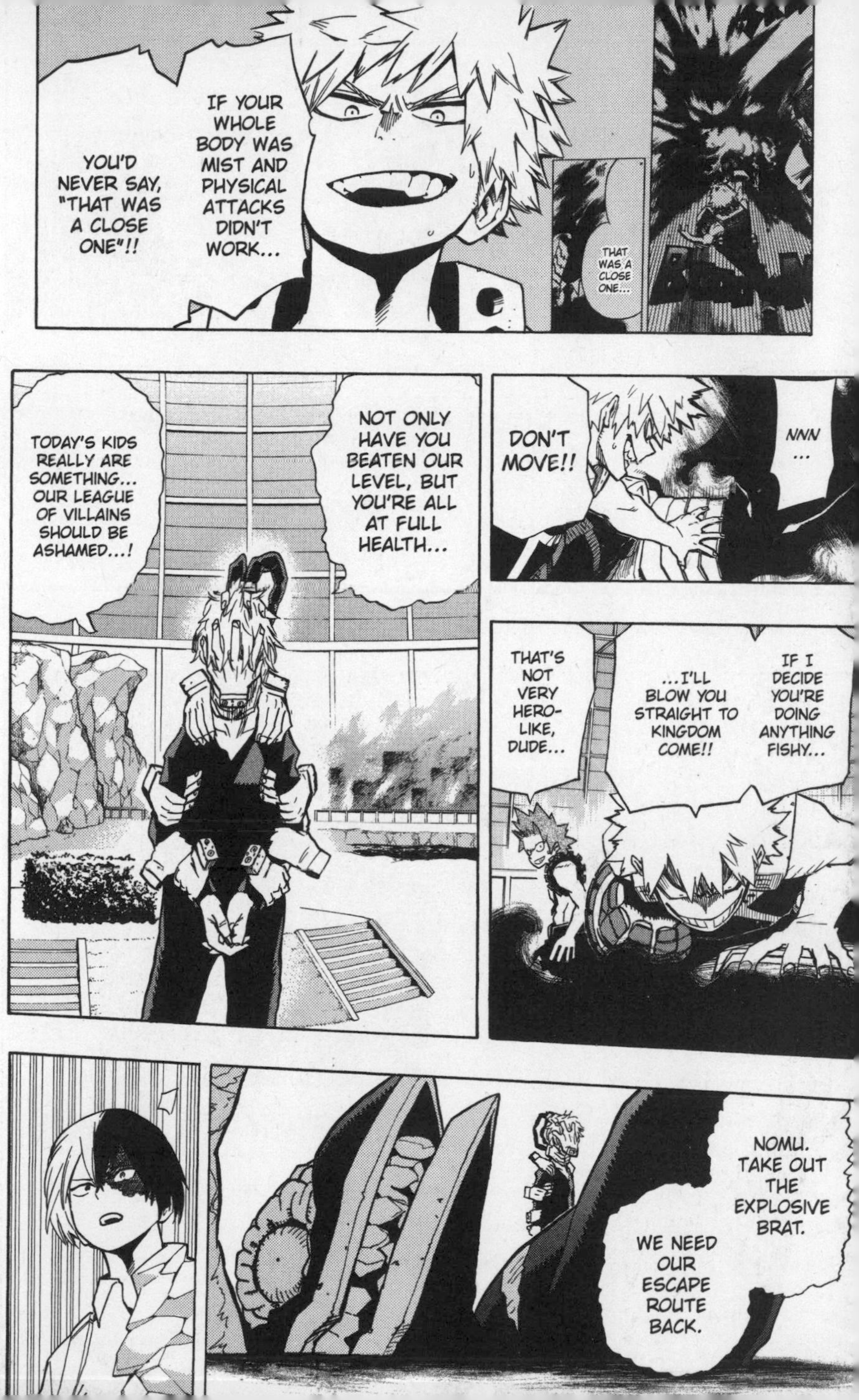
THAT WAS A CLOSE ONE...
IF YOUR WHOLE BODY WAS MIST AND PHYSICAL ATTACKS DIDN'T WORK...
YOU'D NEVER SAY, "THAT WAS A CLOSE ONE"!!
NNN...
DON'T MOVE!!
IF I DECIDE YOU'RE DOING ANYTHING FISHY...
...I'LL BLOW YOU STRAIGHT TO KINGDOM COME!!
THAT'S NOT VERY HERO-LIKE, DUDE...
NOT ONLY HAVE YOU BEATEN OUR LEVEL, BUT YOU'RE ALL AT FULL HEALTH...
TODAY'S KIDS REALLY ARE SOMETHING... OUR LEAGUE OF VILLAINS SHOULD BE ASHAMED...!
NOMU. TAKE OUT THE EXPLOSIVE BRAT.
WE NEED OUR ESCAPE ROUTE BACK.

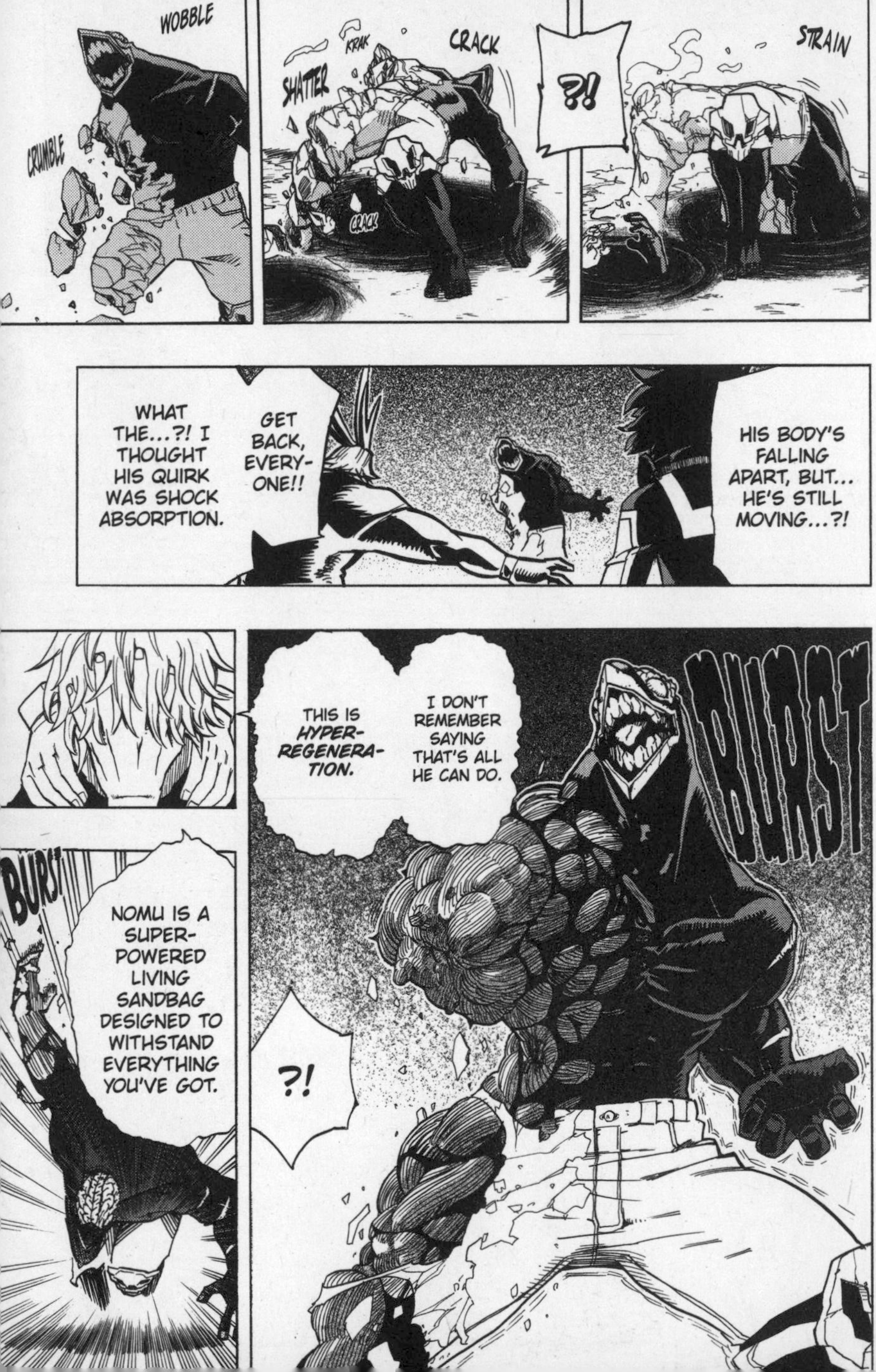
STRAIN
?!
CRACK
KRAK
SHATTER
CRACK
WOBBLE
CRUMBLE
HIS BODY'S FALLING APART, BUT... HE'S STILL MOVING...?!
GET BACK, EVERY-ONE!!
WHAT THE...?! I THOUGHT HIS QUIRK WAS SHOCK ABSORPTION.
BURST
I DON'T REMEMBER SAYING THAT'S ALL HE CAN DO.
THIS IS *HYPER-REGENERA-TION.*
?!
BURST
NOMU IS A SUPER-POWERED LIVING SANDBAG DESIGNED TO WITHSTAND EVERYTHING YOU'VE GOT.

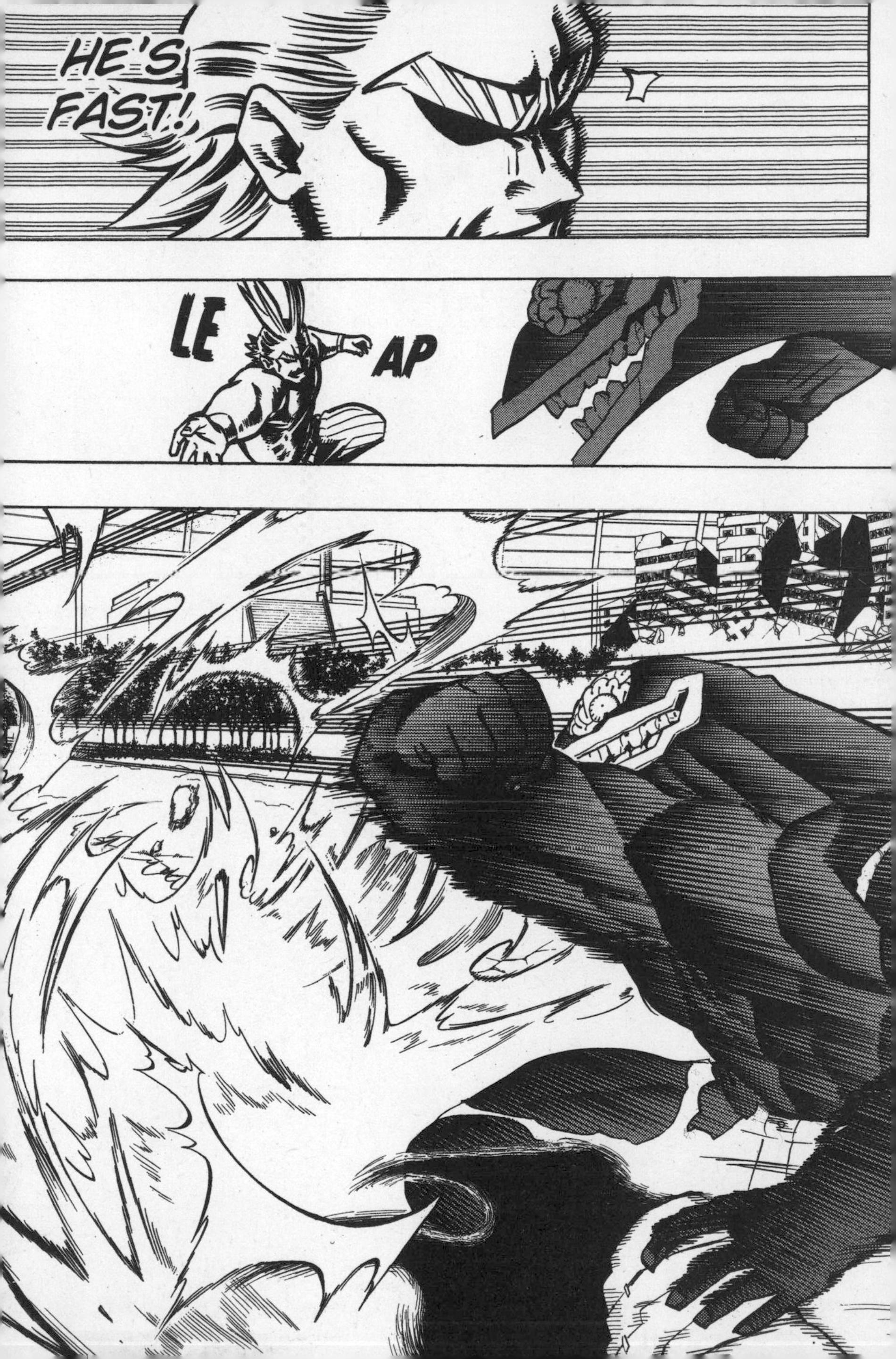
HE'S FAST!
LE
AP

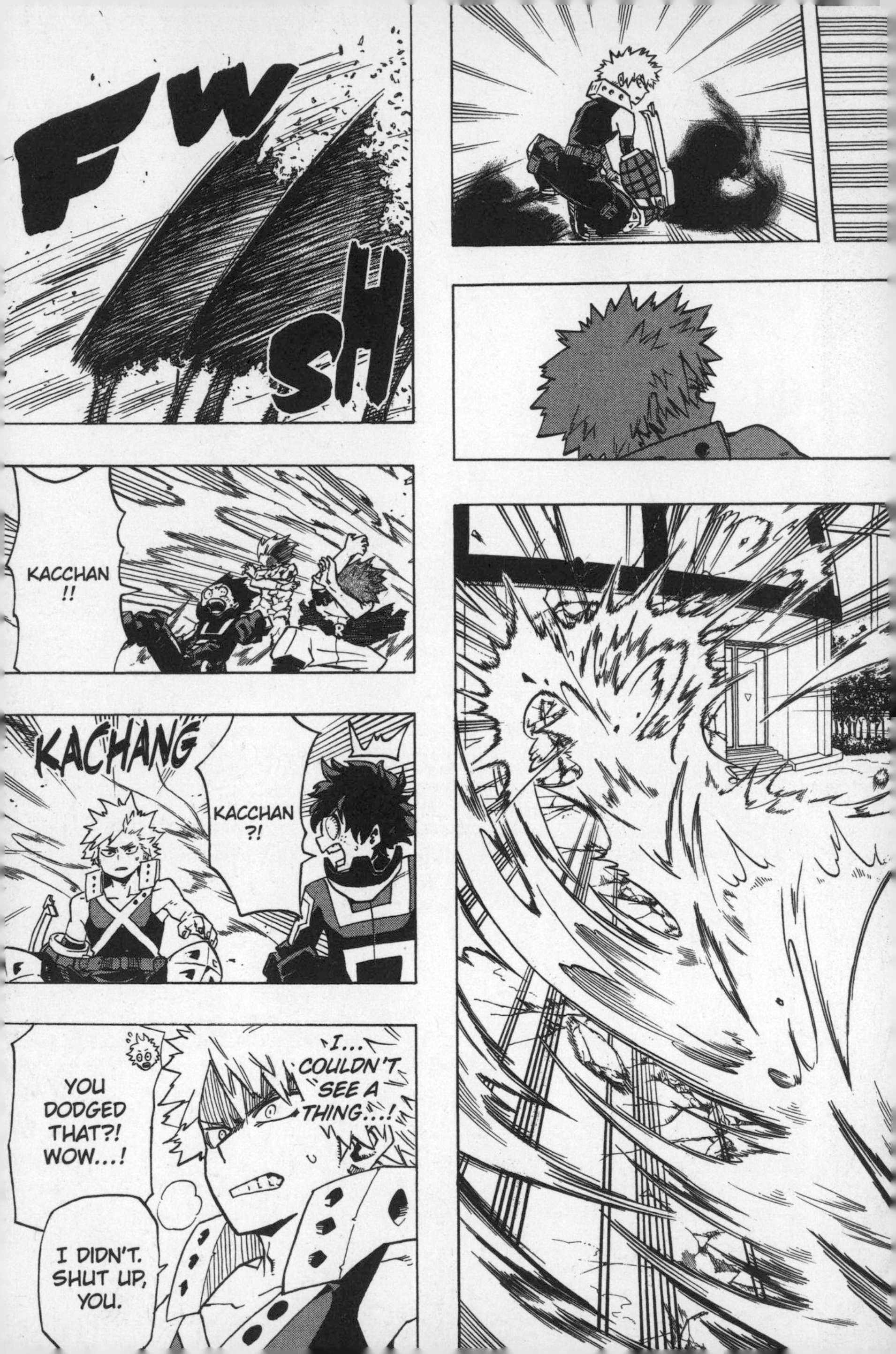
FWSH
KACCHAN !!
KACHANG
KACCHAN ?!
I... COULDN'T SEE A THING...!
YOU DODGED THAT?! WOW...!
I DIDN'T. SHUT UP, YOU.

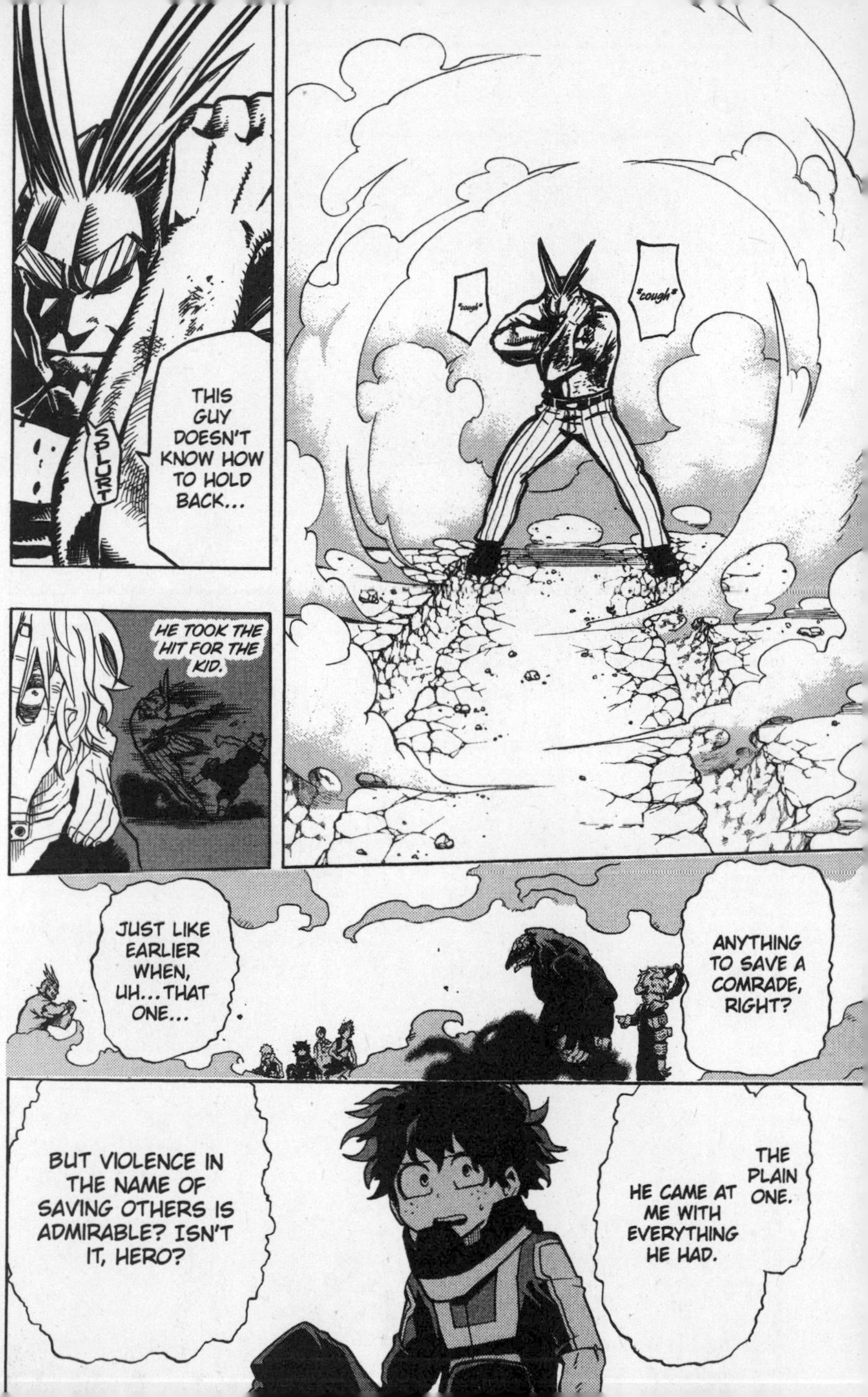
cough
cough
SPLURT
THIS GUY DOESN'T KNOW HOW TO HOLD BACK...
HE TOOK THE HIT FOR THE KID.
ANYTHING TO SAVE A COMRADE, RIGHT?
JUST LIKE EARLIER WHEN, UH...THAT ONE...
THE PLAIN ONE.
HE CAME AT ME WITH EVERYTHING HE HAD.
BUT VIOLENCE IN THE NAME OF SAVING OTHERS IS ADMIRABLE? ISN'T IT, HERO?

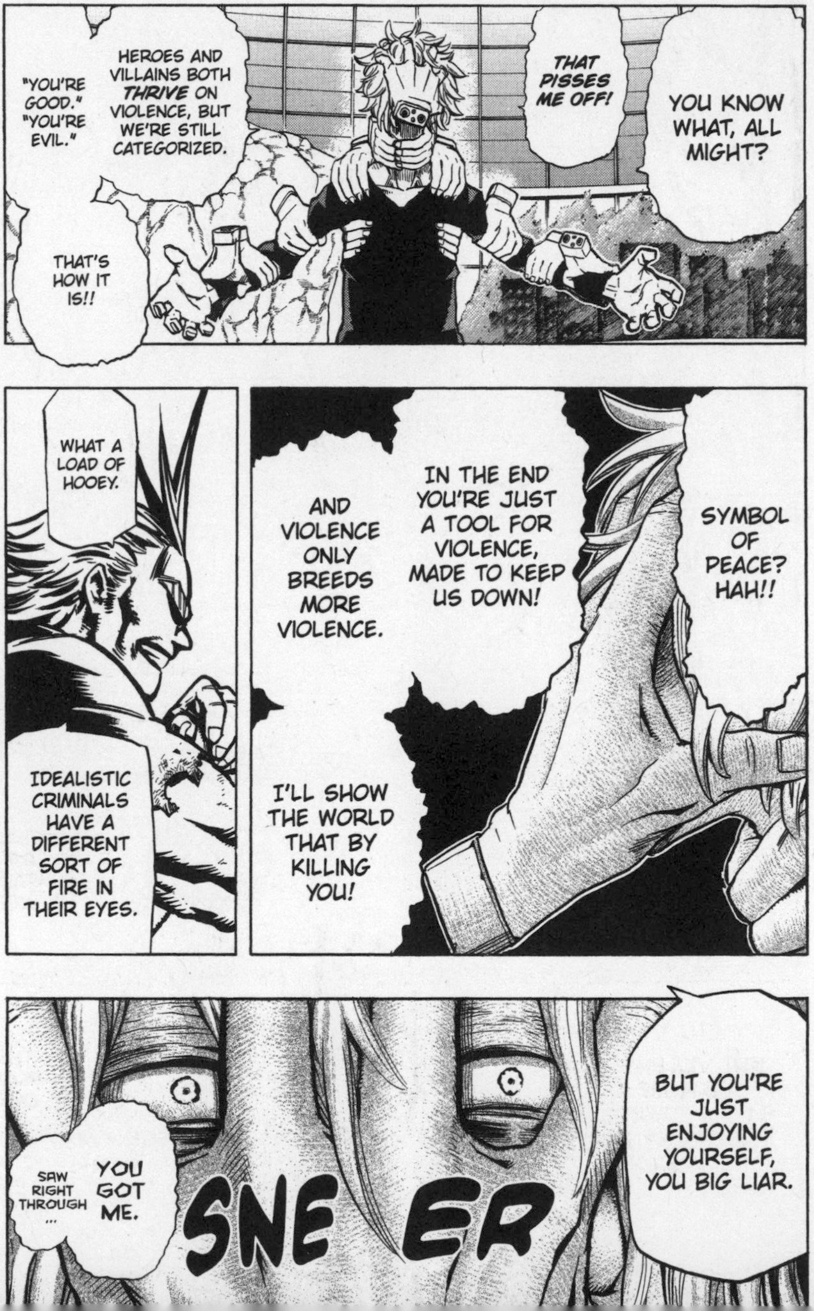
YOU KNOW WHAT, ALL MIGHT?
THAT PISSES ME OFF!
HEROES AND VILLAINS BOTH *THRIVE* ON VIOLENCE, BUT WE'RE STILL CATEGORIZED.
"YOU'RE GOOD." "YOU'RE EVIL."
THAT'S HOW IT IS!!
SYMBOL OF PEACE? HAH!!
IN THE END YOU'RE JUST A TOOL FOR VIOLENCE, MADE TO KEEP US DOWN!
AND VIOLENCE ONLY BREEDS MORE VIOLENCE.
I'LL SHOW THE WORLD THAT BY KILLING YOU!
WHAT A LOAD OF HOOEY.
IDEALISTIC CRIMINALS HAVE A DIFFERENT SORT OF FIRE IN THEIR EYES.
BUT YOU'RE JUST ENJOYING YOURSELF, YOU BIG LIAR.
SNEER
YOU GOT ME.
SAW RIGHT THROUGH ...

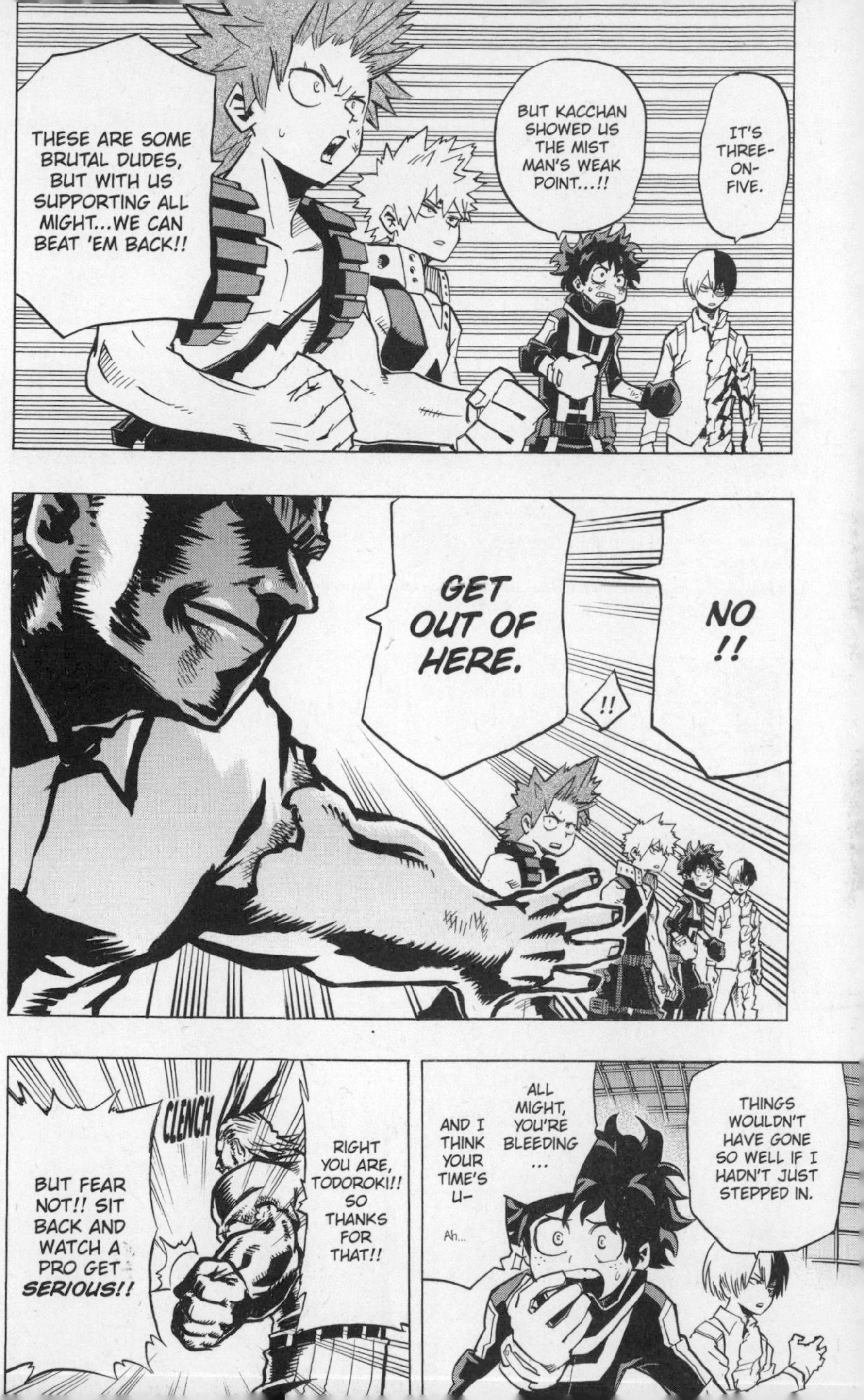
IT'S THREE-ON-FIVE.
BUT KACCHAN SHOWED US THE MIST MAN'S WEAK POINT...!!
THESE ARE SOME BRUTAL DUDES, BUT WITH US SUPPORTING ALL MIGHT...WE CAN BEAT 'EM BACK!!
NO !!
!!
GET OUT OF HERE.
THINGS WOULDN'T HAVE GONE SO WELL IF I HADN'T JUST STEPPED IN.
ALL MIGHT, YOU'RE BLEEDING ...
AND I THINK YOUR TIME'S U-
Ah...
RIGHT YOU ARE, TODOROKI!! SO THANKS FOR THAT!!
CLENCH
BUT FEAR NOT!! SIT BACK AND WATCH A PRO GET SERIOUS!!

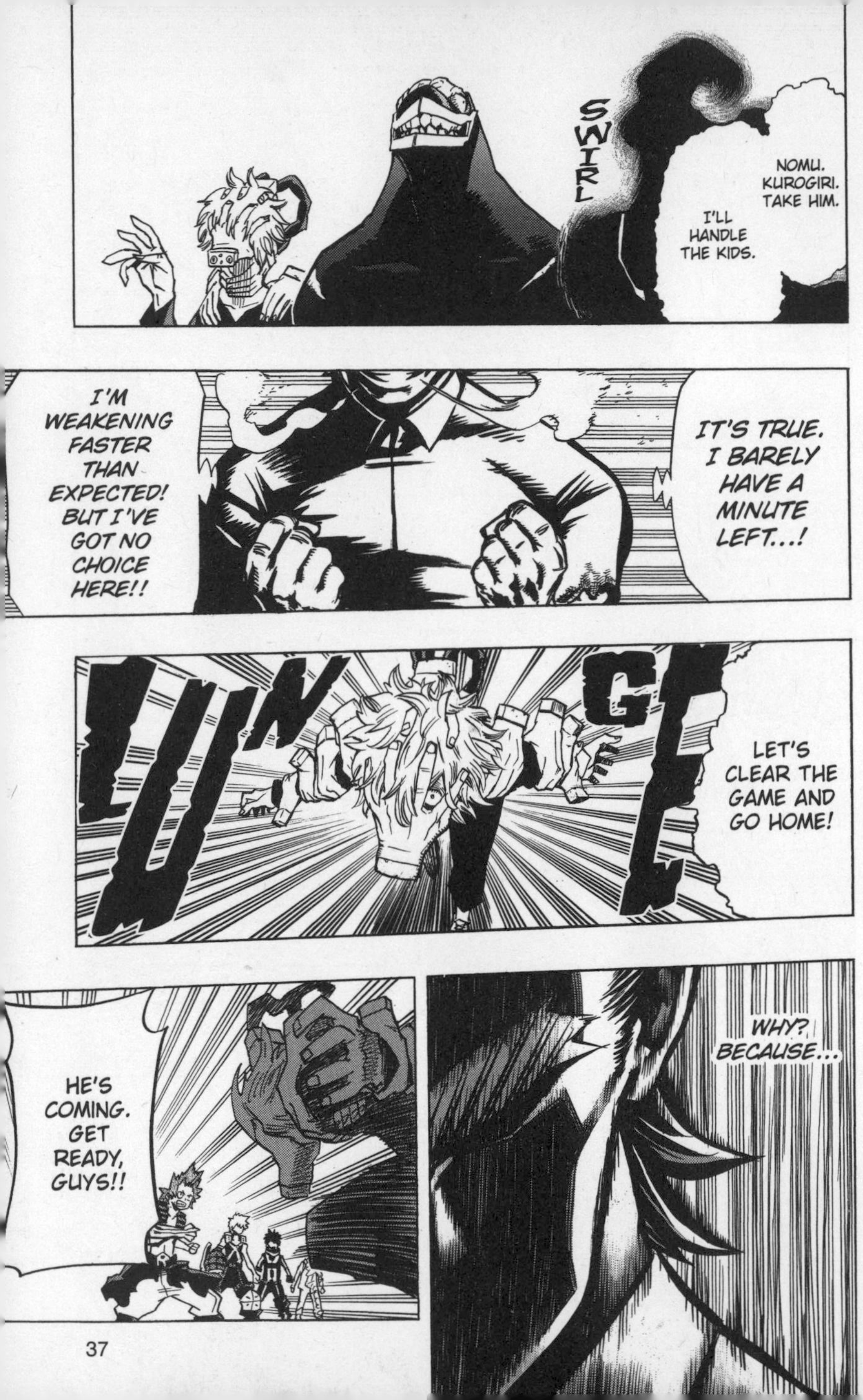
NOMU. KUROGIRI. TAKE HIM.
I'LL HANDLE THE KIDS.
SWIRL
IT'S TRUE. I BARELY HAVE A MINUTE LEFT...!
I'M WEAKENING FASTER THAN EXPECTED! BUT I'VE GOT NO CHOICE HERE!!
LET'S CLEAR THE GAME AND GO HOME!
WHY? BECAUSE...
HE'S COMING. GET READY, GUYS!!

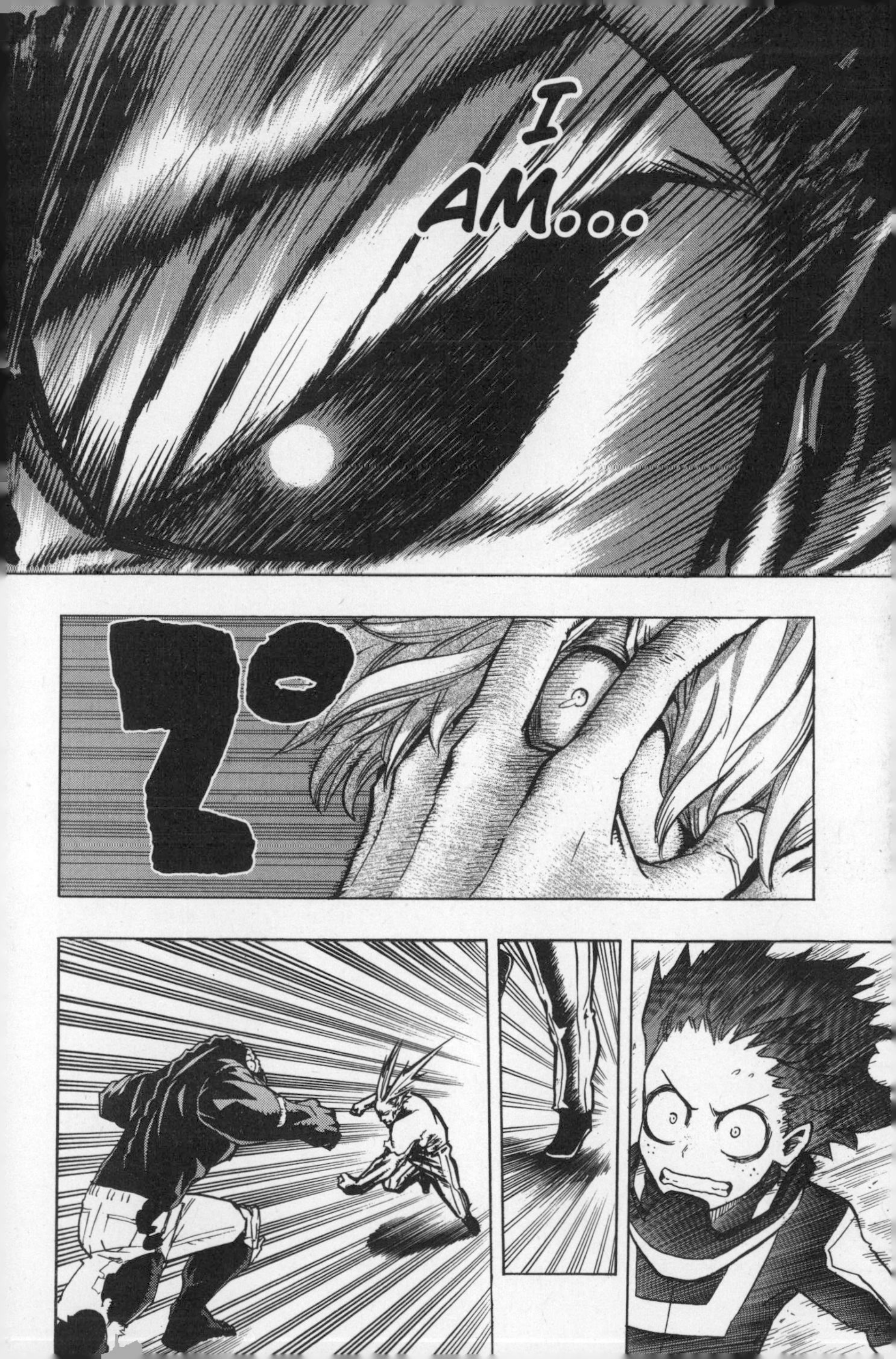
I AM...

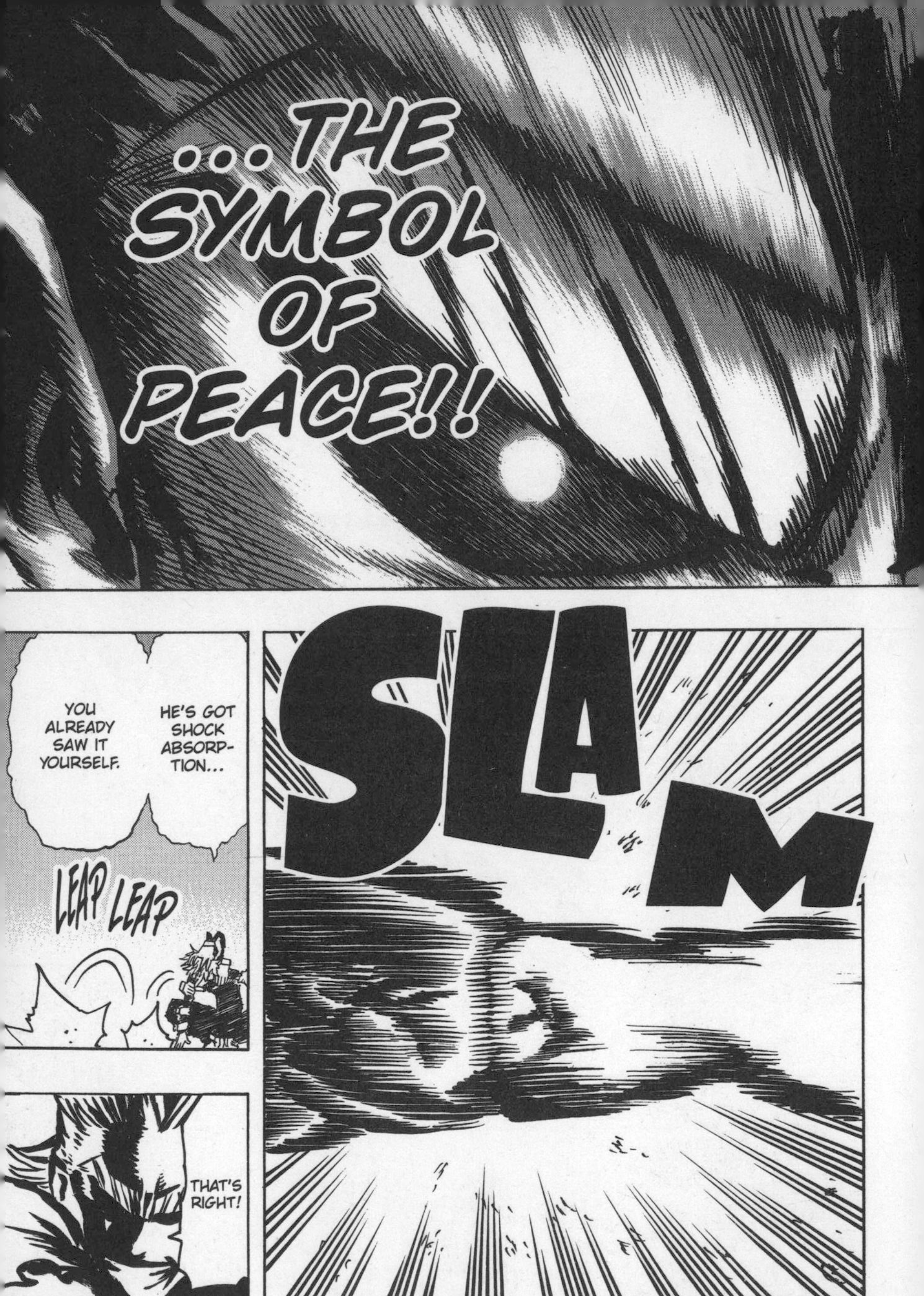
...THE SYMBOL OF PEACE!!
SLAM
HE'S GOT SHOCK ABSORPTION...
YOU ALREADY SAW IT YOURSELF.
LEAP LEAP
THAT'S RIGHT!

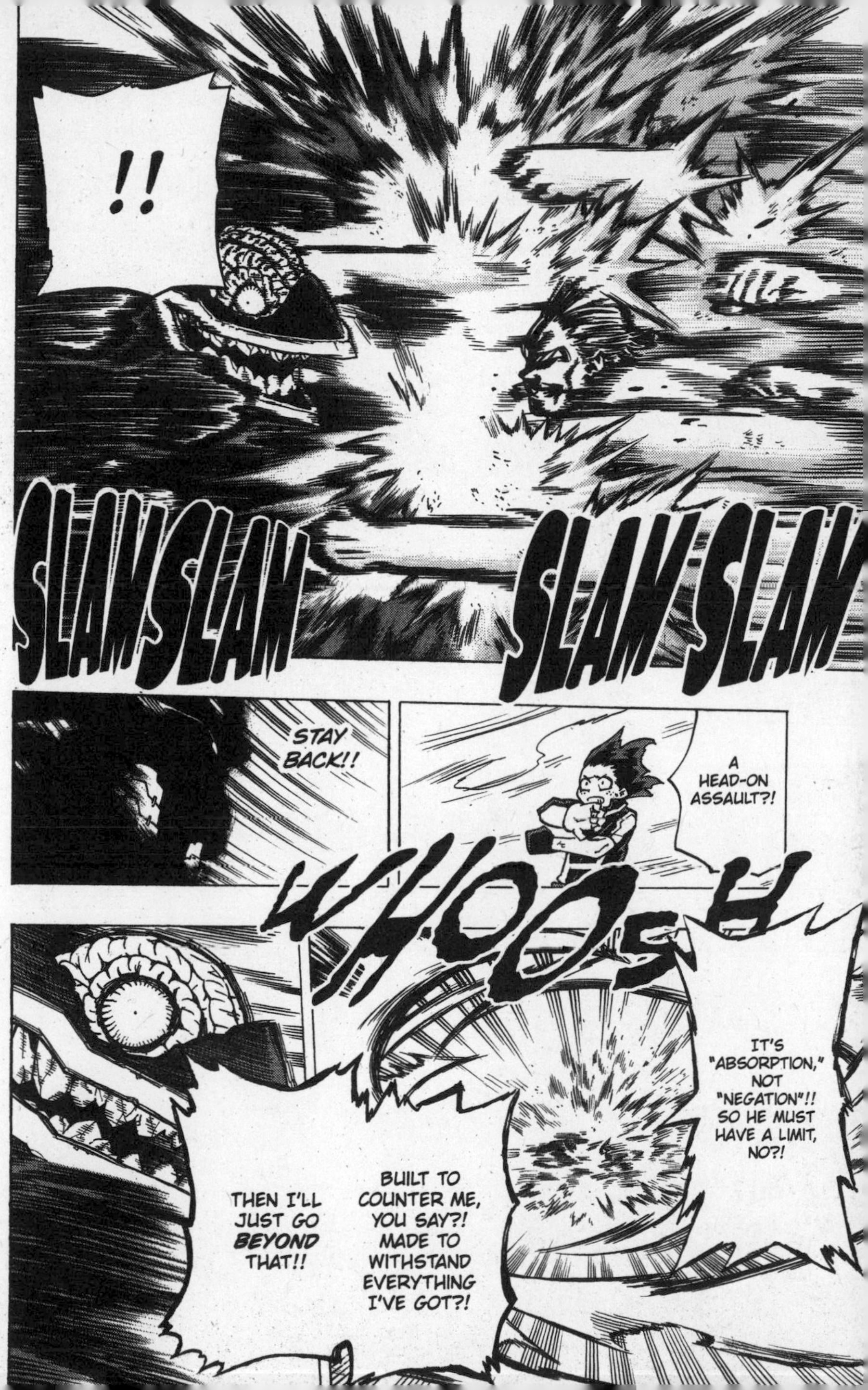
!!
SLAM SLAM
SLAM SLAM
A HEAD-ON ASSAULT?!
STAY BACK!!
WHOOSH
IT'S "ABSORPTION," NOT "NEGATION"!! SO HE MUST HAVE A LIMIT, NO?!
BUILT TO COUNTER ME, YOU SAY?! MADE TO WITHSTAND EVERYTHING I'VE GOT?!
THEN I'LL JUST GO *BEYOND* THAT!!

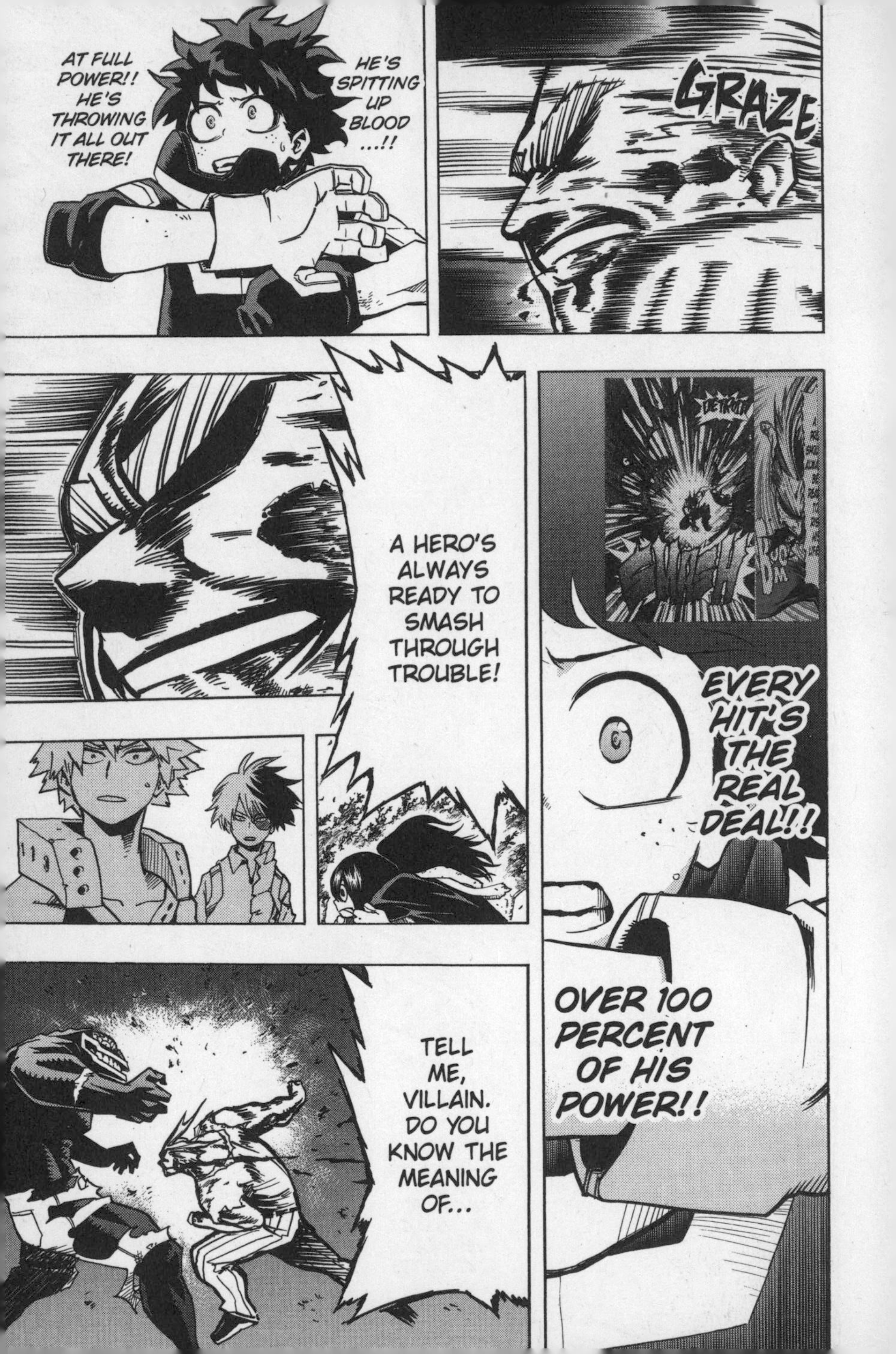
GRAZE
HE'S SPITTING UP BLOOD ...!!
AT FULL POWER!! HE'S THROWING IT ALL OUT THERE!
EVERY HIT'S THE REAL DEAL!!
OVER 100 PERCENT OF HIS POWER!!
A HERO'S ALWAYS READY TO SMASH THROUGH TROUBLE!
TELL ME, VILLAIN. DO YOU KNOW THE MEANING OF...

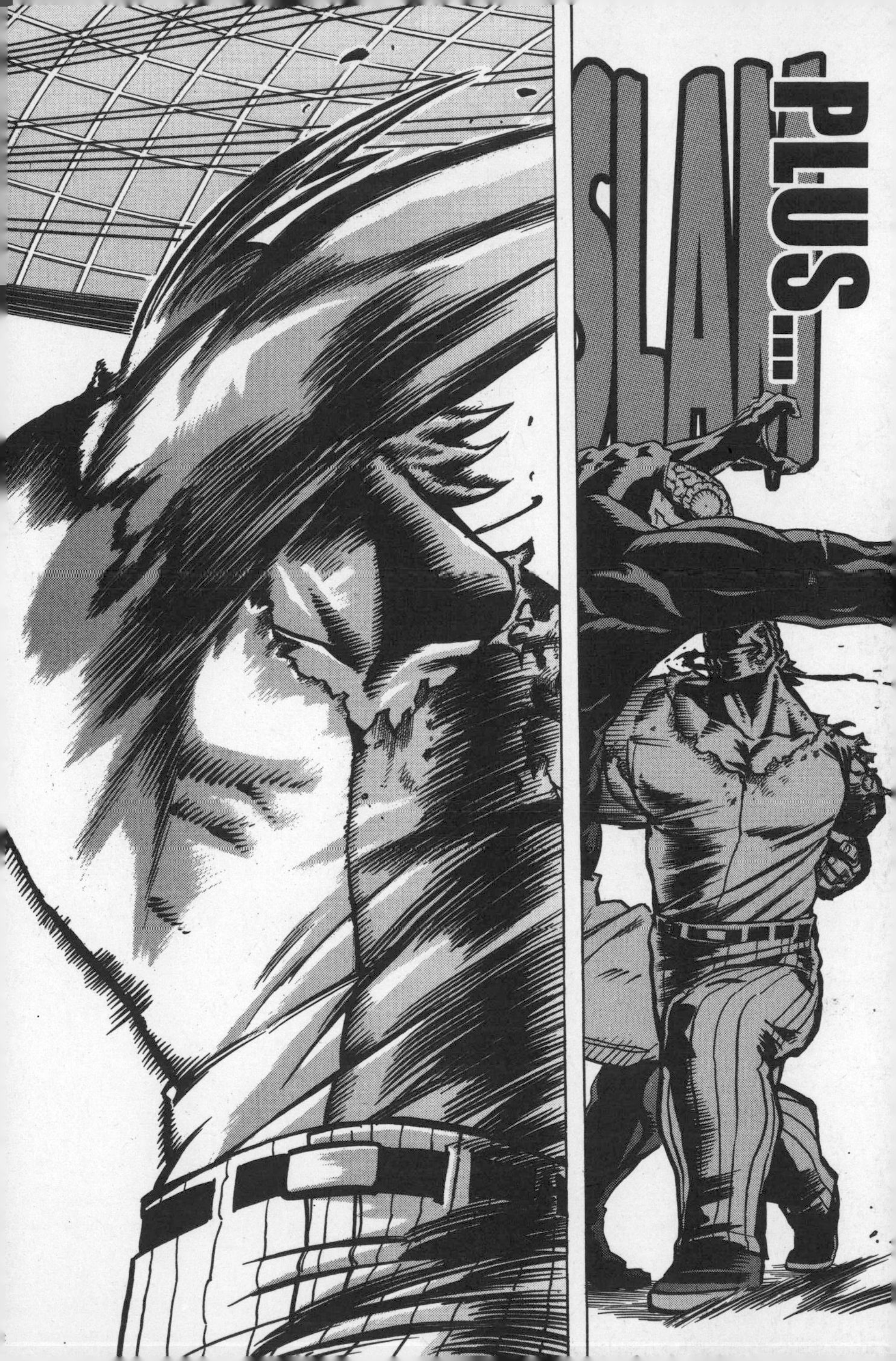
PLUS...
SLAM

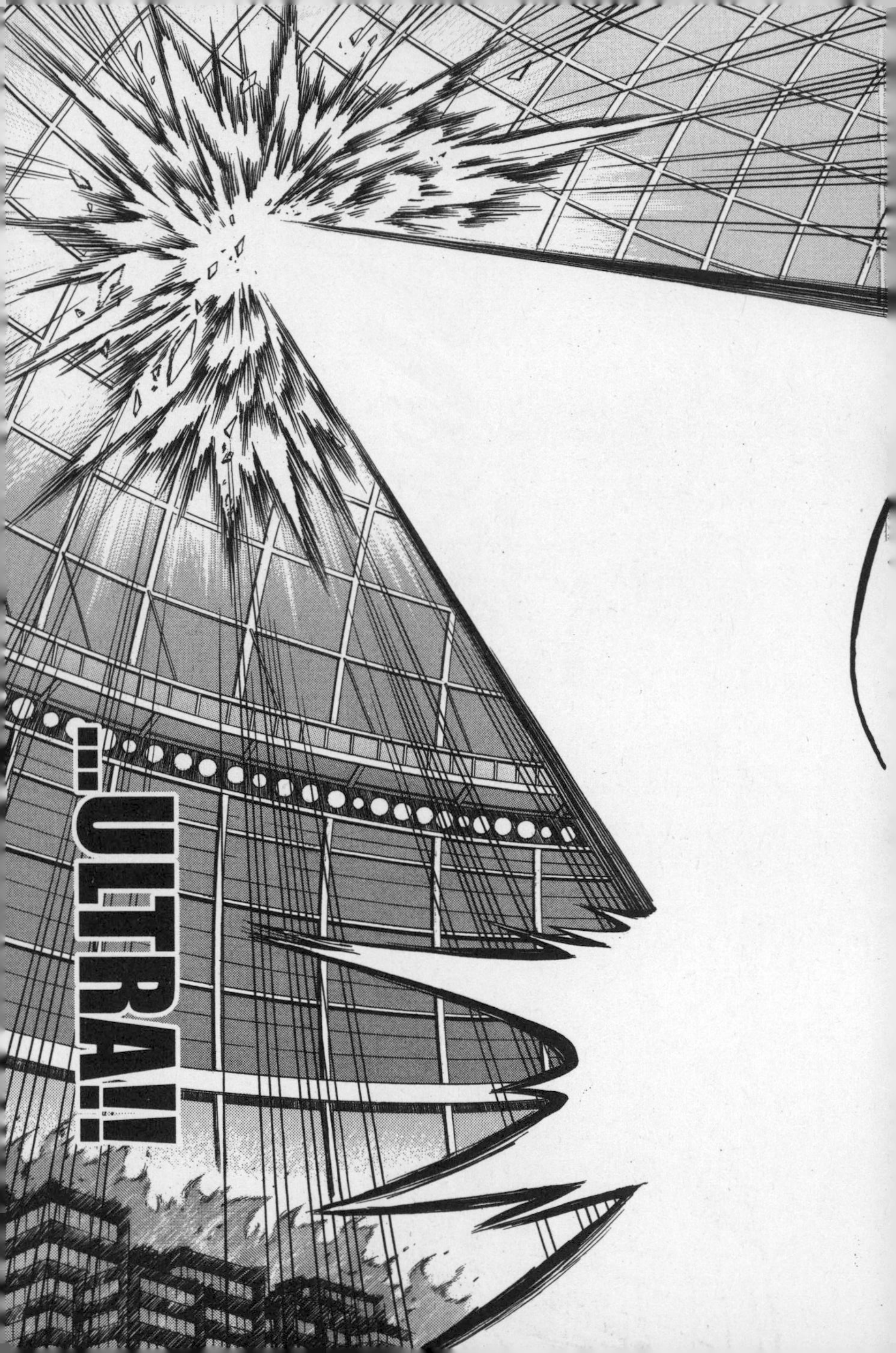
...ULTRA!!

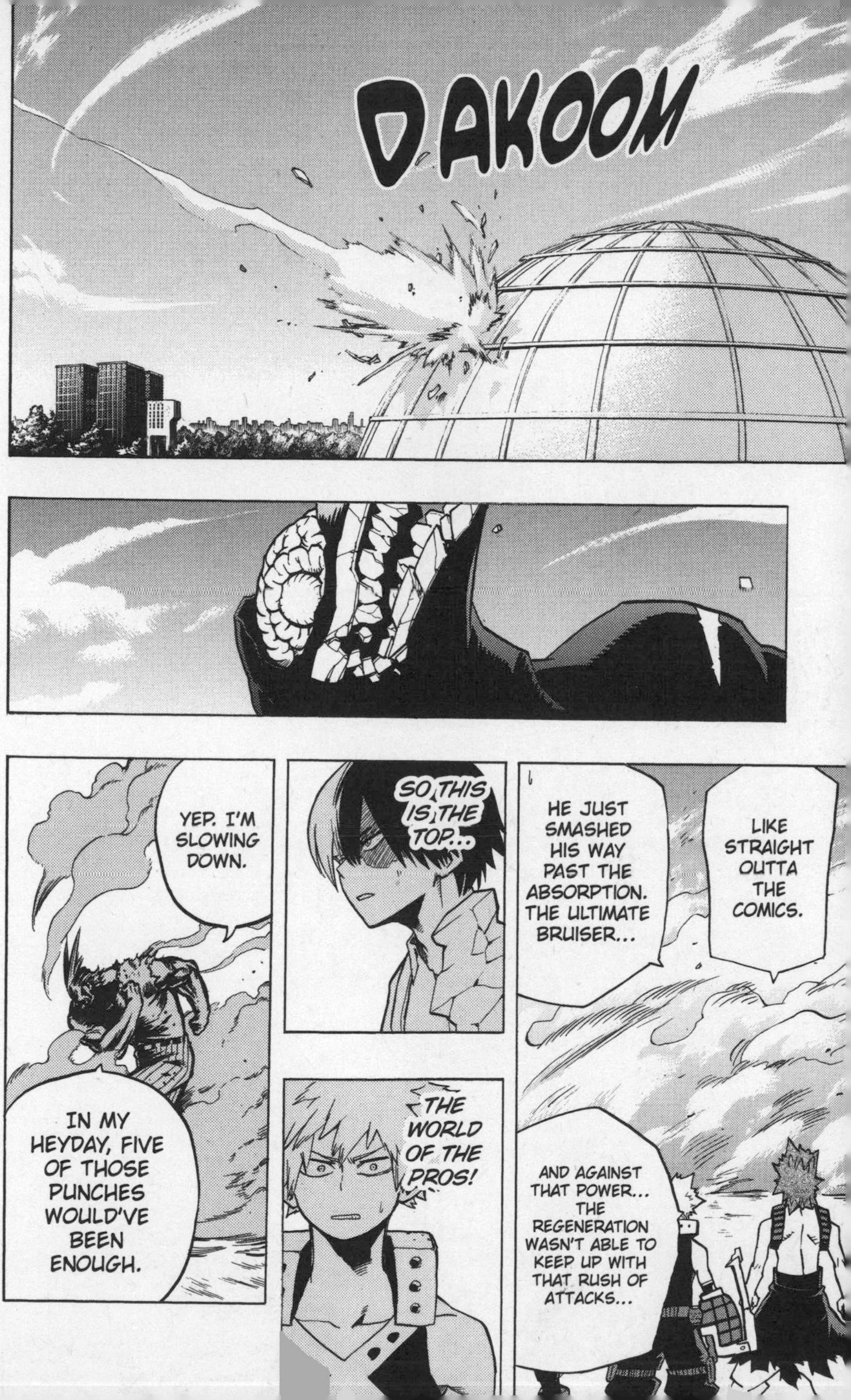
DAKOOM
LIKE STRAIGHT OUTTA THE COMICS.
HE JUST SMASHED HIS WAY PAST THE ABSORPTION. THE ULTIMATE BRUISER...
AND AGAINST THAT POWER... THE REGENERATION WASN'T ABLE TO KEEP UP WITH THAT RUSH OF ATTACKS...
SO THIS IS THE TOP...
THE WORLD OF THE PROS!
YEP. I'M SLOWING DOWN.
IN MY HEYDAY, FIVE OF THOSE PUNCHES WOULD'VE BEEN ENOUGH.

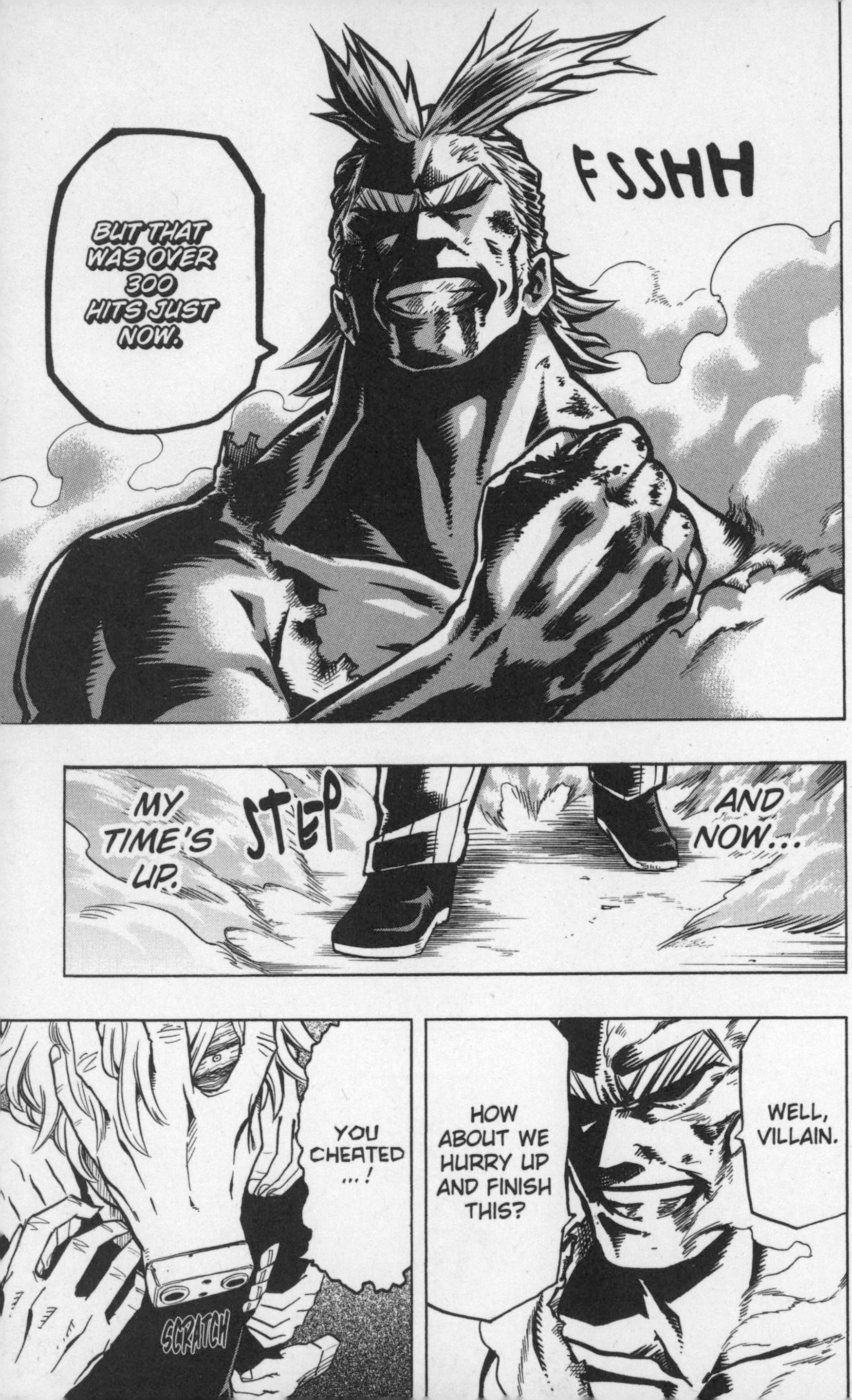
FSSHH
BUT THAT WAS OVER 300 HITS JUST NOW.
AND NOW...
STEP
MY TIME'S UP.
WELL, VILLAIN.
HOW ABOUT WE HURRY UP AND FINISH THIS?
YOU CHEATED ...!
SCRATCH

KYOKA JIRO (15)

BATTLE OF THE BANDS

THE END OF VILLAINS

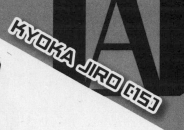

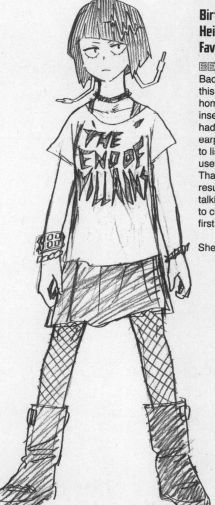

Birthday: 8/1
Height: 154 cm
Favorite Thing: Rock

BEHIND THE SCENES

Back before I even thought up this manga series, I was going home one day, earphones inserted, and I thought "What if I had a character who could plug earphones into all sorts of things to listen to them, or who could use the earphones like whips…! That'd be pretty cool!!" And that resulted in Kyoka. So if we're talking about Quirks as opposed to characters, this is really the first one I came up with.

She looks like she'd play bass.

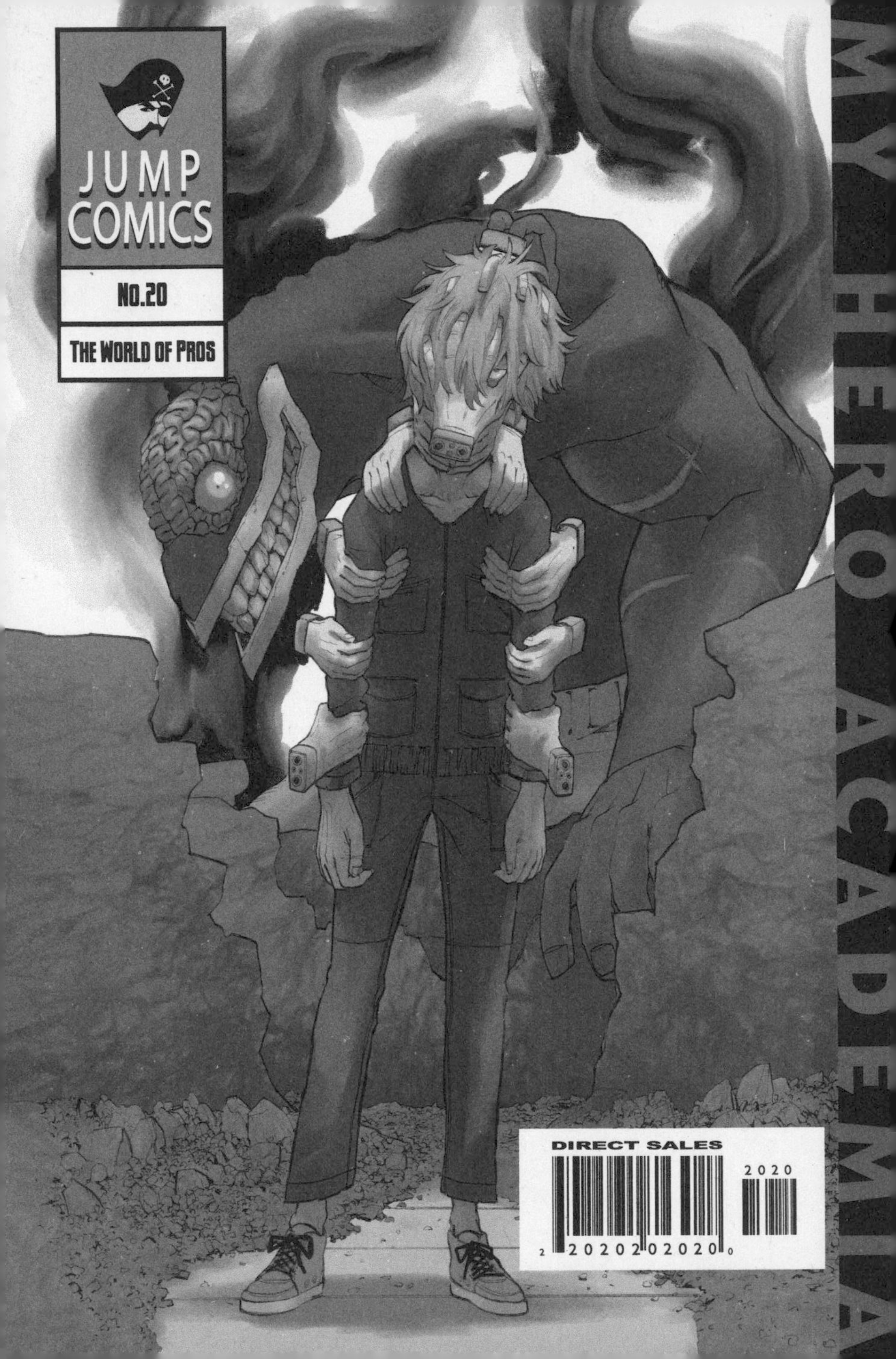
JUMP
COMICS
No.20
THE WORLD OF PROS
MY HERO ACADEMIA
DIRECT SALES
2020
2 20202020200

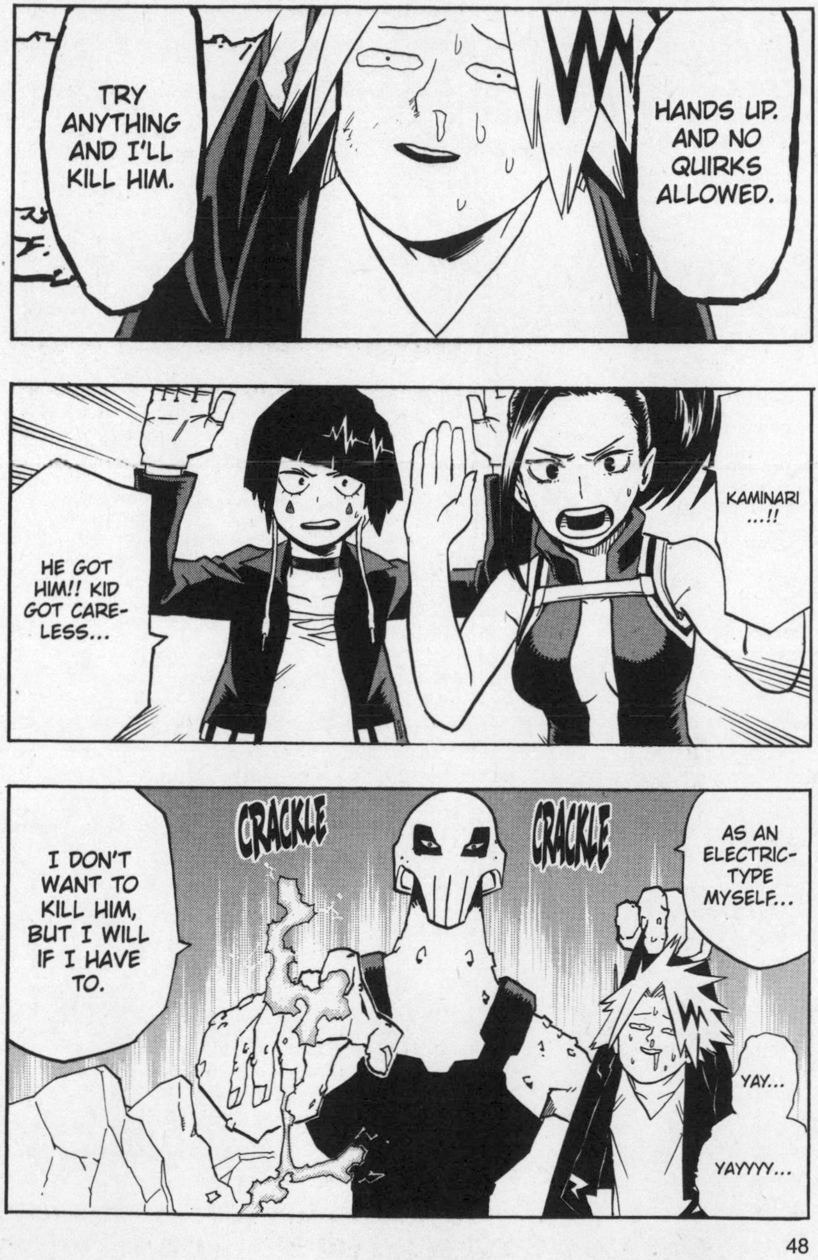
HANDS UP. AND NO QUIRKS ALLOWED.
TRY ANYTHING AND I'LL KILL HIM.
KAMINARI ...!!
HE GOT HIM!! KID GOT CARE-LESS...
AS AN ELECTRIC-TYPE MYSELF...
CRACKLE
CRACKLE
I DON'T WANT TO KILL HIM, BUT I WILL IF I HAVE TO.
YAY...
YAYYYY...

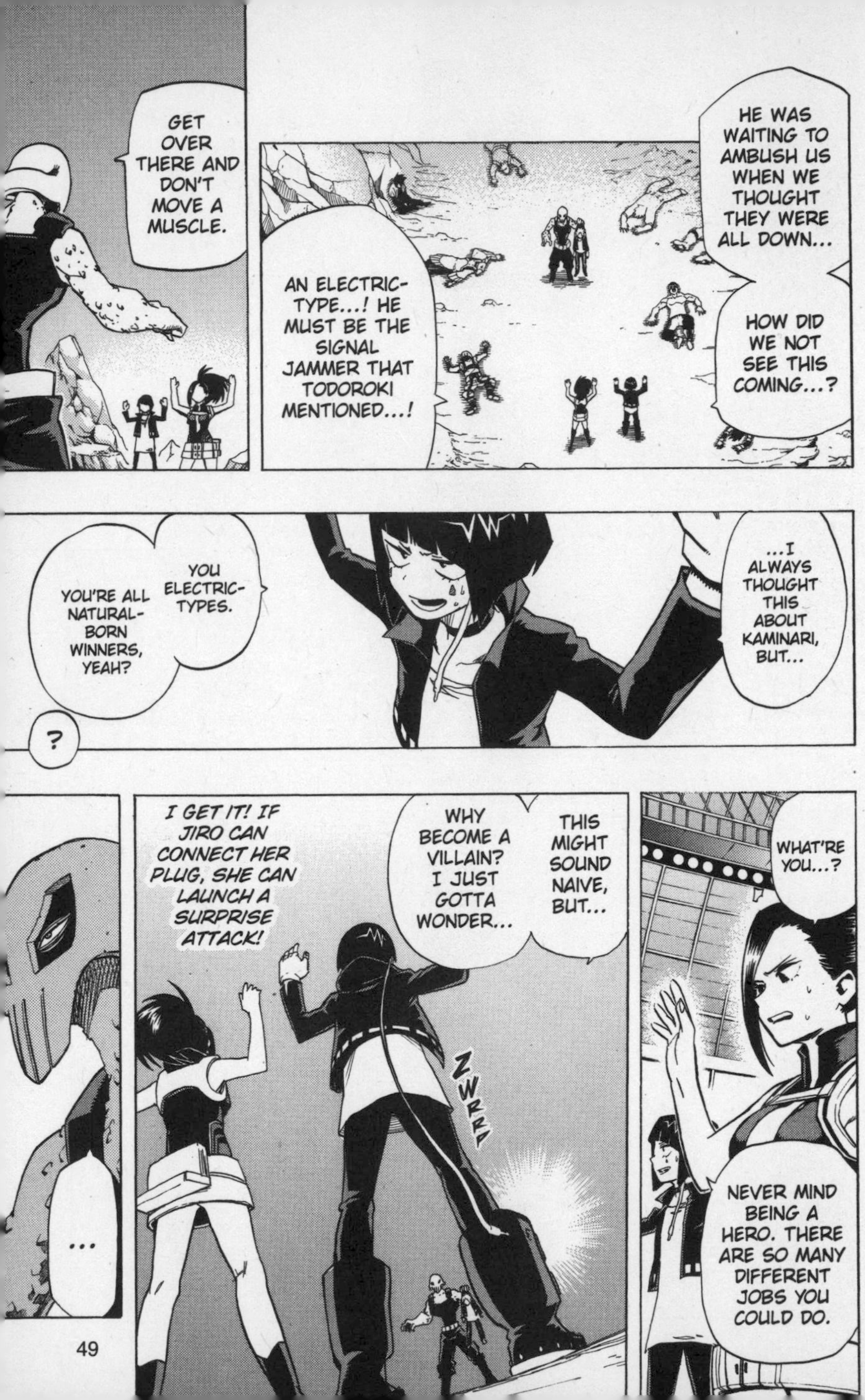
HE WAS WAITING TO AMBUSH US WHEN WE THOUGHT THEY WERE ALL DOWN...
HOW DID WE NOT SEE THIS COMING...?
AN ELECTRIC-TYPE...! HE MUST BE THE SIGNAL JAMMER THAT TODOROKI MENTIONED...!
GET OVER THERE AND DON'T MOVE A MUSCLE.
...I ALWAYS THOUGHT THIS ABOUT KAMINARI, BUT...
YOU ELECTRIC-TYPES.
YOU'RE ALL NATURAL-BORN WINNERS, YEAH?
?
WHAT'RE YOU...?
NEVER MIND BEING A HERO. THERE ARE SO MANY DIFFERENT JOBS YOU COULD DO.
THIS MIGHT SOUND NAIVE, BUT...
WHY BECOME A VILLAIN? I JUST GOTTA WONDER...
I GET IT! IF JIRO CAN CONNECT HER PLUG, SHE CAN LAUNCH A SURPRISE ATTACK!
ZWRRP
...

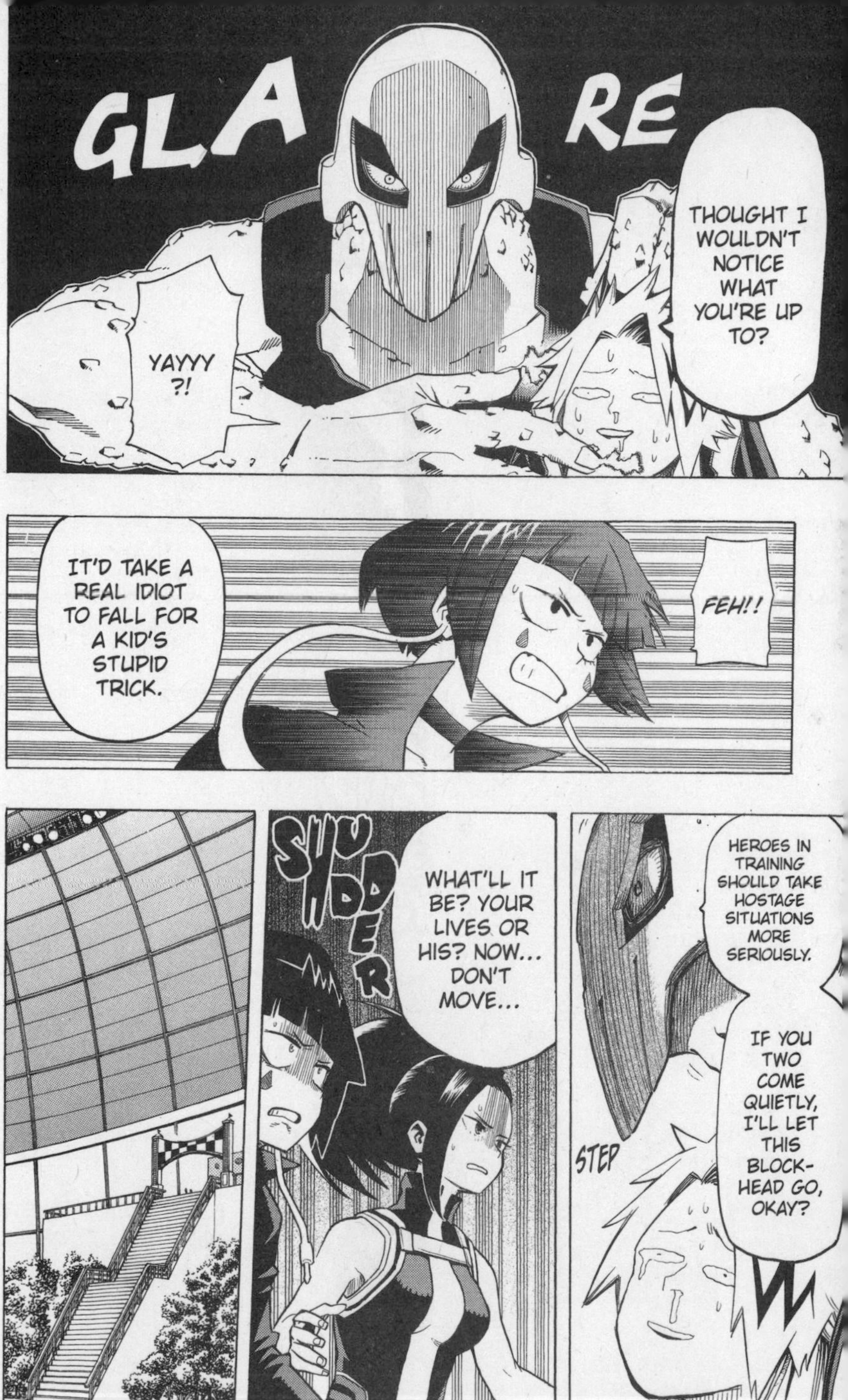
GLARE
THOUGHT I WOULDN'T NOTICE WHAT YOU'RE UP TO?
YAYYY ?!
FEH!!
IT'D TAKE A REAL IDIOT TO FALL FOR A KID'S STUPID TRICK.
HEROES IN TRAINING SHOULD TAKE HOSTAGE SITUATIONS MORE SERIOUSLY.
IF YOU TWO COME QUIETLY, I'LL LET THIS BLOCK-HEAD GO, OKAY?
STEP
SHUDDER
WHAT'LL IT BE? YOUR LIVES OR HIS? NOW... DON'T MOVE...

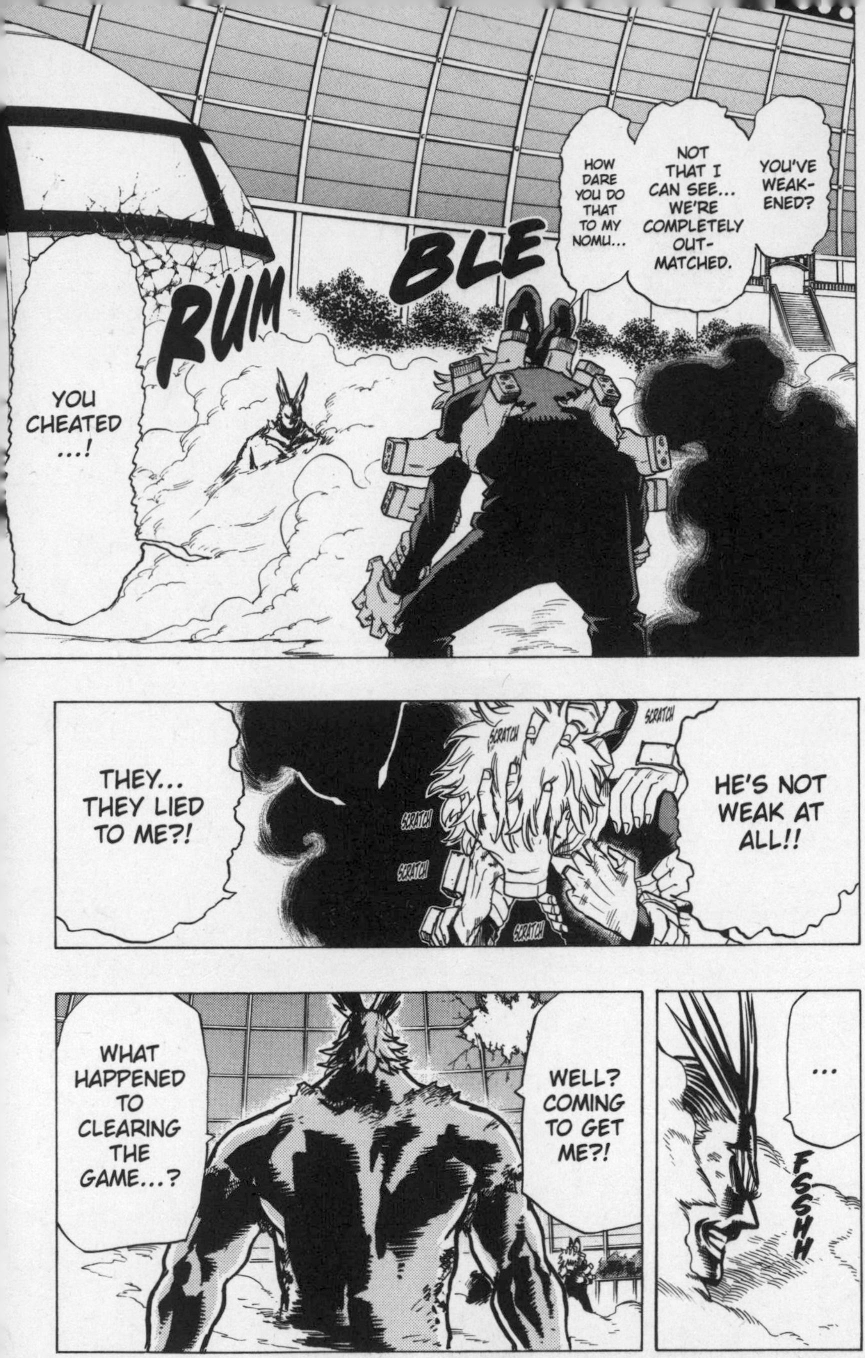
YOU'VE WEAKENED?
NOT THAT I CAN SEE... WE'RE COMPLETELY OUTMATCHED.
HOW DARE YOU DO THAT TO MY NOMU...
RUMBLE
YOU CHEATED ...!
HE'S NOT WEAK AT ALL!!
SCRATCH
SCRATCH
SCRATCH
SCRATCH
SCRATCH
THEY... THEY LIED TO ME?!
...
FSSHH
WELL? COMING TO GET ME?!
WHAT HAPPENED TO CLEARING THE GAME...?

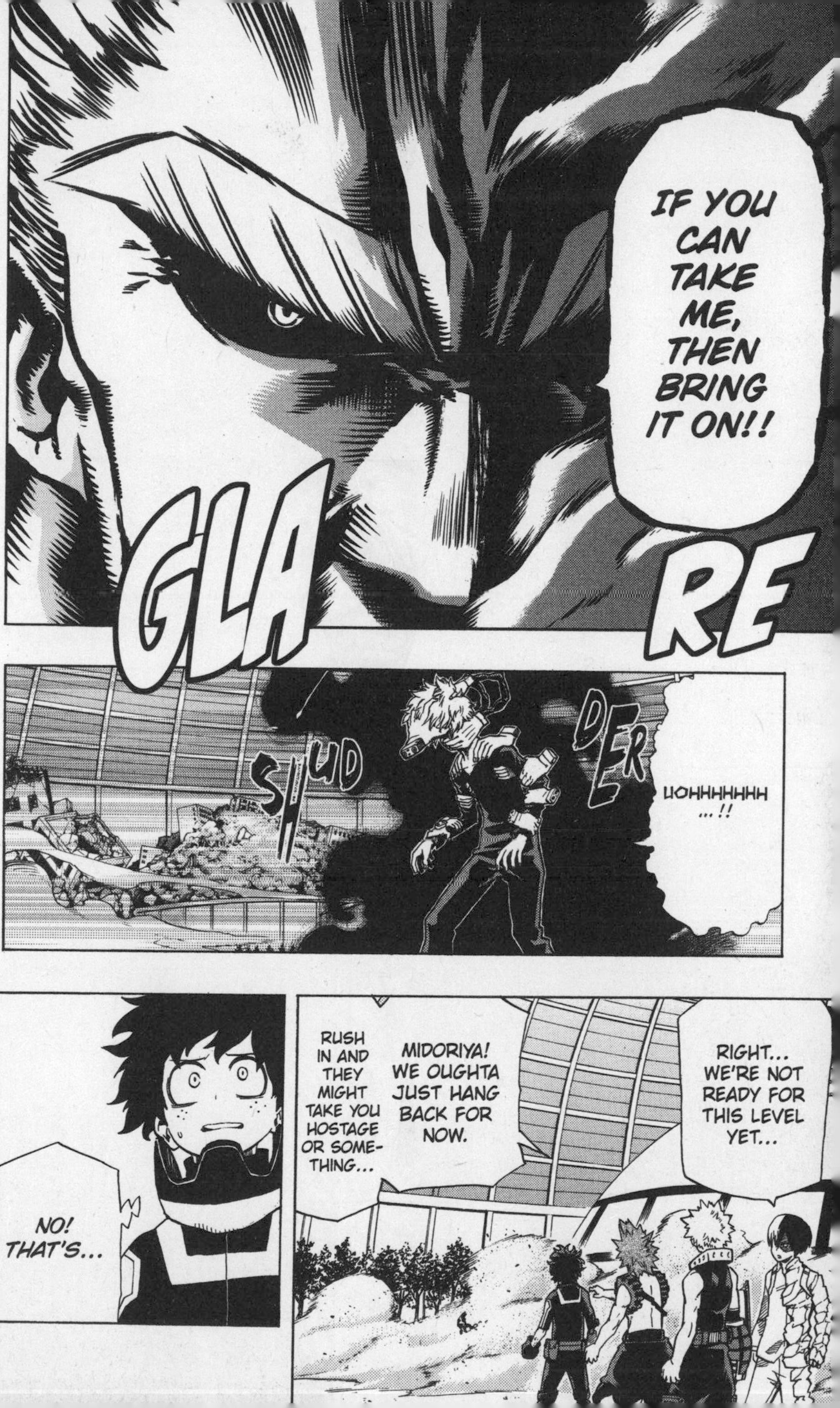
IF YOU CAN TAKE ME, THEN BRING IT ON!!
GLARE
UOHHHHHHH...!!
SHUDDER
RIGHT... WE'RE NOT READY FOR THIS LEVEL YET...
MIDORIYA! WE OUGHTA JUST HANG BACK FOR NOW.
RUSH IN AND THEY MIGHT TAKE YOU HOSTAGE OR SOME-THING...
NO! THAT'S...

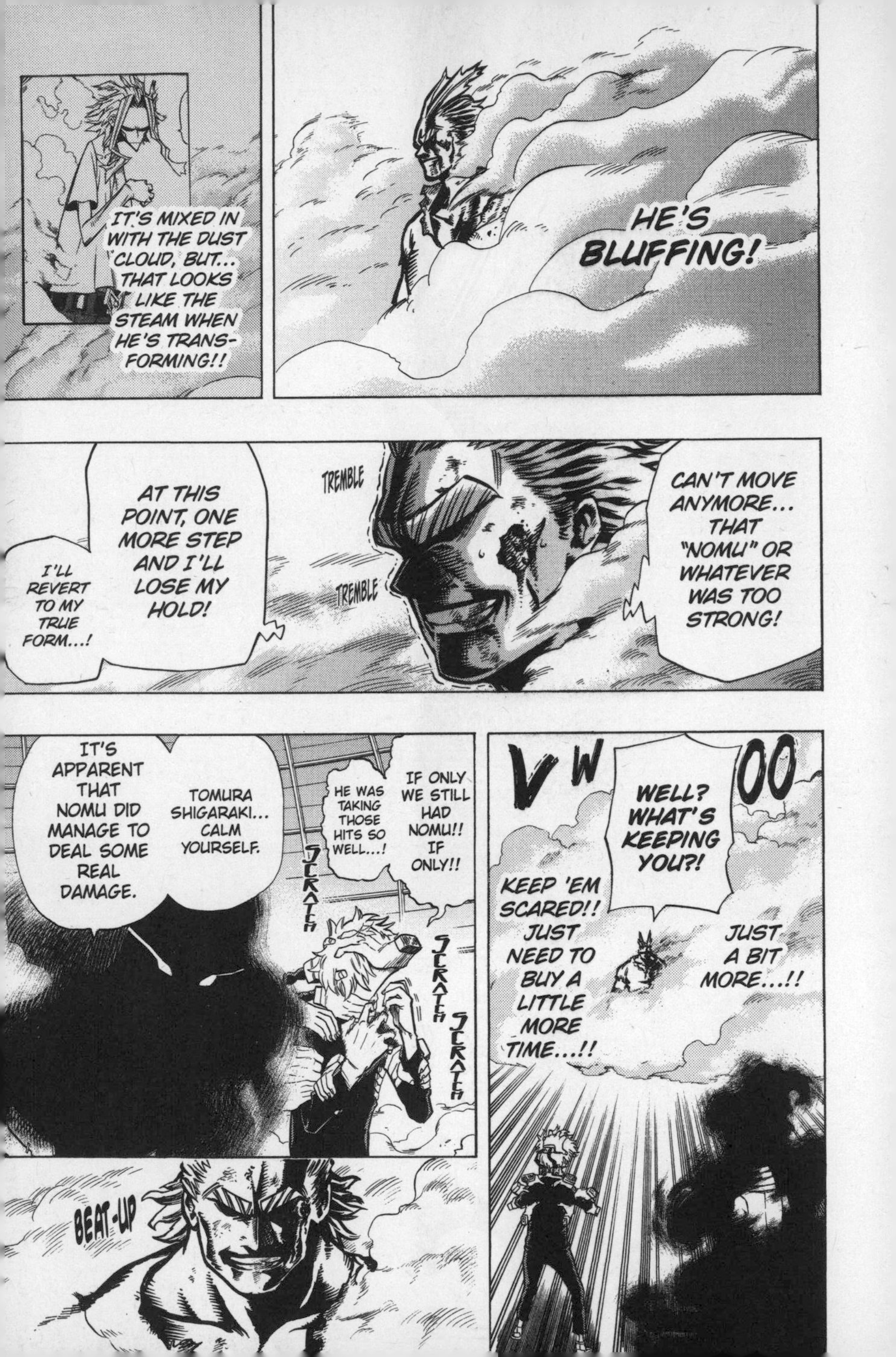
HE'S BLUFFING!
IT'S MIXED IN WITH THE DUST CLOUD, BUT... THAT LOOKS LIKE THE STEAM WHEN HE'S TRANS-FORMING!!
CAN'T MOVE ANYMORE... THAT "NOMU" OR WHATEVER WAS TOO STRONG!
TREMBLE
TREMBLE
AT THIS POINT, ONE MORE STEP AND I'LL LOSE MY HOLD!
I'LL REVERT TO MY TRUE FORM...!
VWOO
WELL? WHAT'S KEEPING YOU?!
JUST A BIT MORE...!!
KEEP 'EM SCARED!! JUST NEED TO BUY A LITTLE MORE TIME...!!
IF ONLY WE STILL HAD NOMU!! IF ONLY!!
HE WAS TAKING THOSE HITS SO WELL...!
TOMURA SHIGARAKI... CALM YOURSELF.
IT'S APPARENT THAT NOMU DID MANAGE TO DEAL SOME REAL DAMAGE.
SCRATCH
SCRATCH
SCRATCH
BEAT-UP

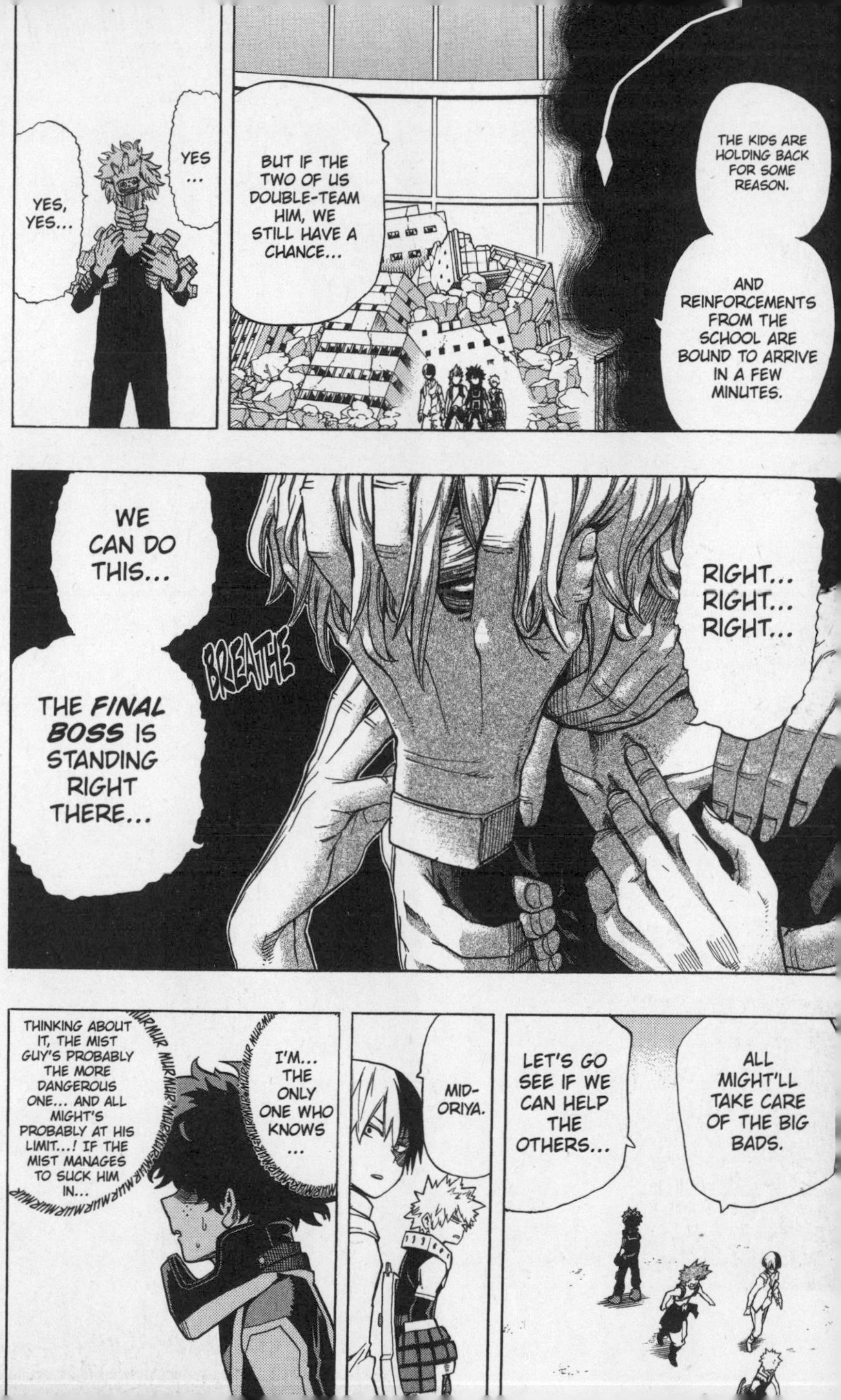
THE KIDS ARE HOLDING BACK FOR SOME REASON.
AND REINFORCEMENTS FROM THE SCHOOL ARE BOUND TO ARRIVE IN A FEW MINUTES.
BUT IF THE TWO OF US DOUBLE-TEAM HIM, WE STILL HAVE A CHANCE...
YES ...
YES, YES...
RIGHT... RIGHT... RIGHT...
WE CAN DO THIS...
BREATHE
THE *FINAL BOSS* IS STANDING RIGHT THERE...
ALL MIGHT'LL TAKE CARE OF THE BIG BADS.
LET'S GO SEE IF WE CAN HELP THE OTHERS...
MID-ORIYA.
I'M... THE ONLY ONE WHO KNOWS ...
MURMUR MURMUR MURMUR MURMUR
THINKING ABOUT IT, THE MIST GUY'S PROBABLY THE MORE DANGEROUS ONE... AND ALL MIGHT'S PROBABLY AT HIS LIMIT...! IF THE MIST MANAGES TO SUCK HIM IN...

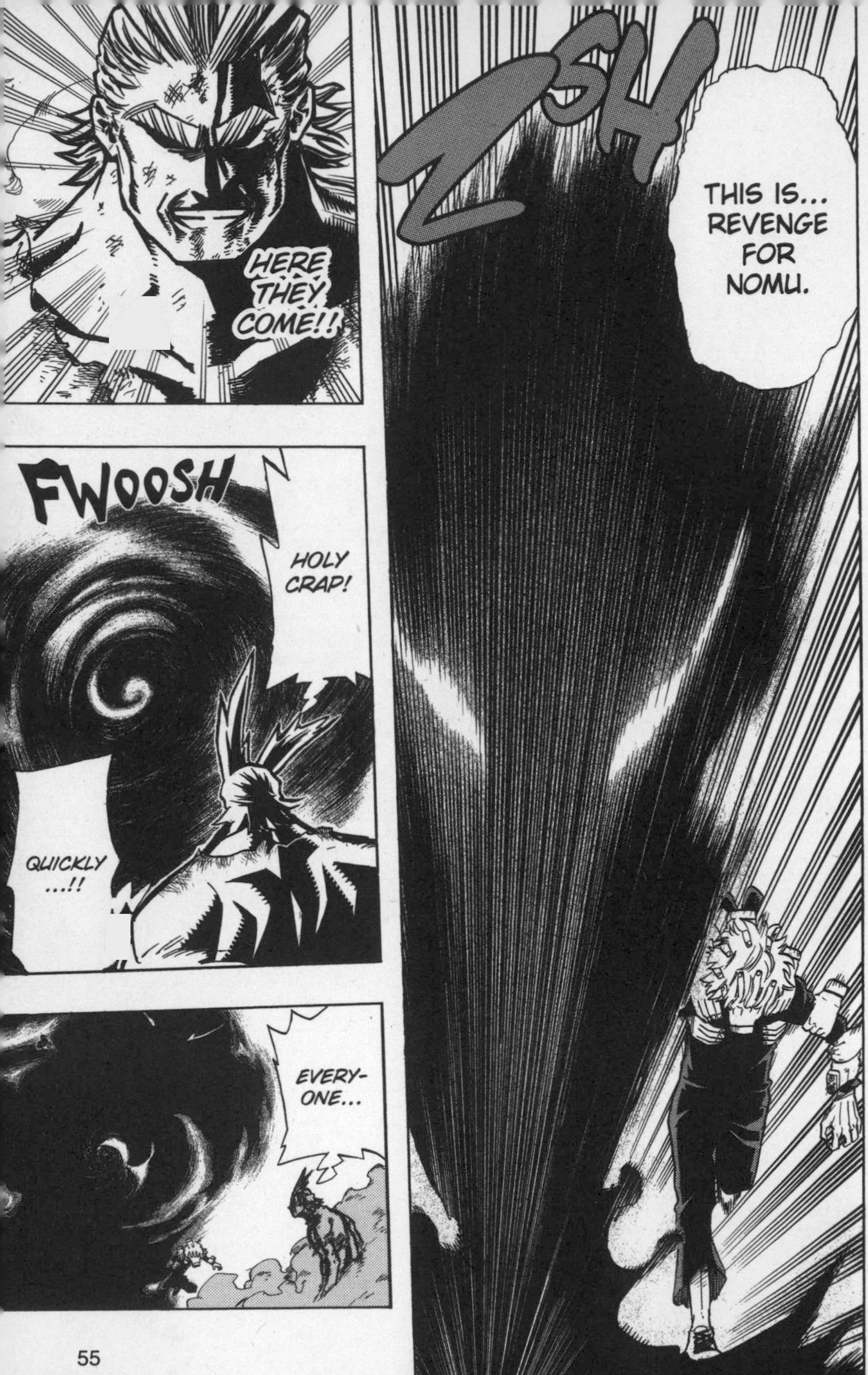
ZSH
THIS IS... REVENGE FOR NOMU.
HERE THEY COME!!
FWOOSH
HOLY CRAP!
QUICKLY ...!!
EVERY-ONE...

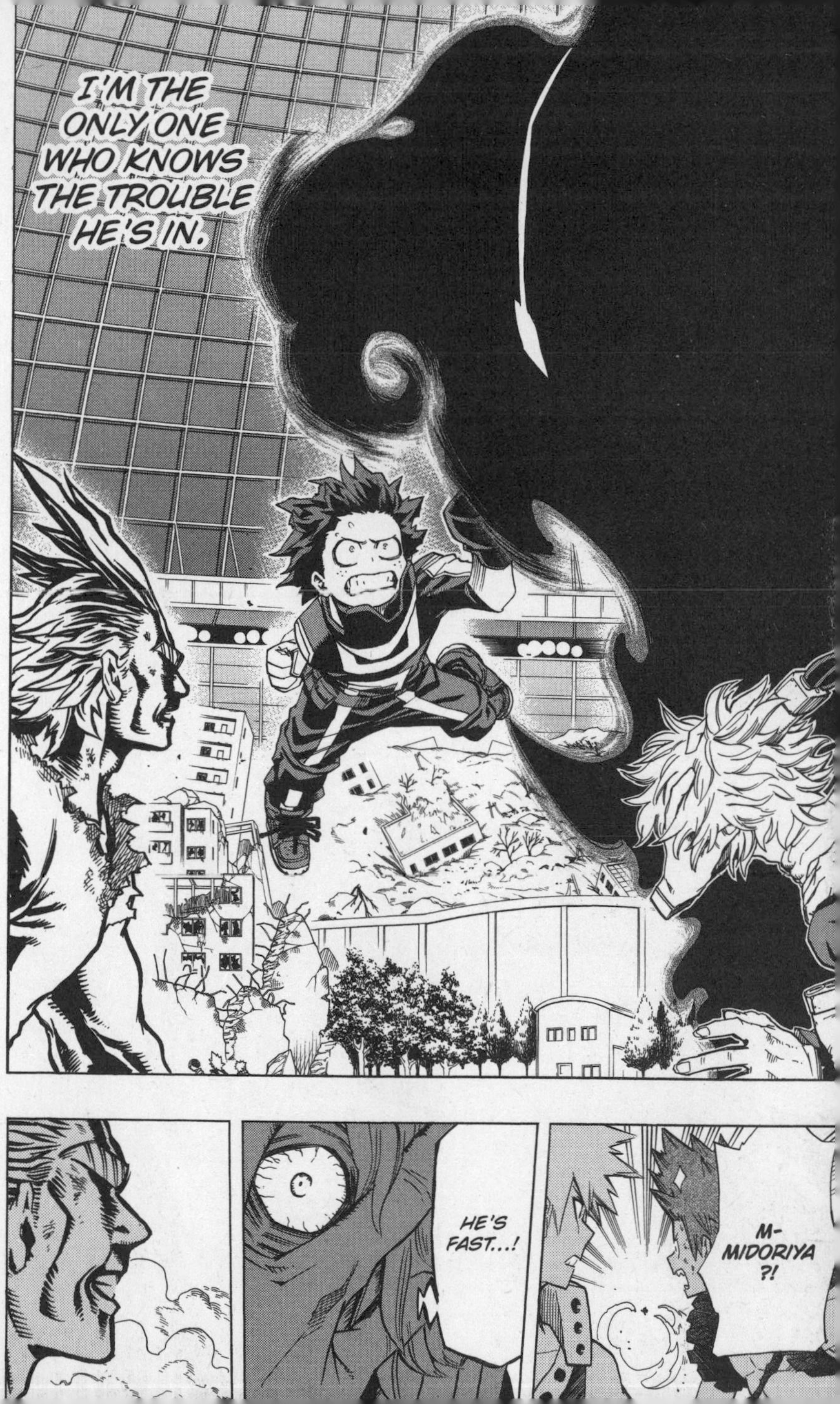
I'M THE ONLY ONE WHO KNOWS THE TROUBLE HE'S IN.
M-MIDORIYA ?!
HE'S FAST...!

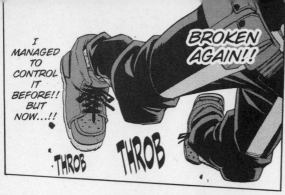

I MANAGED TO CONTROL IT BEFORE!! BUT NOW...!!

BROKEN AGAIN!!

THROB THROB

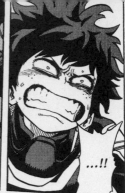

...!!

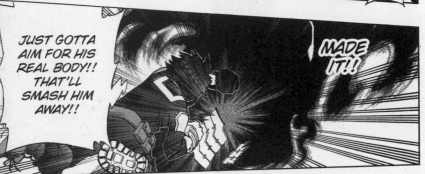

JUST GOTTA AIM FOR HIS REAL BODY!! THAT'LL SMASH HIM AWAY!!

MADE IT!!

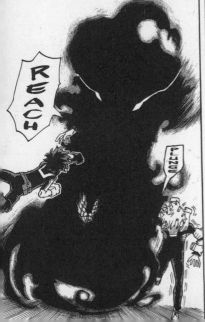

REACH

PLUNGE

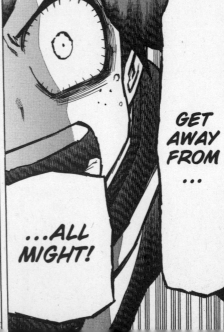

GET AWAY FROM...

...ALL MIGHT!

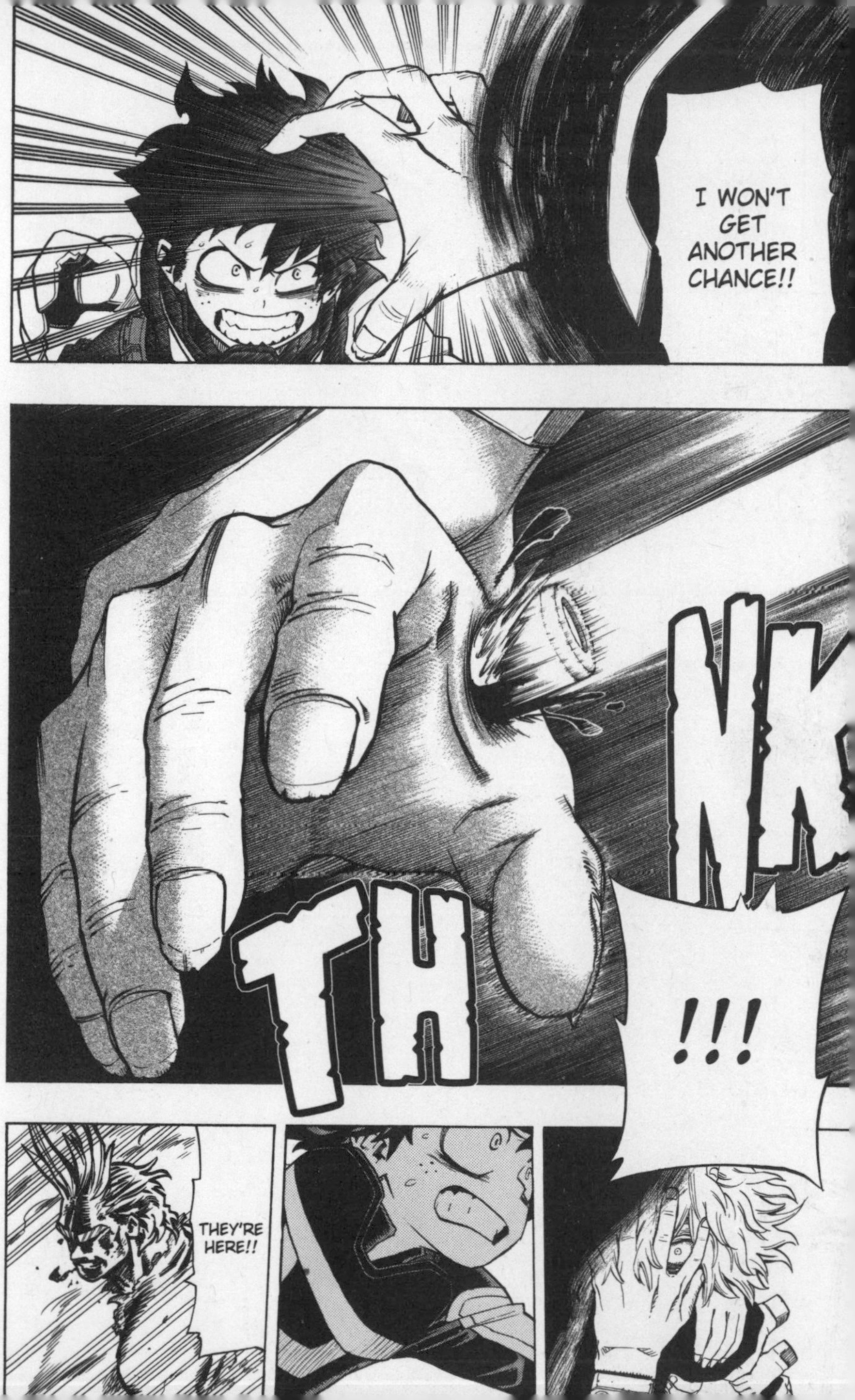
I WON'T GET ANOTHER CHANCE!!
THNK
!!!
THEY'RE HERE!!

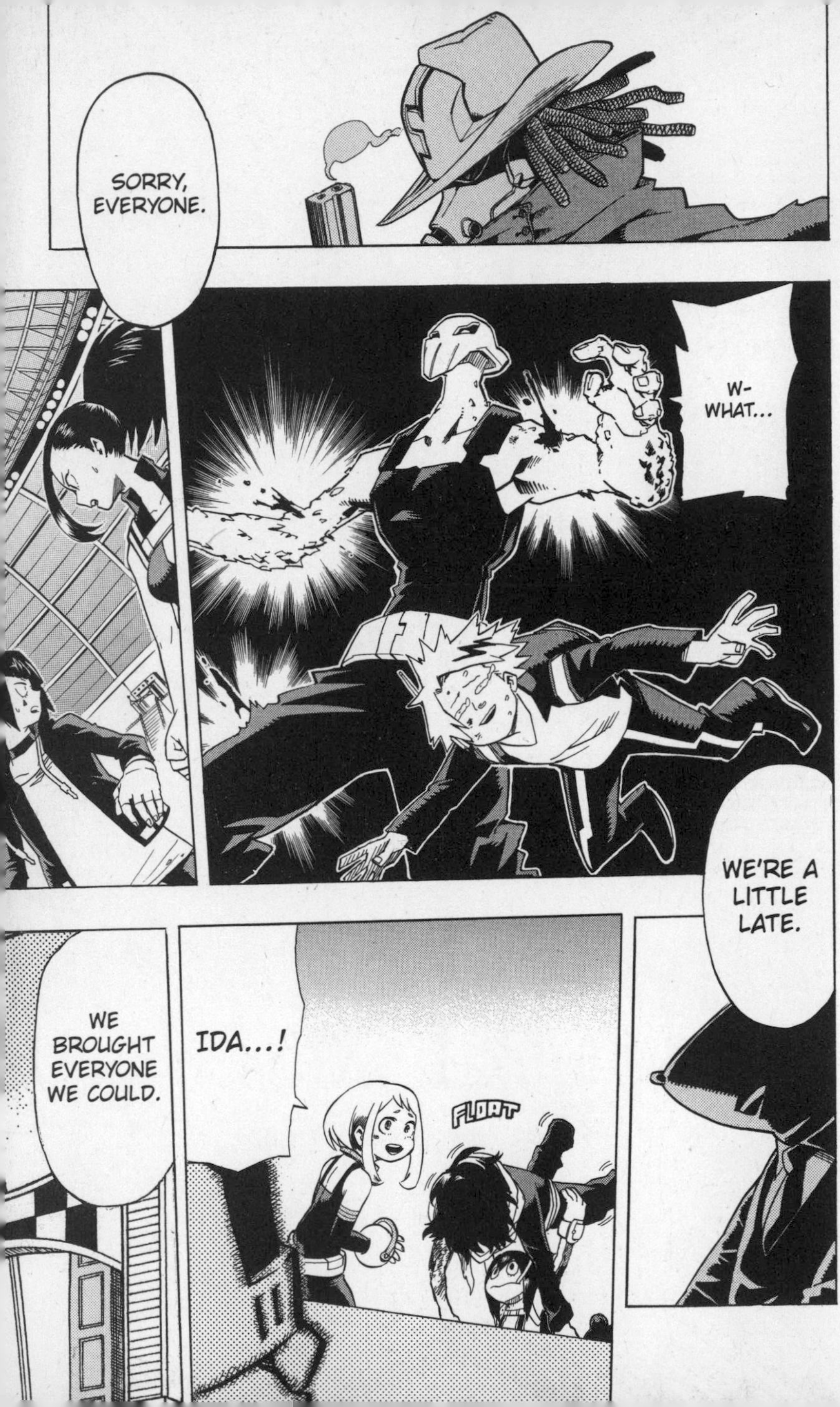
SORRY, EVERYONE.
W- WHAT...
WE'RE A LITTLE LATE.
IDA...!
FLOAT
WE BROUGHT EVERYONE WE COULD.

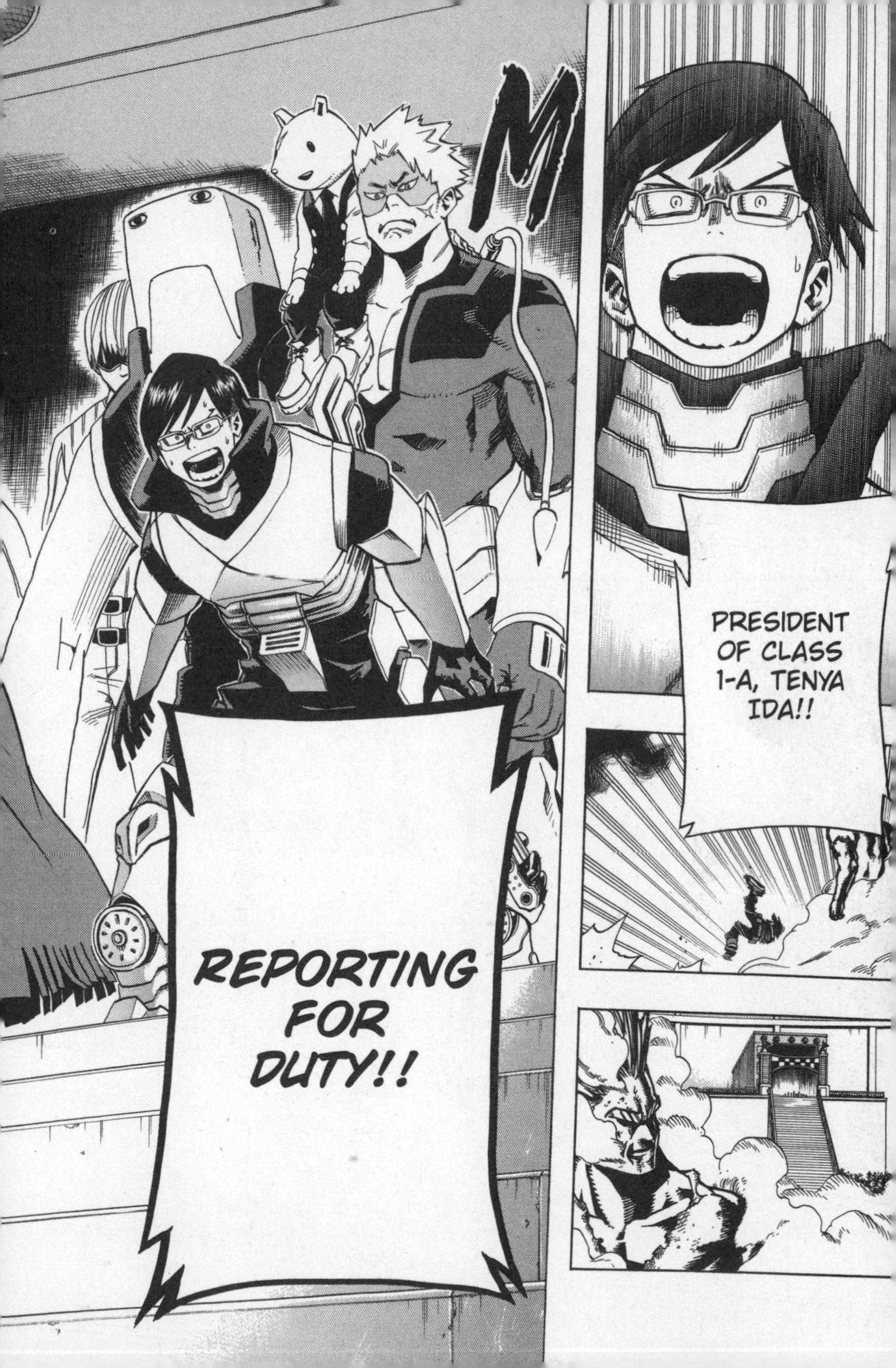
PRESIDENT OF CLASS 1-A, TENYA IDA!!
M
REPORTING FOR DUTY!!

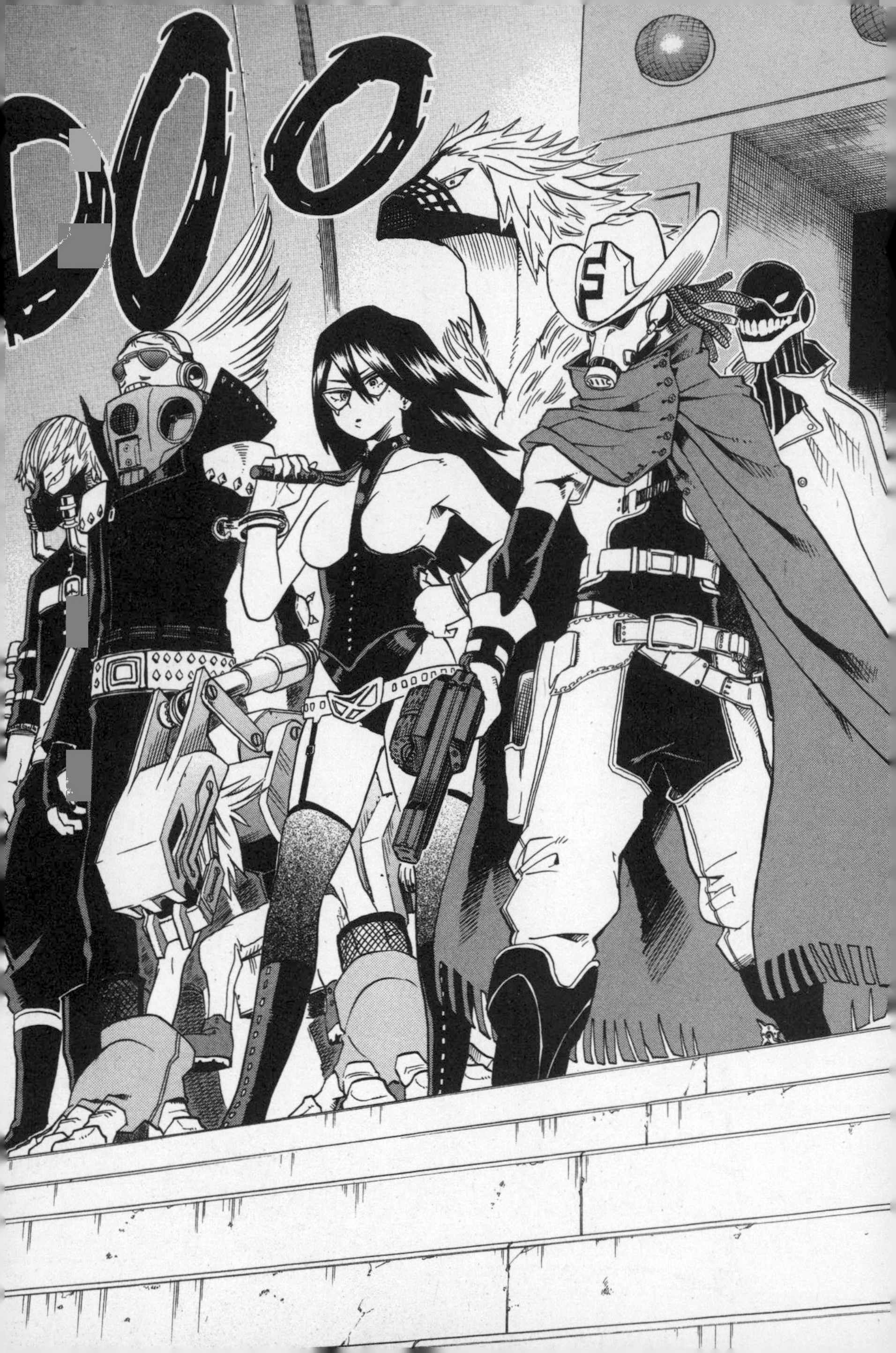
DOO

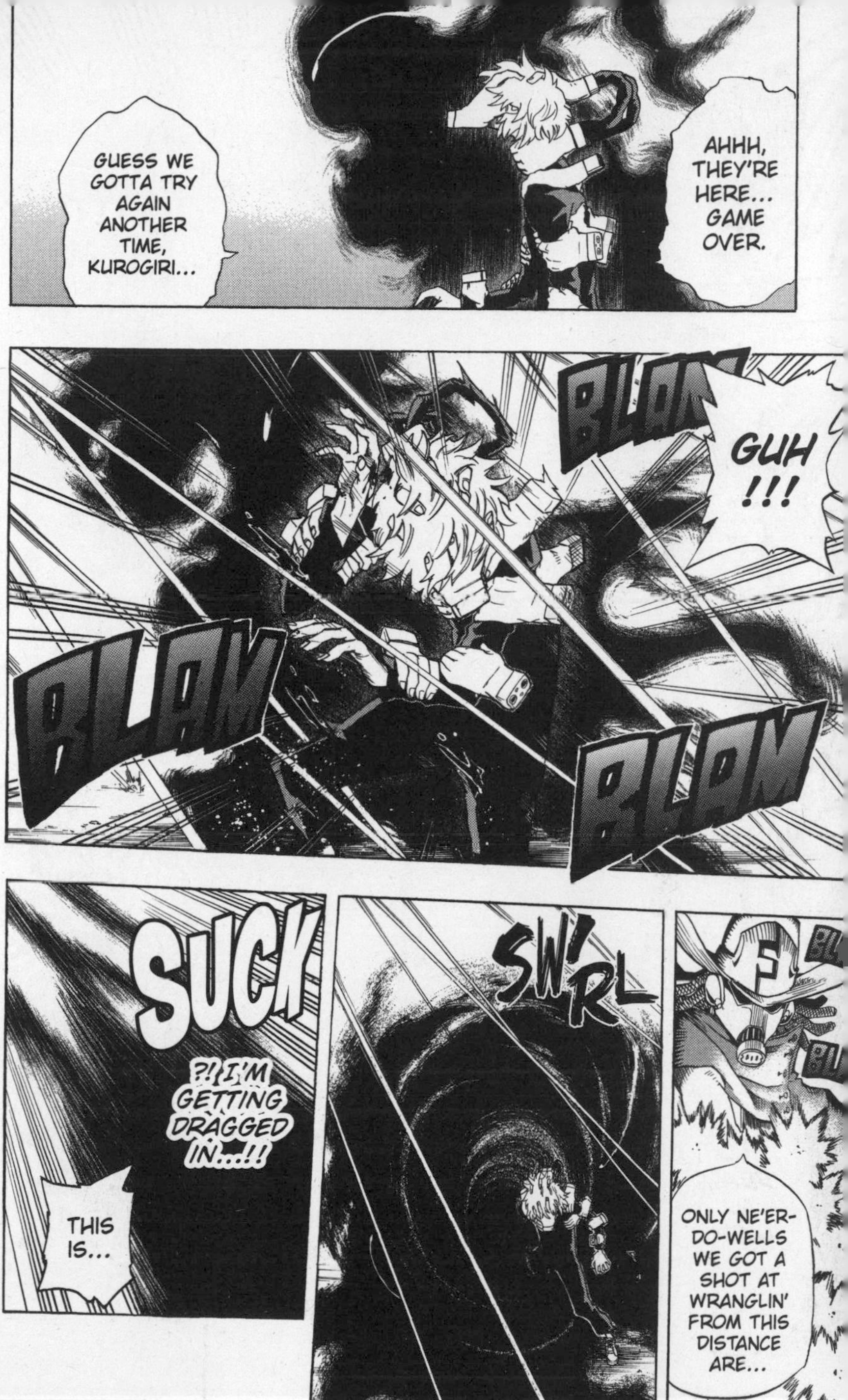
AHHH, THEY'RE HERE... GAME OVER.
GUESS WE GOTTA TRY AGAIN ANOTHER TIME, KUROGIRI...
BLAM
GUH !!!
BLAM
BLAM
ONLY NE'ER-DO-WELLS WE GOT A SHOT AT WRANGLIN' FROM THIS DISTANCE ARE...
SWIRL
SUCK
?! I'M GETTING DRAGGED IN...!!
THIS IS...

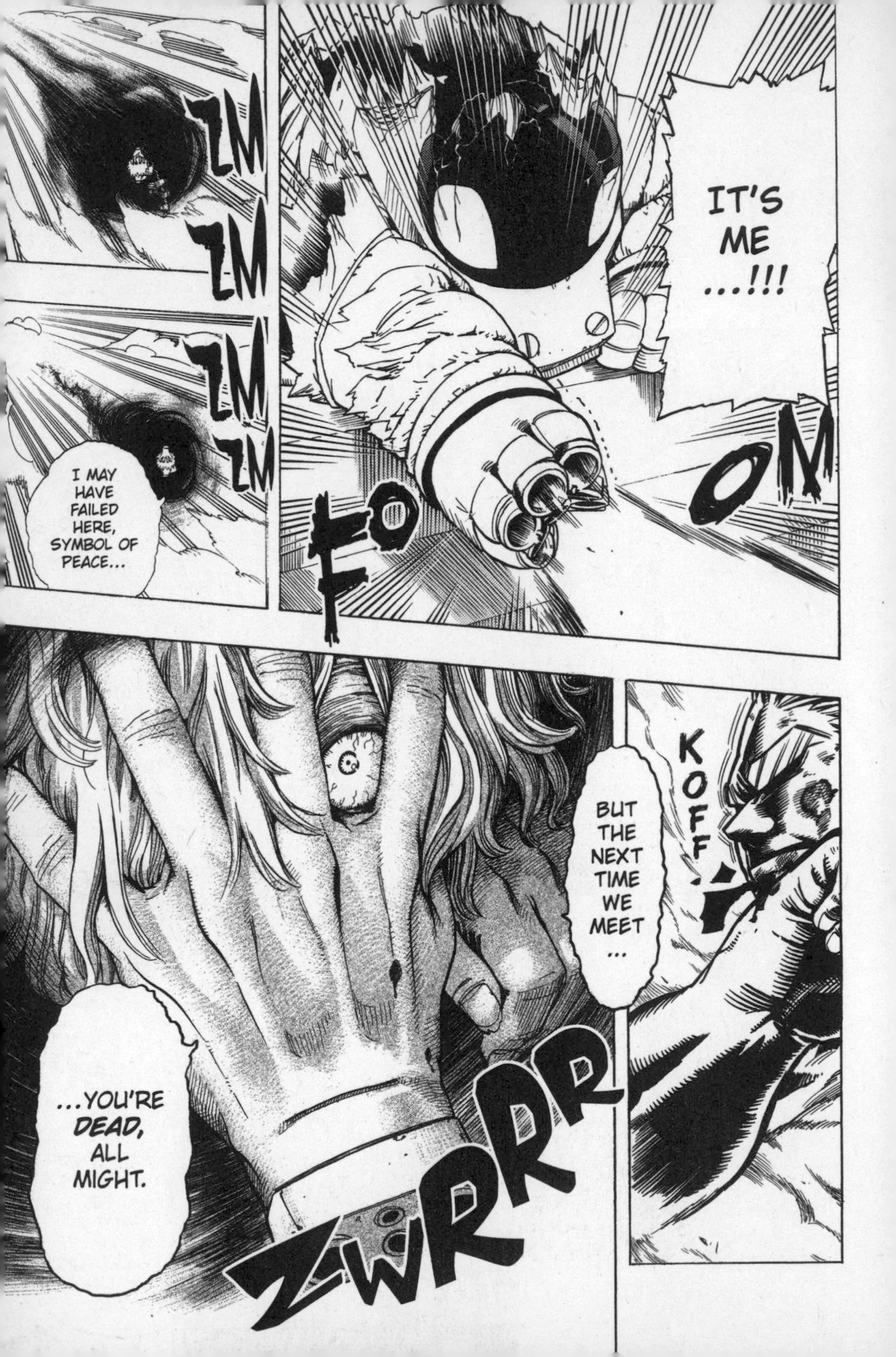
IT'S ME ...!!!
FOOM
ZM ZM
ZM ZM
I MAY HAVE FAILED HERE, SYMBOL OF PEACE...
KOFF
BUT THE NEXT TIME WE MEET ...
...YOU'RE *DEAD*, ALL MIGHT.
ZWRRR

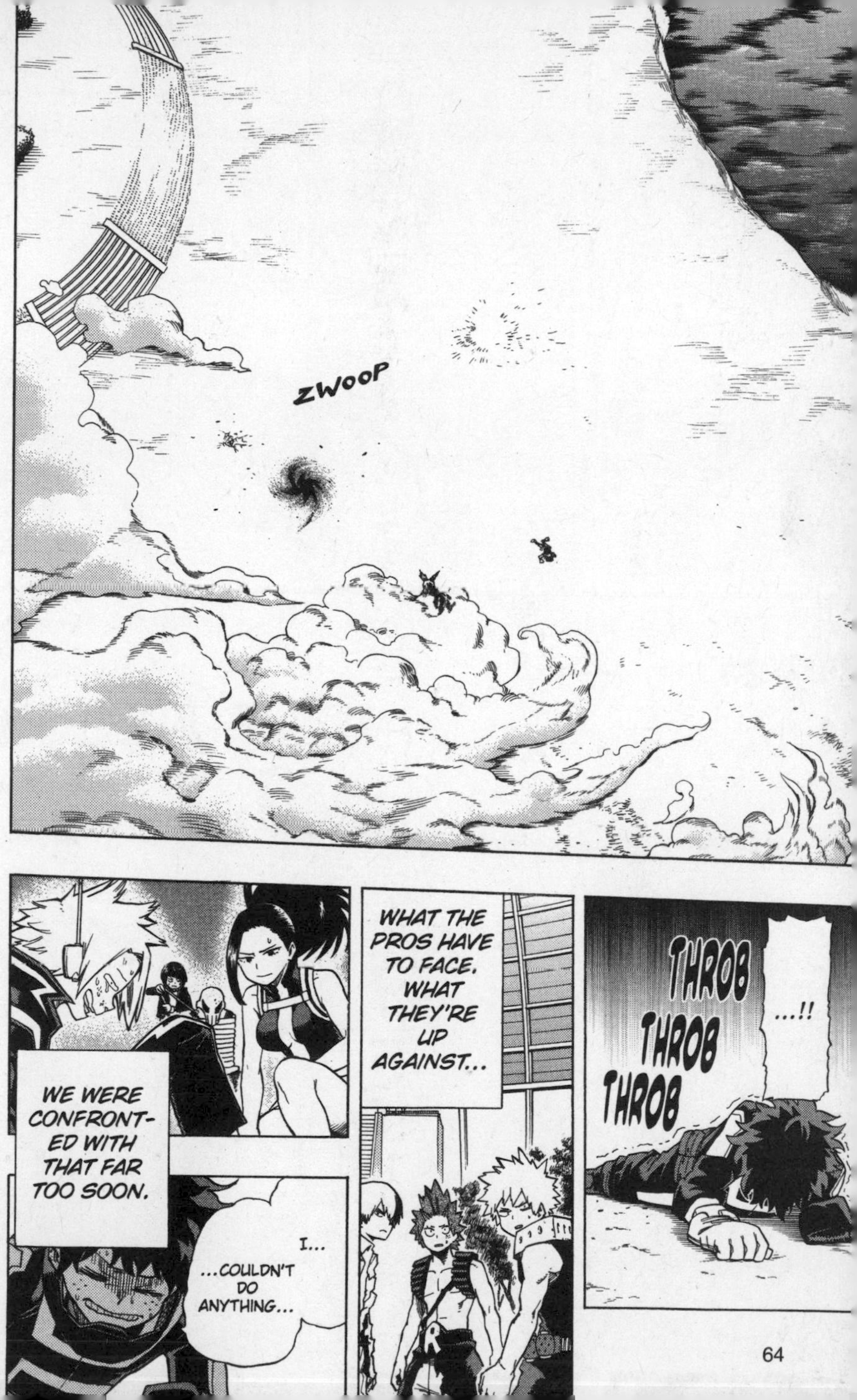
ZWOOP
THROB THROB THROB
...!!
WHAT THE PROS HAVE TO FACE. WHAT THEY'RE UP AGAINST...
WE WERE CONFRONT-ED WITH THAT FAR TOO SOON.
I...
...COULDN'T DO ANYTHING...

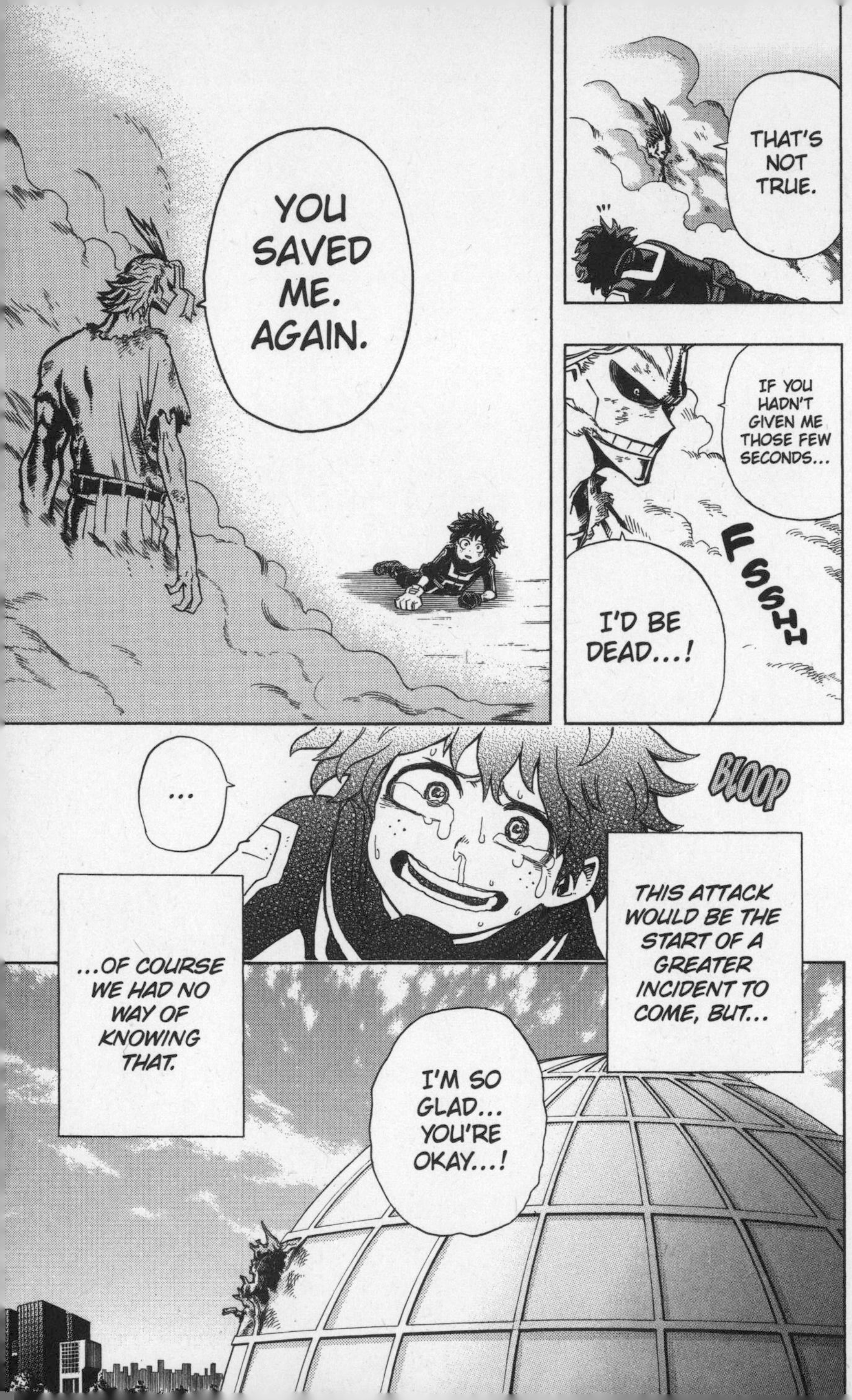
THAT'S NOT TRUE.
IF YOU HADN'T GIVEN ME THOSE FEW SECONDS...
FSSHH
I'D BE DEAD...!
YOU SAVED ME. AGAIN.
BLOOP
...
THIS ATTACK WOULD BE THE START OF A GREATER INCIDENT TO COME, BUT...
...OF COURSE WE HAD NO WAY OF KNOWING THAT.
I'M SO GLAD... YOU'RE OKAY...!

DENKI KAMINARI (15)

STREET CLOTHES

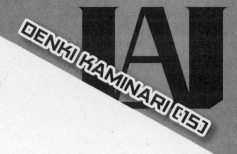

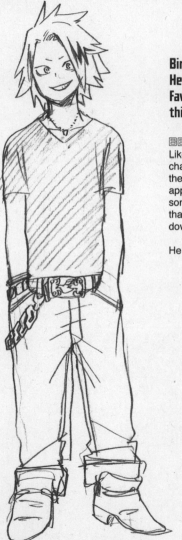

Birthday: 6/29
Height: 168 cm
Favorite Things: Stylish things, hamburgers

BEHIND THE SCENES

Like Kirishima, this is another character who sort of brings the whole class together. His appearance has changed somewhat since his debut, but that wild hairstyle refuses to calm down. It's a pain.

He's fun to draw.

No.21 - In Each of Our Hearts

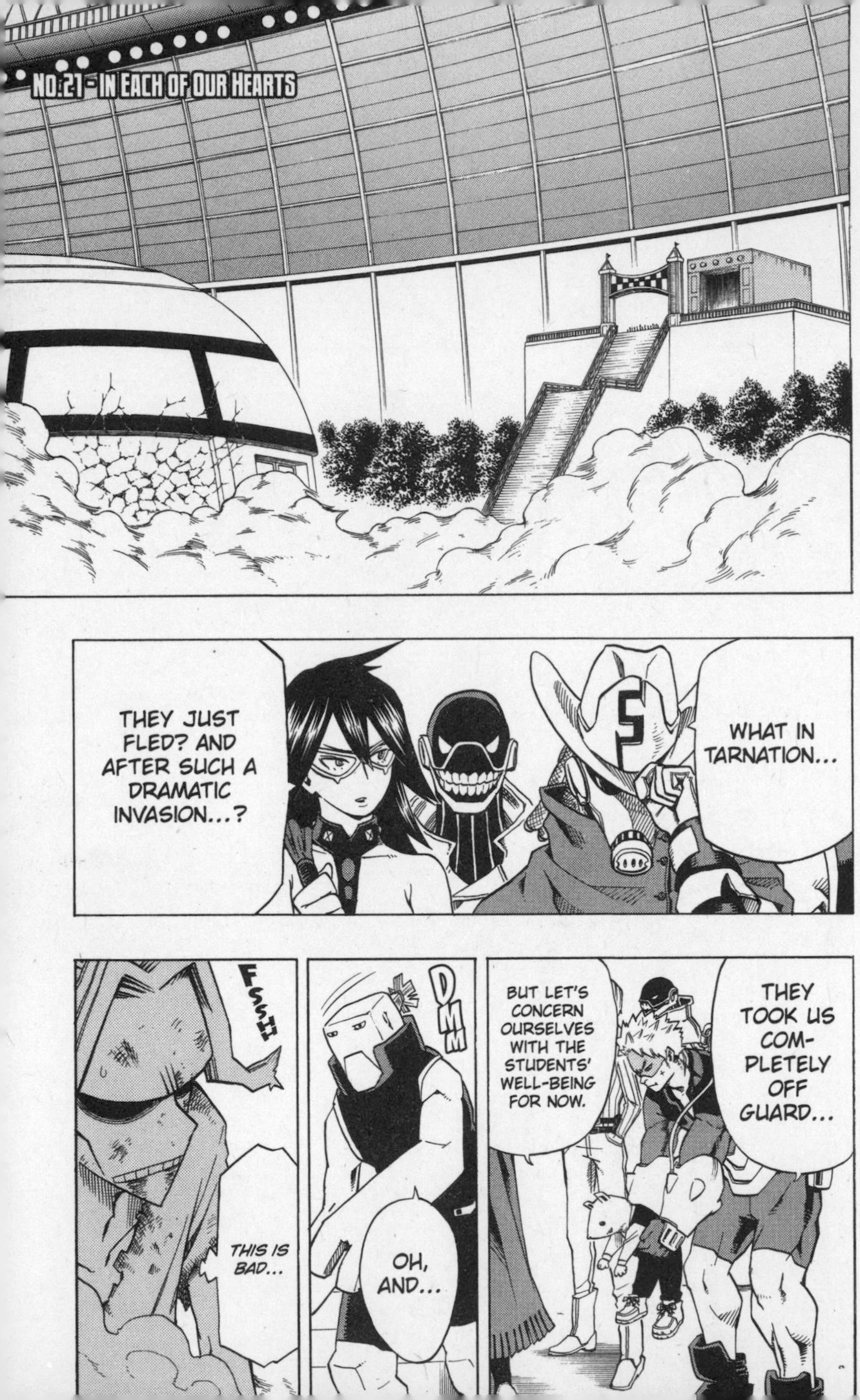

WHAT IN TARNATION...
THEY JUST FLED? AND AFTER SUCH A DRAMATIC INVASION...?
THEY TOOK US COM-PLETELY OFF GUARD...
BUT LET'S CONCERN OURSELVES WITH THE STUDENTS' WELL-BEING FOR NOW.
DMM
OH, AND...
FSSH
THIS IS BAD...

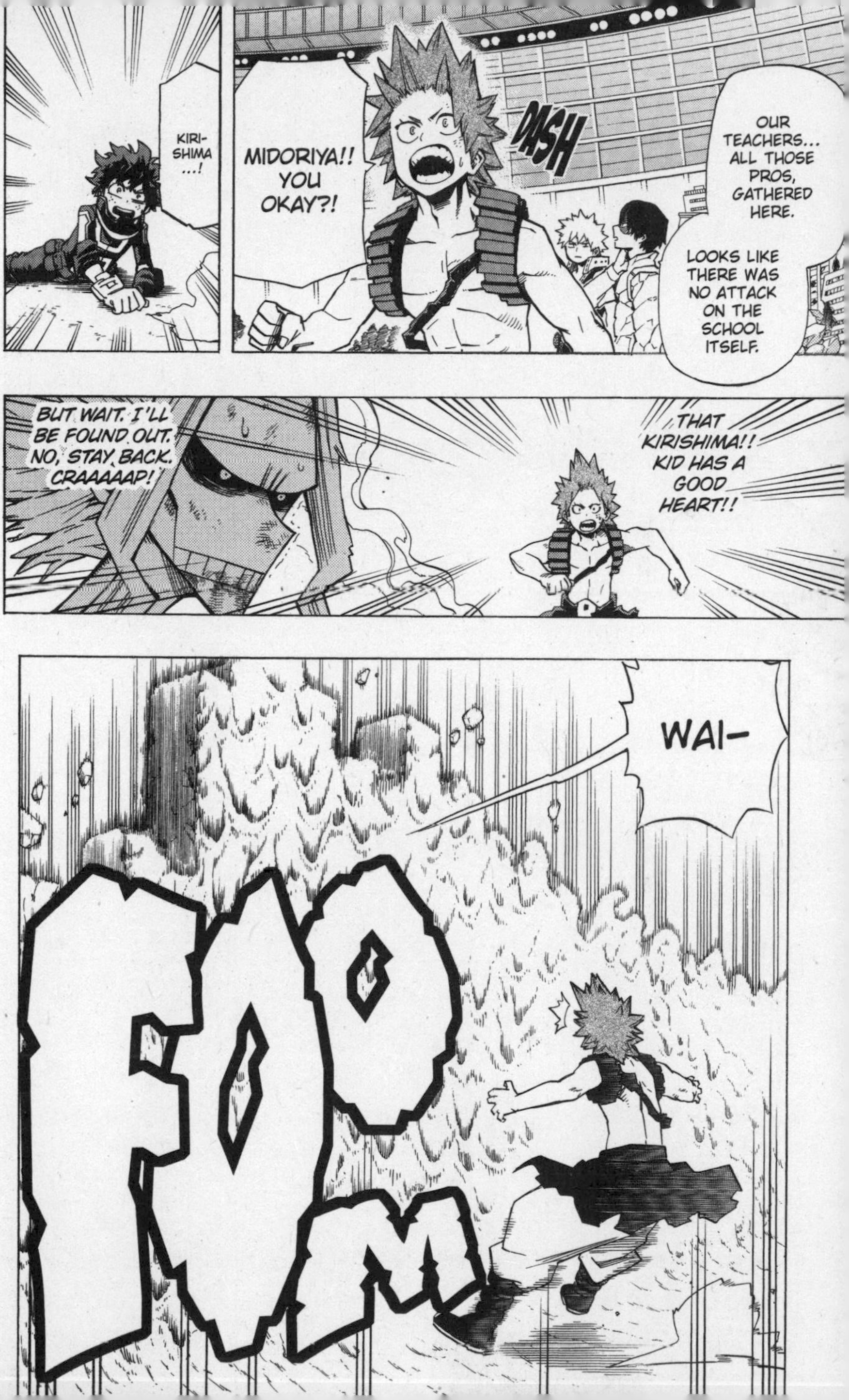
OUR TEACHERS... ALL THOSE PROS, GATHERED HERE.
LOOKS LIKE THERE WAS NO ATTACK ON THE SCHOOL ITSELF.
DASH
MIDORIYA!! YOU OKAY?!
KIRI-SHIMA ...!
THAT KIRISHIMA!! KID HAS A GOOD HEART!!
BUT WAIT. I'LL BE FOUND OUT. NO, STAY BACK. CRAAAAAP!
WAI-
FOOM

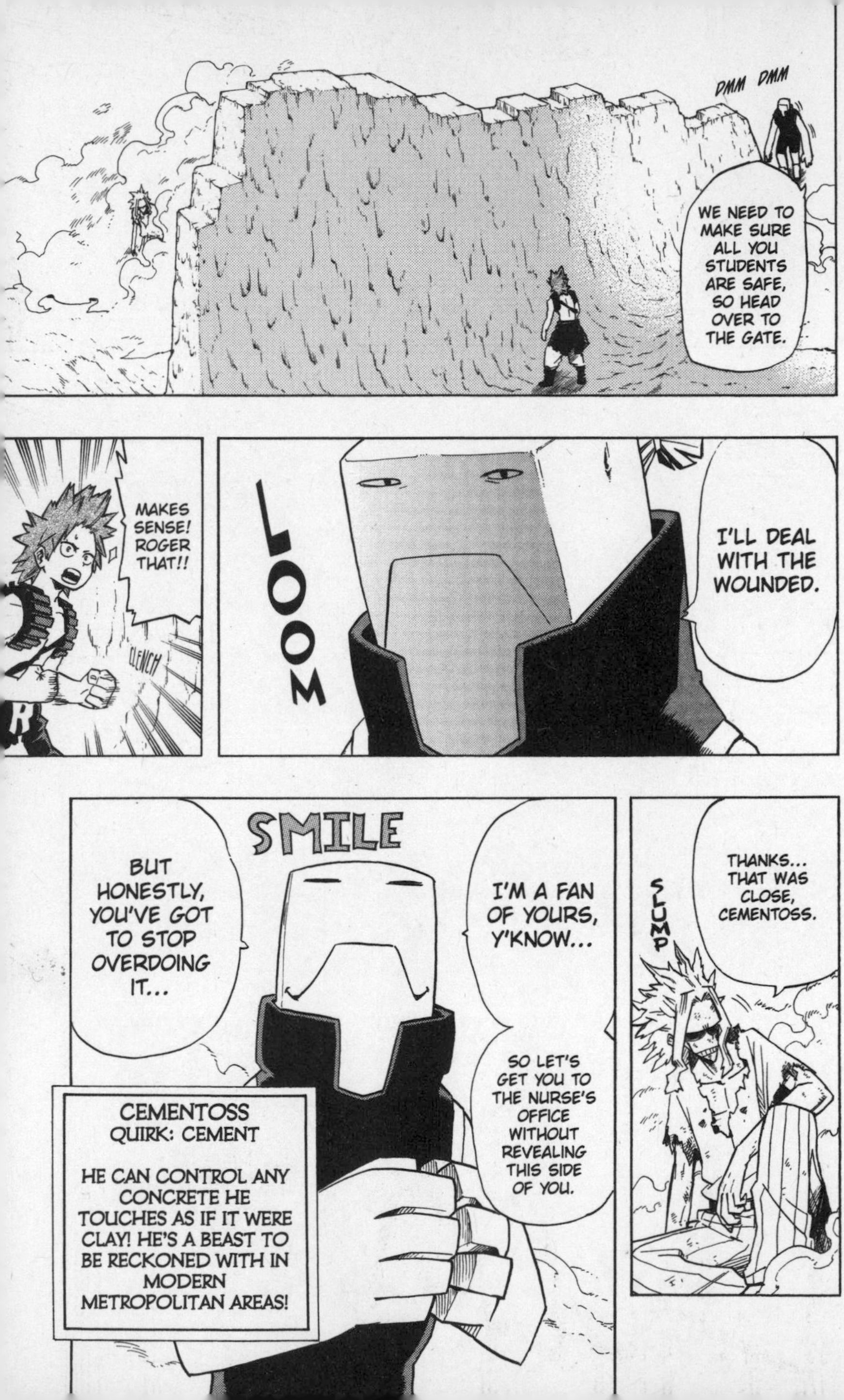
DMM DMM
WE NEED TO MAKE SURE ALL YOU STUDENTS ARE SAFE, SO HEAD OVER TO THE GATE.
I'LL DEAL WITH THE WOUNDED.
LOOM
MAKES SENSE! ROGER THAT!!
CLENCH
THANKS... THAT WAS CLOSE, CEMENTOSS.
SLUMP
SMILE
I'M A FAN OF YOURS, Y'KNOW...
BUT HONESTLY, YOU'VE GOT TO STOP OVERDOING IT...
SO LET'S GET YOU TO THE NURSE'S OFFICE WITHOUT REVEALING THIS SIDE OF YOU.
CEMENTOSS
QUIRK: CEMENT
HE CAN CONTROL ANY CONCRETE HE TOUCHES AS IF IT WERE CLAY! HE'S A BEAST TO BE RECKONED WITH IN MODERN METROPOLITAN AREAS!

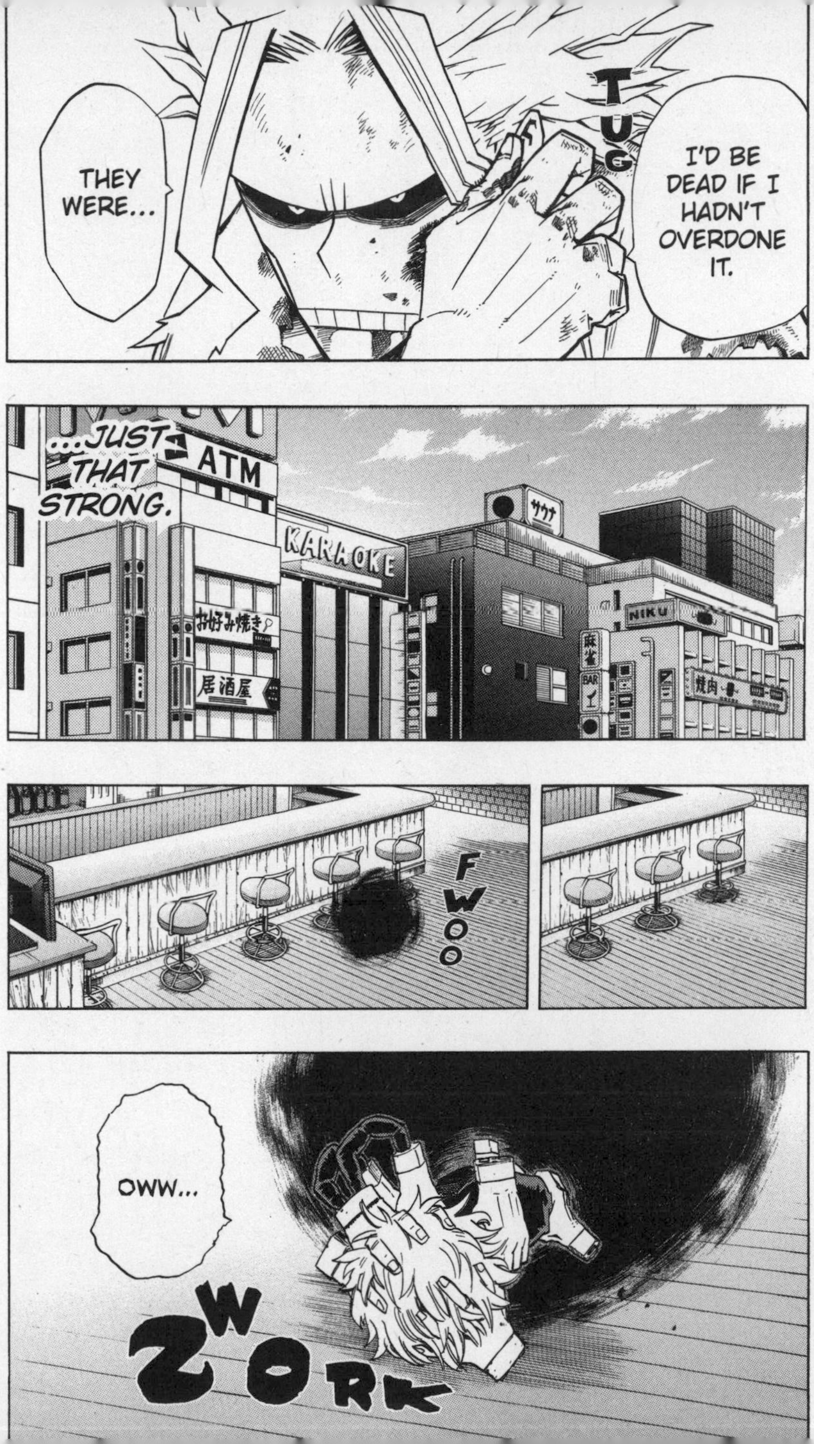

I'D BE DEAD IF I HADN'T OVERDONE IT.
TUG
THEY WERE...
...JUST THAT STRONG.
ATM
KARAOKE
サウナ
お好み焼き
居酒屋
NIKU
麻雀
BAR
焼肉
FWOO
OWW...
ZWORK

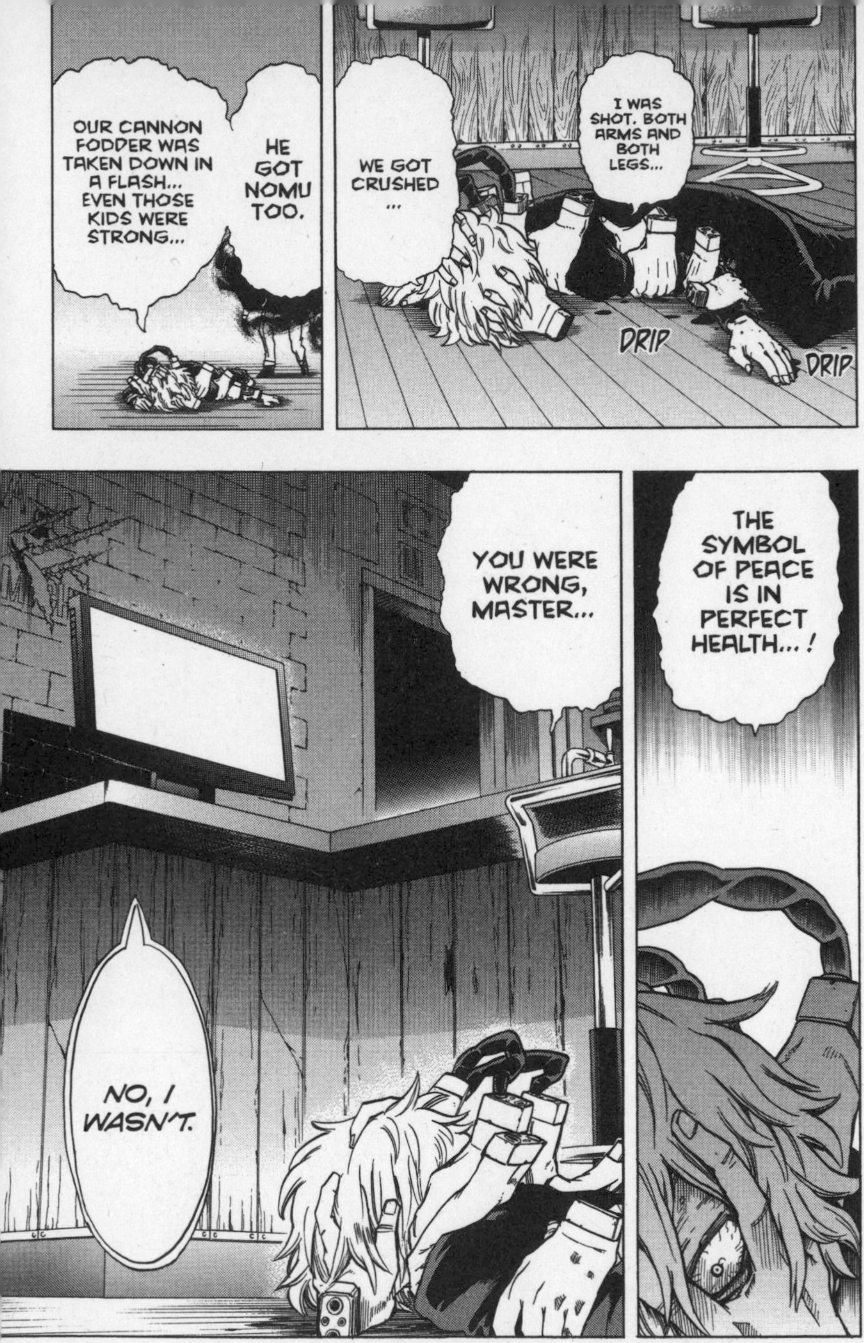

I WAS SHOT. BOTH ARMS AND BOTH LEGS...
WE GOT CRUSHED ...
DRIP
DRIP
HE GOT NOMU TOO.
OUR CANNON FODDER WAS TAKEN DOWN IN A FLASH... EVEN THOSE KIDS WERE STRONG...
THE SYMBOL OF PEACE IS IN PERFECT HEALTH...!
YOU WERE WRONG, MASTER...
NO, I WASN'T.

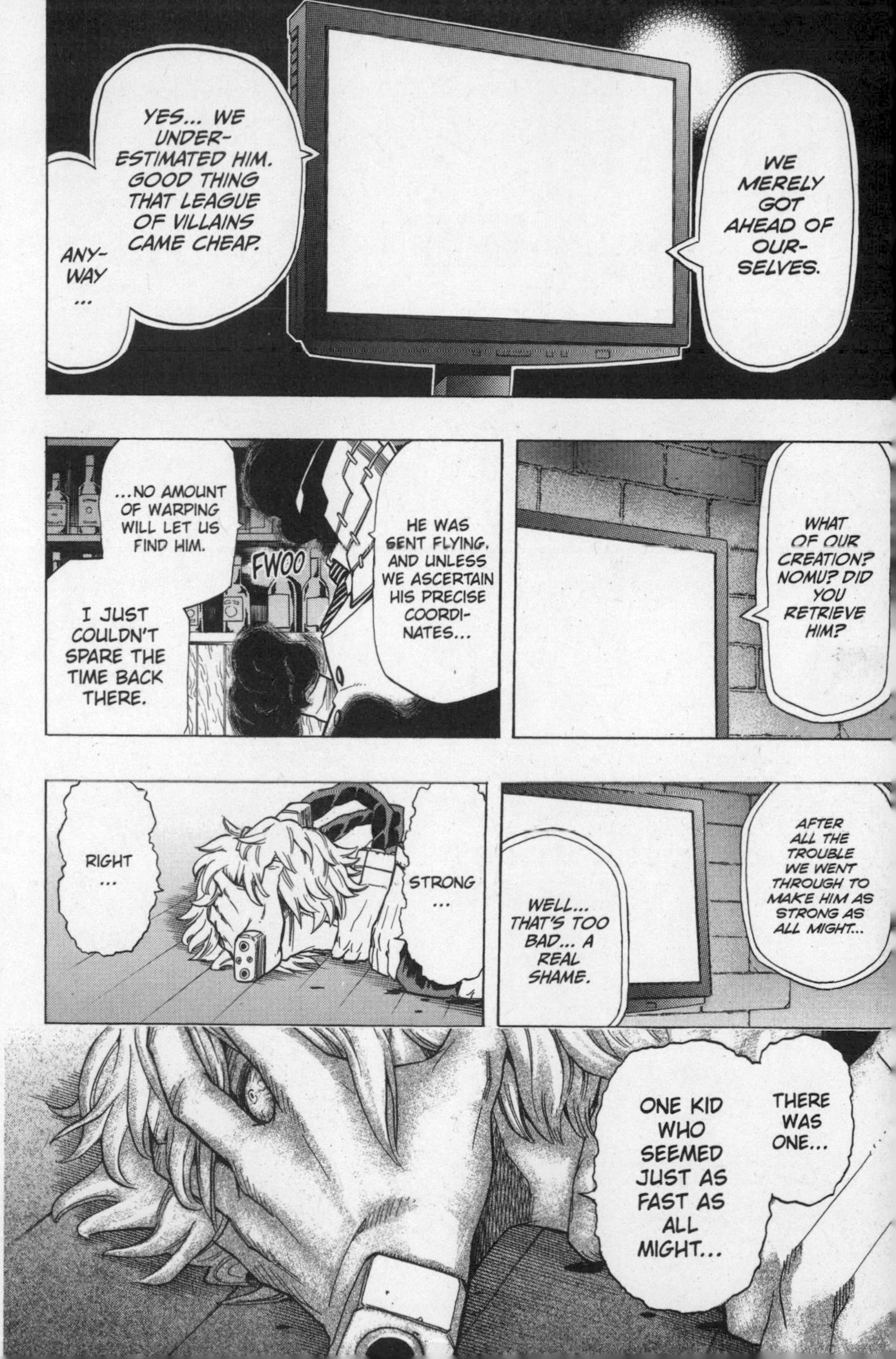
WE MERELY GOT AHEAD OF OURSELVES.
YES... WE UNDERESTIMATED HIM. GOOD THING THAT LEAGUE OF VILLAINS CAME CHEAP.
ANYWAY...
WHAT OF OUR CREATION? NOMU? DID YOU RETRIEVE HIM?
HE WAS SENT FLYING. AND UNLESS WE ASCERTAIN HIS PRECISE COORDINATES...
...NO AMOUNT OF WARPING WILL LET US FIND HIM.
FWOO
I JUST COULDN'T SPARE THE TIME BACK THERE.
AFTER ALL THE TROUBLE WE WENT THROUGH TO MAKE HIM AS STRONG AS ALL MIGHT...
WELL... THAT'S TOO BAD... A REAL SHAME.
STRONG...
RIGHT...
THERE WAS ONE...
ONE KID WHO SEEMED JUST AS FAST AS ALL MIGHT...

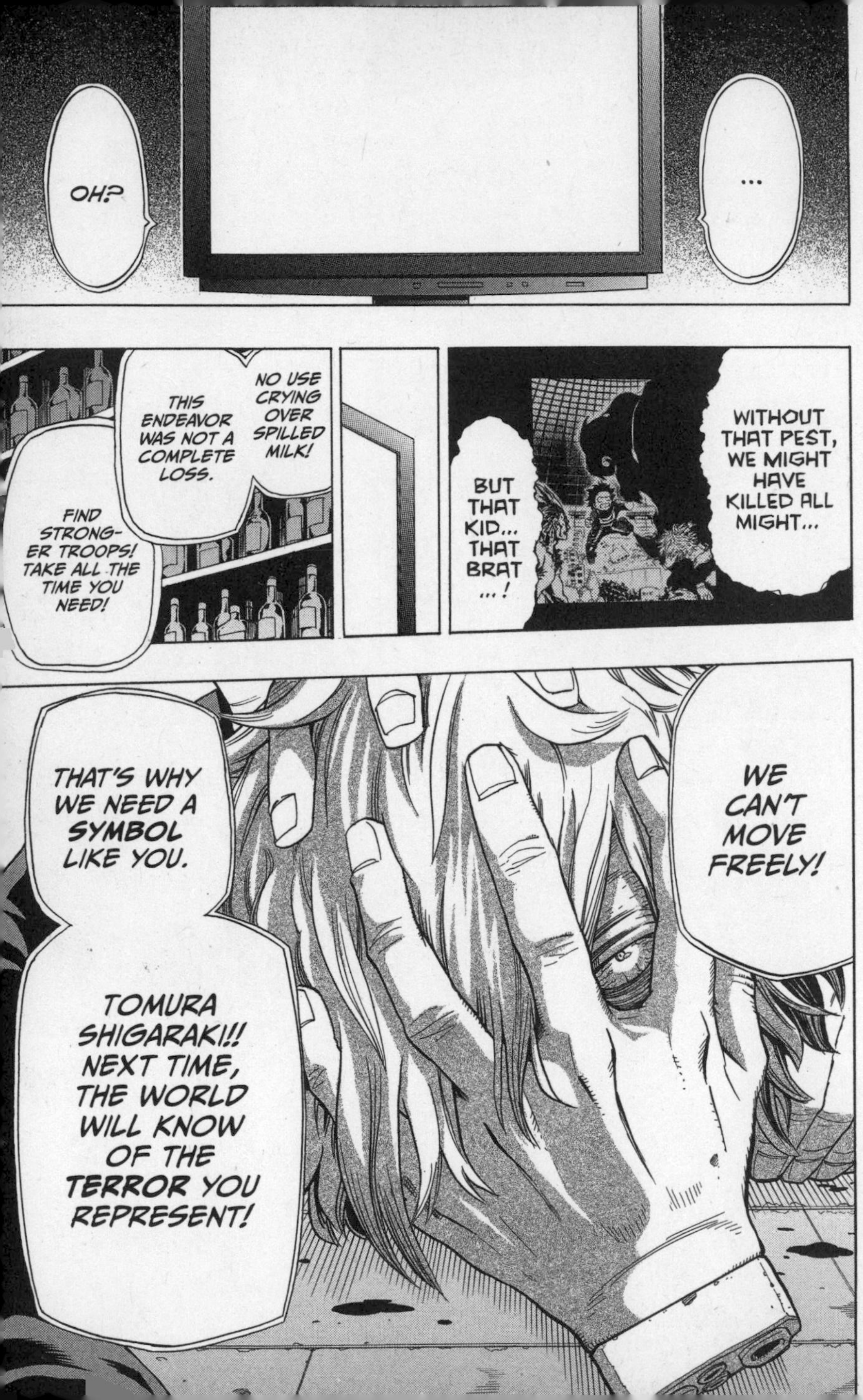
...
OH?
WITHOUT THAT PEST, WE MIGHT HAVE KILLED ALL MIGHT...
BUT THAT KID... THAT BRAT ...!
NO USE CRYING OVER SPILLED MILK!
THIS ENDEAVOR WAS NOT A COMPLETE LOSS.
FIND STRONGER TROOPS! TAKE ALL THE TIME YOU NEED!
WE CAN'T MOVE FREELY!
THAT'S WHY WE NEED A SYMBOL LIKE YOU.
TOMURA SHIGARAKI!! NEXT TIME, THE WORLD WILL KNOW OF THE TERROR YOU REPRESENT!

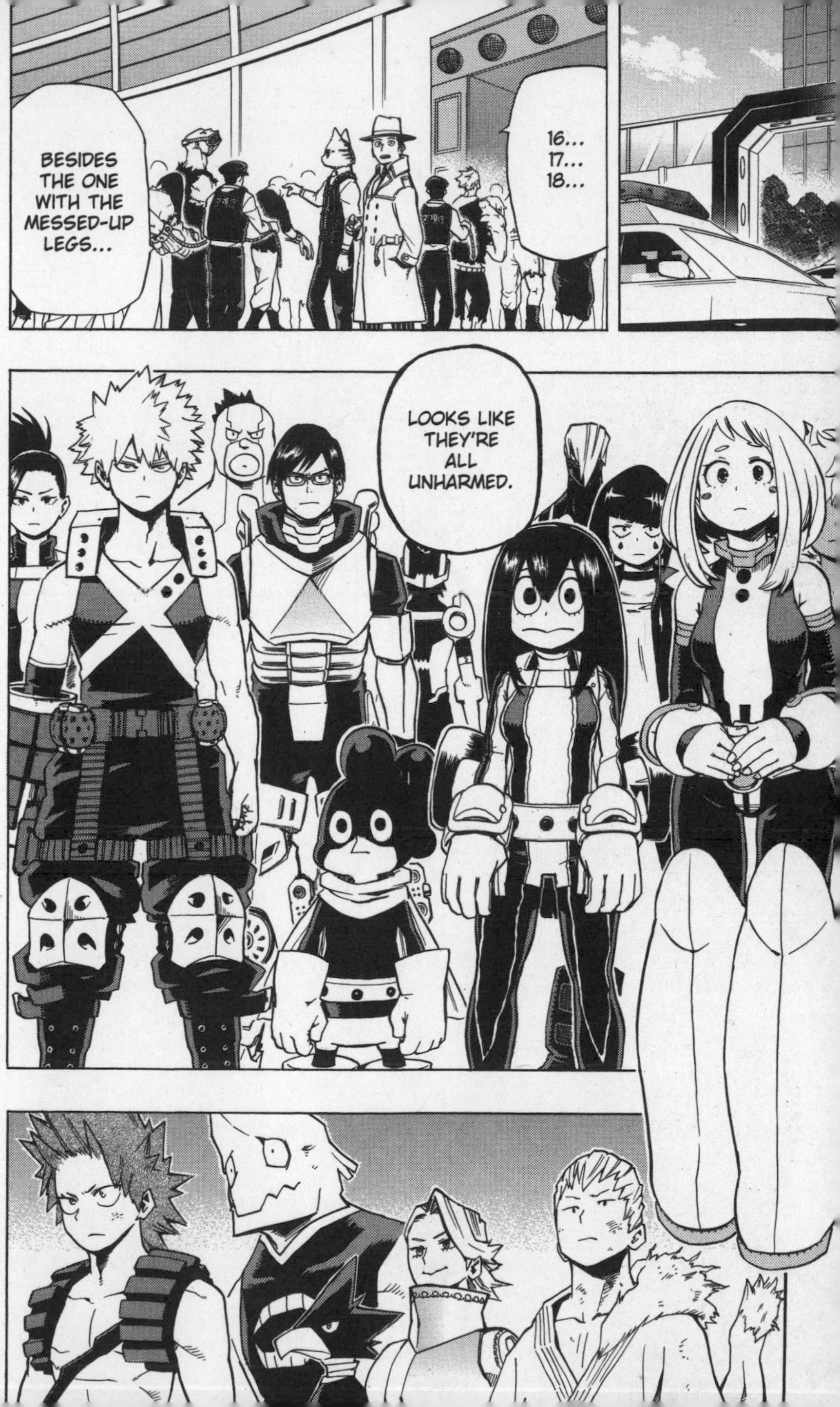
16... 17... 18...
BESIDES THE ONE WITH THE MESSED-UP LEGS...
LOOKS LIKE THEY'RE ALL UNHARMED.

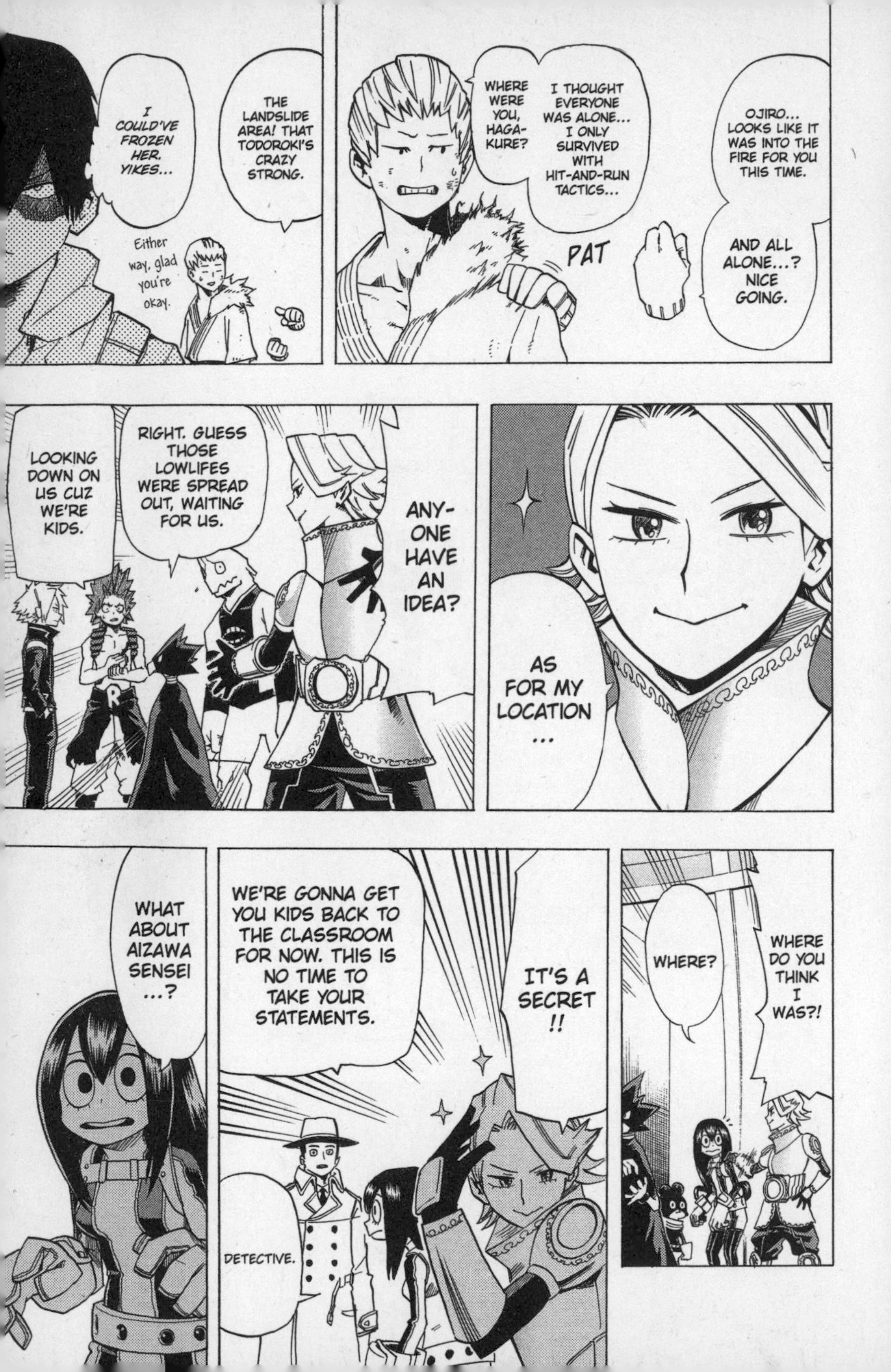
OJIRO... LOOKS LIKE IT WAS INTO THE FIRE FOR YOU THIS TIME.
AND ALL ALONE...? NICE GOING.
PAT
I THOUGHT EVERYONE WAS ALONE... I ONLY SURVIVED WITH HIT-AND-RUN TACTICS...
WHERE WERE YOU, HAGA-KURE?
THE LANDSLIDE AREA! THAT TODOROKI'S CRAZY STRONG.
I COULD'VE FROZEN HER. YIKES...
Either way, glad you're okay.
AS FOR MY LOCATION ...
ANY-ONE HAVE AN IDEA?
RIGHT. GUESS THOSE LOWLIFES WERE SPREAD OUT, WAITING FOR US.
LOOKING DOWN ON US CUZ WE'RE KIDS.
WHERE DO YOU THINK I WAS?!
WHERE?
IT'S A SECRET !!
WE'RE GONNA GET YOU KIDS BACK TO THE CLASSROOM FOR NOW. THIS IS NO TIME TO TAKE YOUR STATEMENTS.
DETECTIVE.
WHAT ABOUT AIZAWA SENSEI ...?

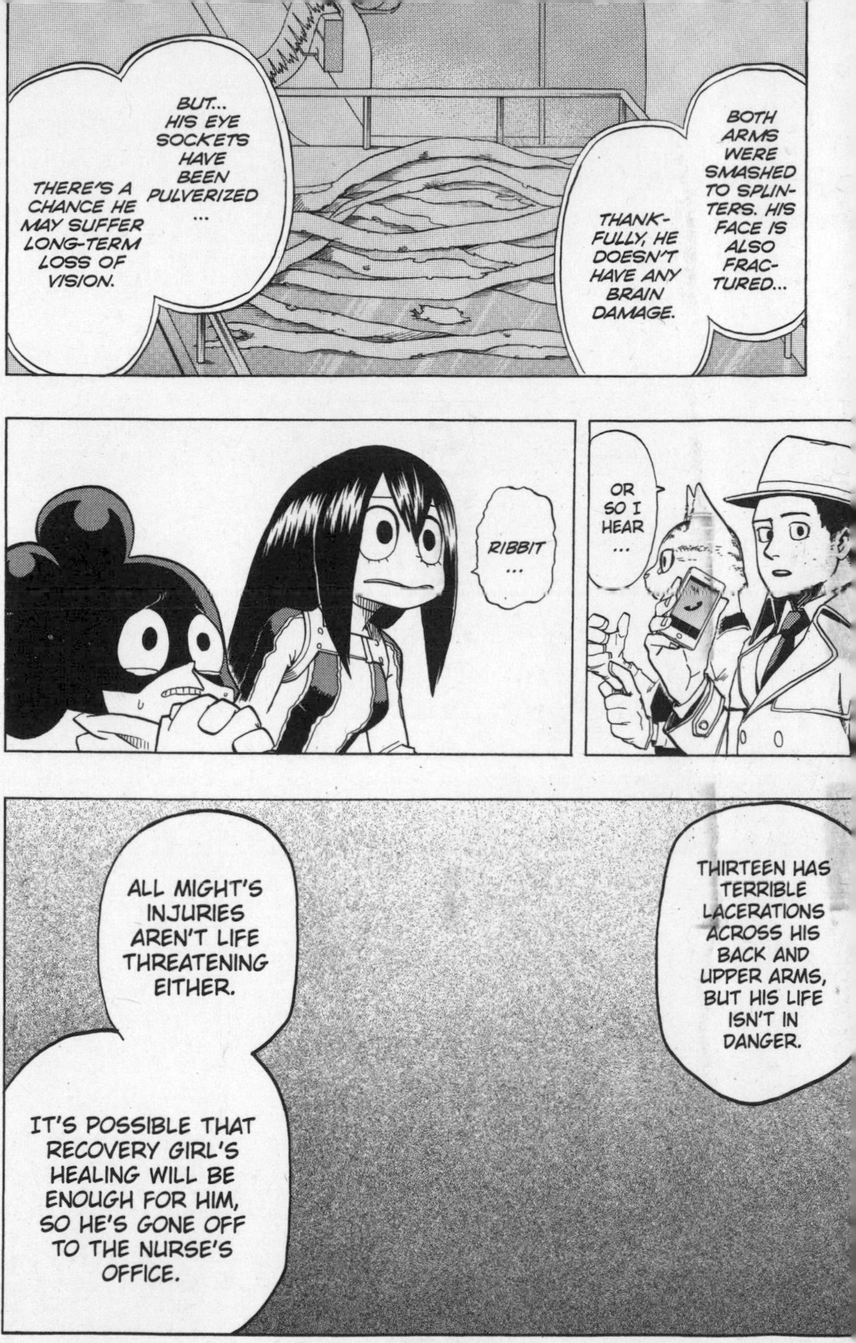
BOTH ARMS WERE SMASHED TO SPLINTERS. HIS FACE IS ALSO FRACTURED...
THANKFULLY, HE DOESN'T HAVE ANY BRAIN DAMAGE.
BUT... HIS EYE SOCKETS HAVE BEEN PULVERIZED ...
THERE'S A CHANCE HE MAY SUFFER LONG-TERM LOSS OF VISION.
OR SO I HEAR ...
RIBBIT ...
THIRTEEN HAS TERRIBLE LACERATIONS ACROSS HIS BACK AND UPPER ARMS, BUT HIS LIFE ISN'T IN DANGER.
ALL MIGHT'S INJURIES AREN'T LIFE THREATENING EITHER.
IT'S POSSIBLE THAT RECOVERY GIRL'S HEALING WILL BE ENOUGH FOR HIM, SO HE'S GONE OFF TO THE NURSE'S OFFICE.

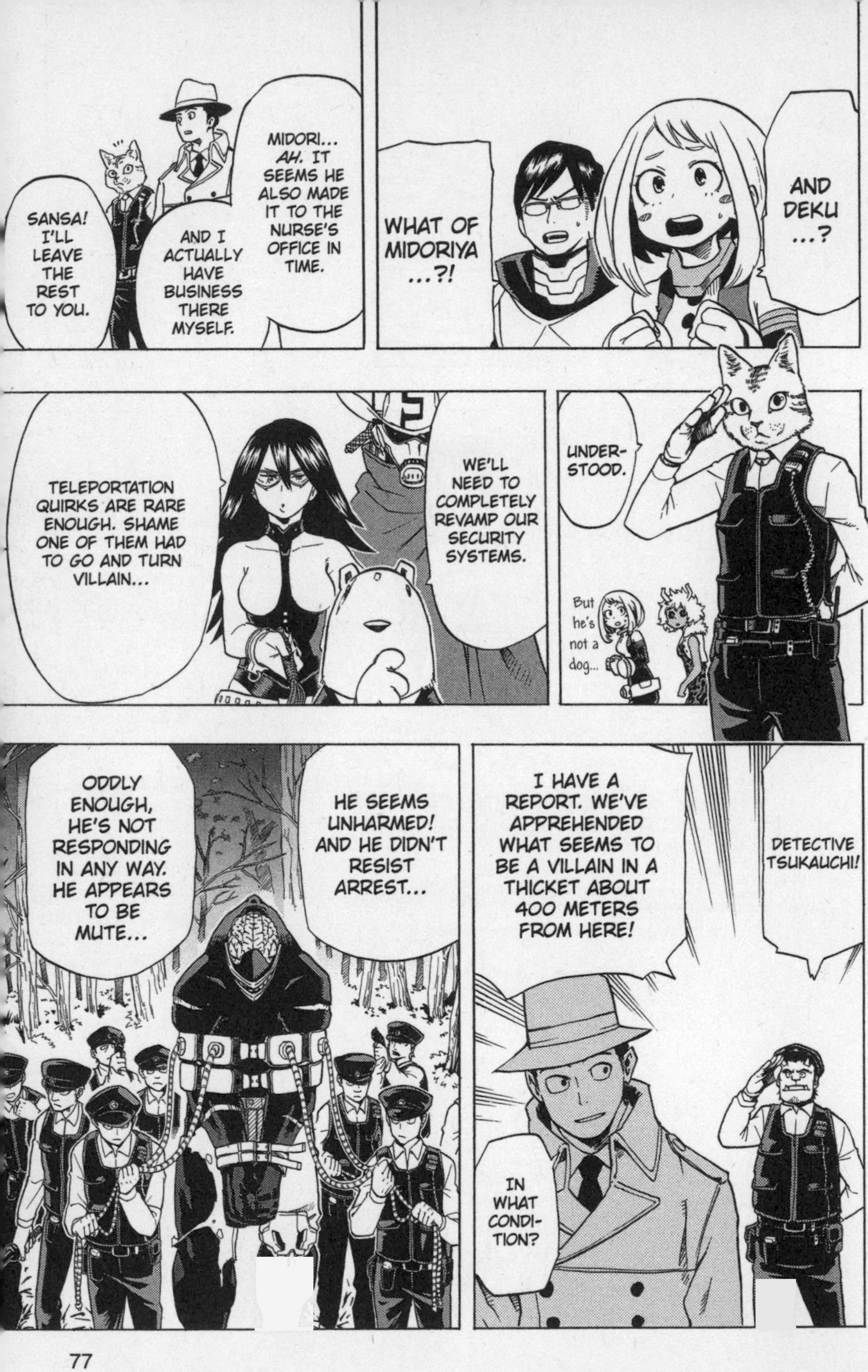
AND DEKU ...?
WHAT OF MIDORIYA ...?!
MIDORI... AH. IT SEEMS HE ALSO MADE IT TO THE NURSE'S OFFICE IN TIME.
AND I ACTUALLY HAVE BUSINESS THERE MYSELF.
SANSA! I'LL LEAVE THE REST TO YOU.
UNDER-STOOD.
But he's not a dog...
WE'LL NEED TO COMPLETELY REVAMP OUR SECURITY SYSTEMS.
TELEPORTATION QUIRKS ARE RARE ENOUGH. SHAME ONE OF THEM HAD TO GO AND TURN VILLAIN...
DETECTIVE TSUKAUCHI!
I HAVE A REPORT. WE'VE APPREHENDED WHAT SEEMS TO BE A VILLAIN IN A THICKET ABOUT 400 METERS FROM HERE!
IN WHAT CONDI-TION?
HE SEEMS UNHARMED! AND HE DIDN'T RESIST ARREST...
ODDLY ENOUGH, HE'S NOT RESPONDING IN ANY WAY. HE APPEARS TO BE MUTE...

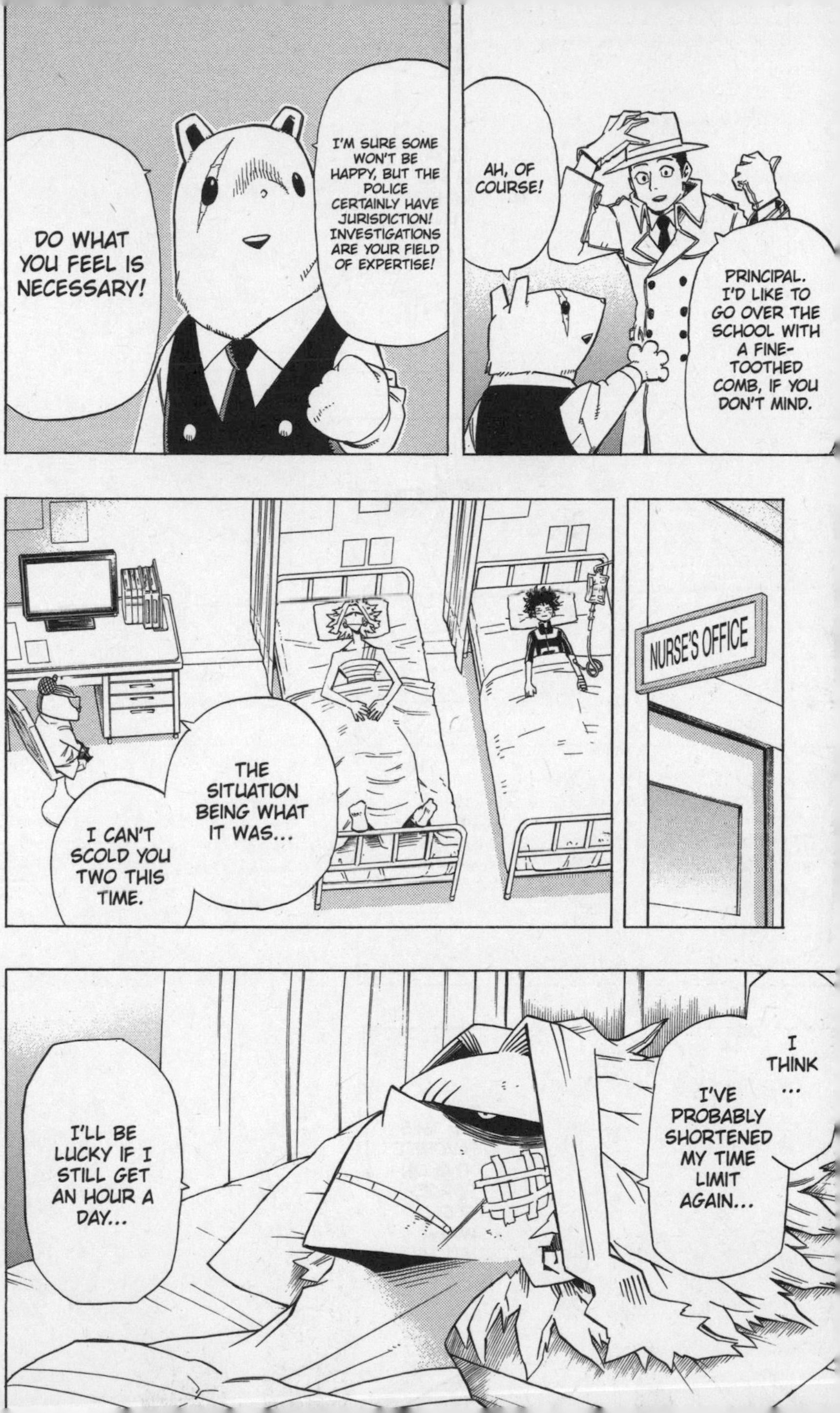
PRINCIPAL. I'D LIKE TO GO OVER THE SCHOOL WITH A FINE-TOOTHED COMB, IF YOU DON'T MIND.
AH, OF COURSE!
I'M SURE SOME WON'T BE HAPPY, BUT THE POLICE CERTAINLY HAVE JURISDICTION! INVESTIGATIONS ARE YOUR FIELD OF EXPERTISE!
DO WHAT YOU FEEL IS NECESSARY!
NURSE'S OFFICE
THE SITUATION BEING WHAT IT WAS...
I CAN'T SCOLD YOU TWO THIS TIME.
I THINK...
I'VE PROBABLY SHORTENED MY TIME LIMIT AGAIN...
I'LL BE LUCKY IF I STILL GET AN HOUR A DAY...

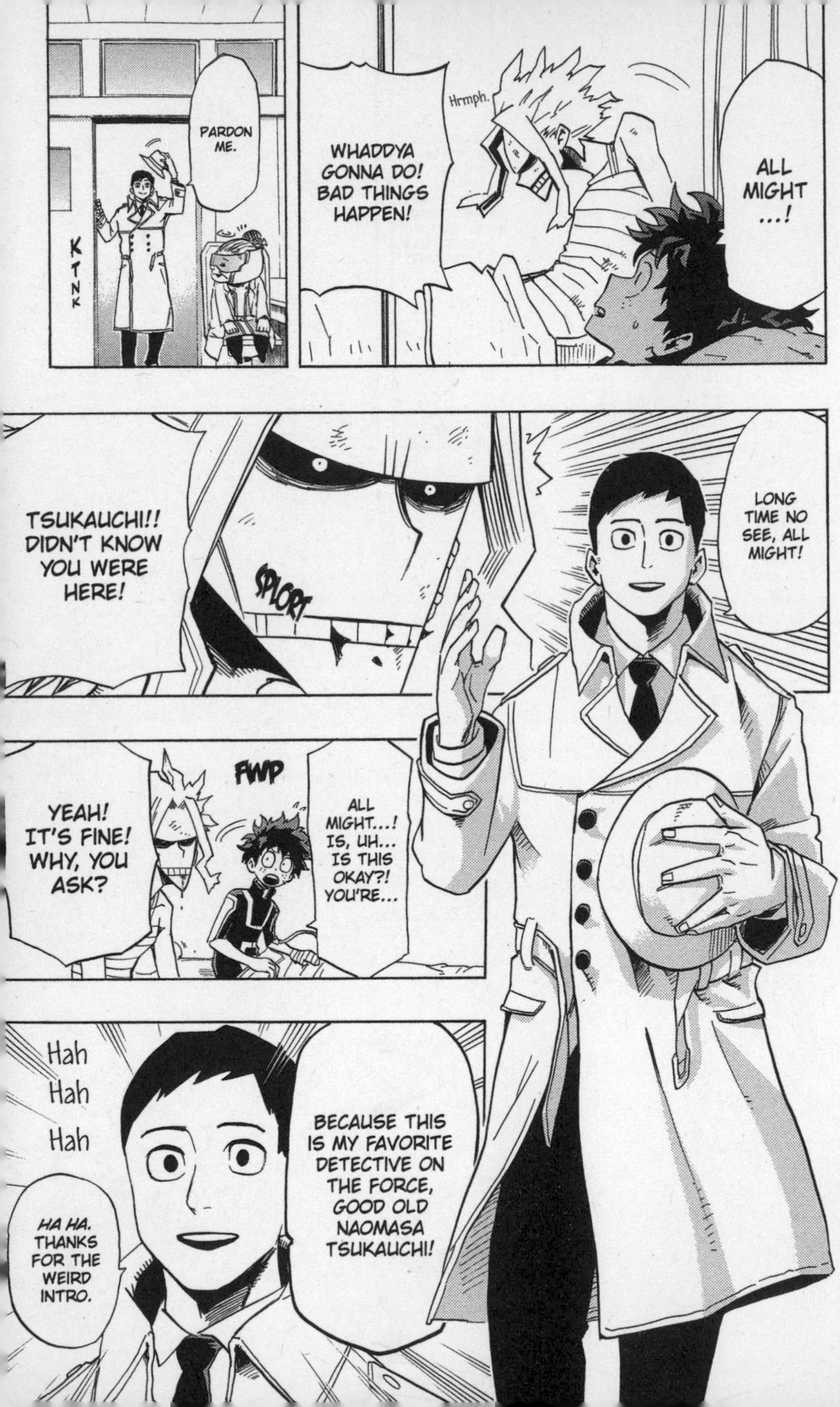
ALL MIGHT ...!
Hrmph.
WHADDYA GONNA DO! BAD THINGS HAPPEN!
PARDON ME.
KTNK
LONG TIME NO SEE, ALL MIGHT!
SPLORT
TSUKAUCHI!! DIDN'T KNOW YOU WERE HERE!
FWIP
ALL MIGHT...! IS, UH... IS THIS OKAY?! YOU'RE...
YEAH! IT'S FINE! WHY, YOU ASK?
BECAUSE THIS IS MY FAVORITE DETECTIVE ON THE FORCE, GOOD OLD NAOMASA TSUKAUCHI!
Hah Hah Hah
HA HA. THANKS FOR THE WEIRD INTRO.

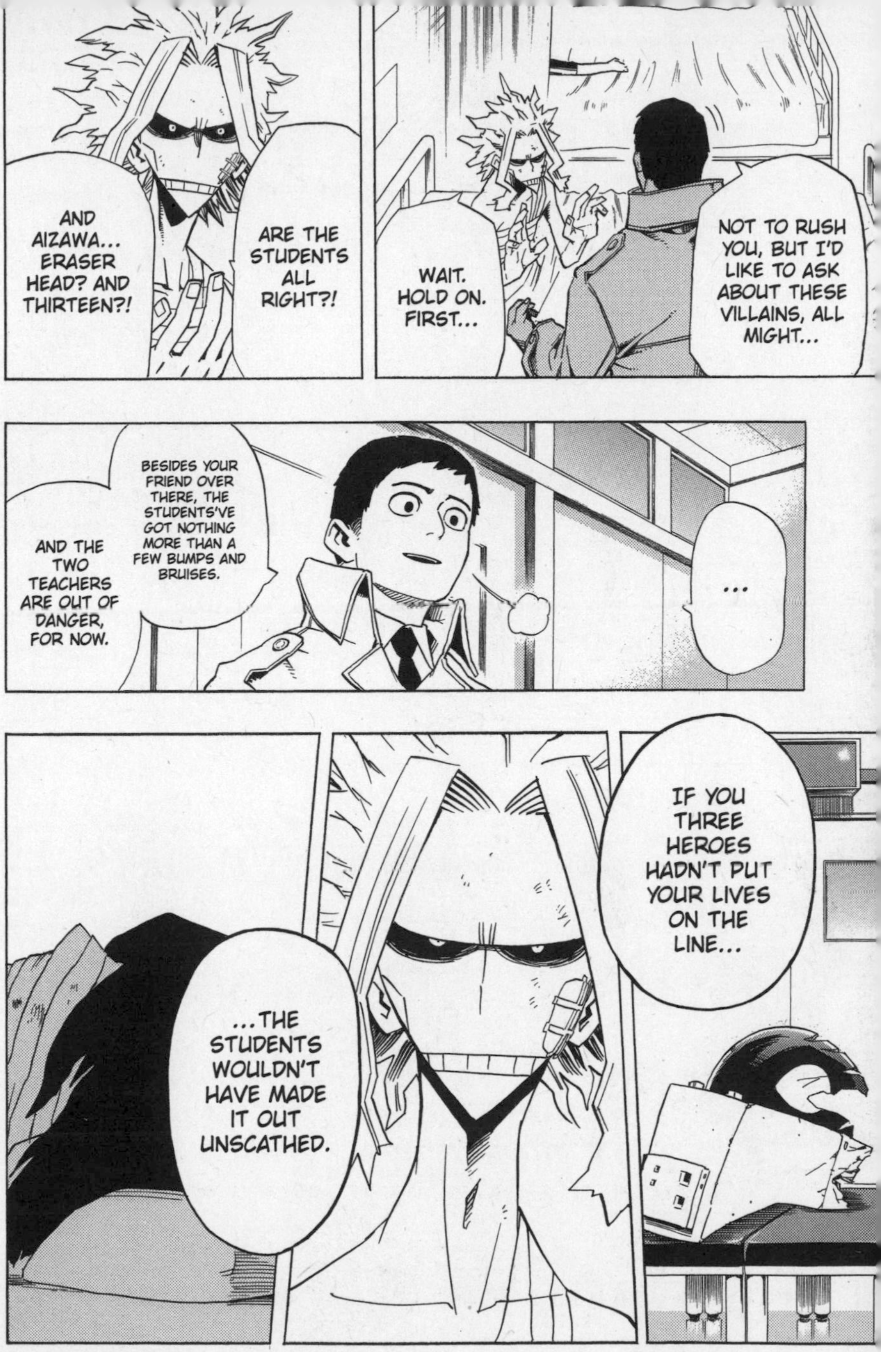
NOT TO RUSH YOU, BUT I'D LIKE TO ASK ABOUT THESE VILLAINS, ALL MIGHT...
WAIT. HOLD ON. FIRST...
ARE THE STUDENTS ALL RIGHT?!
AND AIZAWA... ERASER HEAD? AND THIRTEEN?!
...
BESIDES YOUR FRIEND OVER THERE, THE STUDENTS'VE GOT NOTHING MORE THAN A FEW BUMPS AND BRUISES.
AND THE TWO TEACHERS ARE OUT OF DANGER, FOR NOW.
IF YOU THREE HEROES HADN'T PUT YOUR LIVES ON THE LINE...
...THE STUDENTS WOULDN'T HAVE MADE IT OUT UNSCATHED.

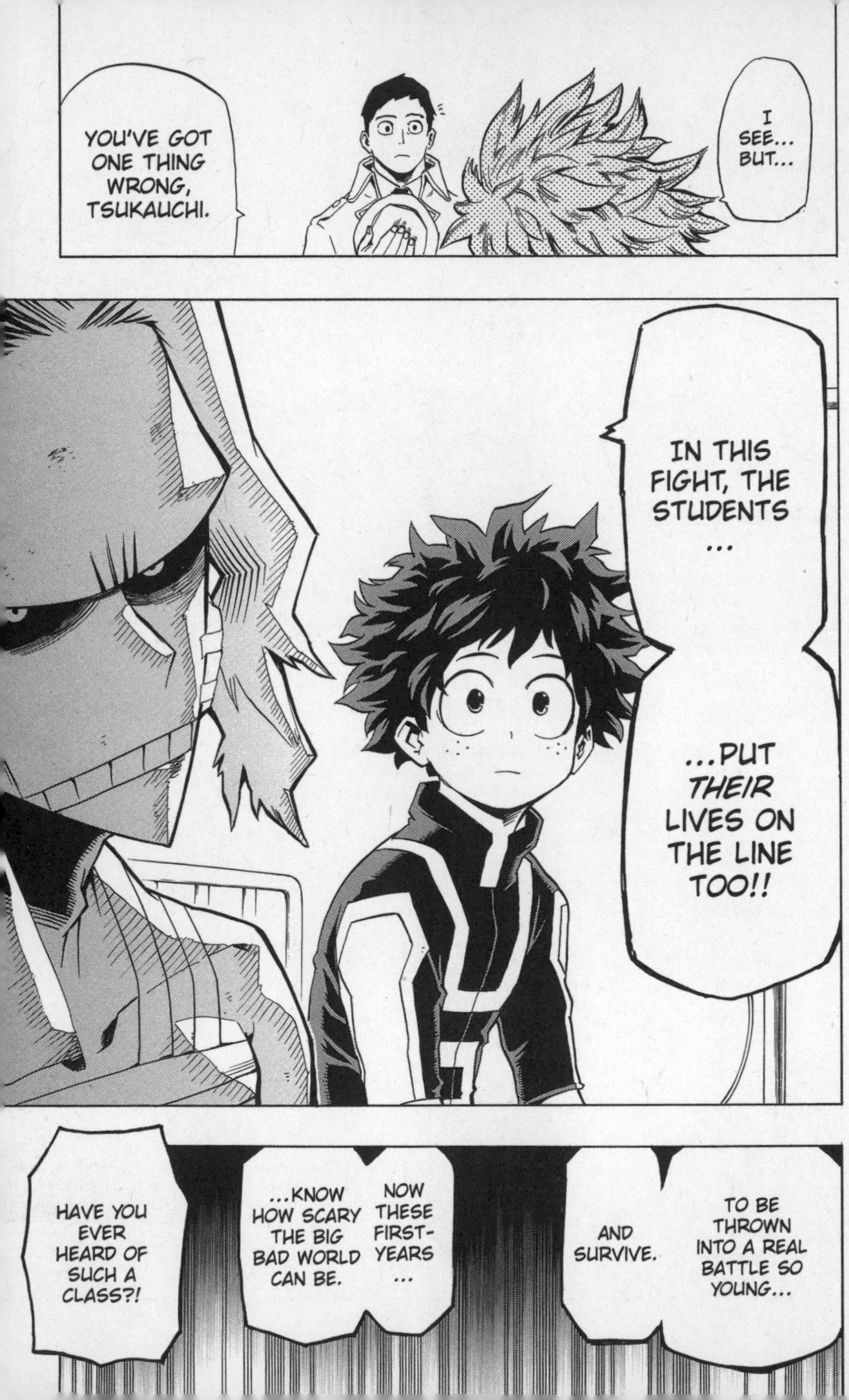
I SEE... BUT...
YOU'VE GOT ONE THING WRONG, TSUKAUCHI.
IN THIS FIGHT, THE STUDENTS ...
...PUT *THEIR* LIVES ON THE LINE TOO!!
TO BE THROWN INTO A REAL BATTLE SO YOUNG...
AND SURVIVE.
NOW THESE FIRST-YEARS ...
...KNOW HOW SCARY THE BIG BAD WORLD CAN BE.
HAVE YOU EVER HEARD OF SUCH A CLASS?!

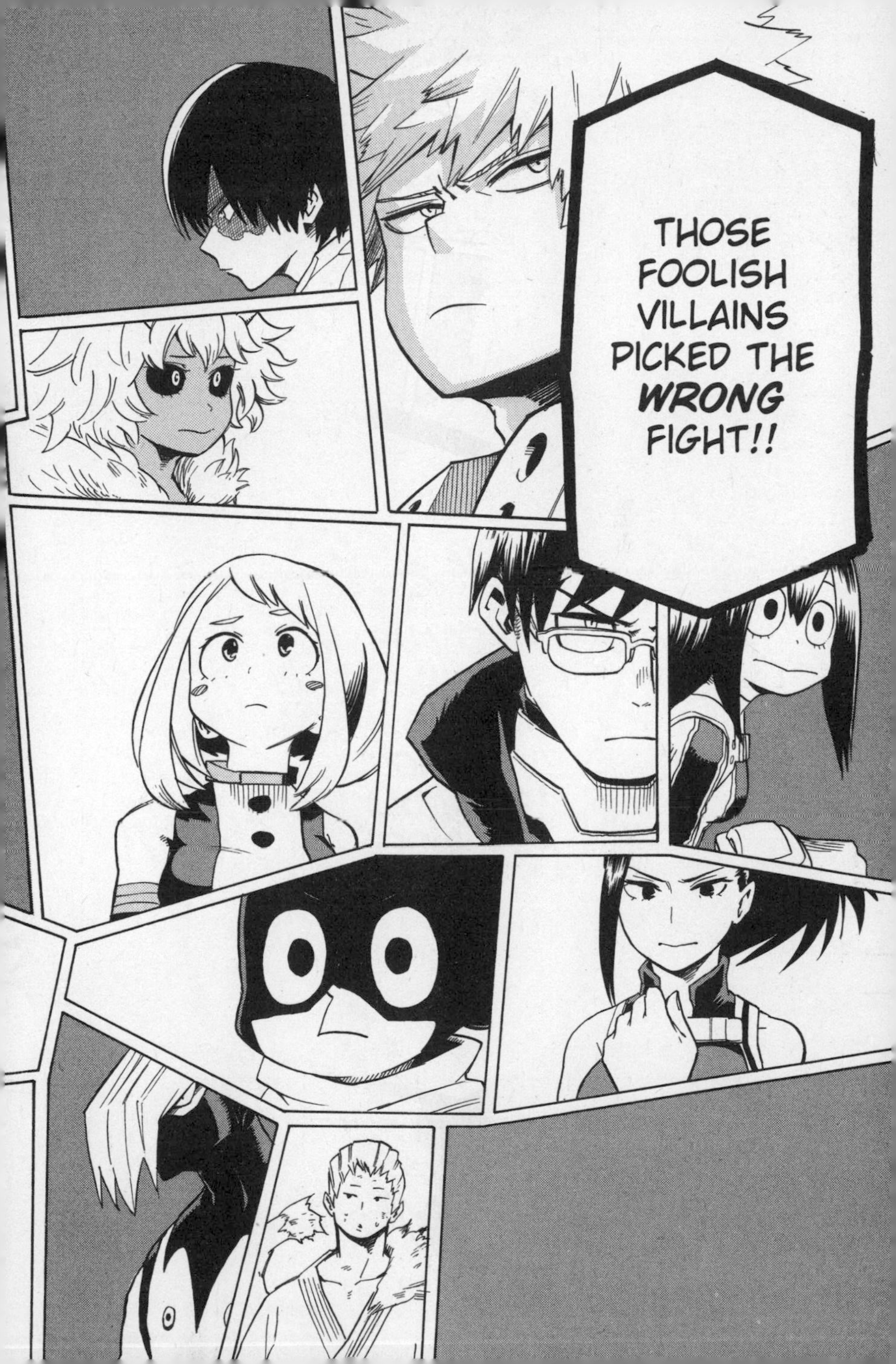
THOSE FOOLISH VILLAINS PICKED THE WRONG FIGHT!!

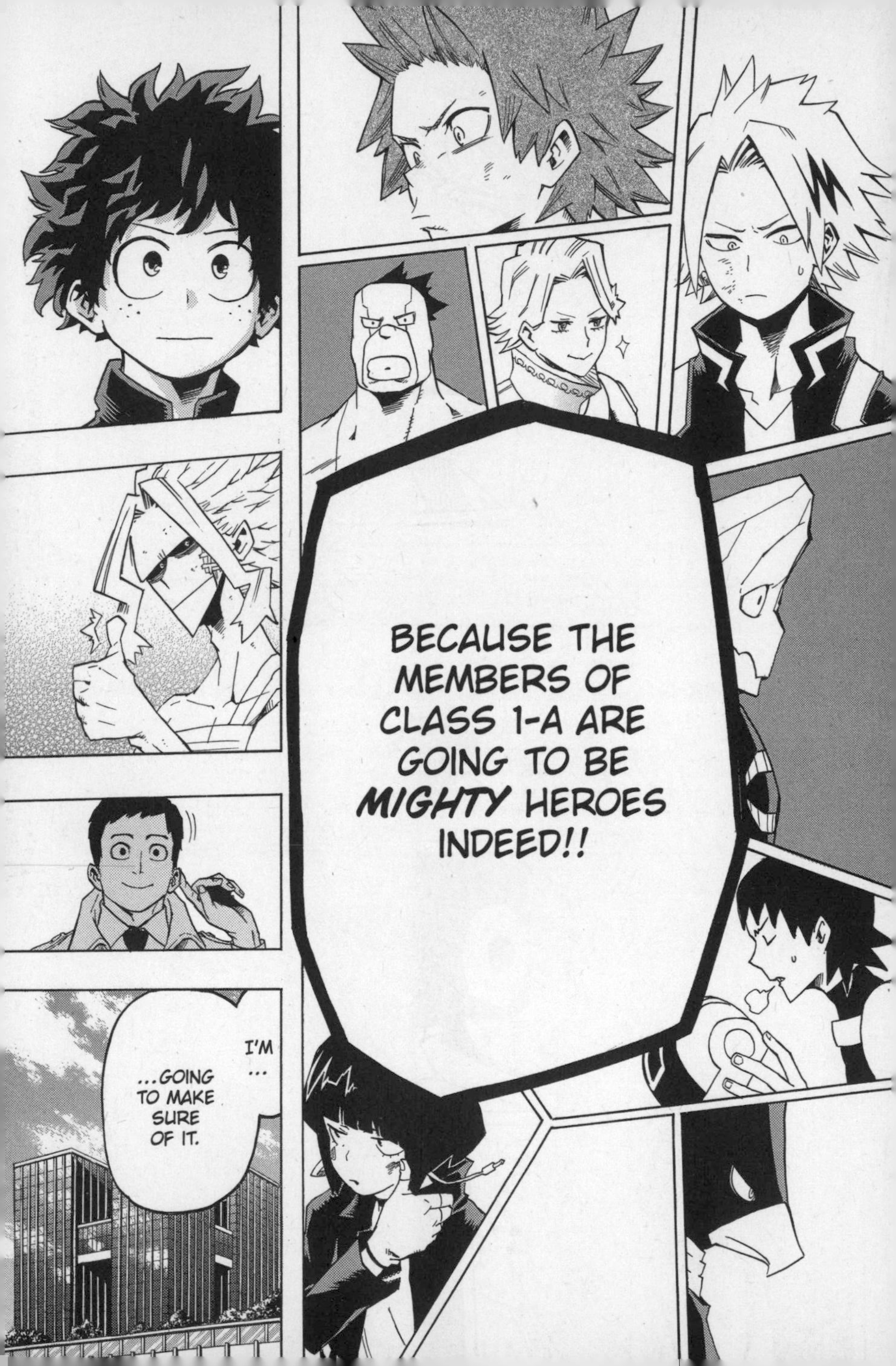
BECAUSE THE MEMBERS OF CLASS 1-A ARE GOING TO BE *MIGHTY* HEROES INDEED!!
I'M ...
...GOING TO MAKE SURE OF IT.

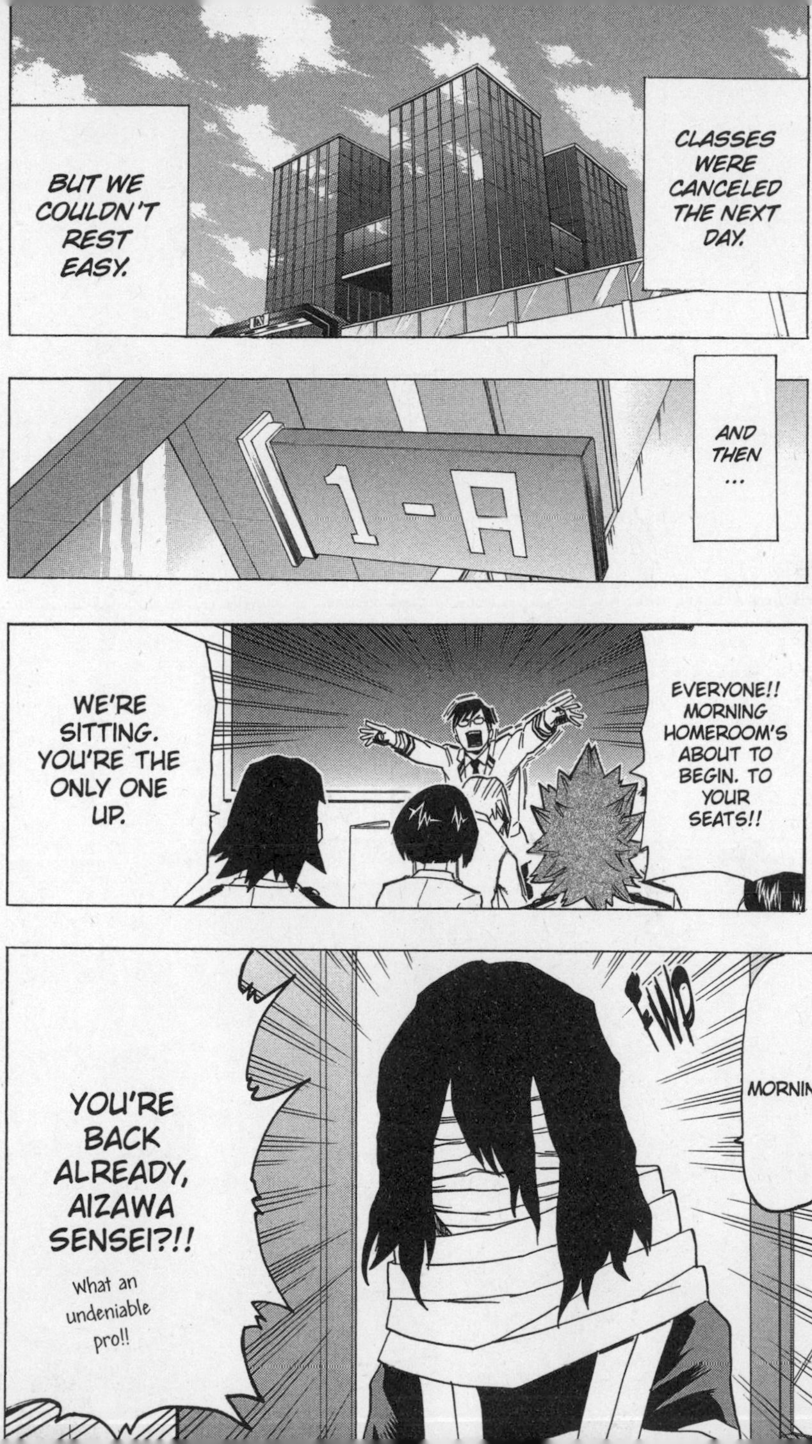
CLASSES WERE CANCELED THE NEXT DAY.
BUT WE COULDN'T REST EASY.
AND THEN ...
1-A
EVERYONE!! MORNING HOMEROOM'S ABOUT TO BEGIN. TO YOUR SEATS!!
WE'RE SITTING. YOU'RE THE ONLY ONE UP.
FWP
MORNING.
YOU'RE BACK ALREADY, AIZAWA SENSEI?!!
What an undeniable pro!!

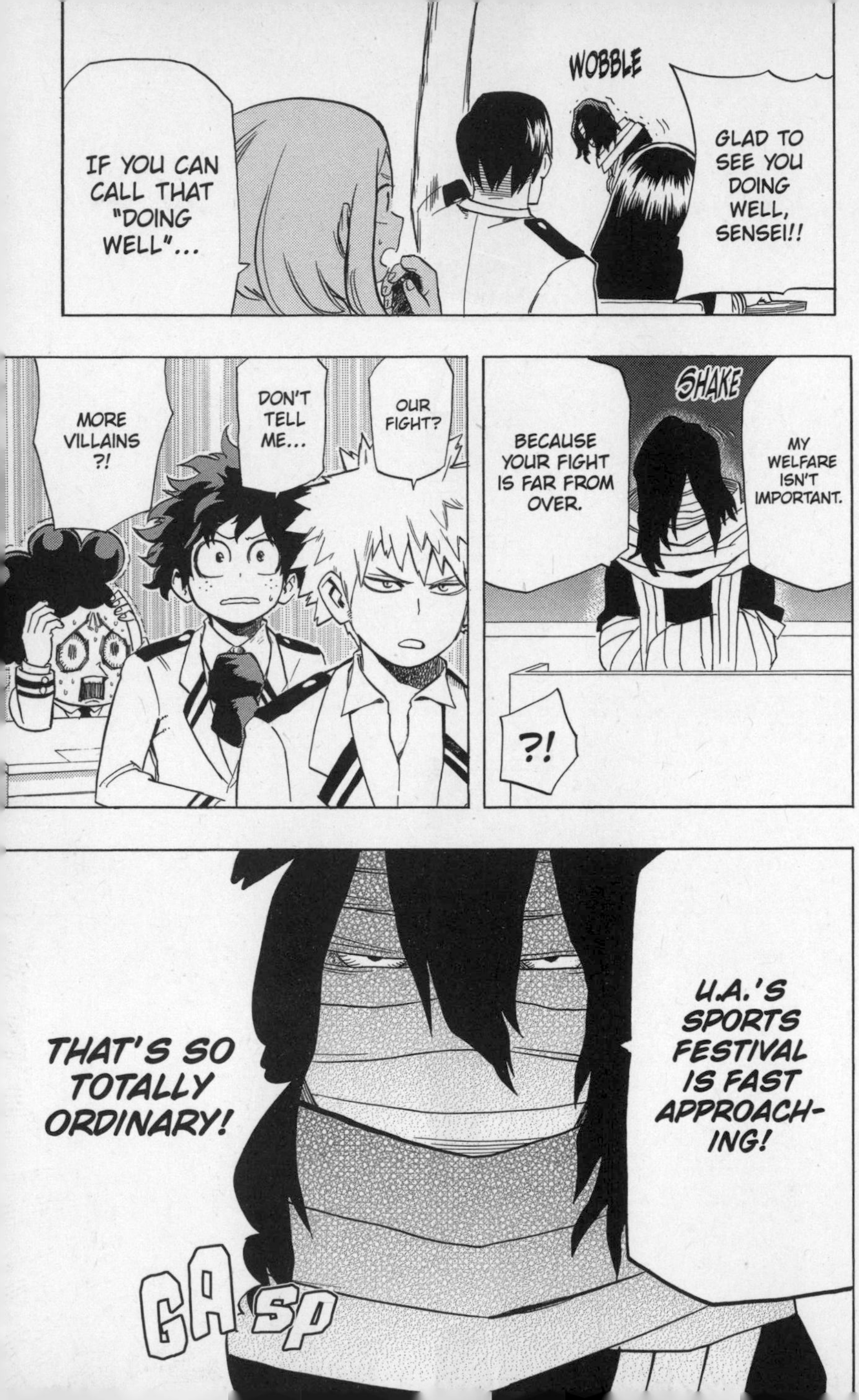
GLAD TO SEE YOU DOING WELL, SENSEI!!
WOBBLE
IF YOU CAN CALL THAT "DOING WELL"...
MY WELFARE ISN'T IMPORTANT.
SHAKE
BECAUSE YOUR FIGHT IS FAR FROM OVER.
?!
OUR FIGHT?
DON'T TELL ME...
MORE VILLAINS ?!
U.A.'S SPORTS FESTIVAL IS FAST APPROACH-ING!
THAT'S SO TOTALLY ORDINARY!
GASP

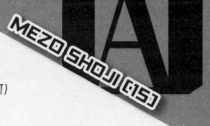

STREET CLOTHES
(HE ENDURES THE WINTER WITH A PONCHO-LIKE GARMENT)

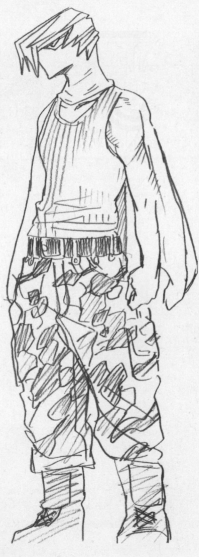

Birthday: 2/15
Height: 187 cm
Favorite Things: Takoyaki,
squid-ink pasta

BEHIND THE SCENES
I've always been fond of drawing these not-quite-humanoid type of characters. He's not the type to stand out in the crowd, but I hope to show how cool he is now and then.

I want to feature him in the story, but I'm not sure when that'll happen…

NO.22 - THAT'S THE IDEA, OCHAKO

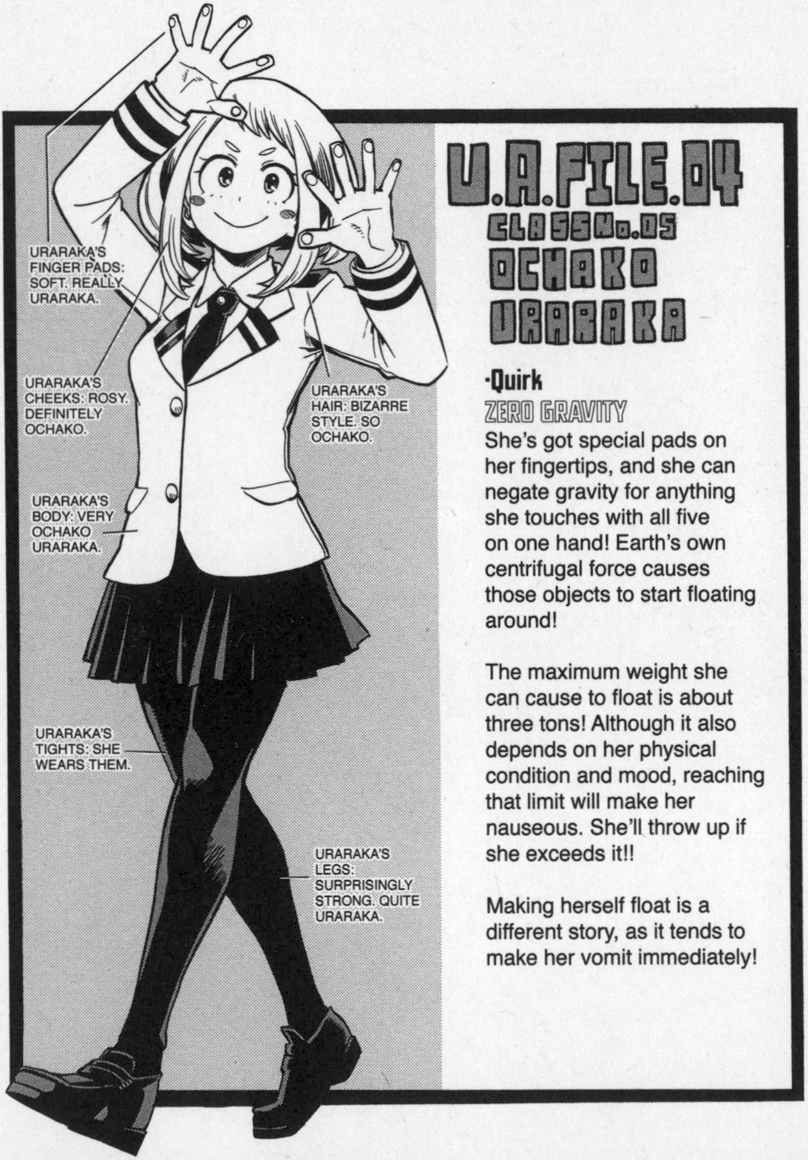
URARAKA'S FINGER PADS: SOFT. REALLY URARAKA.
URARAKA'S CHEEKS: ROSY. DEFINITELY OCHAKO.
URARAKA'S HAIR: BIZARRE STYLE. SO OCHAKO.
URARAKA'S BODY: VERY OCHAKO URARAKA.
URARAKA'S TIGHTS: SHE WEARS THEM.
URARAKA'S LEGS: SURPRISINGLY STRONG. QUITE URARAKA.

U.A. FILE.04
CLASS No.05
OCHAKO URARAKA

·Quirk

ZERO GRAVITY

She's got special pads on her fingertips, and she can negate gravity for anything she touches with all five on one hand! Earth's own centrifugal force causes those objects to start floating around!

The maximum weight she can cause to float is about three tons! Although it also depends on her physical condition and mood, reaching that limit will make her nauseous. She'll throw up if she exceeds it!!

Making herself float is a different story, as it tends to make her vomit immediately!

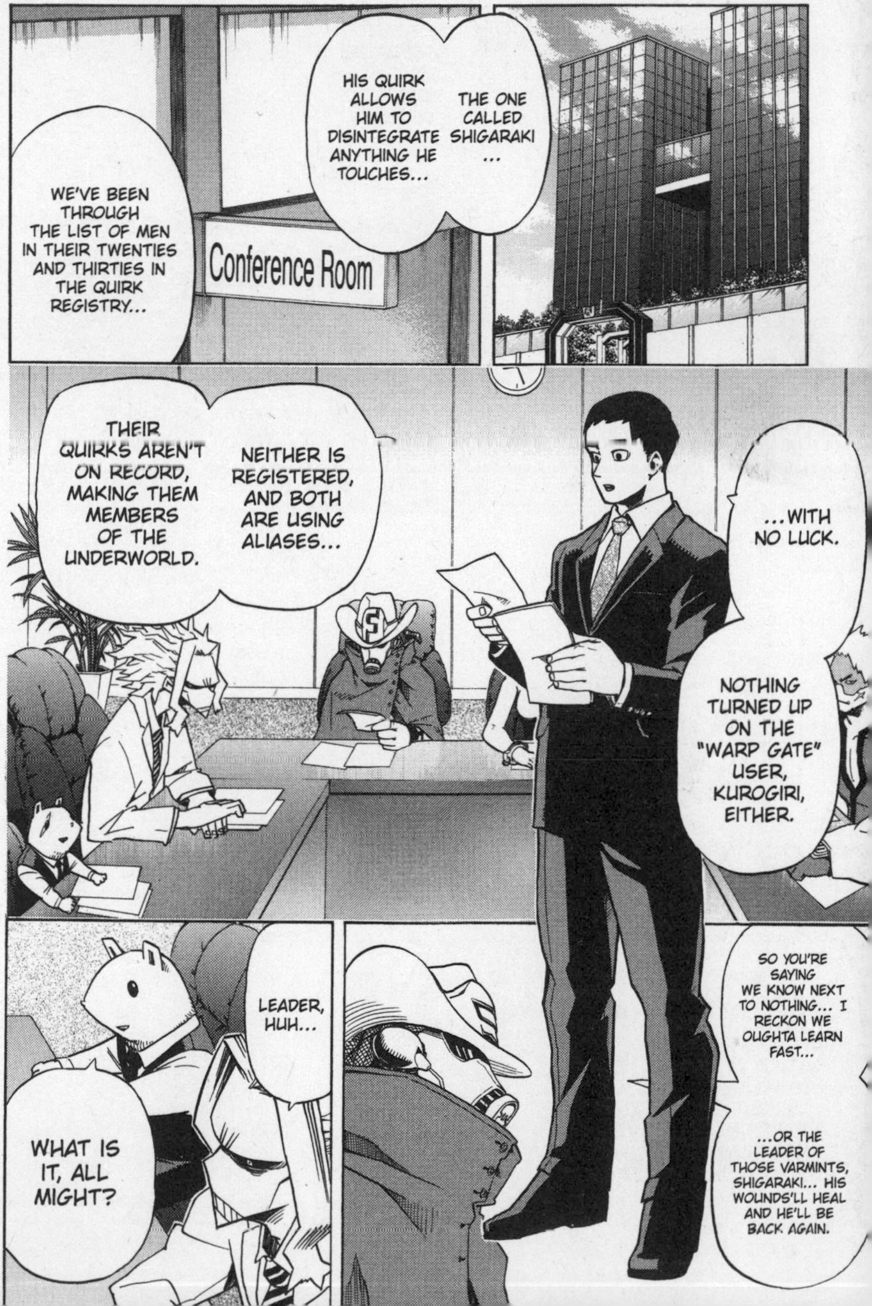
THE ONE CALLED SHIGARAKI...
HIS QUIRK ALLOWS HIM TO DISINTEGRATE ANYTHING HE TOUCHES...
Conference Room
WE'VE BEEN THROUGH THE LIST OF MEN IN THEIR TWENTIES AND THIRTIES IN THE QUIRK REGISTRY...
...WITH NO LUCK.
NOTHING TURNED UP ON THE "WARP GATE" USER, KUROGIRI, EITHER.
NEITHER IS REGISTERED, AND BOTH ARE USING ALIASES...
THEIR QUIRKS AREN'T ON RECORD, MAKING THEM MEMBERS OF THE UNDERWORLD.
SO YOU'RE SAYING WE KNOW NEXT TO NOTHING... I RECKON WE OUGHTA LEARN FAST...
...OR THE LEADER OF THOSE VARMINTS, SHIGARAKI... HIS WOUNDS'LL HEAL AND HE'LL BE BACK AGAIN.
LEADER, HUH...
WHAT IS IT, ALL MIGHT?

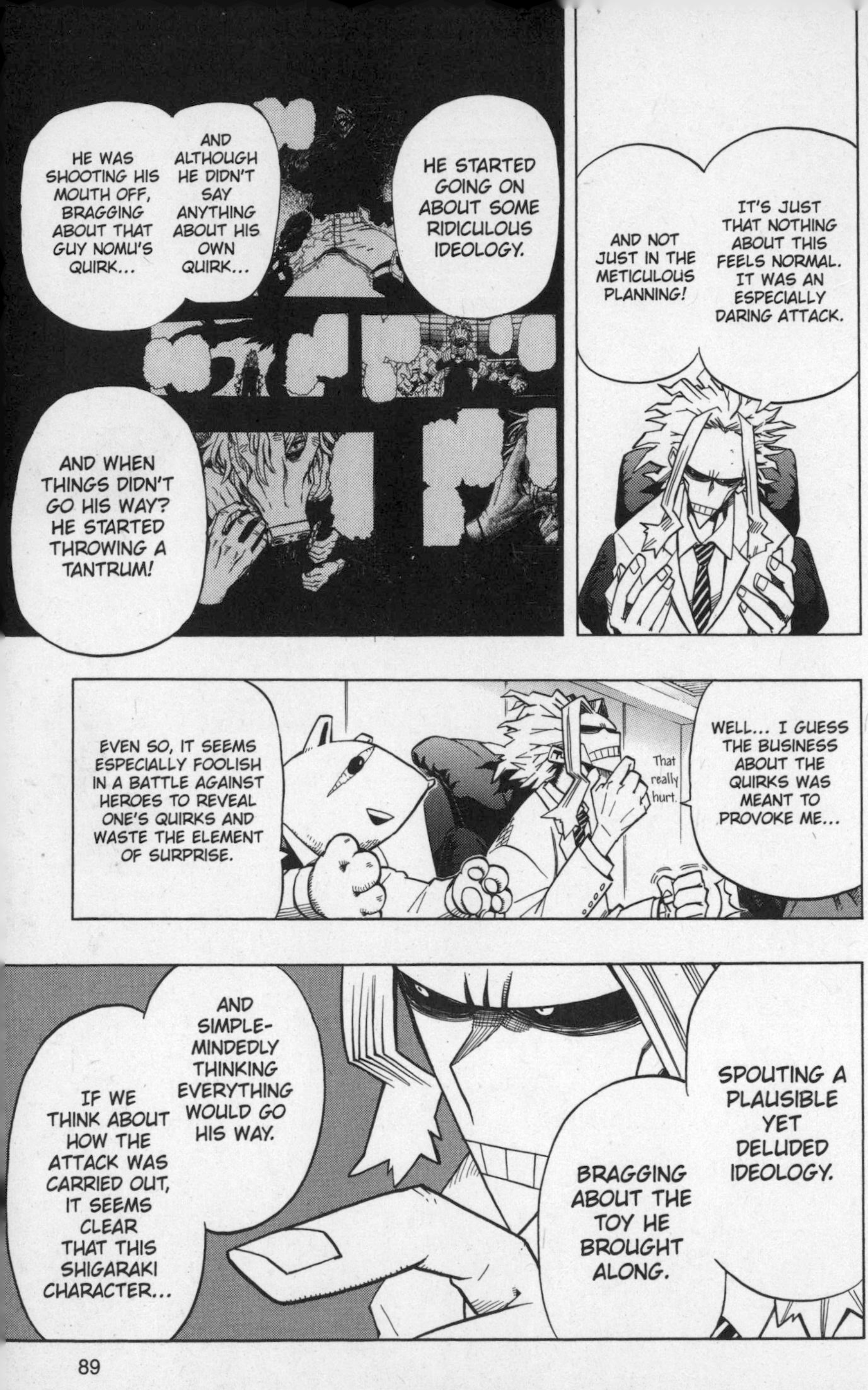
IT'S JUST THAT NOTHING ABOUT THIS FEELS NORMAL. IT WAS AN ESPECIALLY DARING ATTACK.
AND NOT JUST IN THE METICULOUS PLANNING!
HE WAS SHOOTING HIS MOUTH OFF, BRAGGING ABOUT THAT GUY NOMU'S QUIRK...
AND ALTHOUGH HE DIDN'T SAY ANYTHING ABOUT HIS OWN QUIRK...
HE STARTED GOING ON ABOUT SOME RIDICULOUS IDEOLOGY.
AND WHEN THINGS DIDN'T GO HIS WAY? HE STARTED THROWING A TANTRUM!
WELL... I GUESS THE BUSINESS ABOUT THE QUIRKS WAS MEANT TO PROVOKE ME...
That really hurt.
EVEN SO, IT SEEMS ESPECIALLY FOOLISH IN A BATTLE AGAINST HEROES TO REVEAL ONE'S QUIRKS AND WASTE THE ELEMENT OF SURPRISE.
SPOUTING A PLAUSIBLE YET DELUDED IDEOLOGY.
BRAGGING ABOUT THE TOY HE BROUGHT ALONG.
AND SIMPLE-MINDEDLY THINKING EVERYTHING WOULD GO HIS WAY.
IF WE THINK ABOUT HOW THE ATTACK WAS CARRIED OUT, IT SEEMS CLEAR THAT THIS SHIGARAKI CHARACTER...

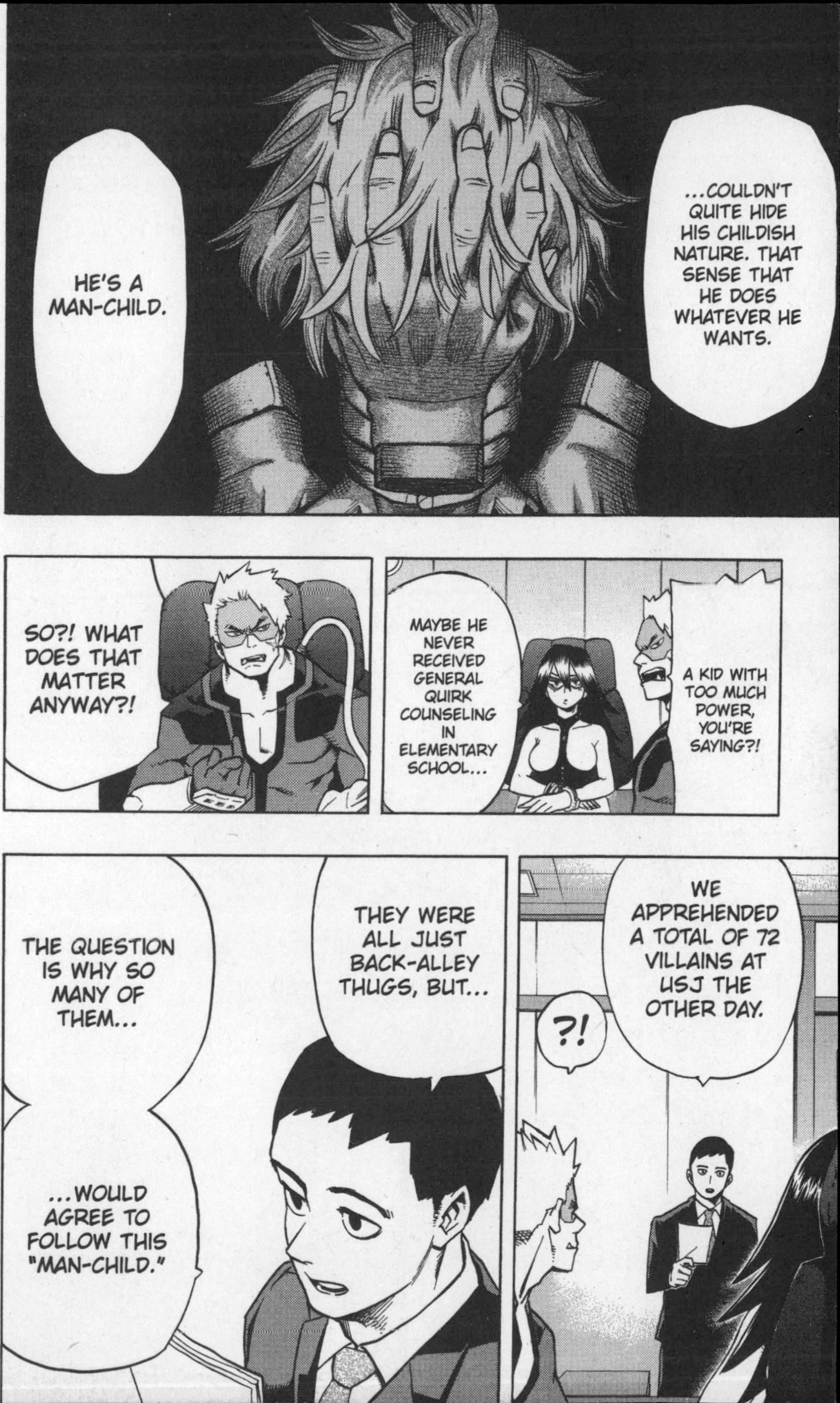
...COULDN'T QUITE HIDE HIS CHILDISH NATURE. THAT SENSE THAT HE DOES WHATEVER HE WANTS.
HE'S A MAN-CHILD.
A KID WITH TOO MUCH POWER, YOU'RE SAYING?!
MAYBE HE NEVER RECEIVED GENERAL QUIRK COUNSELING IN ELEMENTARY SCHOOL...
SO?! WHAT DOES THAT MATTER ANYWAY?!
WE APPREHENDED A TOTAL OF 72 VILLAINS AT USJ THE OTHER DAY.
?!
THEY WERE ALL JUST BACK-ALLEY THUGS, BUT...
THE QUESTION IS WHY SO MANY OF THEM...
...WOULD AGREE TO FOLLOW THIS "MAN-CHILD."

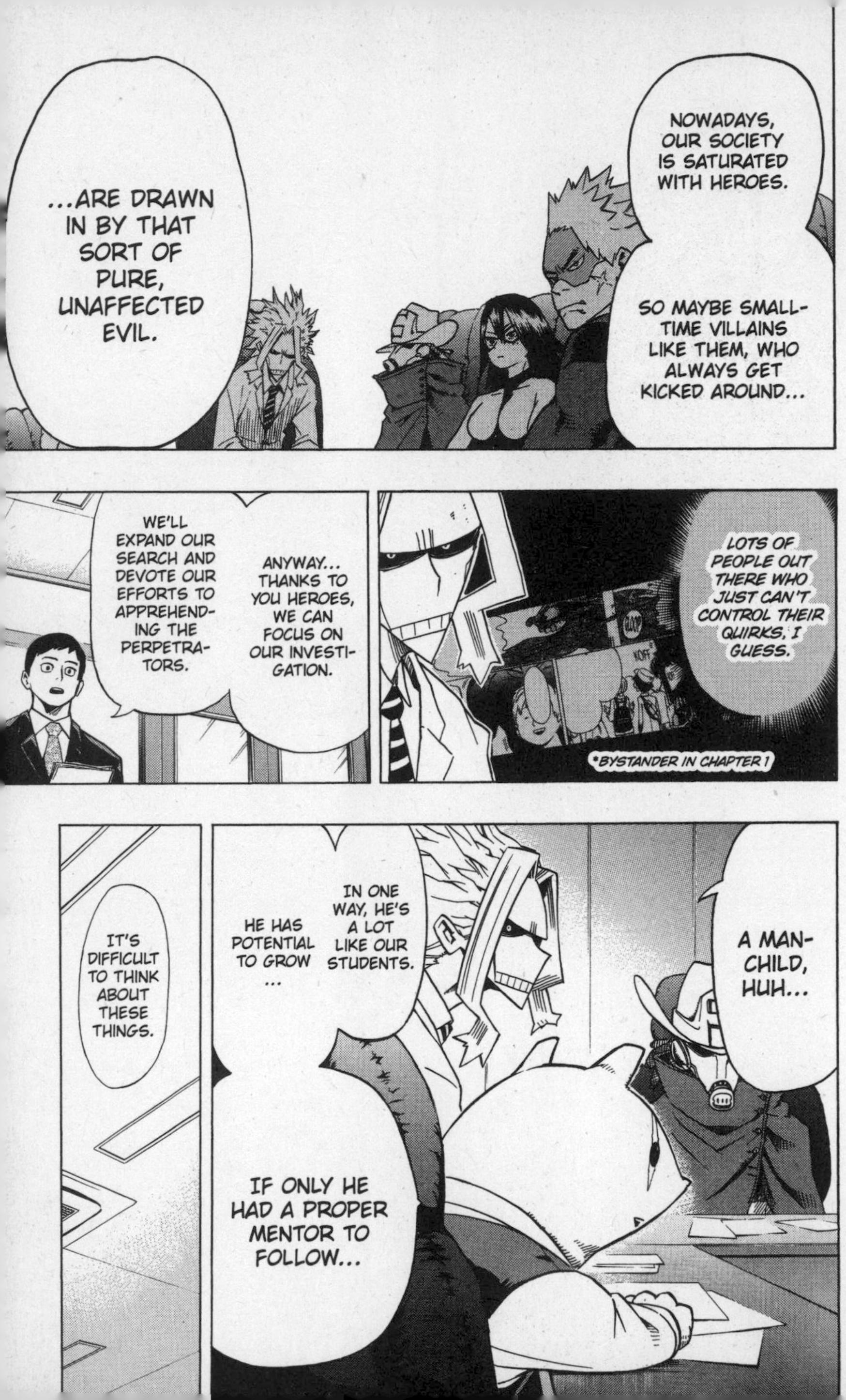
NOWADAYS, OUR SOCIETY IS SATURATED WITH HEROES.
SO MAYBE SMALL-TIME VILLAINS LIKE THEM, WHO ALWAYS GET KICKED AROUND...
...ARE DRAWN IN BY THAT SORT OF PURE, UNAFFECTED EVIL.
LOTS OF PEOPLE OUT THERE WHO JUST CAN'T CONTROL THEIR QUIRKS, I GUESS.
*BYSTANDER IN CHAPTER 1
ANYWAY... THANKS TO YOU HEROES, WE CAN FOCUS ON OUR INVESTIGATION.
WE'LL EXPAND OUR SEARCH AND DEVOTE OUR EFFORTS TO APPREHENDING THE PERPETRATORS.
A MAN-CHILD, HUH...
IN ONE WAY, HE'S A LOT LIKE OUR STUDENTS.
HE HAS POTENTIAL TO GROW...
IF ONLY HE HAD A PROPER MENTOR TO FOLLOW...
IT'S DIFFICULT TO THINK ABOUT THESE THINGS.

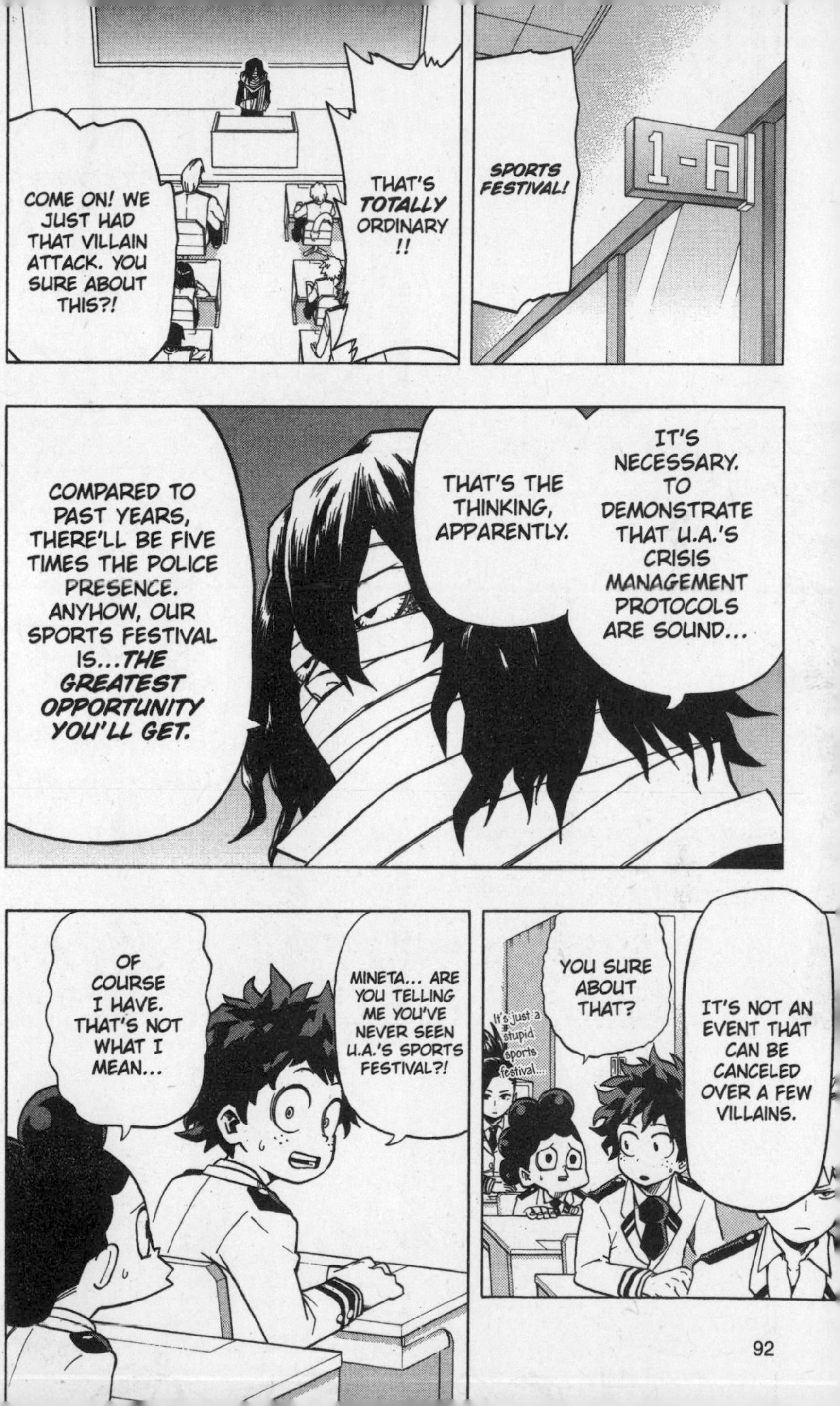
SPORTS FESTIVAL!
THAT'S TOTALLY ORDINARY !!
COME ON! WE JUST HAD THAT VILLAIN ATTACK. YOU SURE ABOUT THIS?!
IT'S NECESSARY. TO DEMONSTRATE THAT U.A.'S CRISIS MANAGEMENT PROTOCOLS ARE SOUND...
THAT'S THE THINKING, APPARENTLY.
COMPARED TO PAST YEARS, THERE'LL BE FIVE TIMES THE POLICE PRESENCE. ANYHOW, OUR SPORTS FESTIVAL IS...THE GREATEST OPPORTUNITY YOU'LL GET.
IT'S NOT AN EVENT THAT CAN BE CANCELED OVER A FEW VILLAINS.
YOU SURE ABOUT THAT?
It's just a stupid sports festival...
MINETA... ARE YOU TELLING ME YOU'VE NEVER SEEN U.A.'S SPORTS FESTIVAL?!
OF COURSE I HAVE. THAT'S NOT WHAT I MEAN...

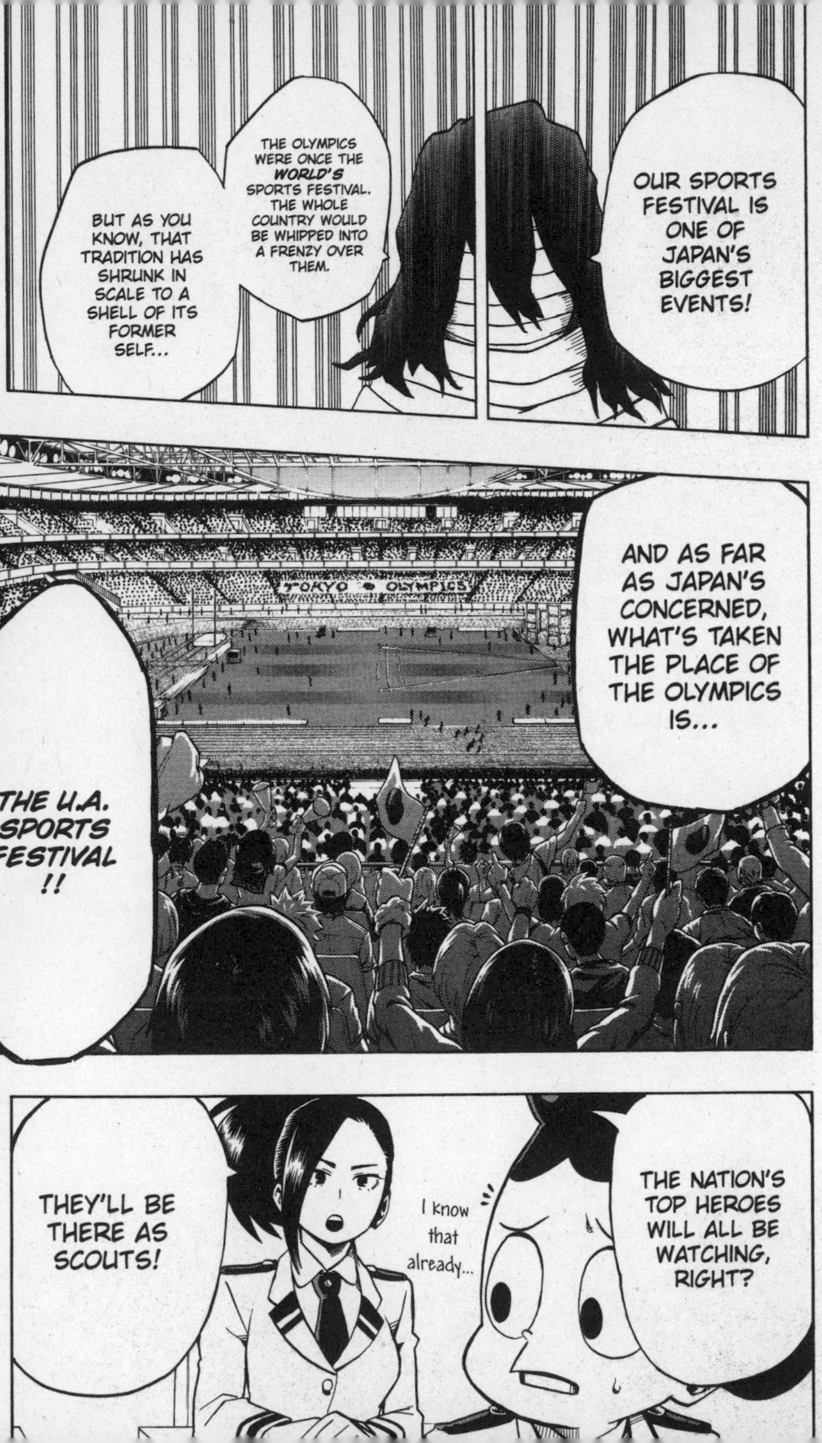
OUR SPORTS FESTIVAL IS ONE OF JAPAN'S BIGGEST EVENTS!
THE OLYMPICS WERE ONCE THE WORLD'S SPORTS FESTIVAL. THE WHOLE COUNTRY WOULD BE WHIPPED INTO A FRENZY OVER THEM.
BUT AS YOU KNOW, THAT TRADITION HAS SHRUNK IN SCALE TO A SHELL OF ITS FORMER SELF...
AND AS FAR AS JAPAN'S CONCERNED, WHAT'S TAKEN THE PLACE OF THE OLYMPICS IS...
TOKYO OLYMPICS
THE U.A. SPORTS FESTIVAL!!
THE NATION'S TOP HEROES WILL ALL BE WATCHING, RIGHT?
I know that already...
THEY'LL BE THERE AS SCOUTS!

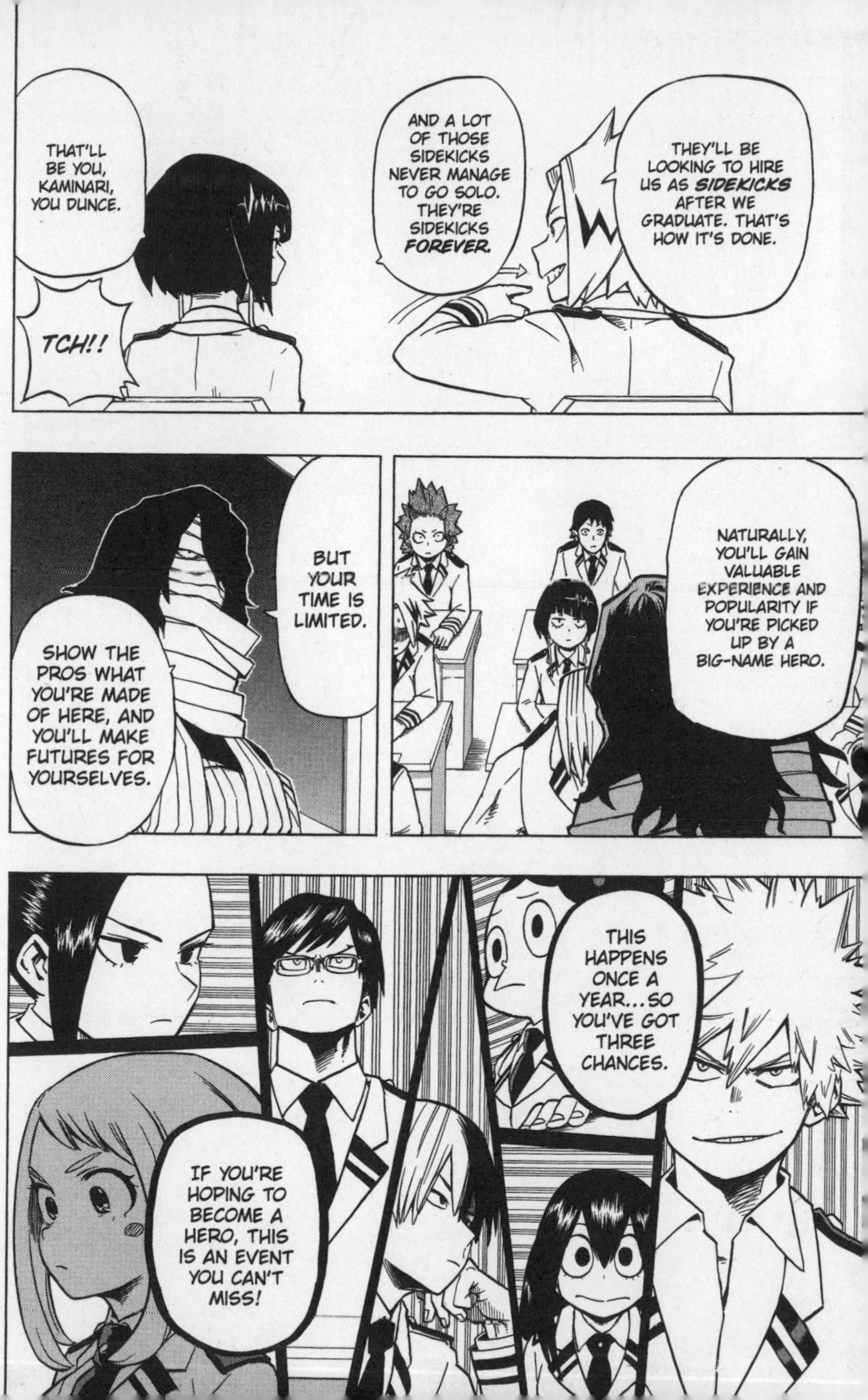
THEY'LL BE LOOKING TO HIRE US AS ***SIDEKICKS*** AFTER WE GRADUATE. THAT'S HOW IT'S DONE.
AND A LOT OF THOSE SIDEKICKS NEVER MANAGE TO GO SOLO. THEY'RE SIDEKICKS ***FOREVER.***
THAT'LL BE YOU, KAMINARI, YOU DUNCE.
TCH!!
NATURALLY, YOU'LL GAIN VALUABLE EXPERIENCE AND POPULARITY IF YOU'RE PICKED UP BY A BIG-NAME HERO.
BUT YOUR TIME IS LIMITED.
SHOW THE PROS WHAT YOU'RE MADE OF HERE, AND YOU'LL MAKE FUTURES FOR YOURSELVES.
THIS HAPPENS ONCE A YEAR...SO YOU'VE GOT THREE CHANCES.
IF YOU'RE HOPING TO BECOME A HERO, THIS IS AN EVENT YOU CAN'T MISS!

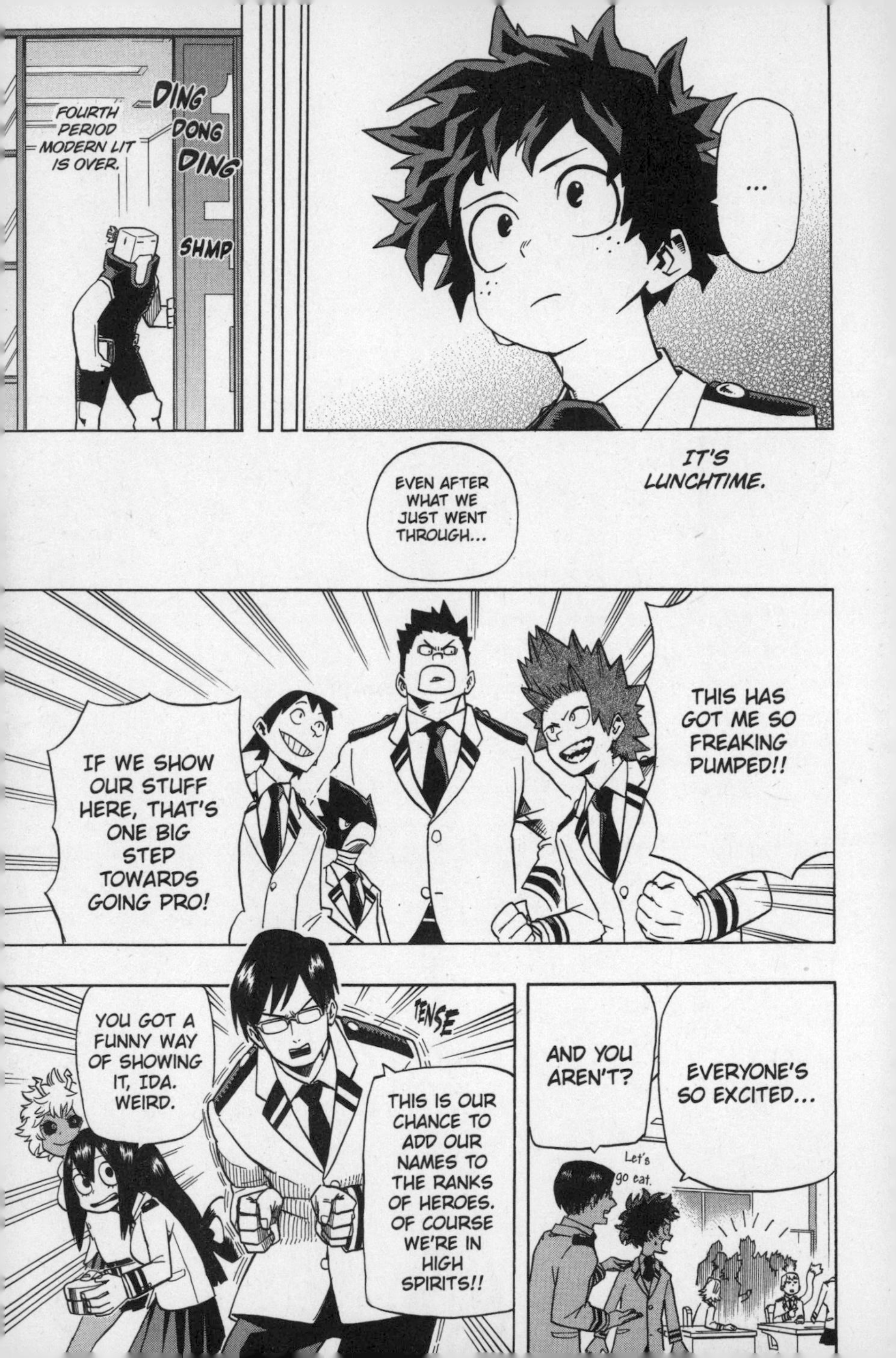
...
FOURTH PERIOD MODERN LIT IS OVER.
DING DONG DING
SHMP
IT'S LUNCHTIME.
EVEN AFTER WHAT WE JUST WENT THROUGH...
THIS HAS GOT ME SO FREAKING PUMPED!!
IF WE SHOW OUR STUFF HERE, THAT'S ONE BIG STEP TOWARDS GOING PRO!
EVERYONE'S SO EXCITED...
AND YOU AREN'T?
Let's go eat.
TENSE
THIS IS OUR CHANCE TO ADD OUR NAMES TO THE RANKS OF HEROES. OF COURSE WE'RE IN HIGH SPIRITS!!
YOU GOT A FUNNY WAY OF SHOWING IT, IDA. WEIRD.

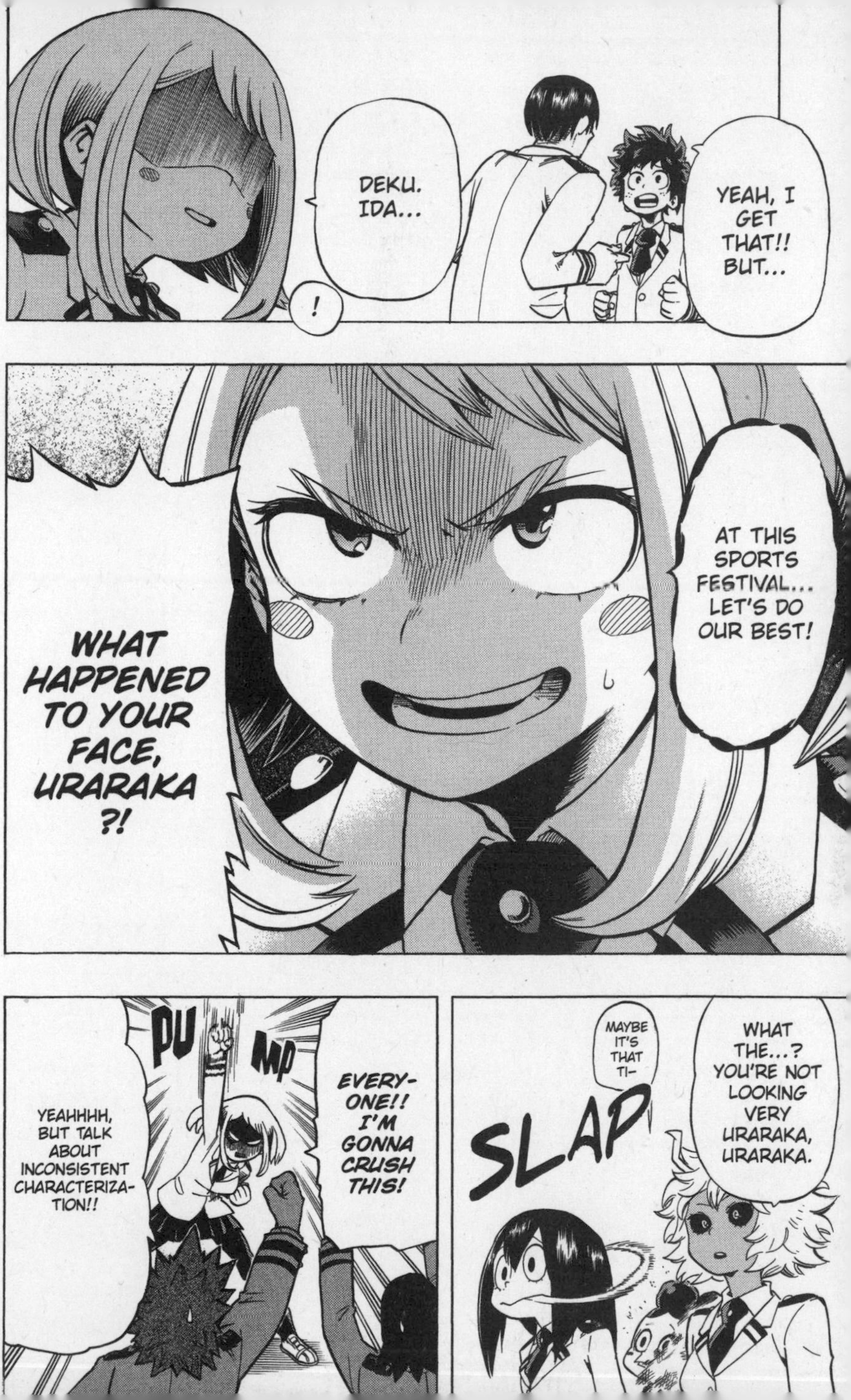
YEAH, I GET THAT!! BUT...
DEKU. IDA...
!
AT THIS SPORTS FESTIVAL... LET'S DO OUR BEST!
WHAT HAPPENED TO YOUR FACE, URARAKA?!
WHAT THE...? YOU'RE NOT LOOKING VERY URARAKA, URARAKA.
MAYBE IT'S THAT TI-
SLAP
PUMP
EVERY-ONE!! I'M GONNA CRUSH THIS!
YEAHHHH, BUT TALK ABOUT INCONSISTENT CHARACTERIZA-TION!!

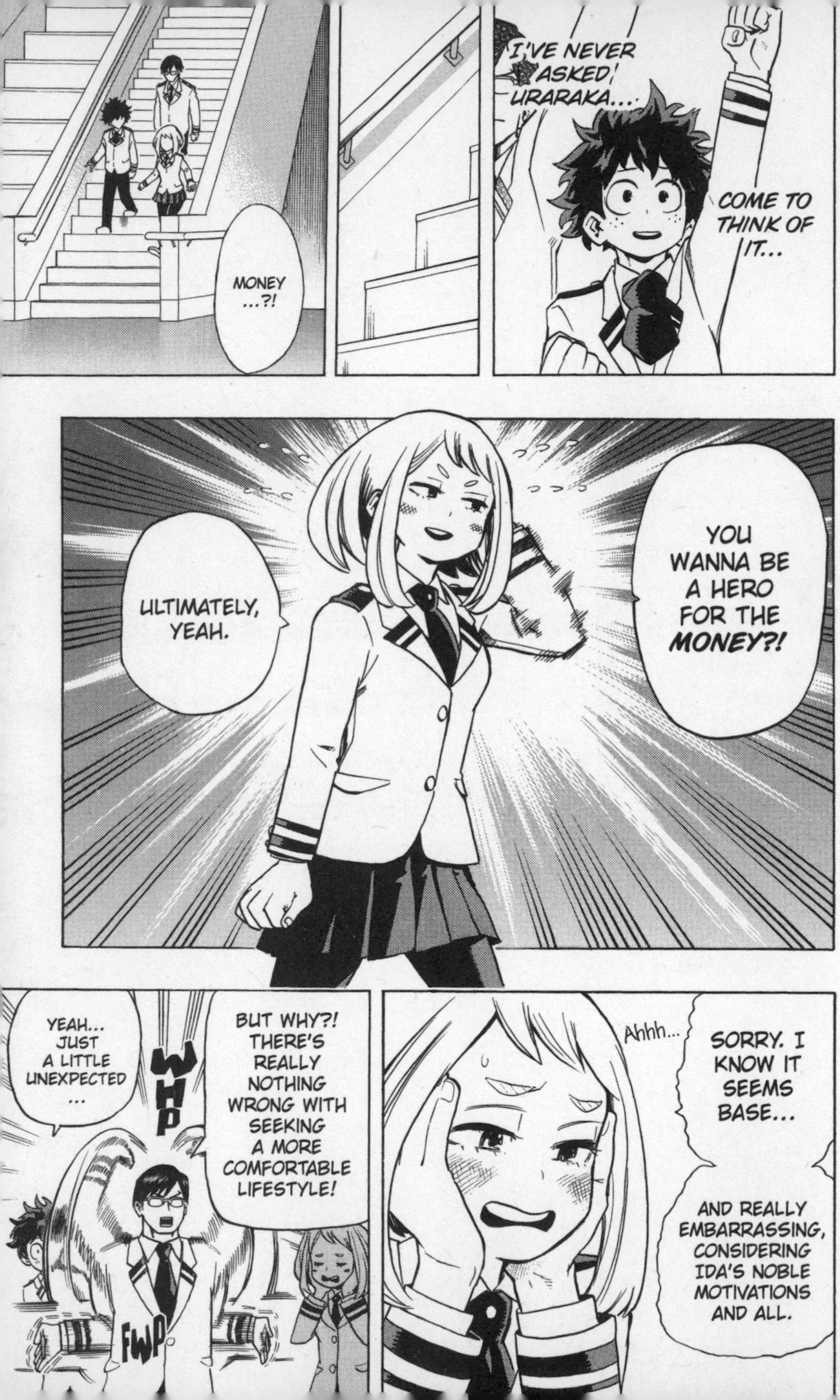
COME TO THINK OF IT...
I'VE NEVER ASKED URARAKA...
MONEY ...?!
YOU WANNA BE A HERO FOR THE MONEY?!
ULTIMATELY, YEAH.
Ahhh...
SORRY. I KNOW IT SEEMS BASE...
AND REALLY EMBARRASSING, CONSIDERING IDA'S NOBLE MOTIVATIONS AND ALL.
BUT WHY?! THERE'S REALLY NOTHING WRONG WITH SEEKING A MORE COMFORTABLE LIFESTYLE!
WHP
FWP
YEAH... JUST A LITTLE UNEXPECTED ...

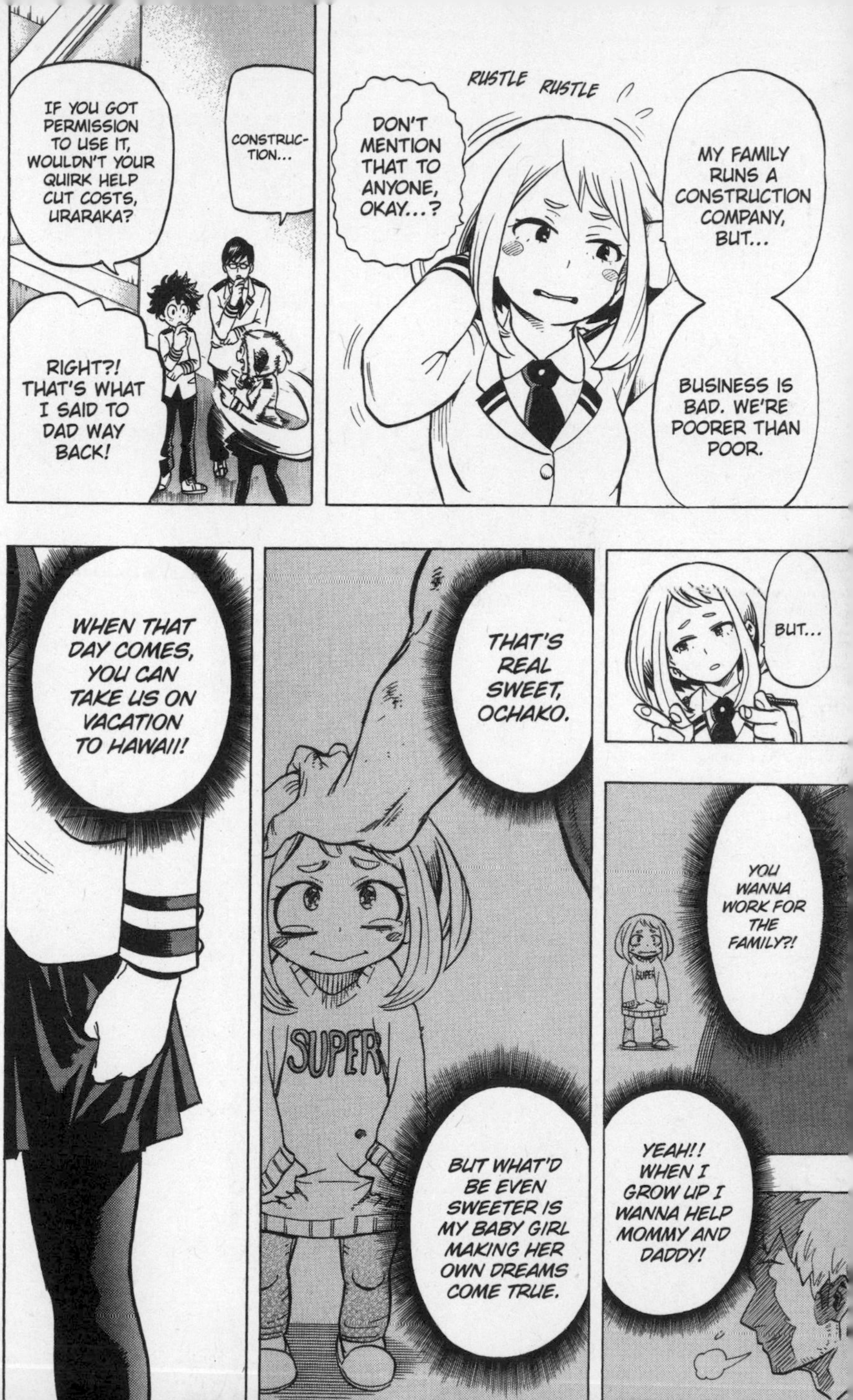
RUSTLE RUSTLE
MY FAMILY RUNS A CONSTRUCTION COMPANY, BUT...
BUSINESS IS BAD. WE'RE POORER THAN POOR.
DON'T MENTION THAT TO ANYONE, OKAY...?
CONSTRUC-TION...
IF YOU GOT PERMISSION TO USE IT, WOULDN'T YOUR QUIRK HELP CUT COSTS, URARAKA?
RIGHT?! THAT'S WHAT I SAID TO DAD WAY BACK!
BUT...
YOU WANNA WORK FOR THE FAMILY?!
YEAH!! WHEN I GROW UP I WANNA HELP MOMMY AND DADDY!
THAT'S REAL SWEET, OCHAKO.
BUT WHAT'D BE EVEN SWEETER IS MY BABY GIRL MAKING HER OWN DREAMS COME TRUE.
WHEN THAT DAY COMES, YOU CAN TAKE US ON VACATION TO HAWAII!
SUPER

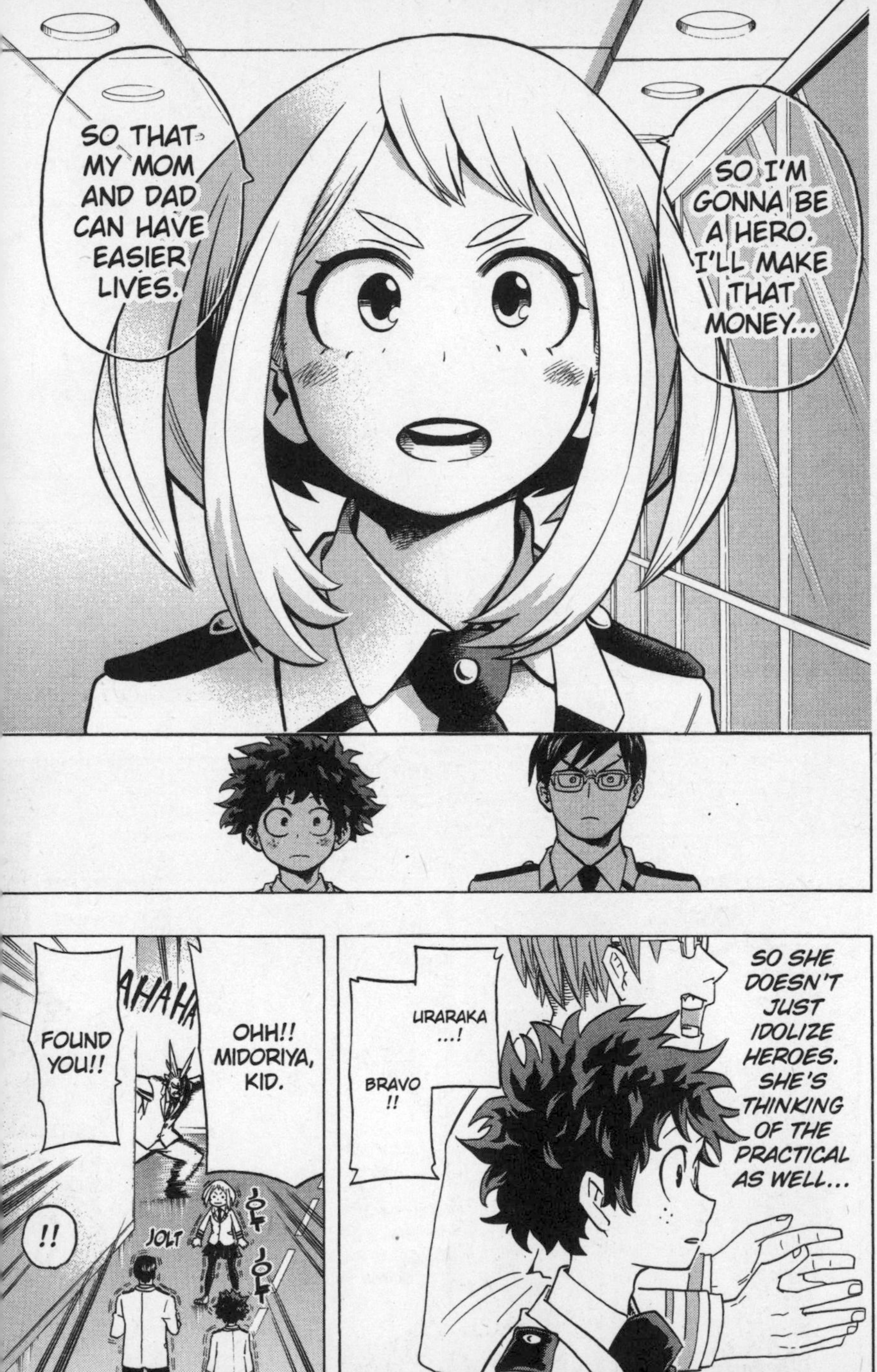
SO I'M GONNA BE A HERO. I'LL MAKE THAT MONEY...
SO THAT MY MOM AND DAD CAN HAVE EASIER LIVES.
SO SHE DOESN'T JUST IDOLIZE HEROES. SHE'S THINKING OF THE PRACTICAL AS WELL...
URARAKA ...!
BRAVO !!
AHAHA
OHH!! MIDORIYA, KID.
FOUND YOU!!
JOLT
JOLT
JOLT
!!

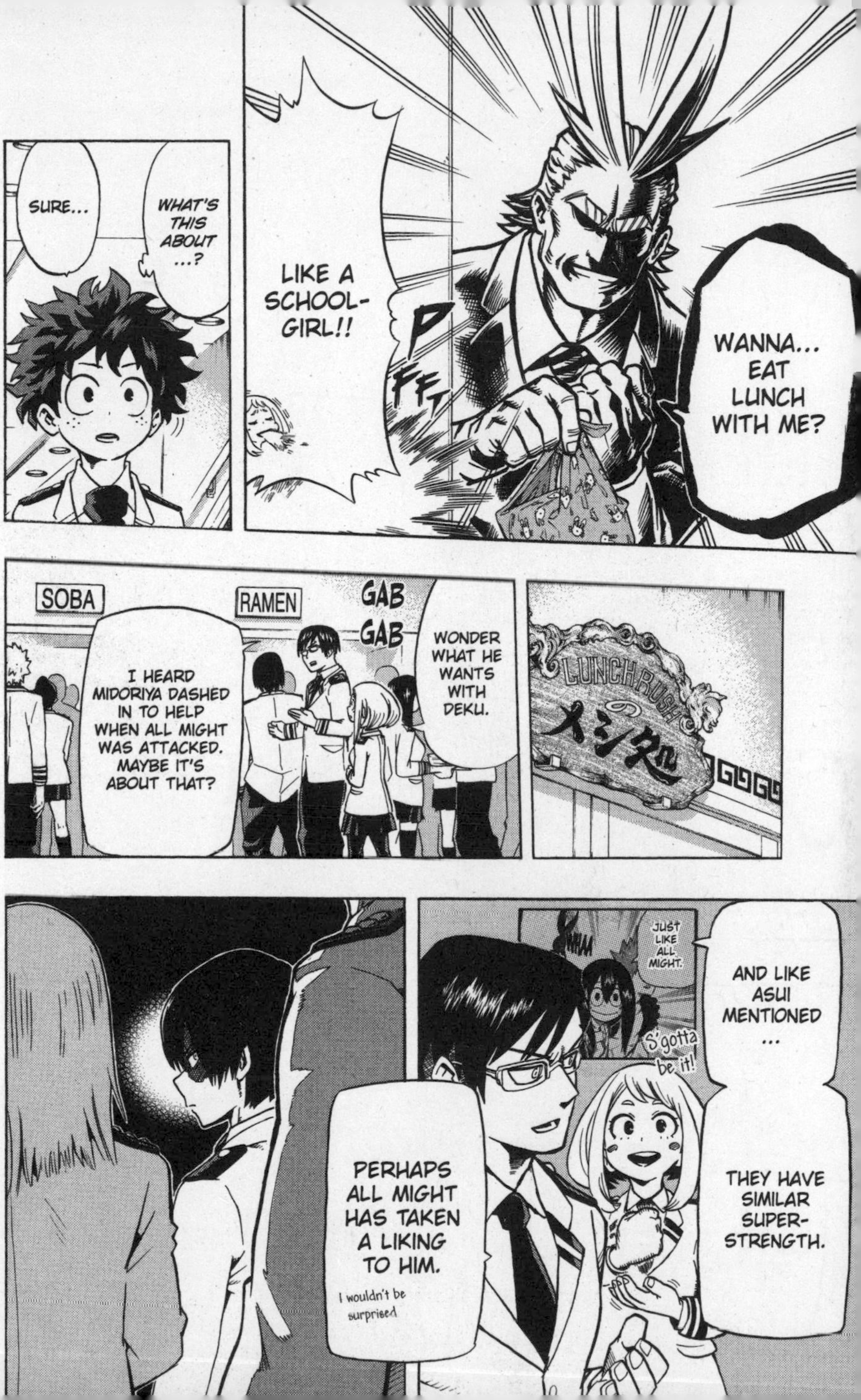

WANNA... EAT LUNCH WITH ME?
PFFT
LIKE A SCHOOL-GIRL!!
WHAT'S THIS ABOUT ...?
SURE...
LUNCHRUSH の メシ処
WONDER WHAT HE WANTS WITH DEKU.
GAB GAB
RAMEN
I HEARD MIDORIYA DASHED IN TO HELP WHEN ALL MIGHT WAS ATTACKED. MAYBE IT'S ABOUT THAT?
SOBA
JUST LIKE ALL MIGHT.
AND LIKE ASUI MENTIONED ...
S'gotta be it!
THEY HAVE SIMILAR SUPER-STRENGTH.
PERHAPS ALL MIGHT HAS TAKEN A LIKING TO HIM.
I wouldn't be surprised

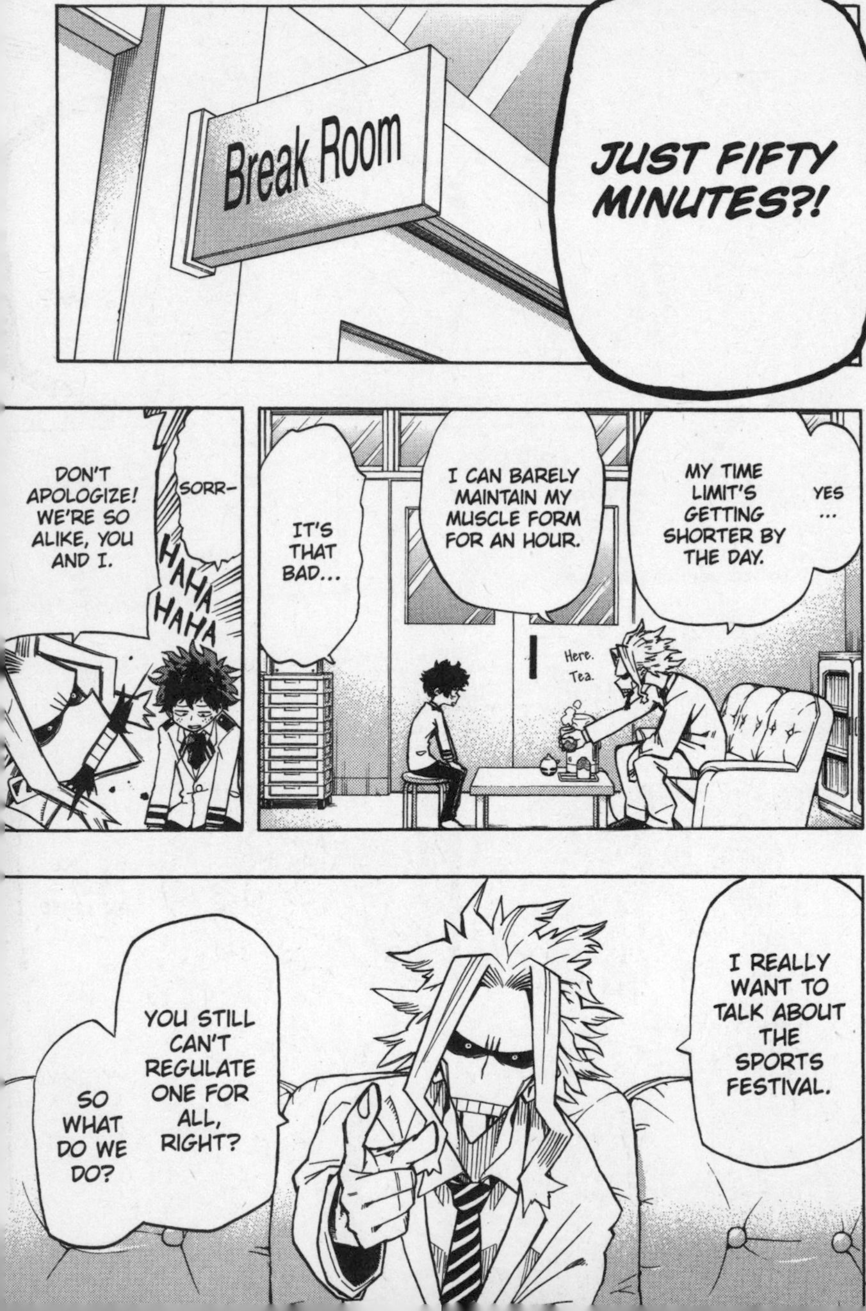
JUST FIFTY MINUTES?!
Break Room
YES ...
MY TIME LIMIT'S GETTING SHORTER BY THE DAY.
I CAN BARELY MAINTAIN MY MUSCLE FORM FOR AN HOUR.
IT'S THAT BAD...
Here. Tea.
SORR-
HAHA HAHA
DON'T APOLOGIZE! WE'RE SO ALIKE, YOU AND I.
I REALLY WANT TO TALK ABOUT THE SPORTS FESTIVAL.
YOU STILL CAN'T REGULATE ONE FOR ALL, RIGHT?
SO WHAT DO WE DO?

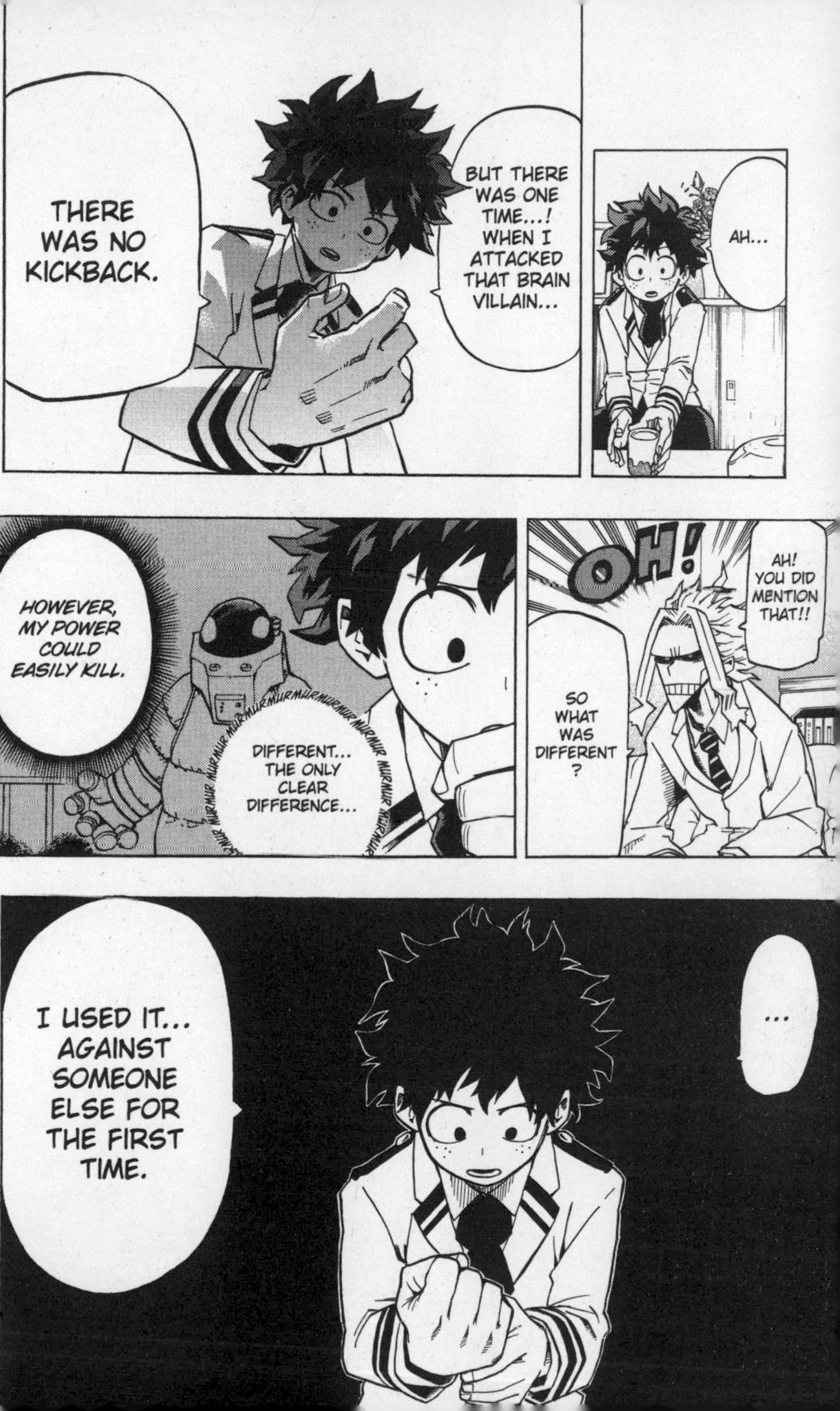
AH...
BUT THERE WAS ONE TIME...! WHEN I ATTACKED THAT BRAIN VILLAIN...
THERE WAS NO KICKBACK.
OH!
AH! YOU DID MENTION THAT!!
SO WHAT WAS DIFFERENT?
DIFFERENT... THE ONLY CLEAR DIFFERENCE...
HOWEVER, MY POWER COULD EASILY KILL.
...
I USED IT... AGAINST SOMEONE ELSE FOR THE FIRST TIME.

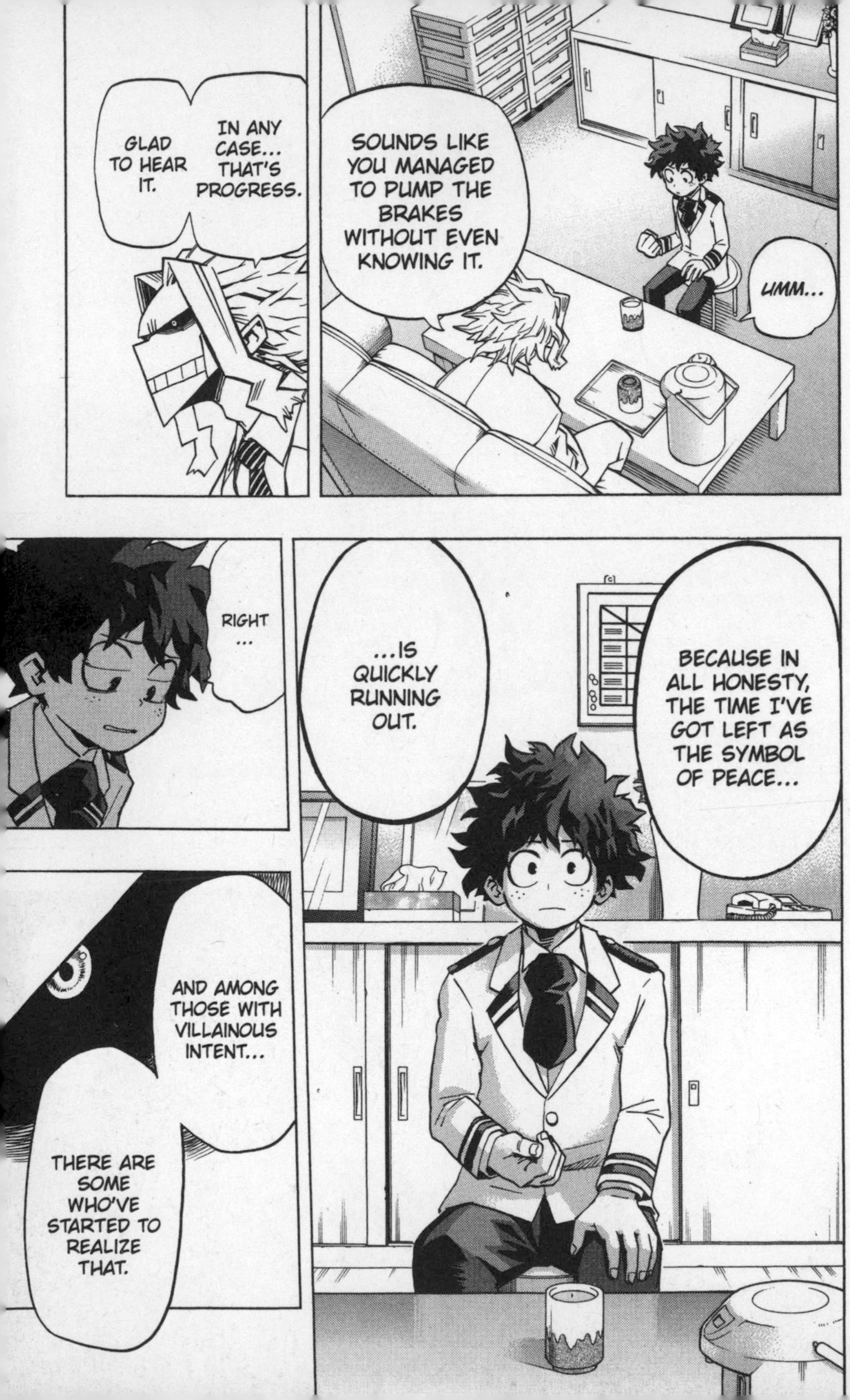
SOUNDS LIKE YOU MANAGED TO PUMP THE BRAKES WITHOUT EVEN KNOWING IT.
UMM...
IN ANY CASE... THAT'S PROGRESS.
GLAD TO HEAR IT.
BECAUSE IN ALL HONESTY, THE TIME I'VE GOT LEFT AS THE SYMBOL OF PEACE...
...IS QUICKLY RUNNING OUT.
RIGHT...
AND AMONG THOSE WITH VILLAINOUS INTENT...
THERE ARE SOME WHO'VE STARTED TO REALIZE THAT.

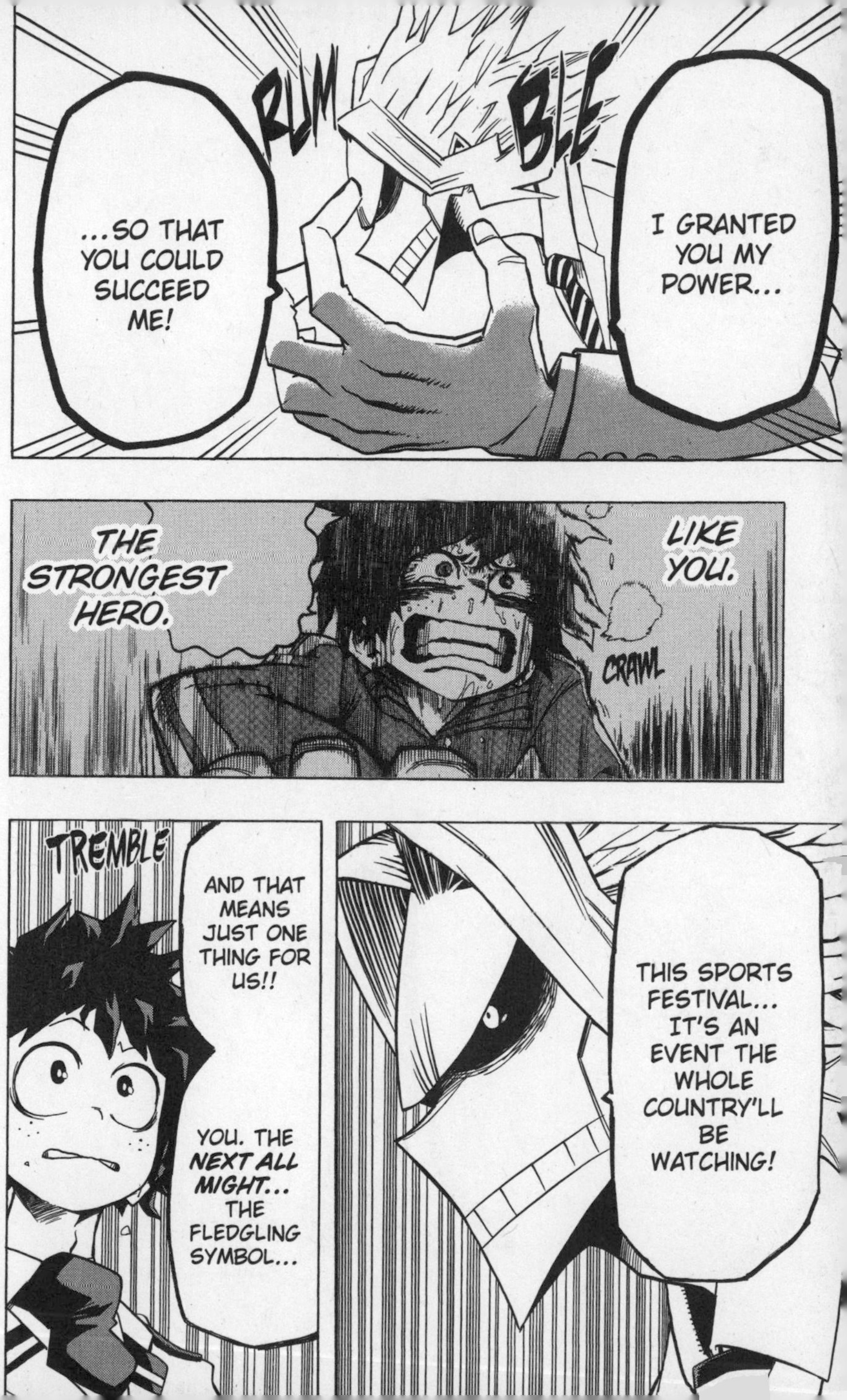
RUMBLE
I GRANTED YOU MY POWER...
...SO THAT YOU COULD SUCCEED ME!
LIKE YOU.
THE STRONGEST HERO.
CRAWL
THIS SPORTS FESTIVAL... IT'S AN EVENT THE WHOLE COUNTRY'LL BE WATCHING!
TREMBLE
AND THAT MEANS JUST ONE THING FOR US!!
YOU. THE NEXT ALL MIGHT... THE FLEDGLING SYMBOL...

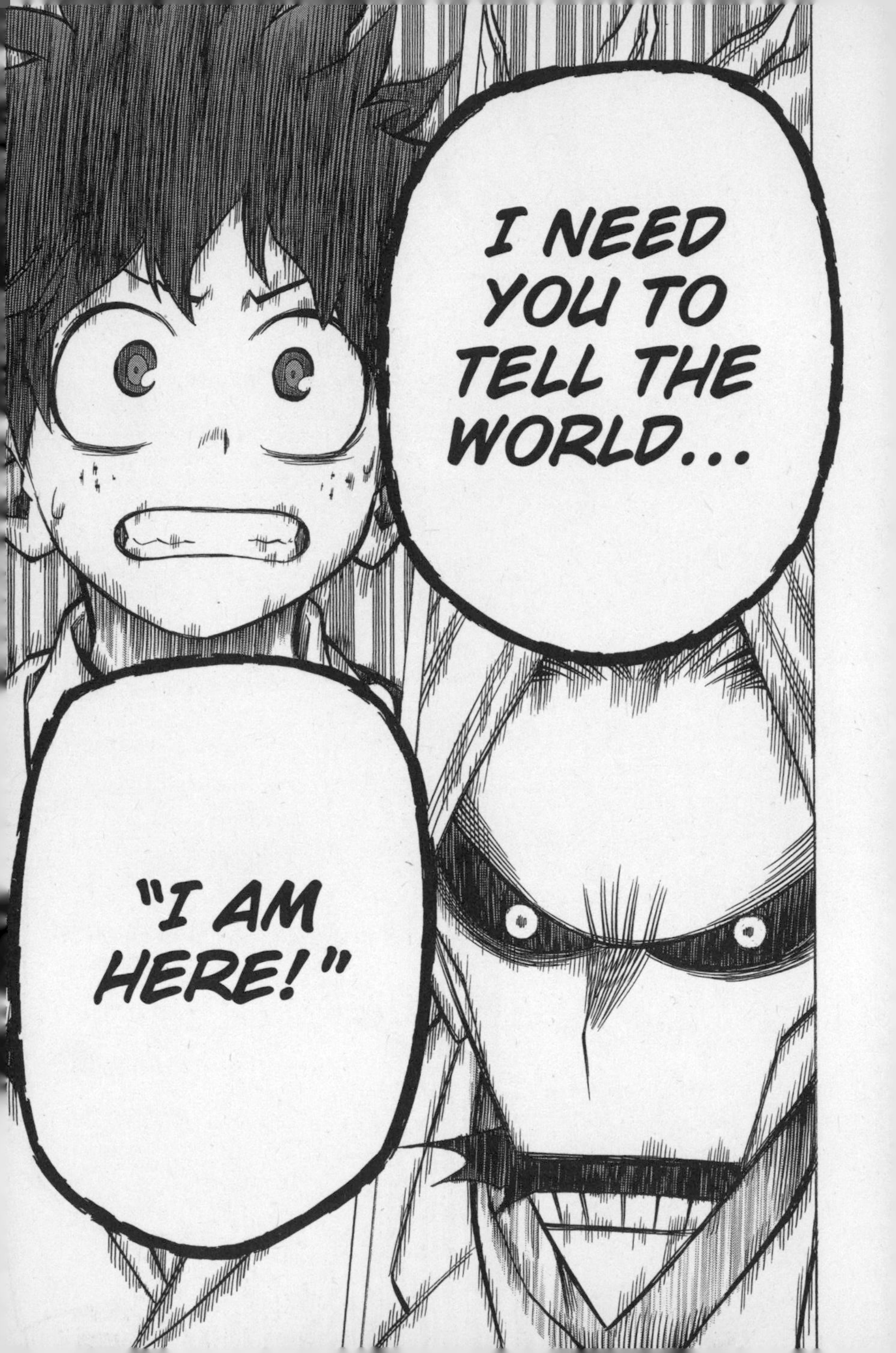
I NEED YOU TO TELL THE WORLD...
"I AM HERE!"

PRINCIPAL [NEZU] [AGE UNKNOWN]

SMOKE BREAK

Birthday: 1/1
Height: 85 cm
Favorite Thing: Brushing

BEHIND THE SCENES
He isn't human. He's an exceedingly rare example of an animal that's manifested a Quirk.

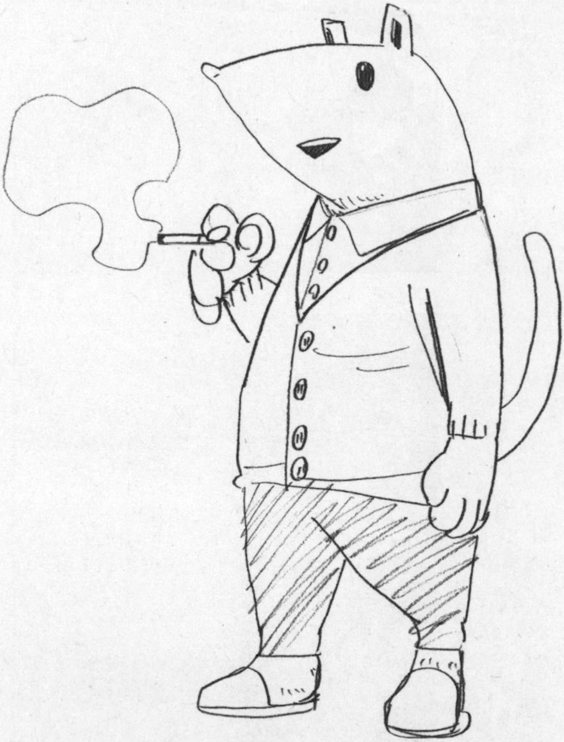

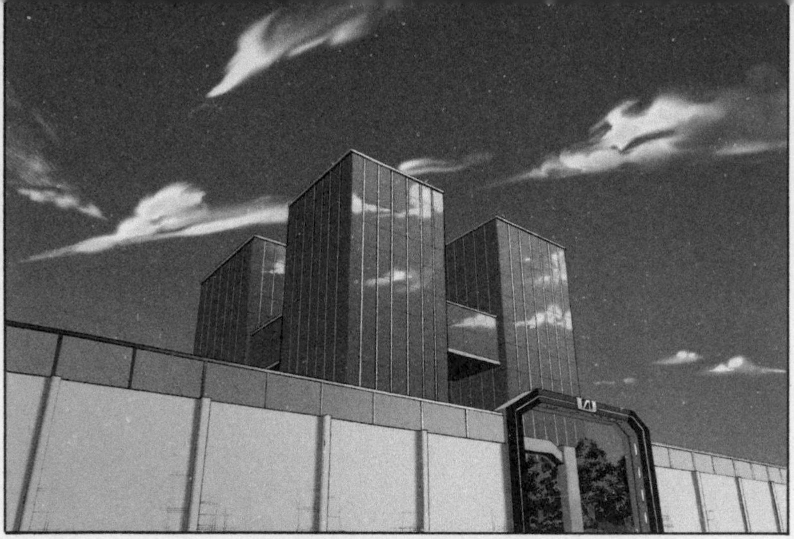

No.23 - Roaring Sports Festival

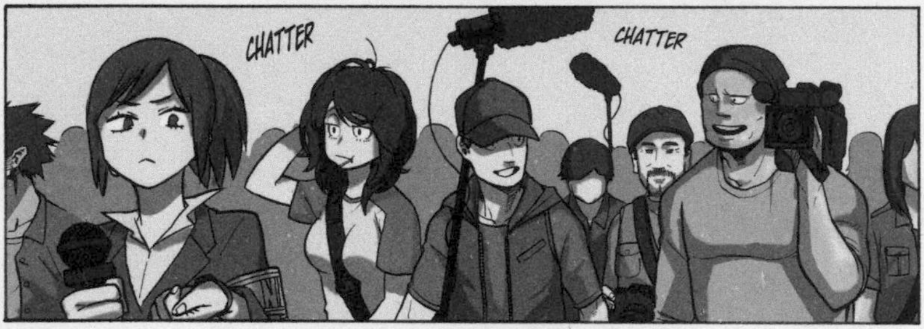
CHATTER
CHATTER

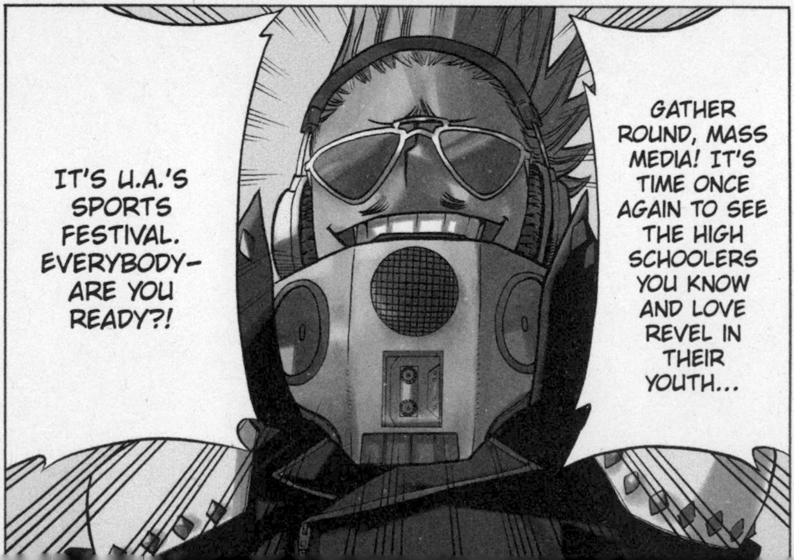
GATHER ROUND, MASS MEDIA! IT'S TIME ONCE AGAIN TO SEE THE HIGH SCHOOLERS YOU KNOW AND LOVE REVEL IN THEIR YOUTH...
IT'S U.A.'S SPORTS FESTIVAL. EVERYBODY- ARE YOU READY?!

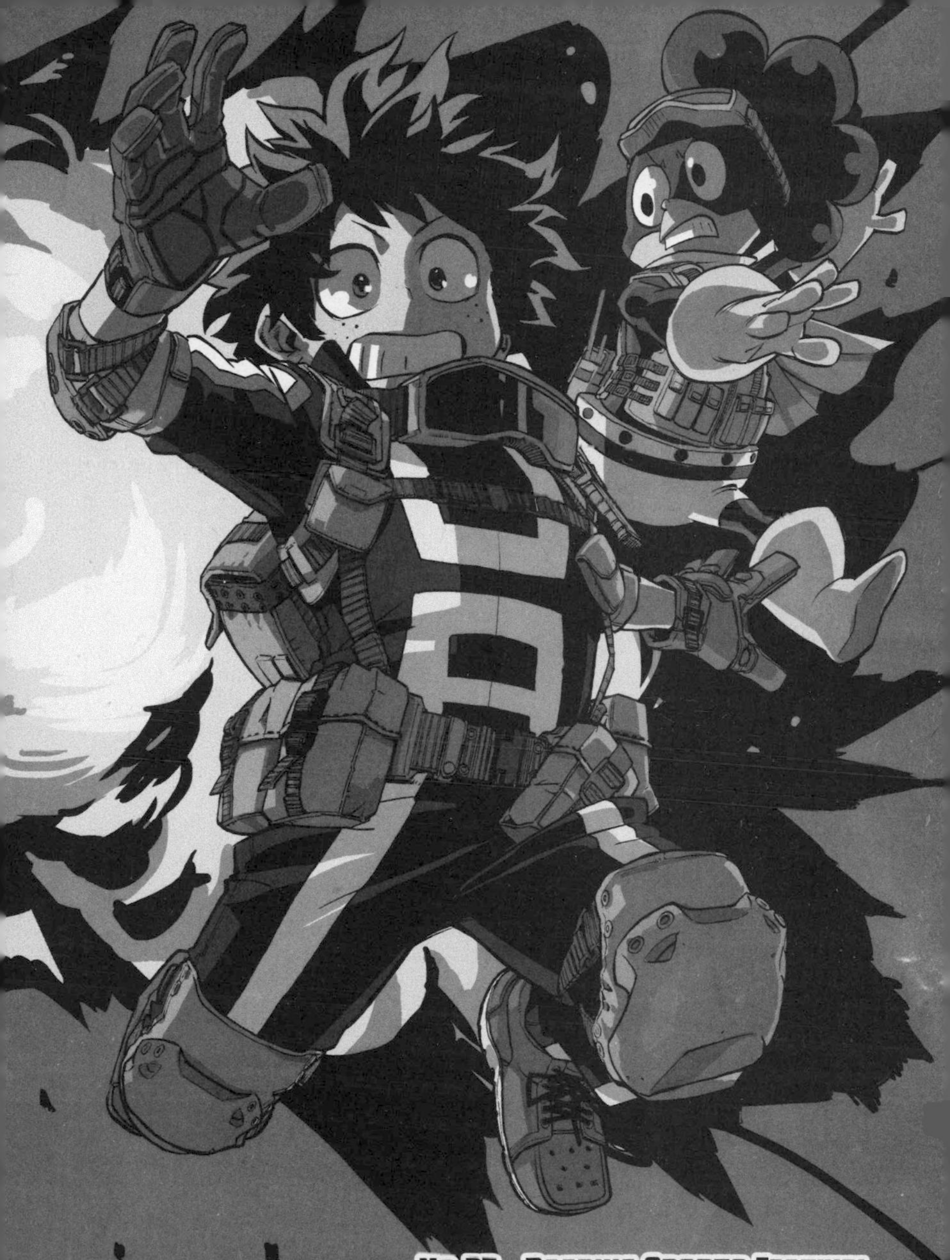

No.23 - Roaring Sports Festival

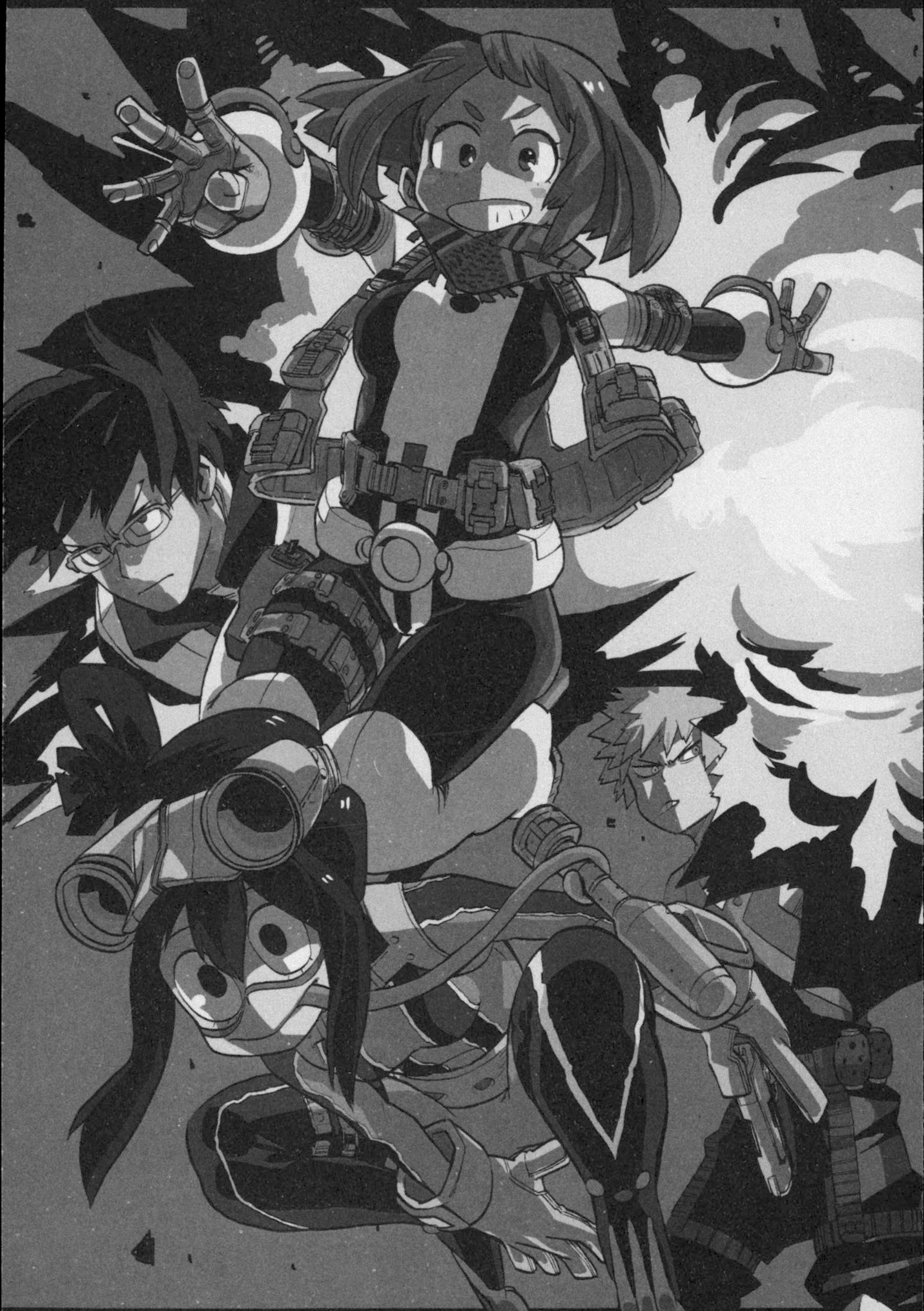

MY HERO ACADEMIA

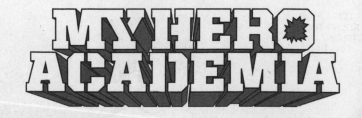

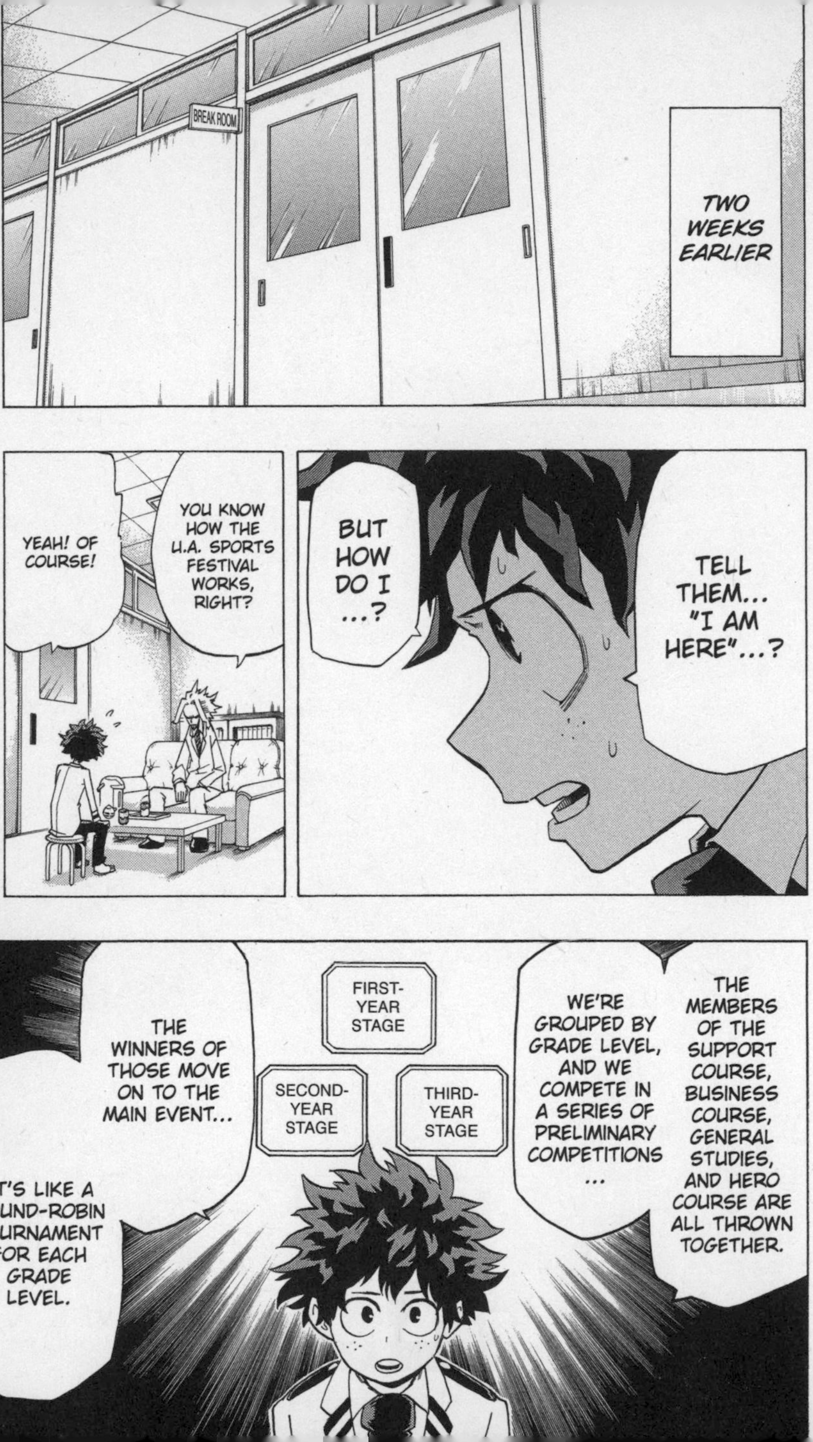
BREAK ROOM
TWO WEEKS EARLIER
TELL THEM... "I AM HERE"...?
BUT HOW DO I ...?
YOU KNOW HOW THE U.A. SPORTS FESTIVAL WORKS, RIGHT?
YEAH! OF COURSE!
THE MEMBERS OF THE SUPPORT COURSE, BUSINESS COURSE, GENERAL STUDIES, AND HERO COURSE ARE ALL THROWN TOGETHER.
WE'RE GROUPED BY GRADE LEVEL, AND WE COMPETE IN A SERIES OF PRELIMINARY COMPETITIONS ...
FIRST-YEAR STAGE
THIRD-YEAR STAGE
SECOND-YEAR STAGE
THE WINNERS OF THOSE MOVE ON TO THE MAIN EVENT...
IT'S LIKE A ROUND-ROBIN TOURNAMENT FOR EACH GRADE LEVEL.

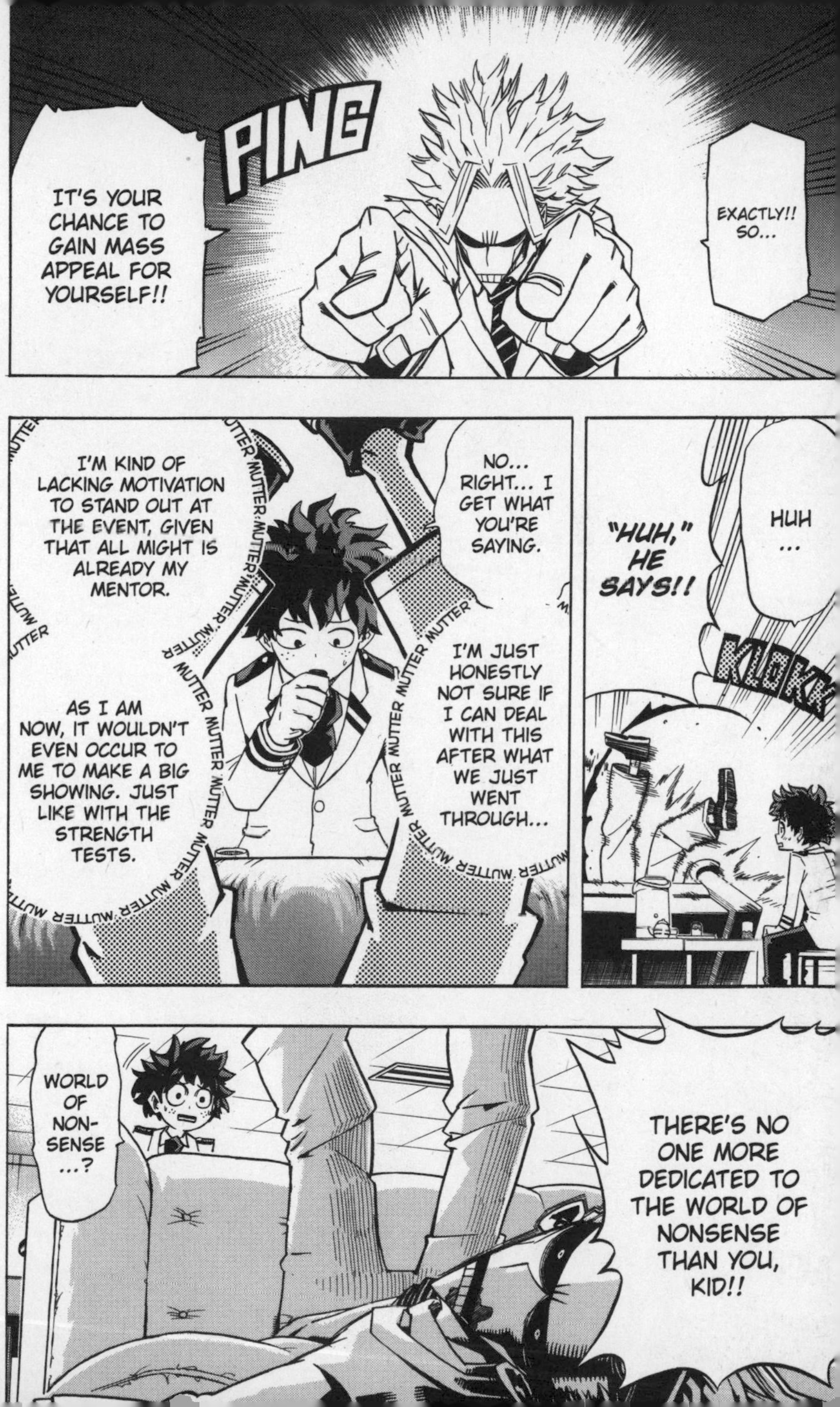
EXACTLY!! SO...
PING
IT'S YOUR CHANCE TO GAIN MASS APPEAL FOR YOURSELF!!
HUH ...
"HUH," HE SAYS!!
NO... RIGHT... I GET WHAT YOU'RE SAYING.
I'M KIND OF LACKING MOTIVATION TO STAND OUT AT THE EVENT, GIVEN THAT ALL MIGHT IS ALREADY MY MENTOR.
I'M JUST HONESTLY NOT SURE IF I CAN DEAL WITH THIS AFTER WHAT WE JUST WENT THROUGH...
AS I AM NOW, IT WOULDN'T EVEN OCCUR TO ME TO MAKE A BIG SHOWING. JUST LIKE WITH THE STRENGTH TESTS.
MUTTER MUTTER MUTTER MUTTER
THERE'S NO ONE MORE DEDICATED TO THE WORLD OF NONSENSE THAN YOU, KID!!
WORLD OF NON-SENSE ...?

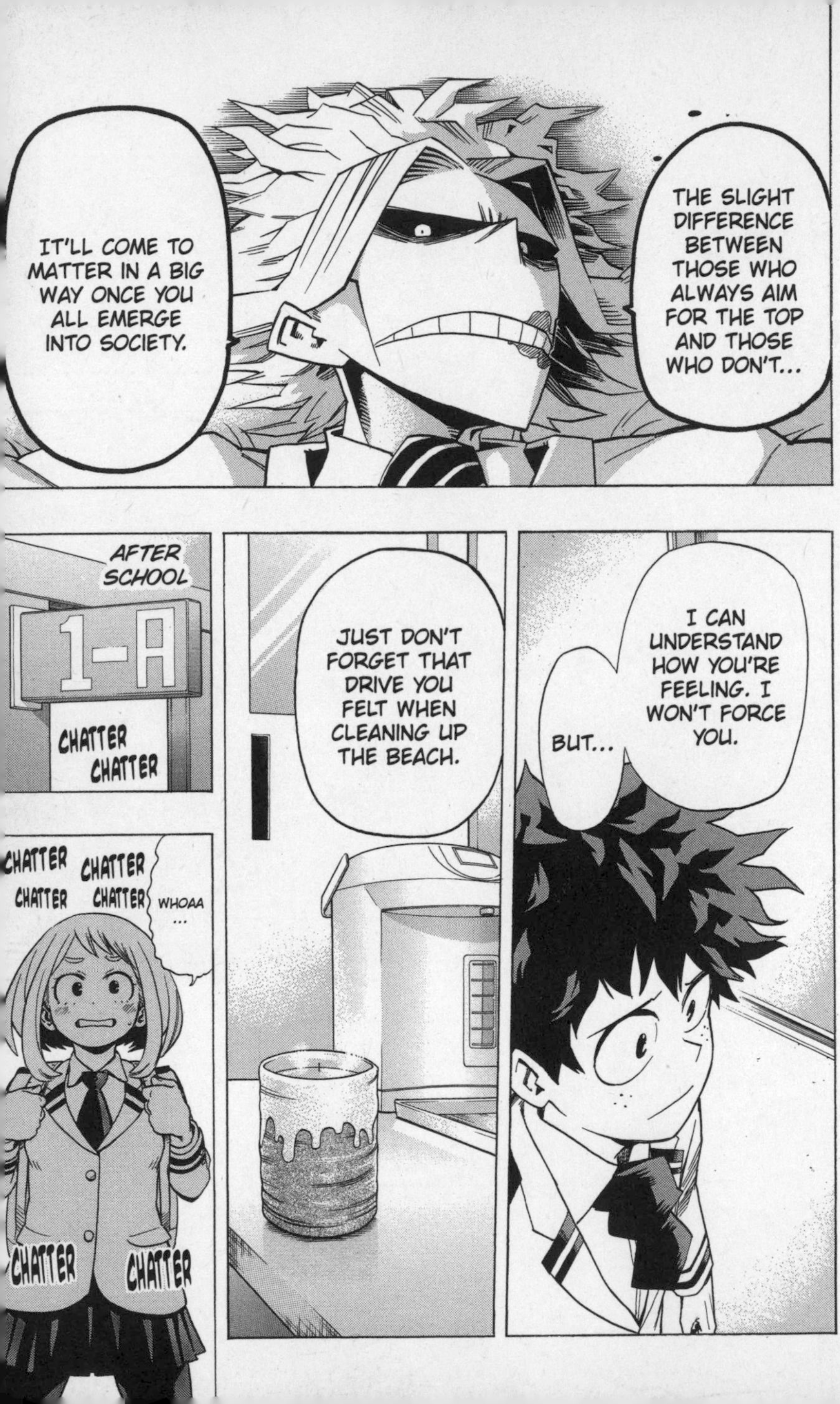
THE SLIGHT DIFFERENCE BETWEEN THOSE WHO ALWAYS AIM FOR THE TOP AND THOSE WHO DON'T...
IT'LL COME TO MATTER IN A BIG WAY ONCE YOU ALL EMERGE INTO SOCIETY.
I CAN UNDERSTAND HOW YOU'RE FEELING. I WON'T FORCE YOU.
BUT...
JUST DON'T FORGET THAT DRIVE YOU FELT WHEN CLEANING UP THE BEACH.
AFTER SCHOOL
1-A
CHATTER CHATTER
CHATTER CHATTER
WHOAA ...
CHATTER CHATTER
CHATTER
CHATTER

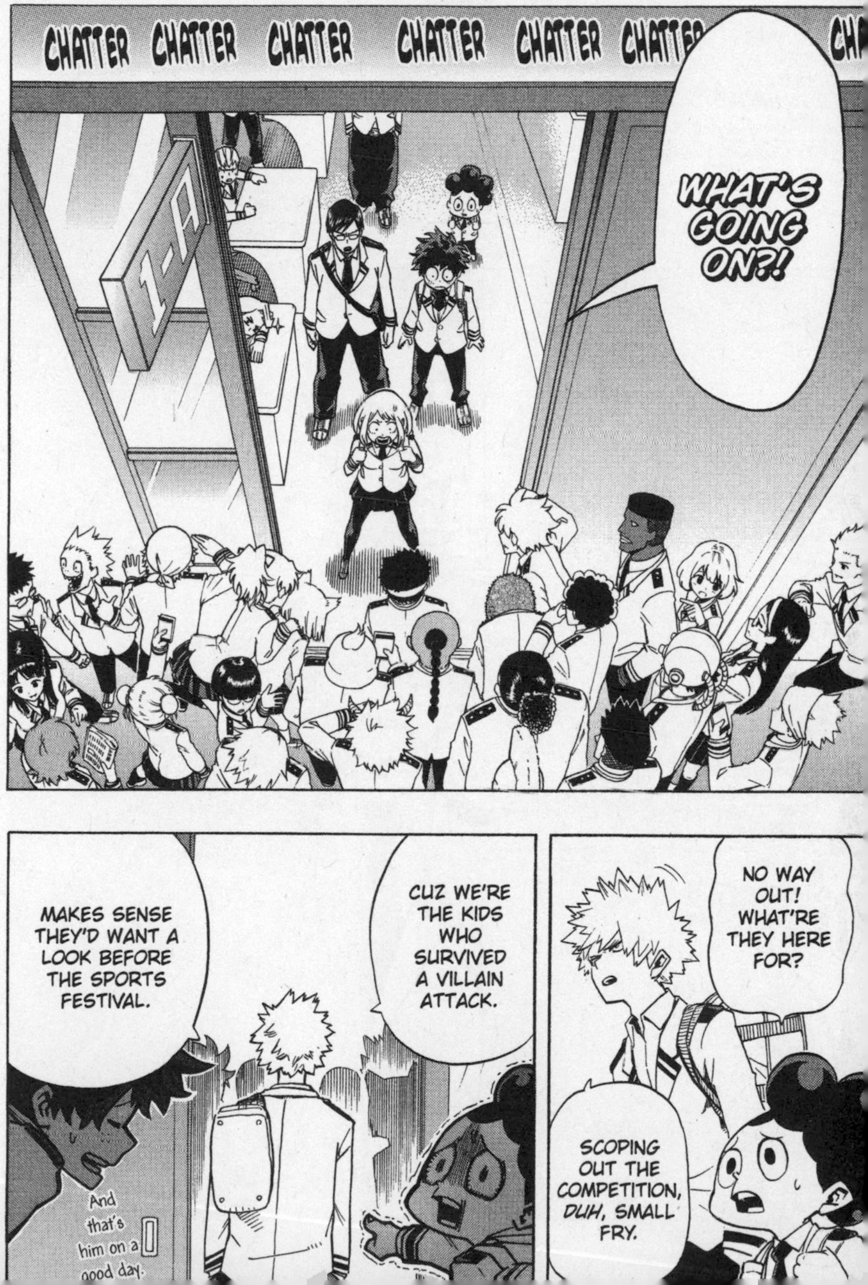
CHATTER CHATTER CHATTER CHATTER CHATTER CHATTER
WHAT'S GOING ON?!
NO WAY OUT! WHAT'RE THEY HERE FOR?
SCOPING OUT THE COMPETITION, *DUH*, SMALL FRY.
CUZ WE'RE THE KIDS WHO SURVIVED A VILLAIN ATTACK.
MAKES SENSE THEY'D WANT A LOOK BEFORE THE SPORTS FESTIVAL.
And that's him on a good day.

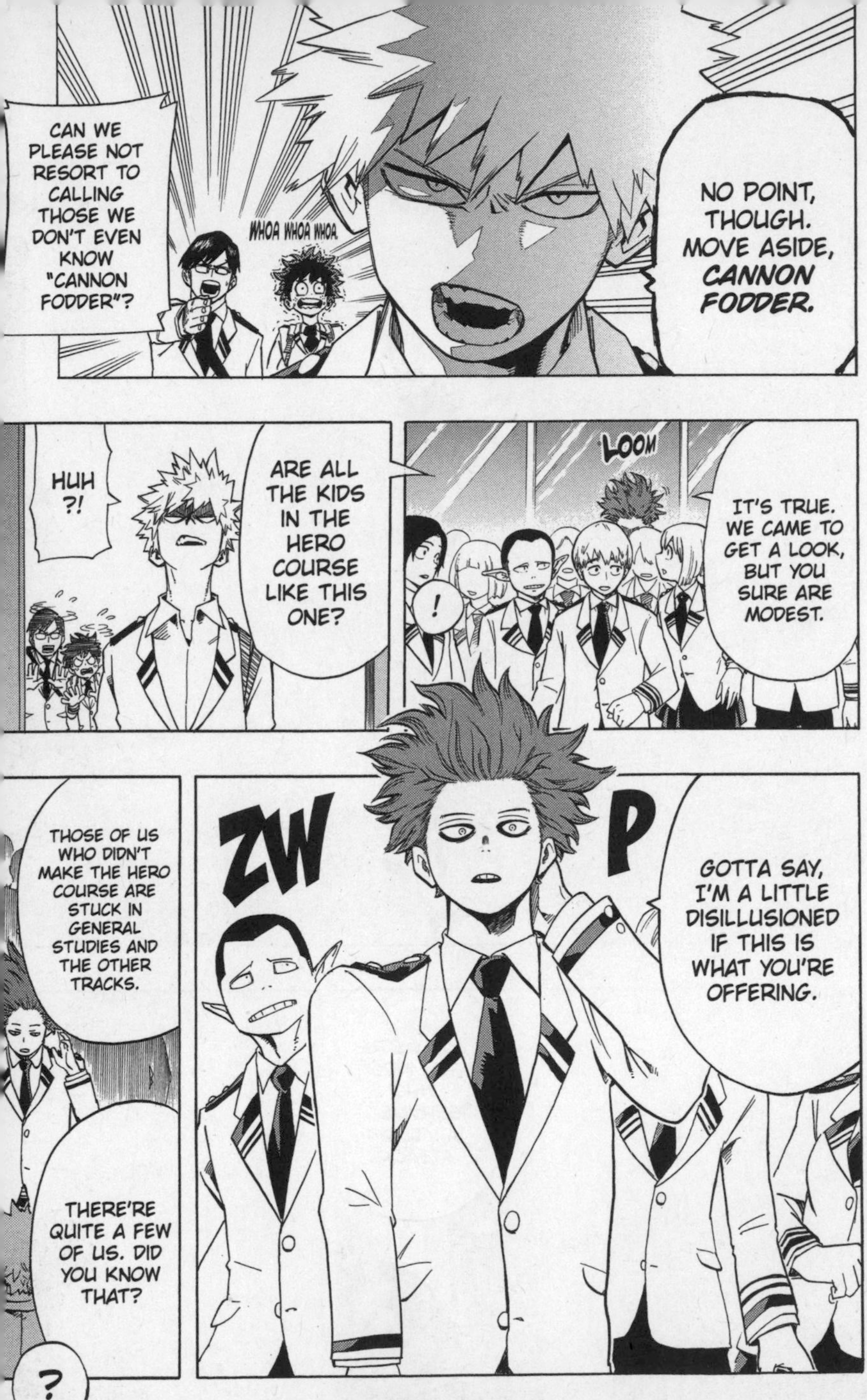
NO POINT, THOUGH. MOVE ASIDE, CANNON FODDER.
WHOA WHOA WHOA.
CAN WE PLEASE NOT RESORT TO CALLING THOSE WE DON'T EVEN KNOW "CANNON FODDER"?
LOOM
IT'S TRUE. WE CAME TO GET A LOOK, BUT YOU SURE ARE MODEST.
!
ARE ALL THE KIDS IN THE HERO COURSE LIKE THIS ONE?
HUH ?!
ZWP
GOTTA SAY, I'M A LITTLE DISILLUSIONED IF THIS IS WHAT YOU'RE OFFERING.
THOSE OF US WHO DIDN'T MAKE THE HERO COURSE ARE STUCK IN GENERAL STUDIES AND THE OTHER TRACKS.
THERE'RE QUITE A FEW OF US. DID YOU KNOW THAT?
?

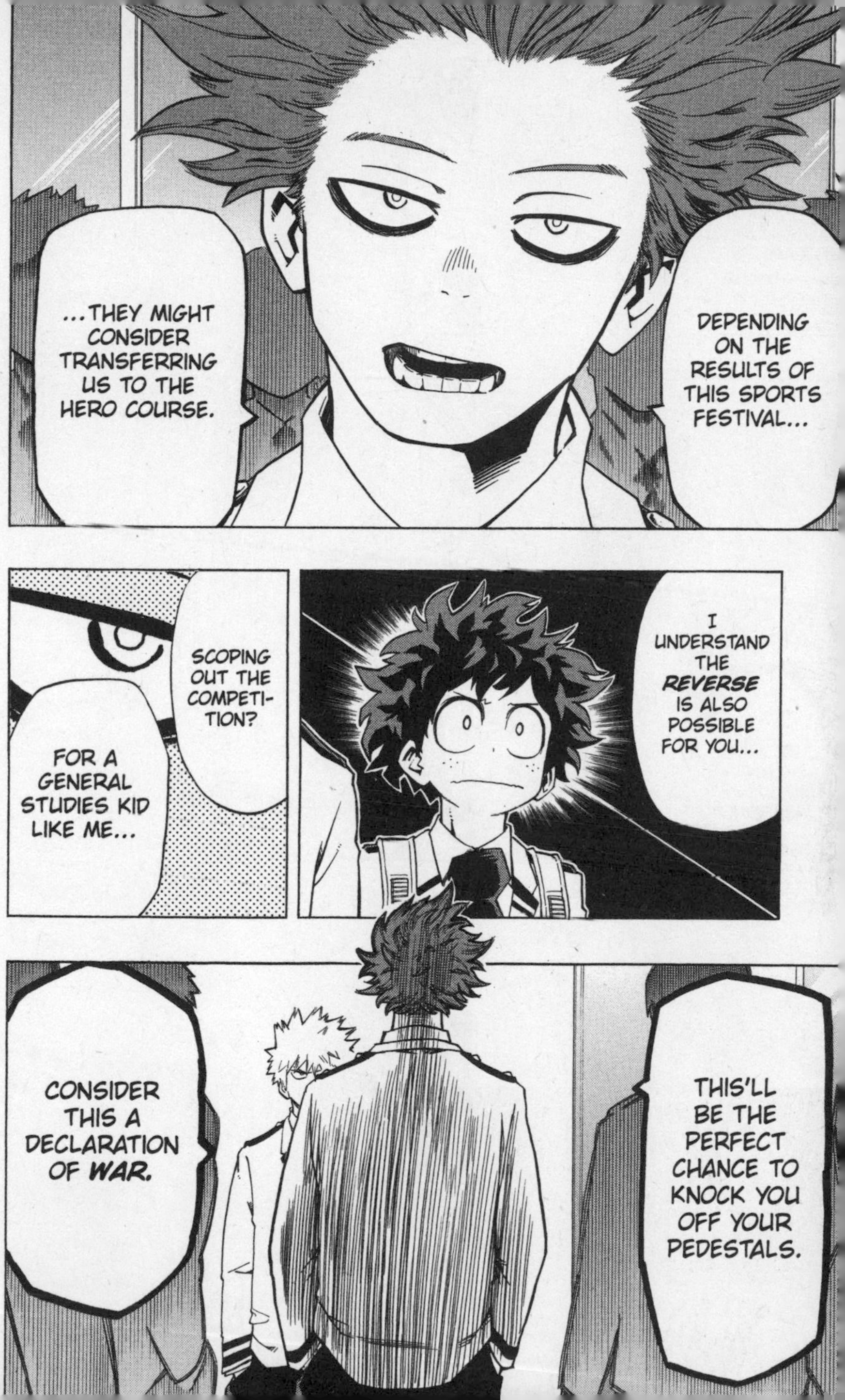
DEPENDING ON THE RESULTS OF THIS SPORTS FESTIVAL...
...THEY MIGHT CONSIDER TRANSFERRING US TO THE HERO COURSE.
I UNDERSTAND THE *REVERSE* IS ALSO POSSIBLE FOR YOU...
SCOPING OUT THE COMPETI- TION?
FOR A GENERAL STUDIES KID LIKE ME...
THIS'LL BE THE PERFECT CHANCE TO KNOCK YOU OFF YOUR PEDESTALS.
CONSIDER THIS A DECLARATION OF *WAR.*

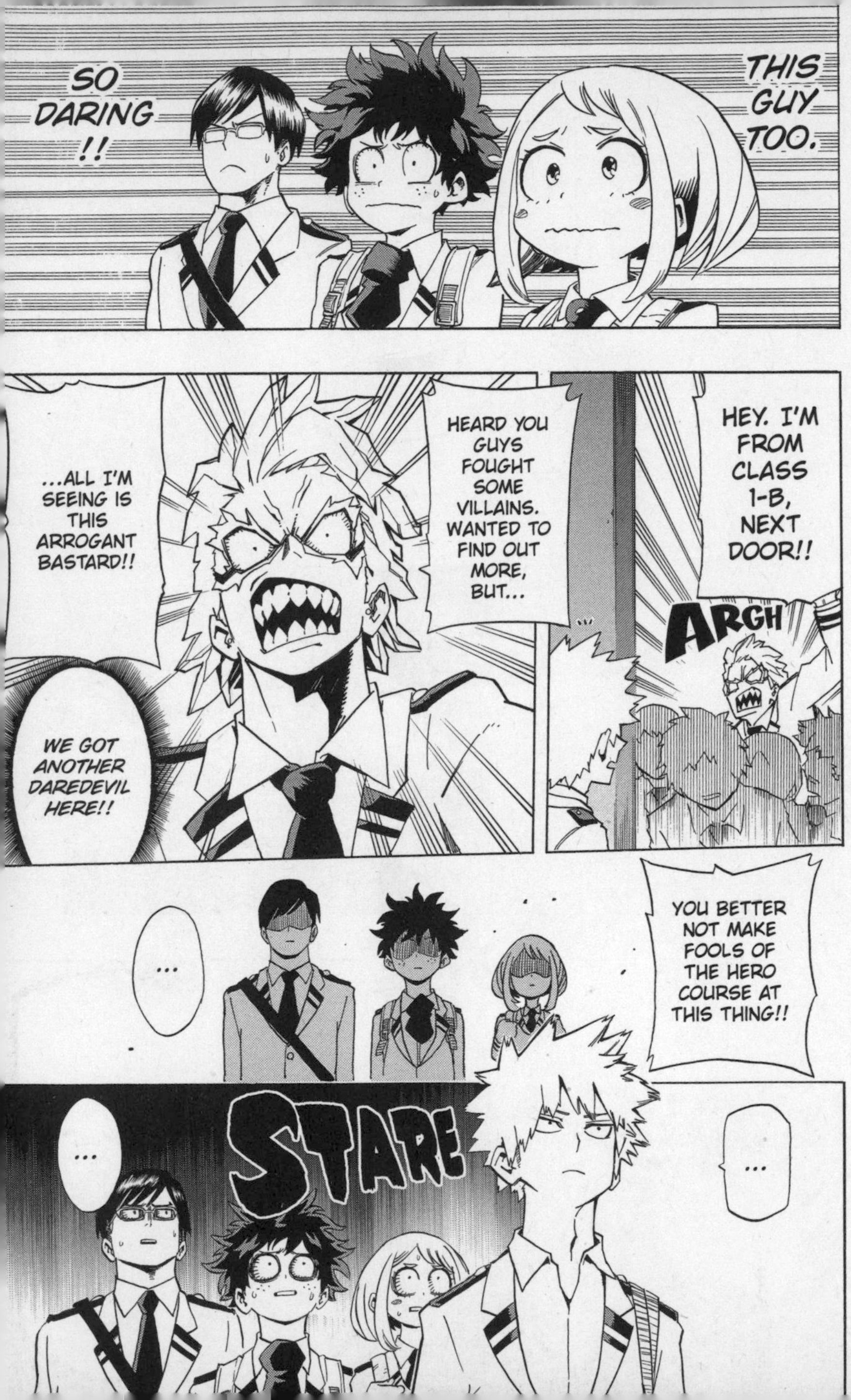
THIS GUY TOO.
SO DARING !!
HEY. I'M FROM CLASS 1-B, NEXT DOOR!!
ARGH
HEARD YOU GUYS FOUGHT SOME VILLAINS. WANTED TO FIND OUT MORE, BUT...
...ALL I'M SEEING IS THIS ARROGANT BASTARD!!
WE GOT ANOTHER DAREDEVIL HERE!!
YOU BETTER NOT MAKE FOOLS OF THE HERO COURSE AT THIS THING!!
...
...
STARE
...

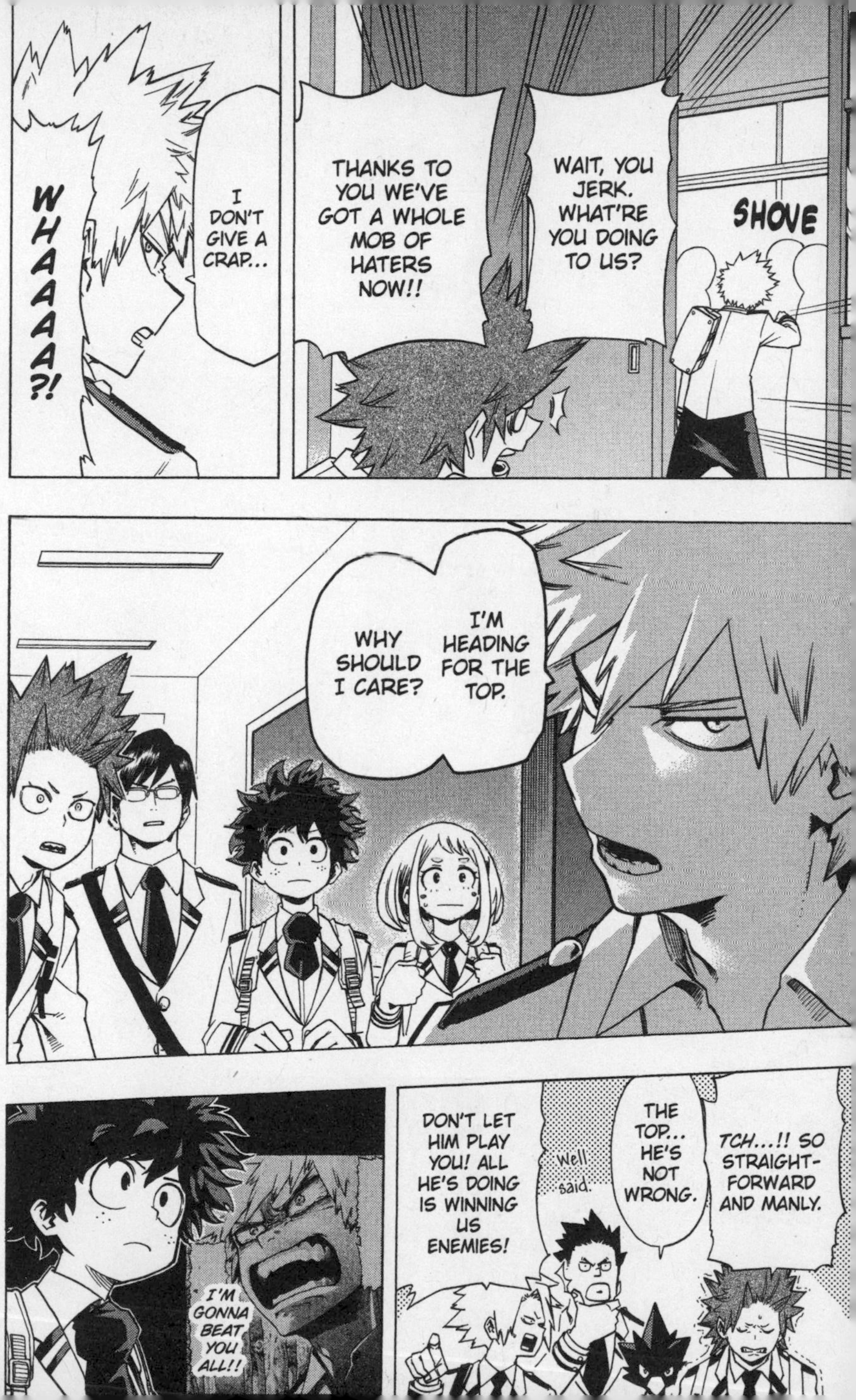
SHOVE
WAIT, YOU JERK. WHAT'RE YOU DOING TO US?
THANKS TO YOU WE'VE GOT A WHOLE MOB OF HATERS NOW!!
I DON'T GIVE A CRAP...
WHAAAAAA?!
I'M HEADING FOR THE TOP.
WHY SHOULD I CARE?
TCH...!! SO STRAIGHT-FORWARD AND MANLY.
THE TOP... HE'S NOT WRONG.
Well said.
DON'T LET HIM PLAY YOU! ALL HE'S DOING IS WINNING US ENEMIES!
I'M GONNA BEAT YOU ALL!!

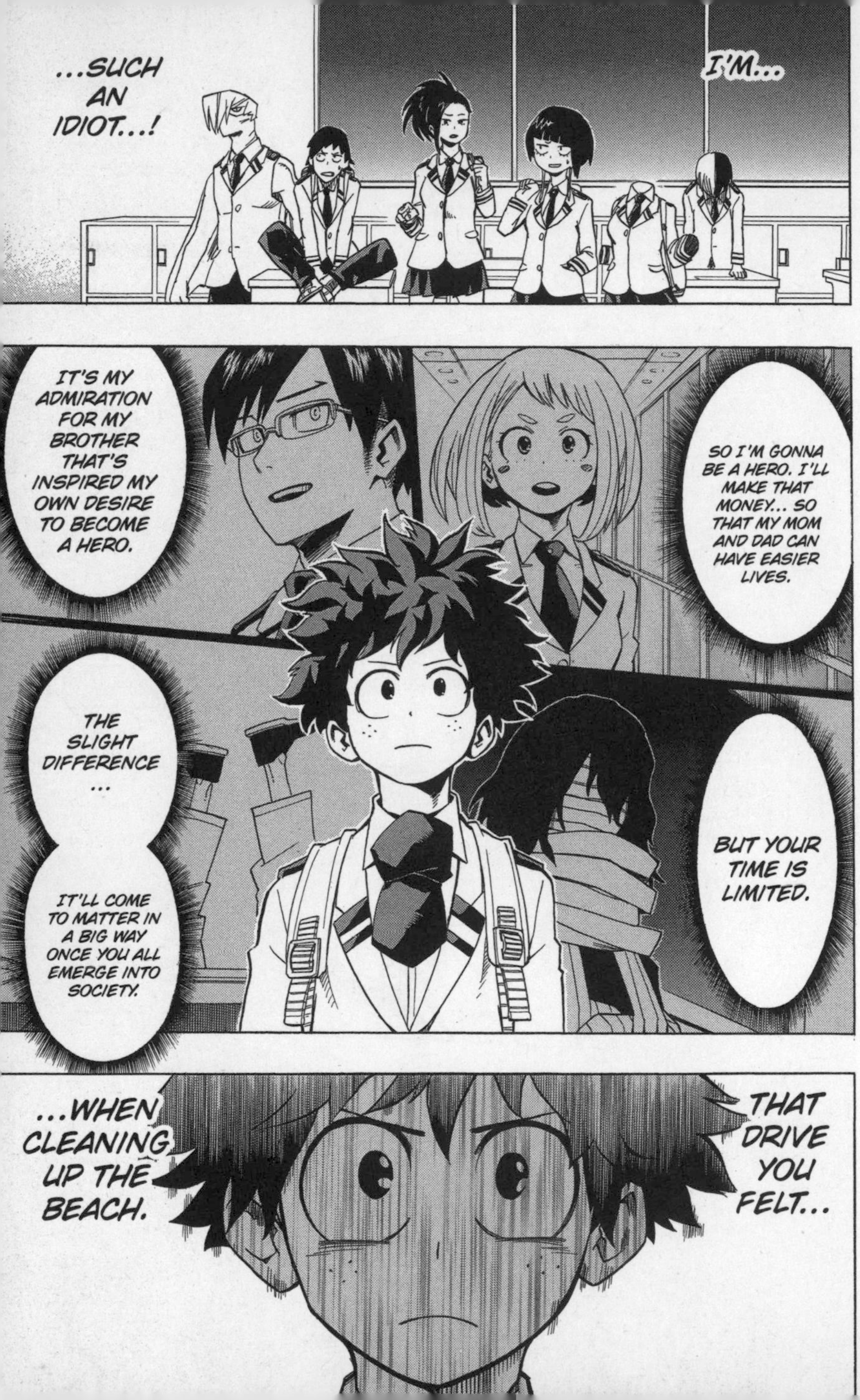
I'M...
...SUCH AN IDIOT...!
SO I'M GONNA BE A HERO. I'LL MAKE THAT MONEY... SO THAT MY MOM AND DAD CAN HAVE EASIER LIVES.
IT'S MY ADMIRATION FOR MY BROTHER THAT'S INSPIRED MY OWN DESIRE TO BECOME A HERO.
BUT YOUR TIME IS LIMITED.
THE SLIGHT DIFFERENCE...
IT'LL COME TO MATTER IN A BIG WAY ONCE YOU ALL EMERGE INTO SOCIETY.
THAT DRIVE YOU FELT...
...WHEN CLEANING UP THE BEACH.

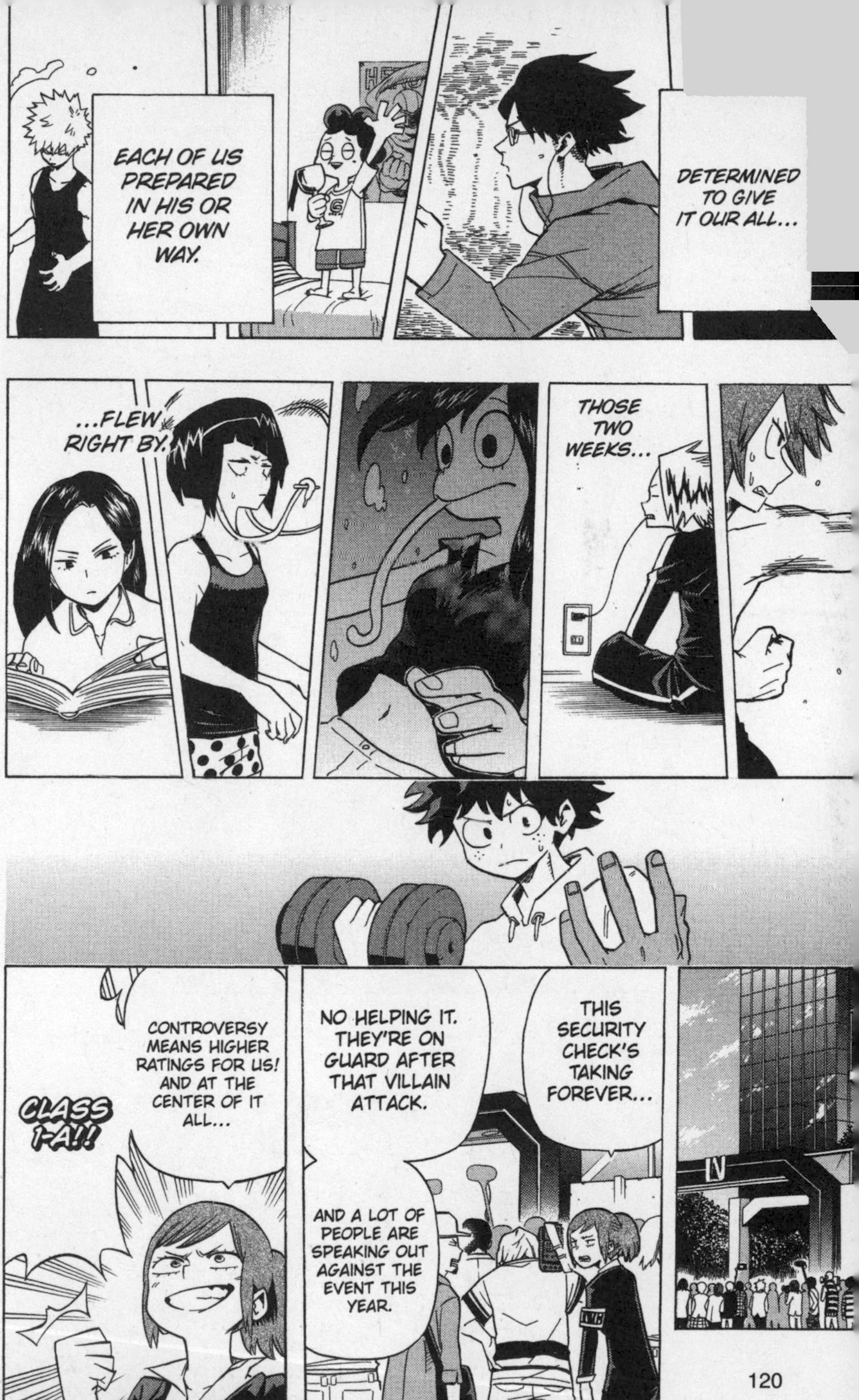
DETERMINED TO GIVE IT OUR ALL...
EACH OF US PREPARED IN HIS OR HER OWN WAY.
THOSE TWO WEEKS...
...FLEW RIGHT BY.
THIS SECURITY CHECK'S TAKING FOREVER...
NO HELPING IT. THEY'RE ON GUARD AFTER THAT VILLAIN ATTACK.
AND A LOT OF PEOPLE ARE SPEAKING OUT AGAINST THE EVENT THIS YEAR.
CONTROVERSY MEANS HIGHER RATINGS FOR US! AND AT THE CENTER OF IT ALL...
CLASS 1-A!!

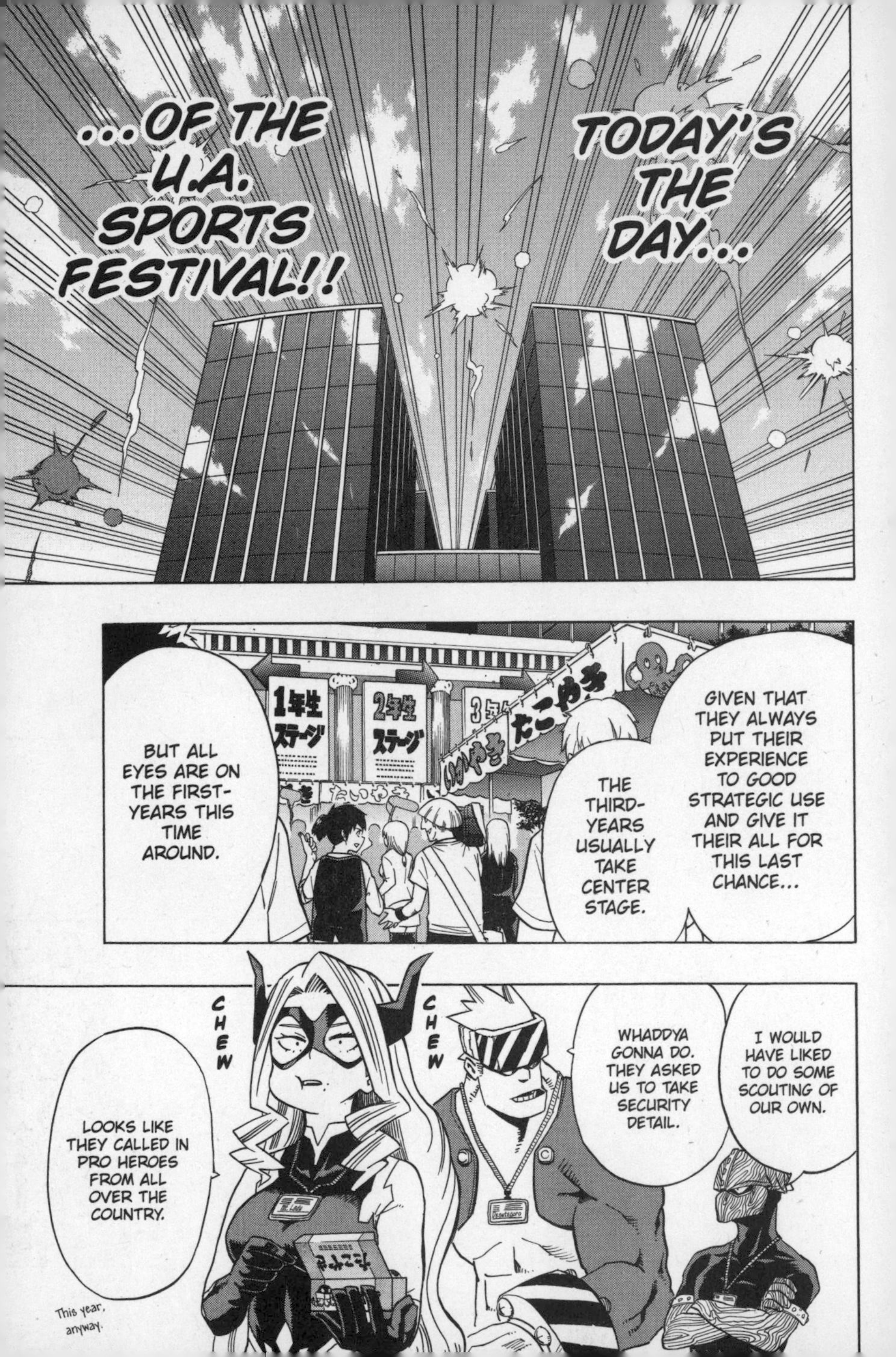
TODAY'S THE DAY...
...OF THE U.A. SPORTS FESTIVAL!!
GIVEN THAT THEY ALWAYS PUT THEIR EXPERIENCE TO GOOD STRATEGIC USE AND GIVE IT THEIR ALL FOR THIS LAST CHANCE...
THE THIRD-YEARS USUALLY TAKE CENTER STAGE.
たこやき
2年生 ステージ
1年生 ステージ
BUT ALL EYES ARE ON THE FIRST-YEARS THIS TIME AROUND.
I WOULD HAVE LIKED TO DO SOME SCOUTING OF OUR OWN.
WHADDYA GONNA DO. THEY ASKED US TO TAKE SECURITY DETAIL.
CHEW
CHEW
LOOKS LIKE THEY CALLED IN PRO HEROES FROM ALL OVER THE COUNTRY.
This year, anyway.

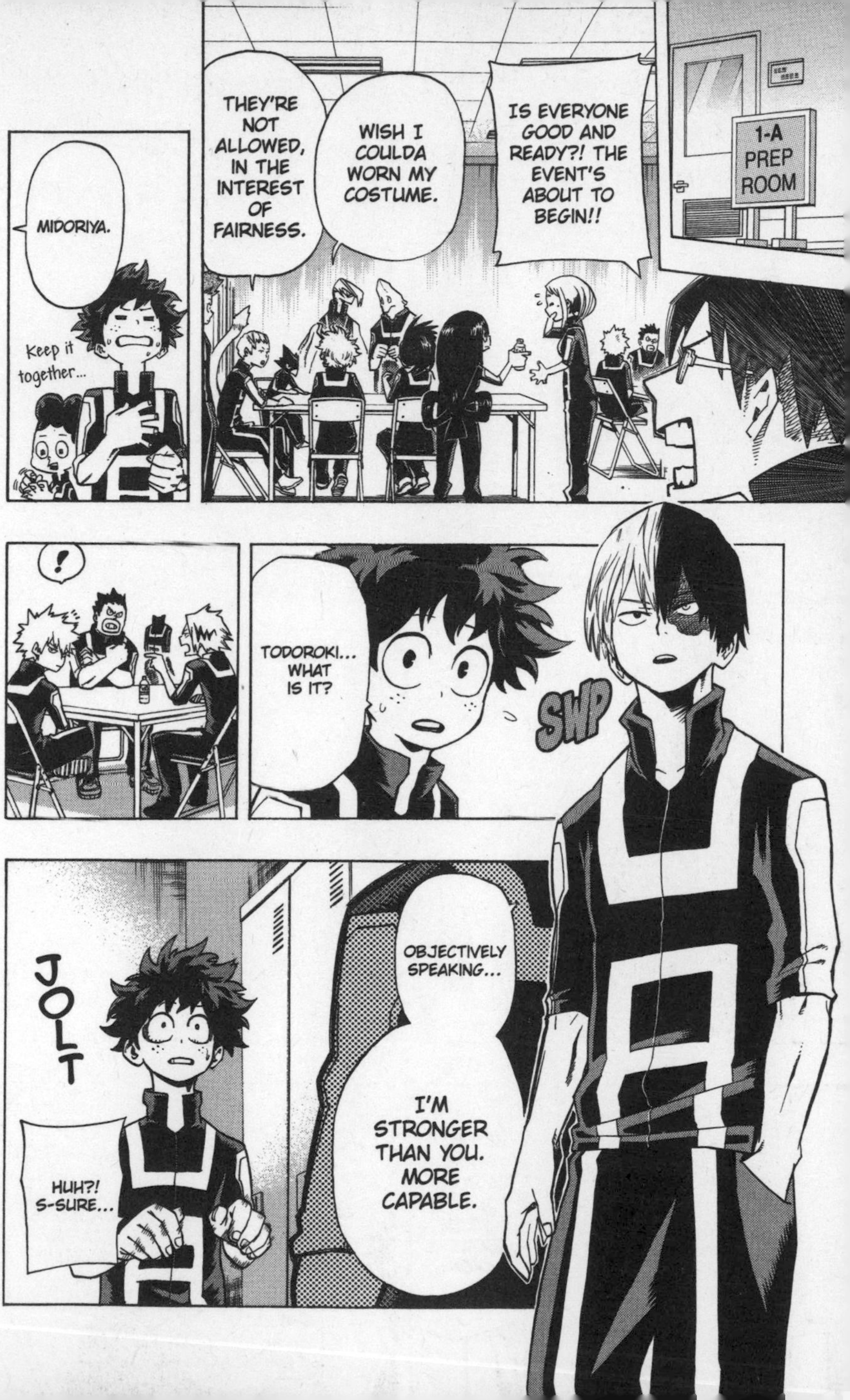
1-A PREP ROOM
IS EVERYONE GOOD AND READY?! THE EVENT'S ABOUT TO BEGIN!!
WISH I COULDA WORN MY COSTUME.
THEY'RE NOT ALLOWED, IN THE INTEREST OF FAIRNESS.
MIDORIYA.
Keep it together...
SWP
TODOROKI... WHAT IS IT?
!
OBJECTIVELY SPEAKING...
I'M STRONGER THAN YOU. MORE CAPABLE.
JOLT
HUH?! S-SURE...

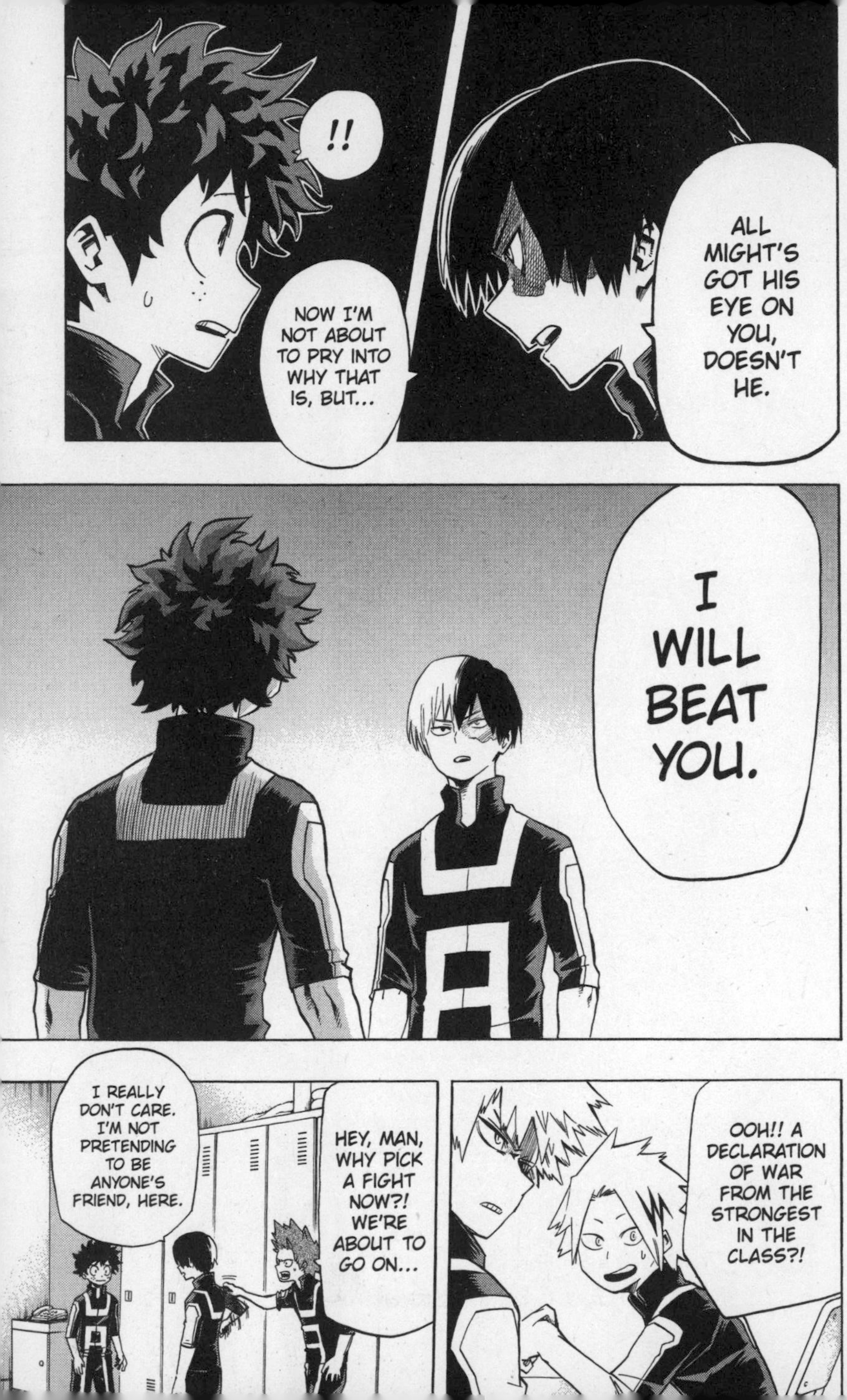
ALL MIGHT'S GOT HIS EYE ON YOU, DOESN'T HE.
!!
NOW I'M NOT ABOUT TO PRY INTO WHY THAT IS, BUT...
I WILL BEAT YOU.
OOH!! A DECLARATION OF WAR FROM THE STRONGEST IN THE CLASS?!
HEY, MAN, WHY PICK A FIGHT NOW?! WE'RE ABOUT TO GO ON...
I REALLY DON'T CARE. I'M NOT PRETENDING TO BE ANYONE'S FRIEND, HERE.

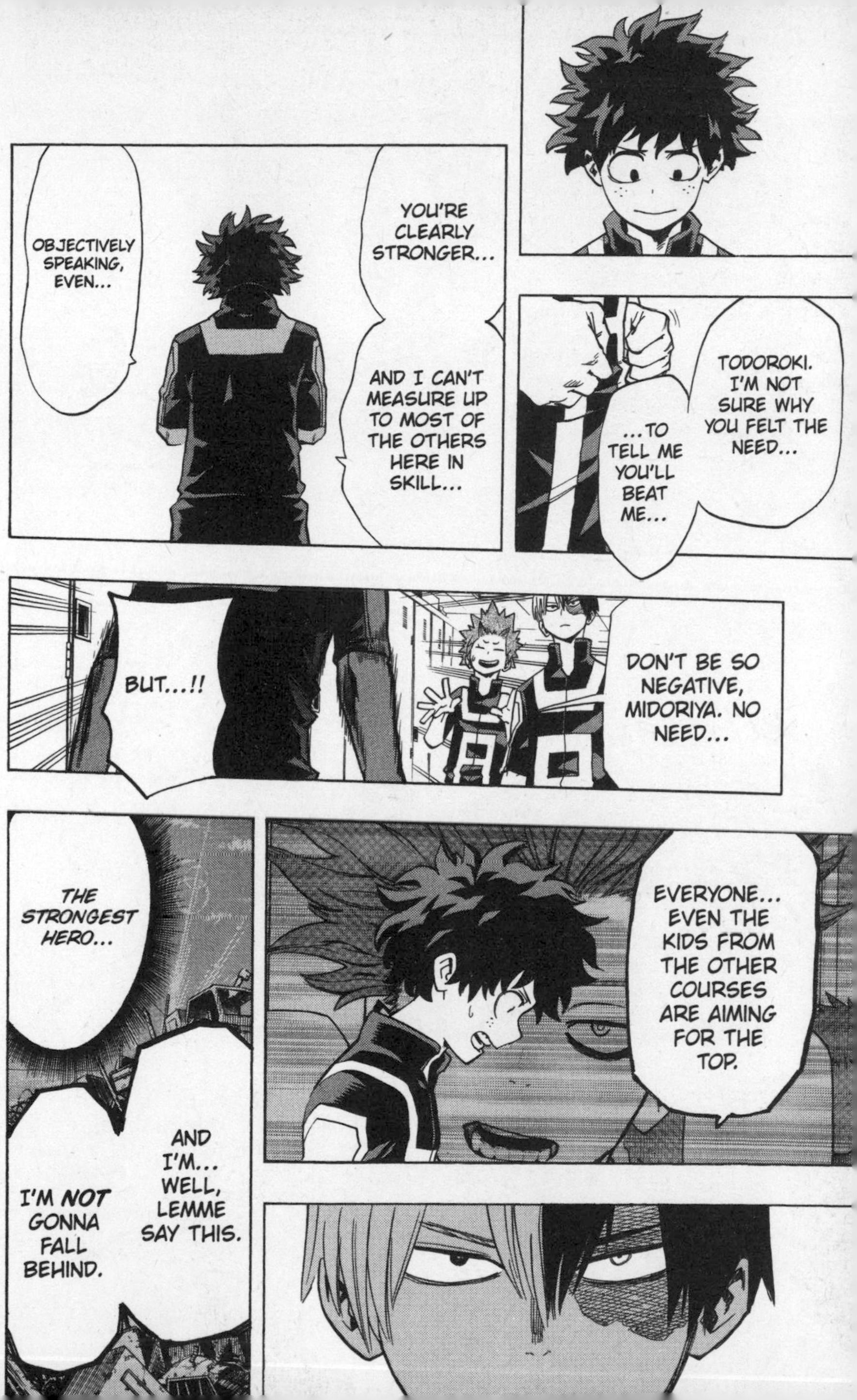
TODOROKI. I'M NOT SURE WHY YOU FELT THE NEED...
...TO TELL ME YOU'LL BEAT ME...
YOU'RE CLEARLY STRONGER...
OBJECTIVELY SPEAKING, EVEN...
AND I CAN'T MEASURE UP TO MOST OF THE OTHERS HERE IN SKILL...
DON'T BE SO NEGATIVE, MIDORIYA. NO NEED...
BUT...!!
EVERYONE... EVEN THE KIDS FROM THE OTHER COURSES ARE AIMING FOR THE TOP.
THE STRONGEST HERO...
AND I'M... WELL, LEMME SAY THIS.
I'M *NOT* GONNA FALL BEHIND.

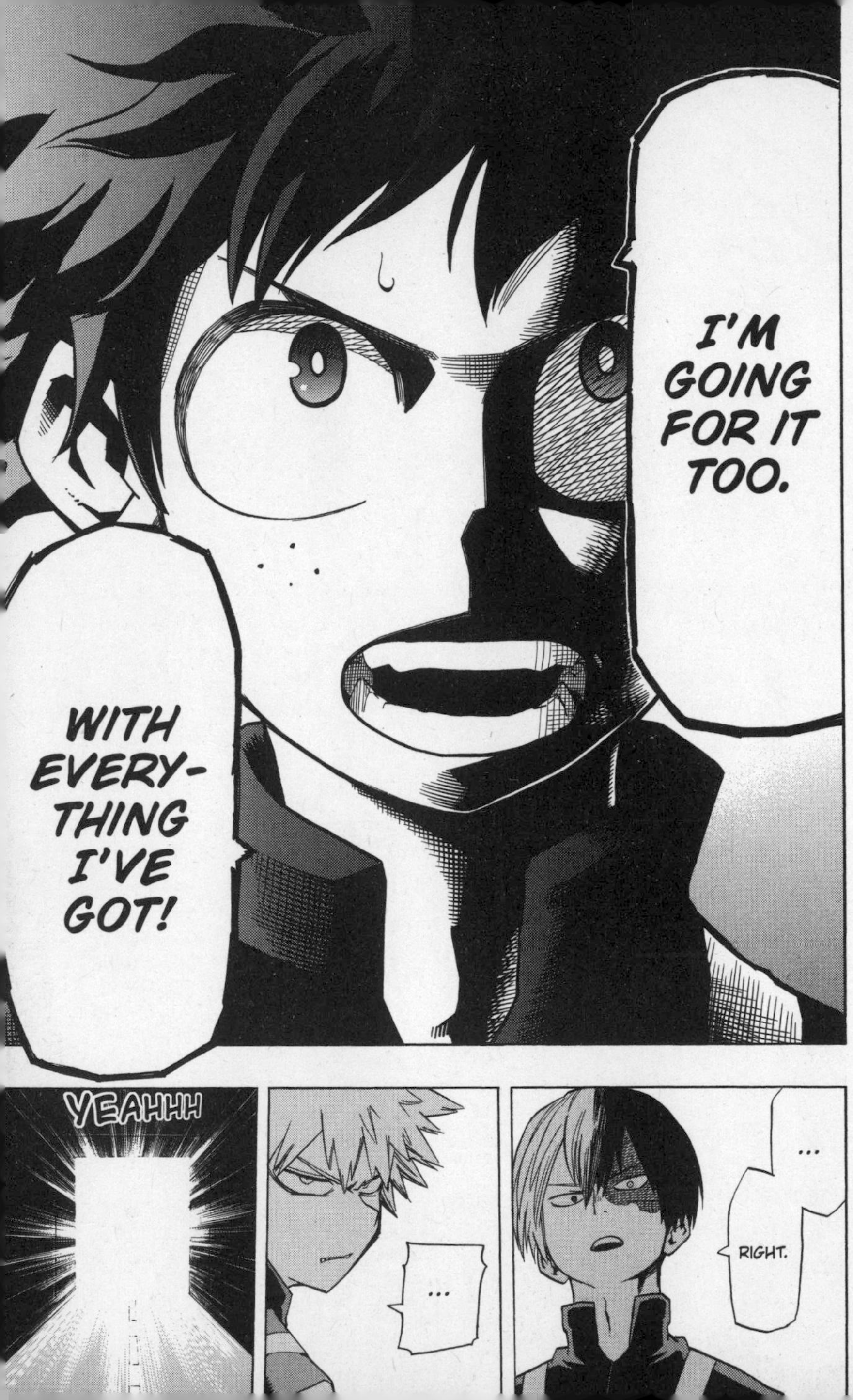
I'M GOING FOR IT TOO.
WITH EVERY-THING I'VE GOT!
...
RIGHT.
...
YEAHHH

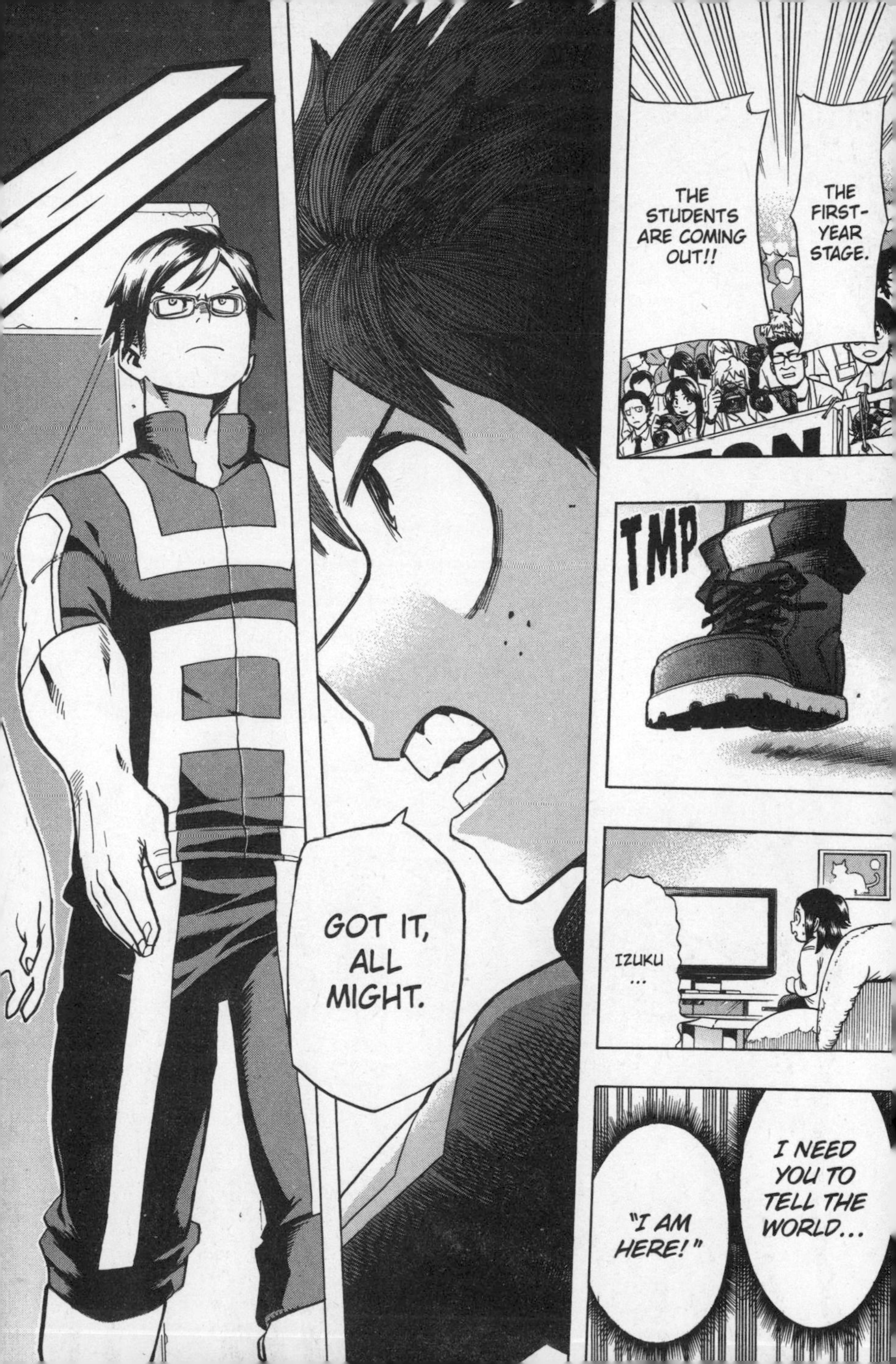
THE FIRST-YEAR STAGE.
THE STUDENTS ARE COMING OUT!!
TMP
IZUKU ...
I NEED YOU TO TELL THE WORLD...
"I AM HERE!"
GOT IT, ALL MIGHT.

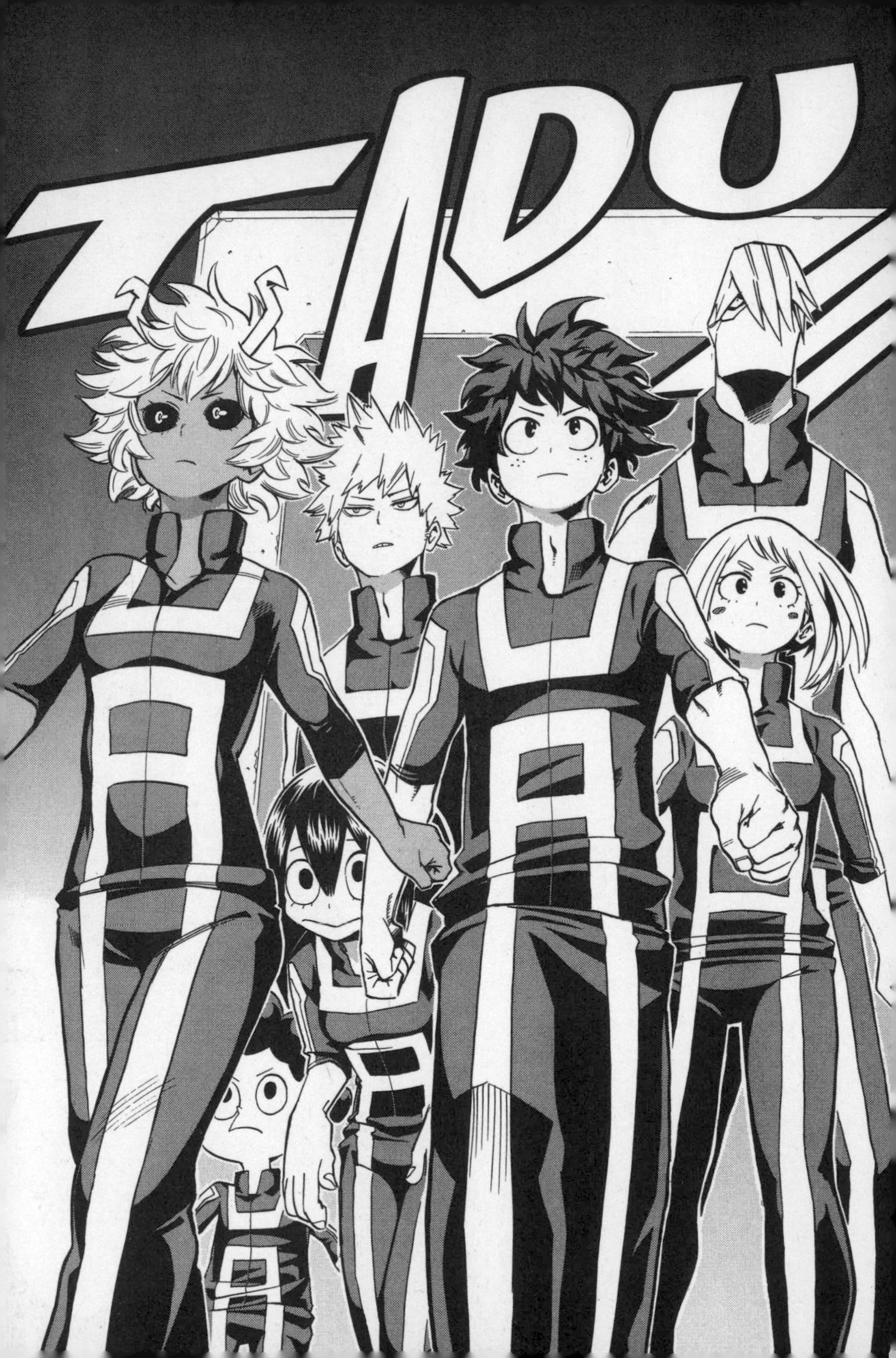
ZADU

STREET CLOTHES

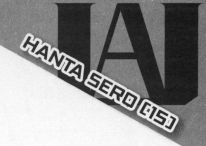

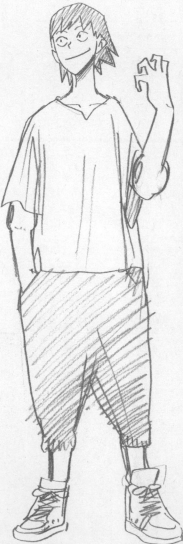

Birthday: 7/28
Height: 177 cm
Favorite Things: Oranges, soy products, things that seem healthy for you

BEHIND THE SCENES

I think I might like his Quirk best of all.

I came up with it when I spotted some tape at a convenience store.

He's mostly just for one-liners in the background, but he's a good guy, and I'd like to feature him more. At some point. For sure.

Nothing to do with Hanta specifically, but I just realized that I have way too many characters with their hands in their pockets on these profile pages.

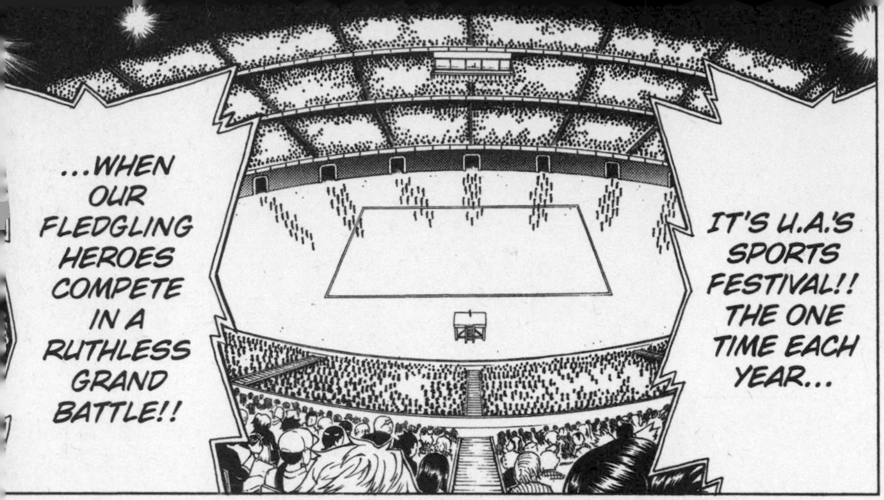
IT'S U.A.'S SPORTS FESTIVAL!! THE ONE TIME EACH YEAR...
...WHEN OUR FLEDGLING HEROES COMPETE IN A RUTHLESS GRAND BATTLE!!

No.24 - Mad Dash and Knockdown

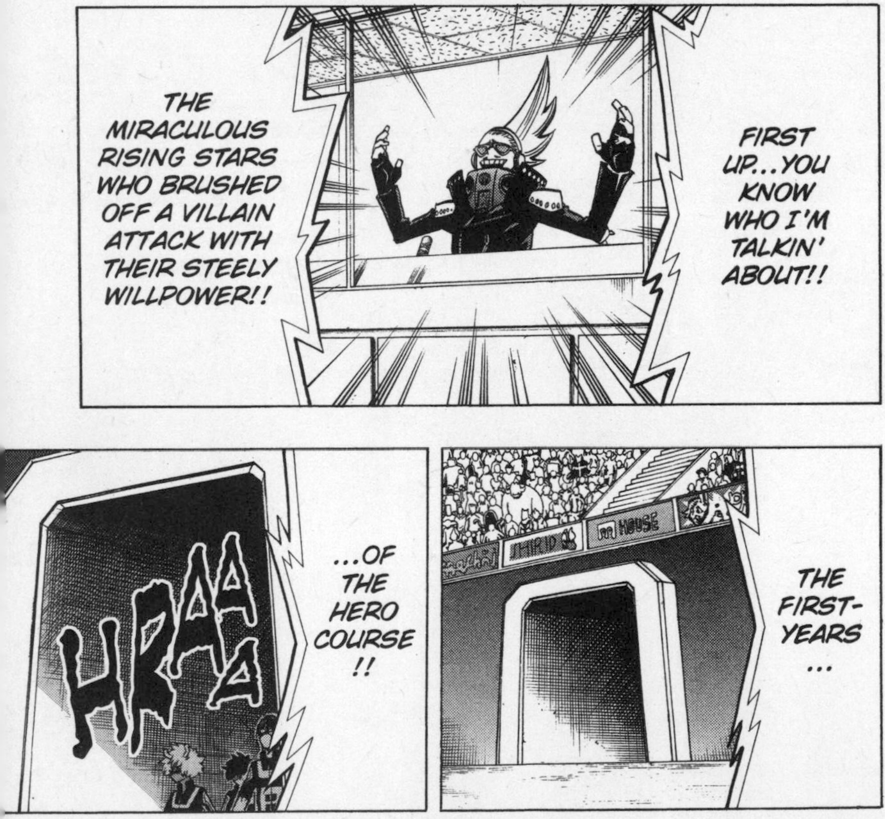
FIRST UP...YOU KNOW WHO I'M TALKIN' ABOUT!!
THE MIRACULOUS RISING STARS WHO BRUSHED OFF A VILLAIN ATTACK WITH THEIR STEELY WILLPOWER!!
HOUSE
THE FIRST-YEARS...
...OF THE HERO COURSE!!
HRAAAA

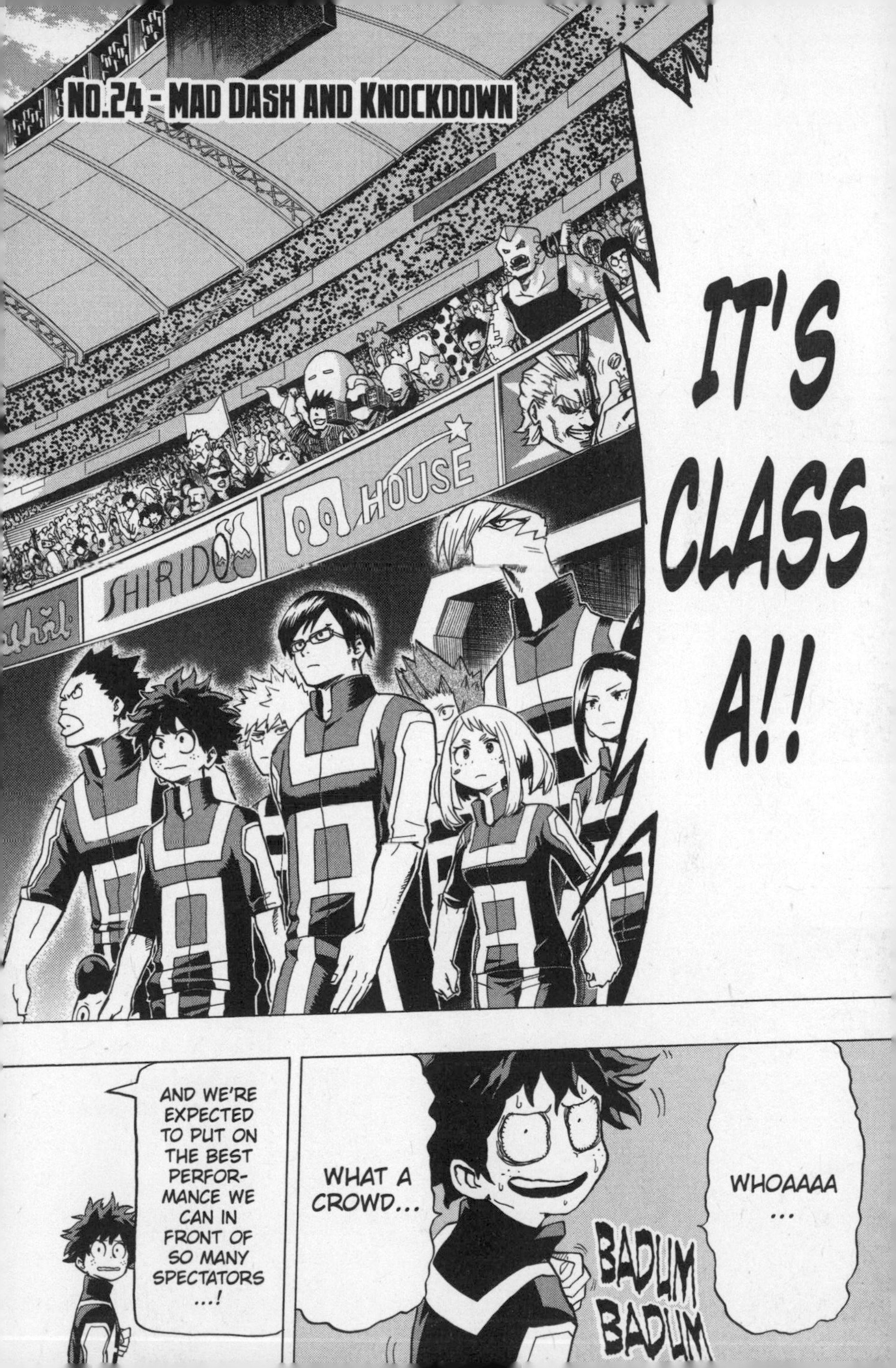
No.24 - Mad Dash and Knockdown
IT'S CLASS A!!
HOUSE
SHIRIDO
WHOAAAA ...
BADUM BADUM
WHAT A CROWD...
AND WE'RE EXPECTED TO PUT ON THE BEST PERFORMANCE WE CAN IN FRONT OF SO MANY SPECTATORS ...!

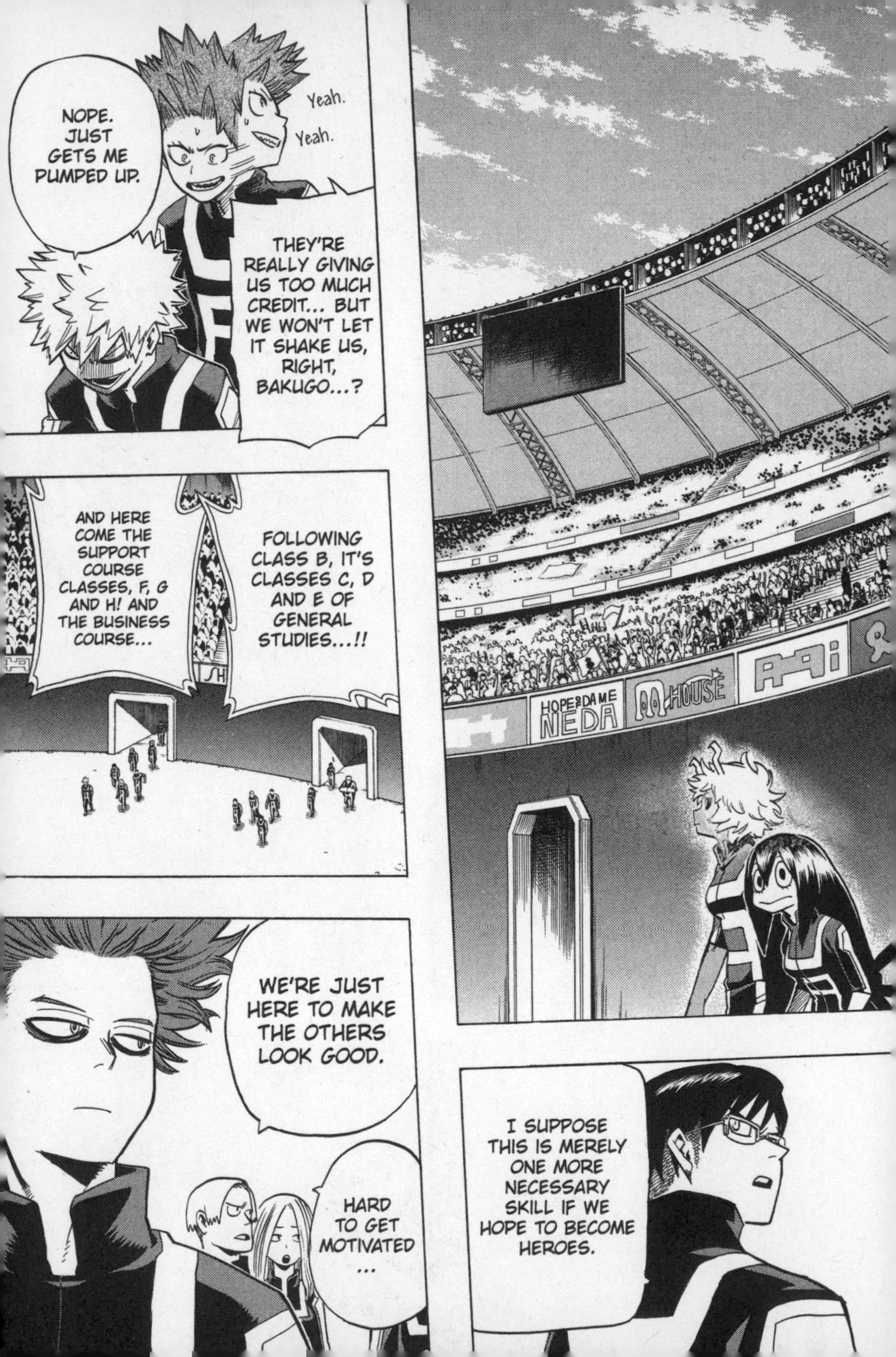
THEY'RE REALLY GIVING US TOO MUCH CREDIT... BUT WE WON'T LET IT SHAKE US, RIGHT, BAKUGO...?
NOPE. JUST GETS ME PUMPED UP.
Yeah.
Yeah.
FOLLOWING CLASS B, IT'S CLASSES C, D AND E OF GENERAL STUDIES...!!
AND HERE COME THE SUPPORT COURSE CLASSES, F, G AND H! AND THE BUSINESS COURSE...
I SUPPOSE THIS IS MERELY ONE MORE NECESSARY SKILL IF WE HOPE TO BECOME HEROES.
WE'RE JUST HERE TO MAKE THE OTHERS LOOK GOOD.
HARD TO GET MOTIVATED ...

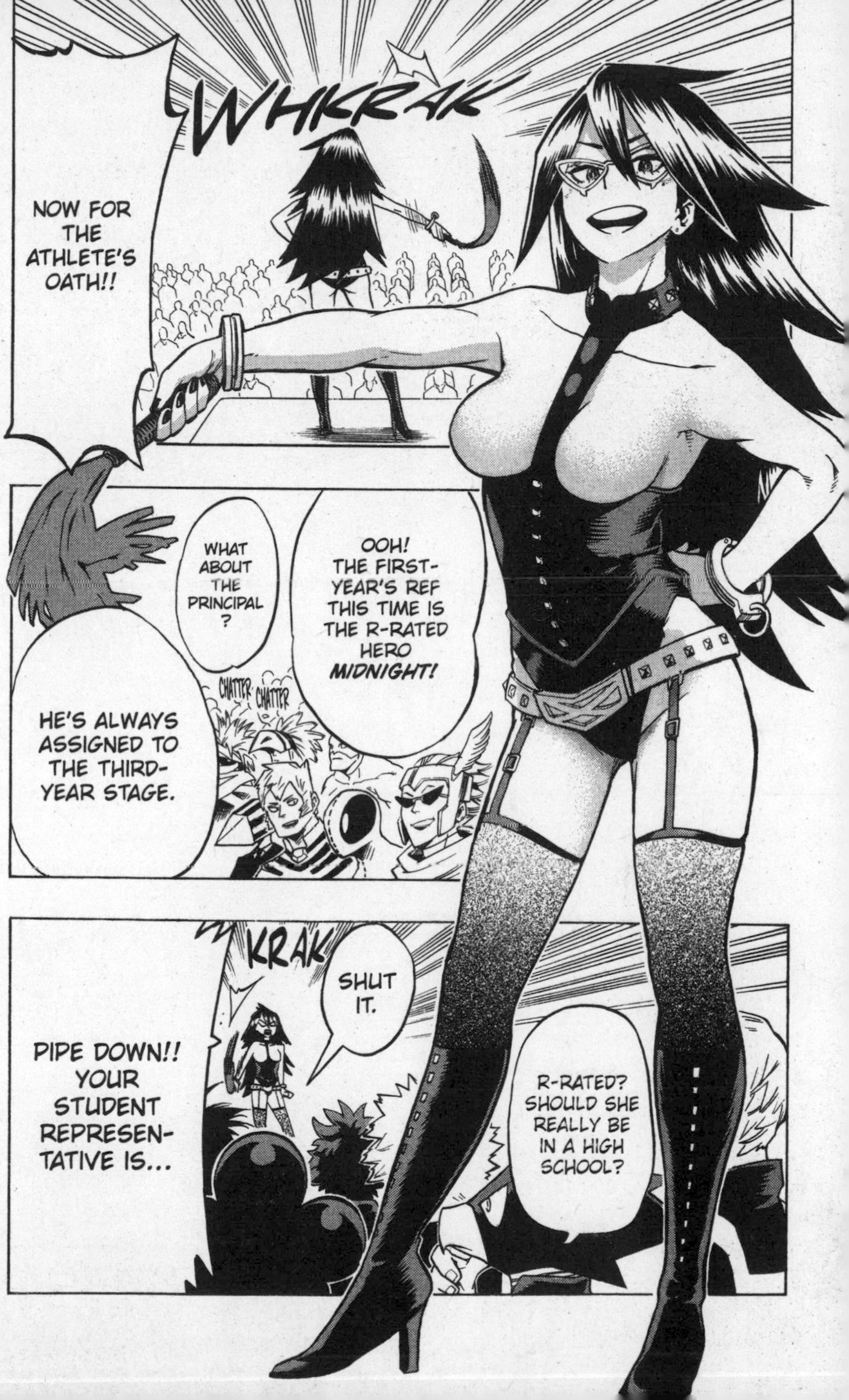
WHKRAK
NOW FOR THE ATHLETE'S OATH!!
OOH! THE FIRST-YEAR'S REF THIS TIME IS THE R-RATED HERO *MIDNIGHT!*
WHAT ABOUT THE PRINCIPAL?
CHATTER CHATTER
HE'S ALWAYS ASSIGNED TO THE THIRD-YEAR STAGE.
R-RATED? SHOULD SHE REALLY BE IN A HIGH SCHOOL?
KRAK
SHUT IT.
PIPE DOWN!! YOUR STUDENT REPRESENTATIVE IS...

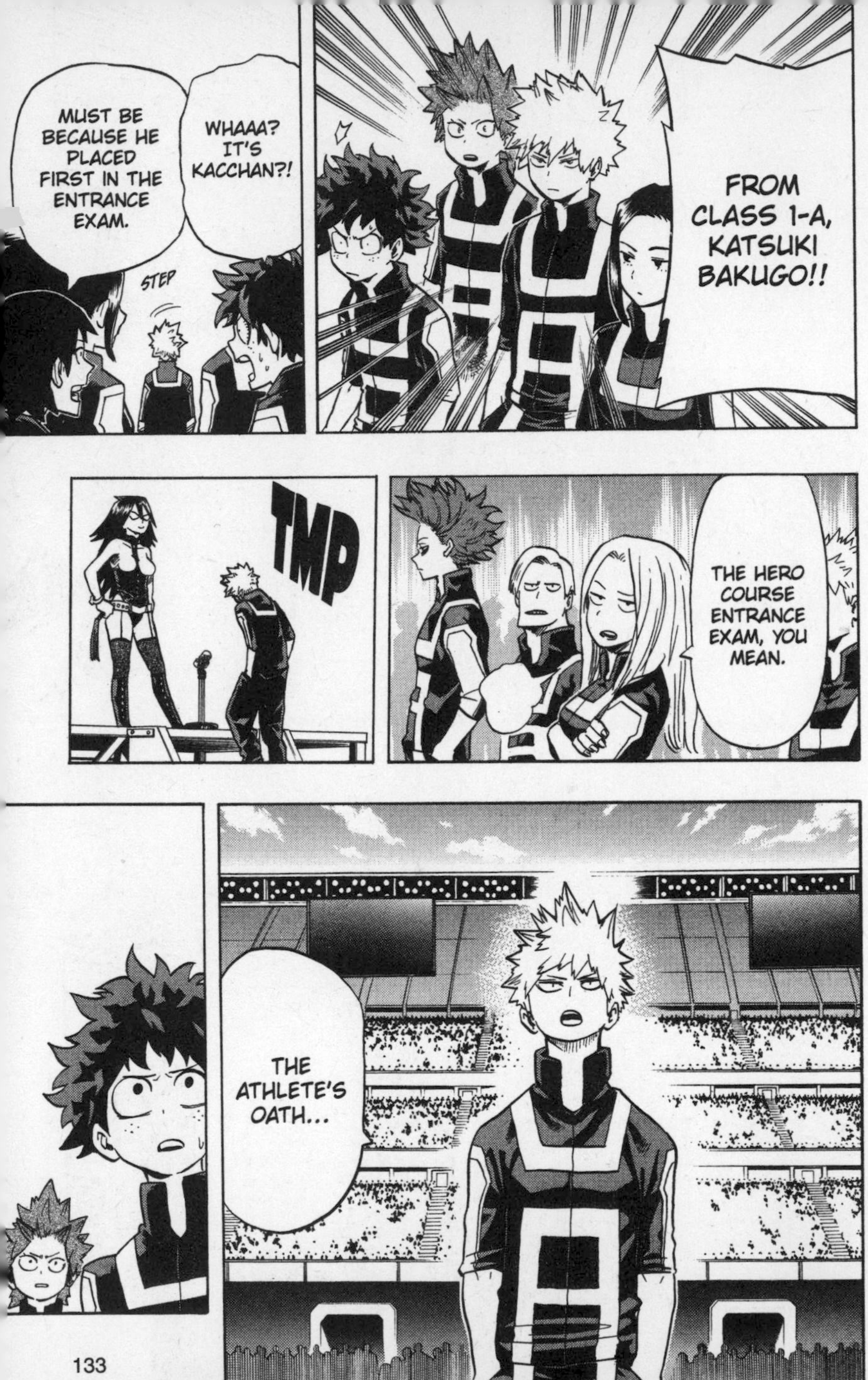
FROM CLASS 1-A, KATSUKI BAKUGO!!
WHAAA? IT'S KACCHAN?!
MUST BE BECAUSE HE PLACED FIRST IN THE ENTRANCE EXAM.
STEP
THE HERO COURSE ENTRANCE EXAM, YOU MEAN.
TMP
THE ATHLETE'S OATH...

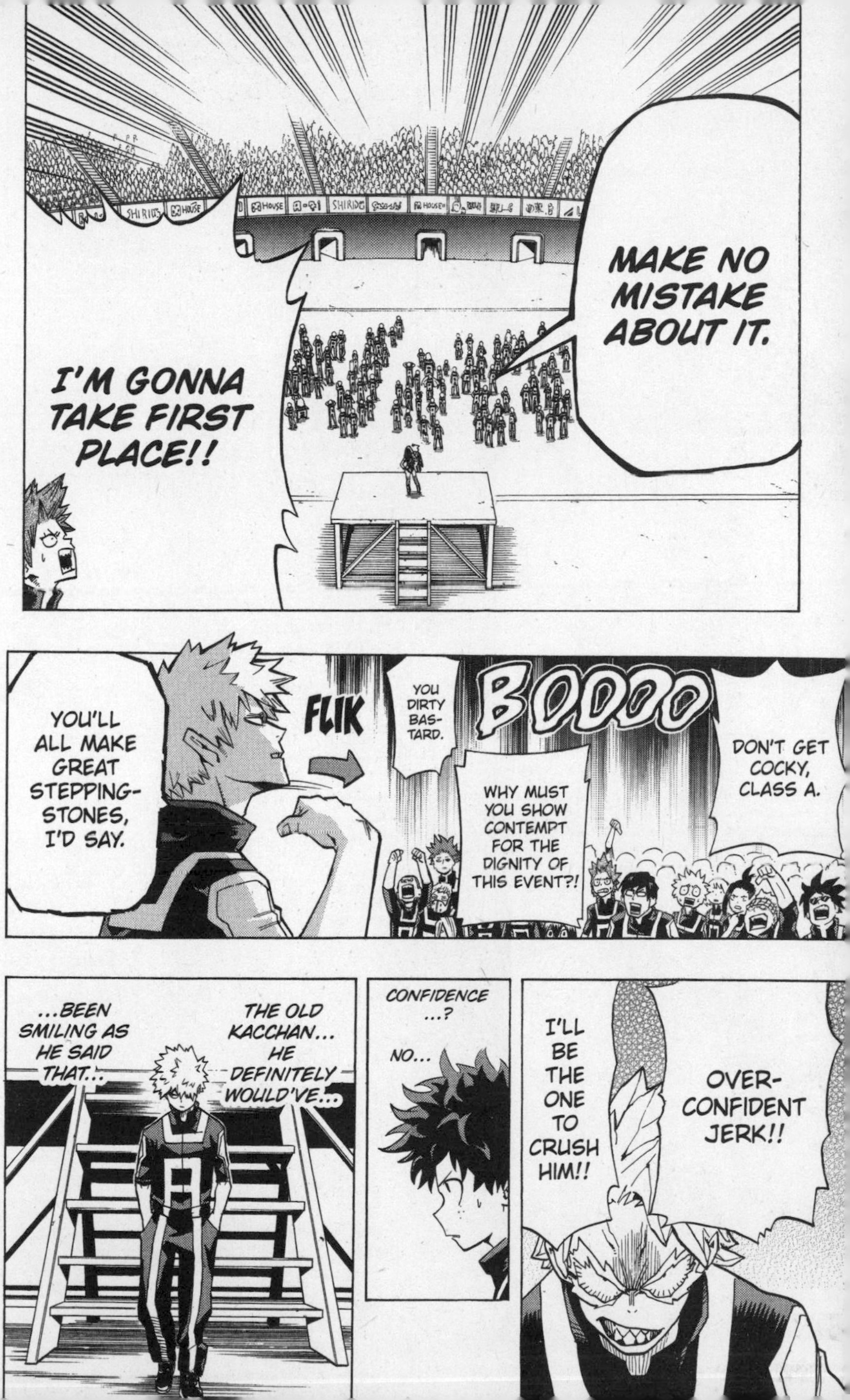
MAKE NO MISTAKE ABOUT IT.
I'M GONNA TAKE FIRST PLACE!!
DON'T GET COCKY, CLASS A.
BOOOO
YOU DIRTY BAS-TARD.
WHY MUST YOU SHOW CONTEMPT FOR THE DIGNITY OF THIS EVENT?!
FLIK
YOU'LL ALL MAKE GREAT STEPPING-STONES, I'D SAY.
OVER-CONFIDENT JERK!!
I'LL BE THE ONE TO CRUSH HIM!!
CONFIDENCE ...?
NO...
THE OLD KACCHAN... HE DEFINITELY WOULD'VE...
...BEEN SMILING AS HE SAID THAT...

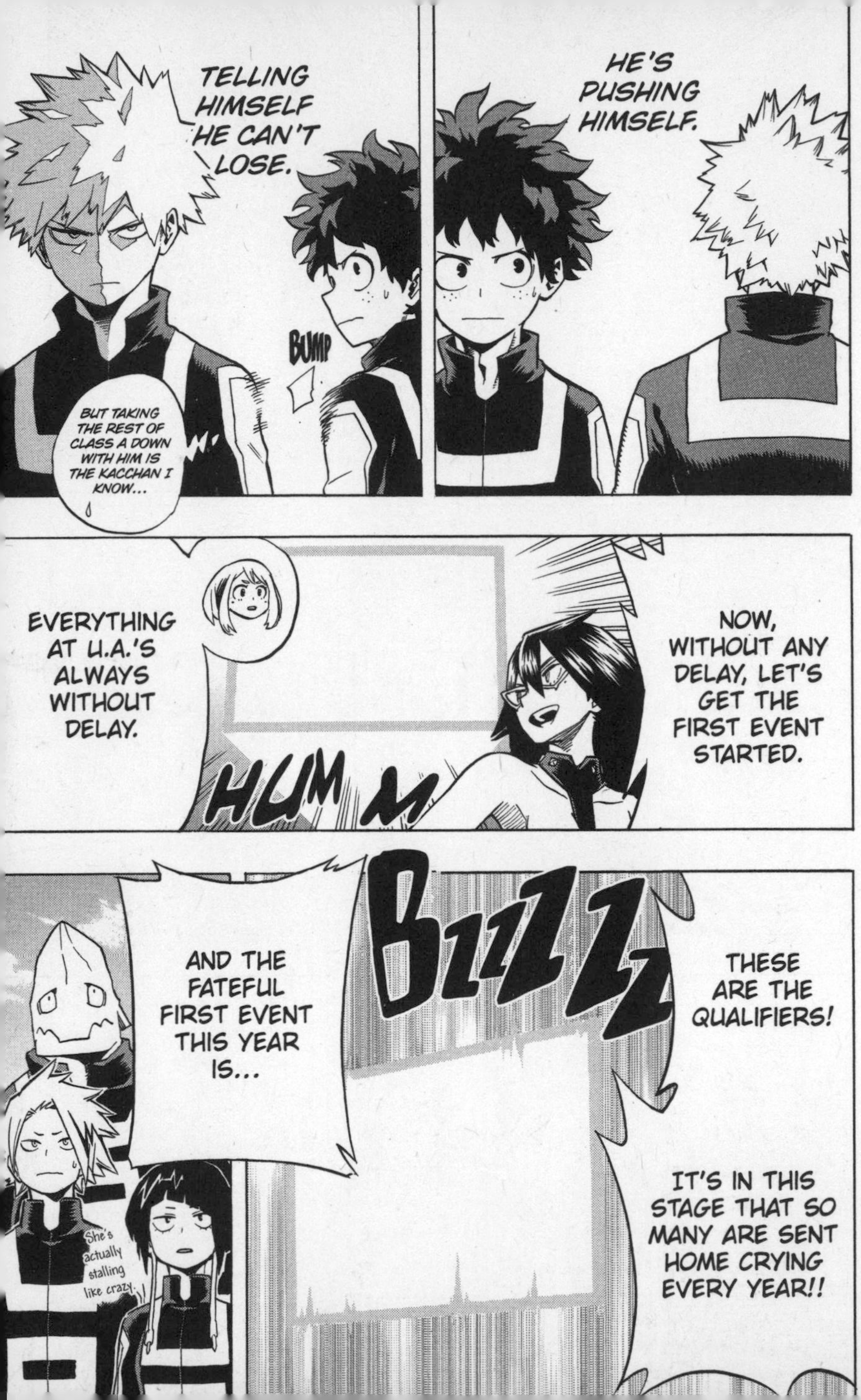
HE'S PUSHING HIMSELF.
TELLING HIMSELF HE CAN'T LOSE.
BUMP
BUT TAKING THE REST OF CLASS A DOWN WITH HIM IS THE KACCHAN I KNOW...
NOW, WITHOUT ANY DELAY, LET'S GET THE FIRST EVENT STARTED.
HUMM
EVERYTHING AT U.A.'S ALWAYS WITHOUT DELAY.
AND THE FATEFUL FIRST EVENT THIS YEAR IS...
BZZZZ
THESE ARE THE QUALIFIERS!
IT'S IN THIS STAGE THAT SO MANY ARE SENT HOME CRYING EVERY YEAR!!
She's actually stalling like crazy.

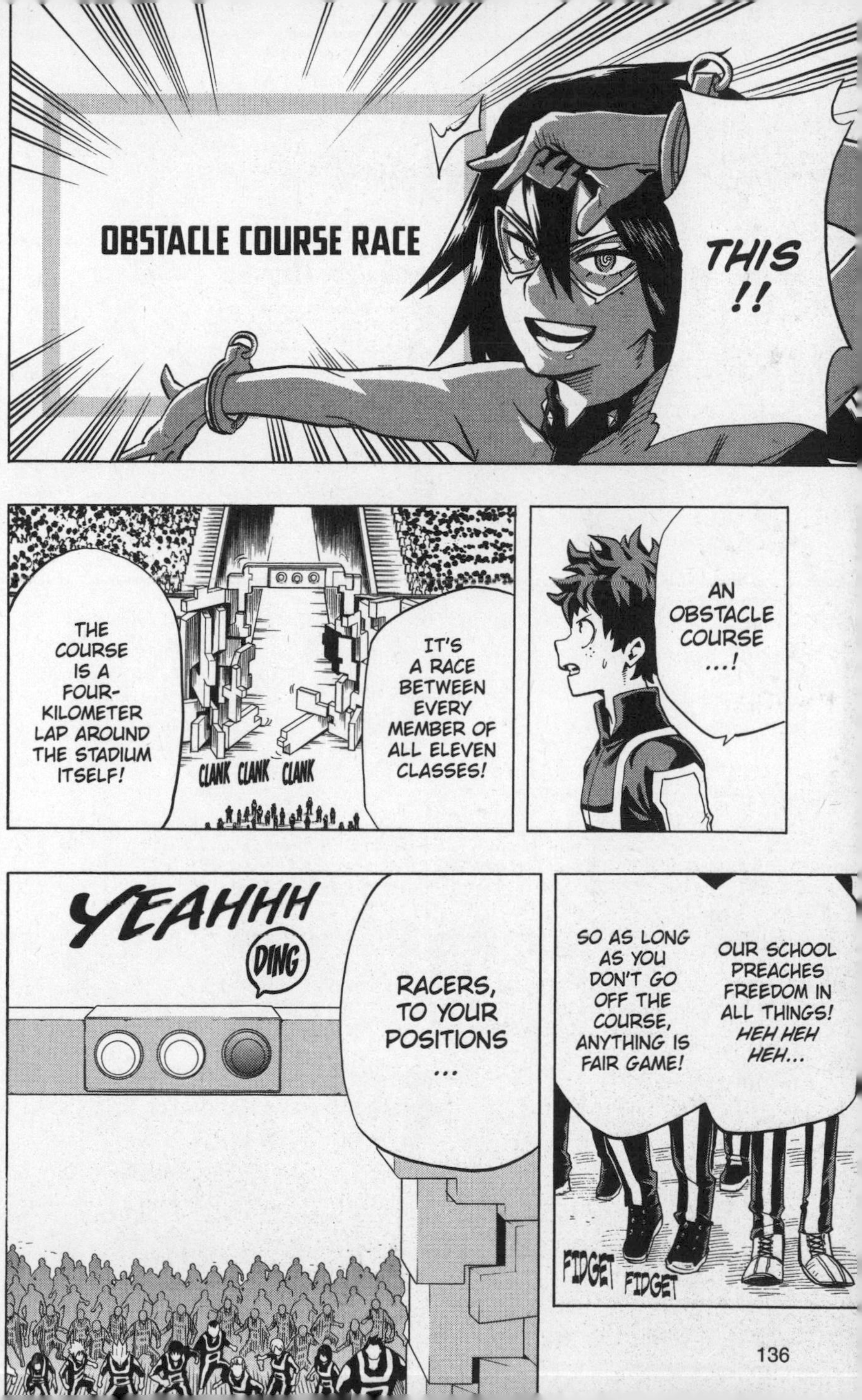
THIS !!
OBSTACLE COURSE RACE
AN OBSTACLE COURSE ...!
IT'S A RACE BETWEEN EVERY MEMBER OF ALL ELEVEN CLASSES!
THE COURSE IS A FOUR-KILOMETER LAP AROUND THE STADIUM ITSELF!
CLANK CLANK CLANK
OUR SCHOOL PREACHES FREEDOM IN ALL THINGS! HEH HEH HEH...
SO AS LONG AS YOU DON'T GO OFF THE COURSE, ANYTHING IS FAIR GAME!
FIDGET FIDGET
RACERS, TO YOUR POSITIONS ...
DING
YEAHHH

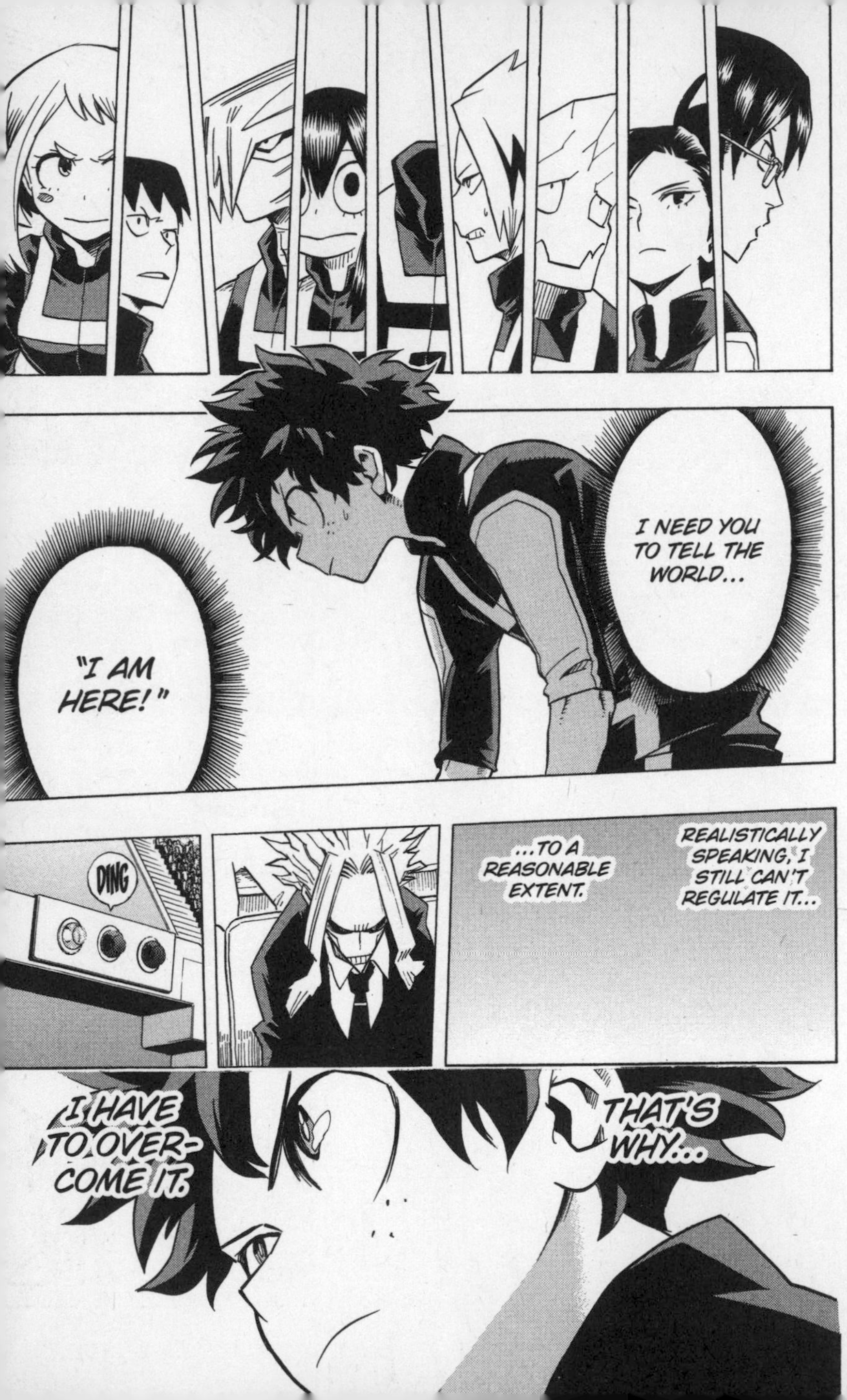
I NEED YOU TO TELL THE WORLD...
"I AM HERE!"
REALISTICALLY SPEAKING, I STILL CAN'T REGULATE IT...
...TO A REASONABLE EXTENT.
DING
THAT'S WHY...
I HAVE TO OVER-COME IT.

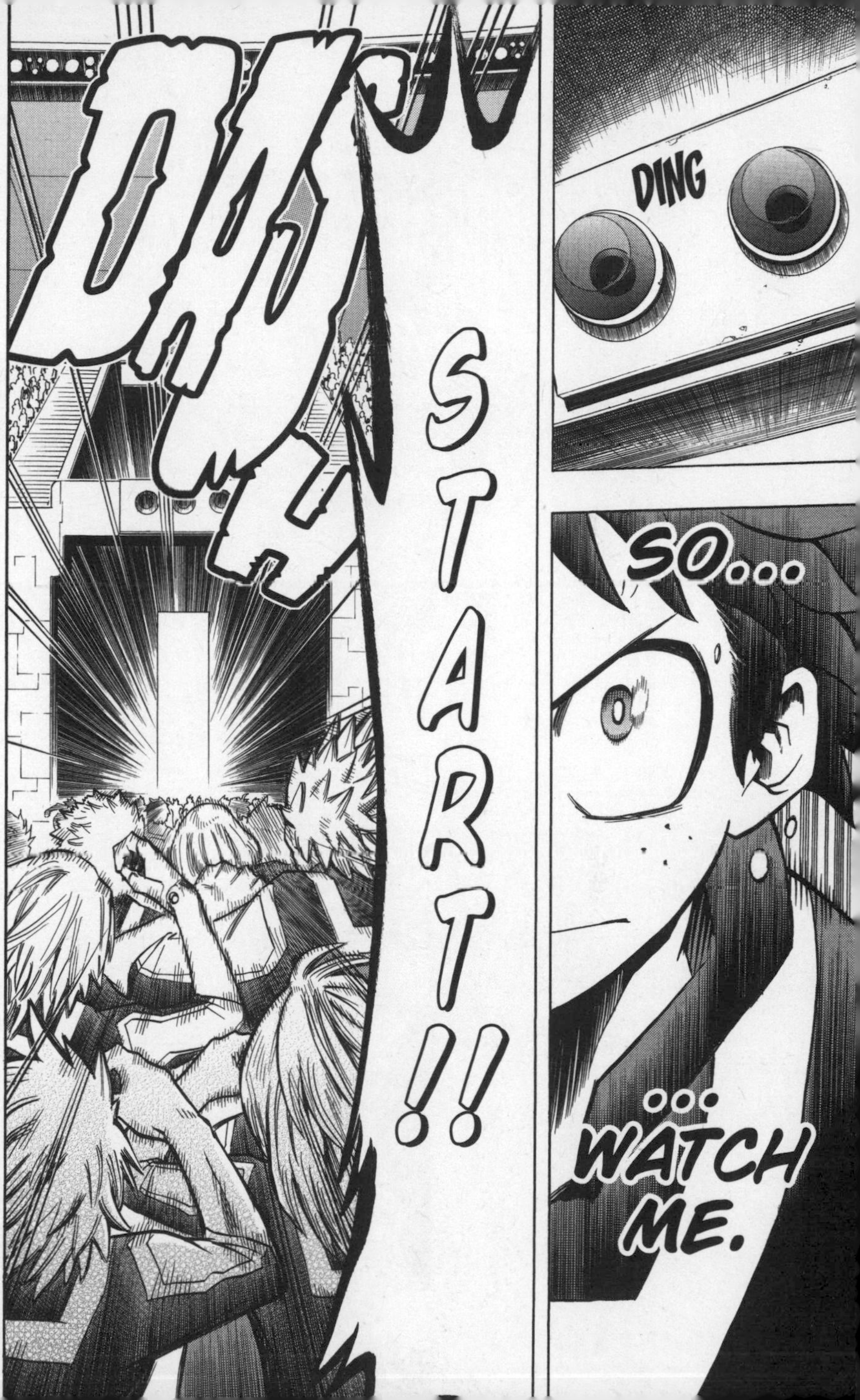
DING
SO...
...WATCH ME.
START!!

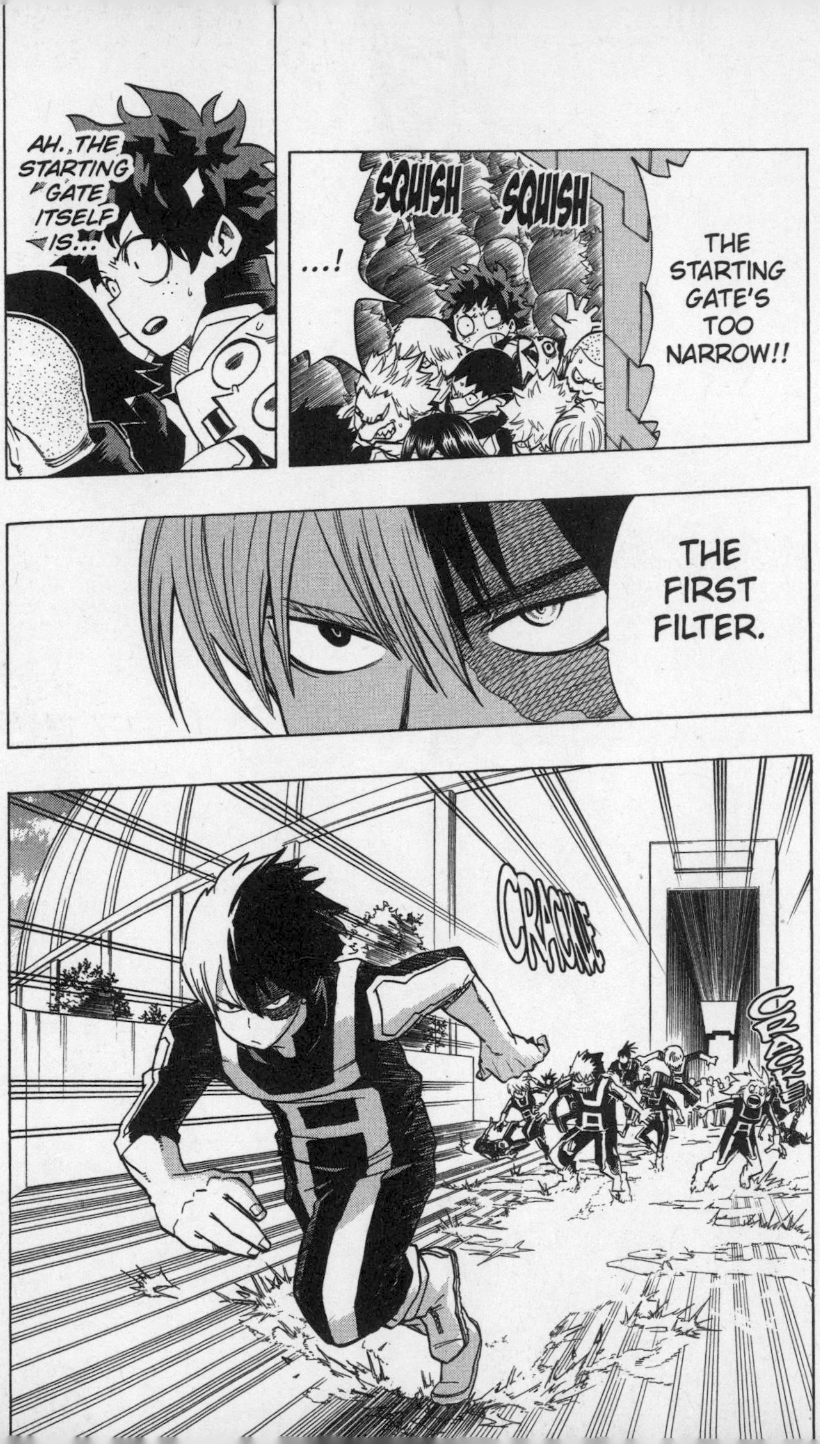
SQUISH SQUISH
...!
THE STARTING GATE'S TOO NARROW!!
AH.. THE STARTING GATE ITSELF IS...!
THE FIRST FILTER.
CRACKLE

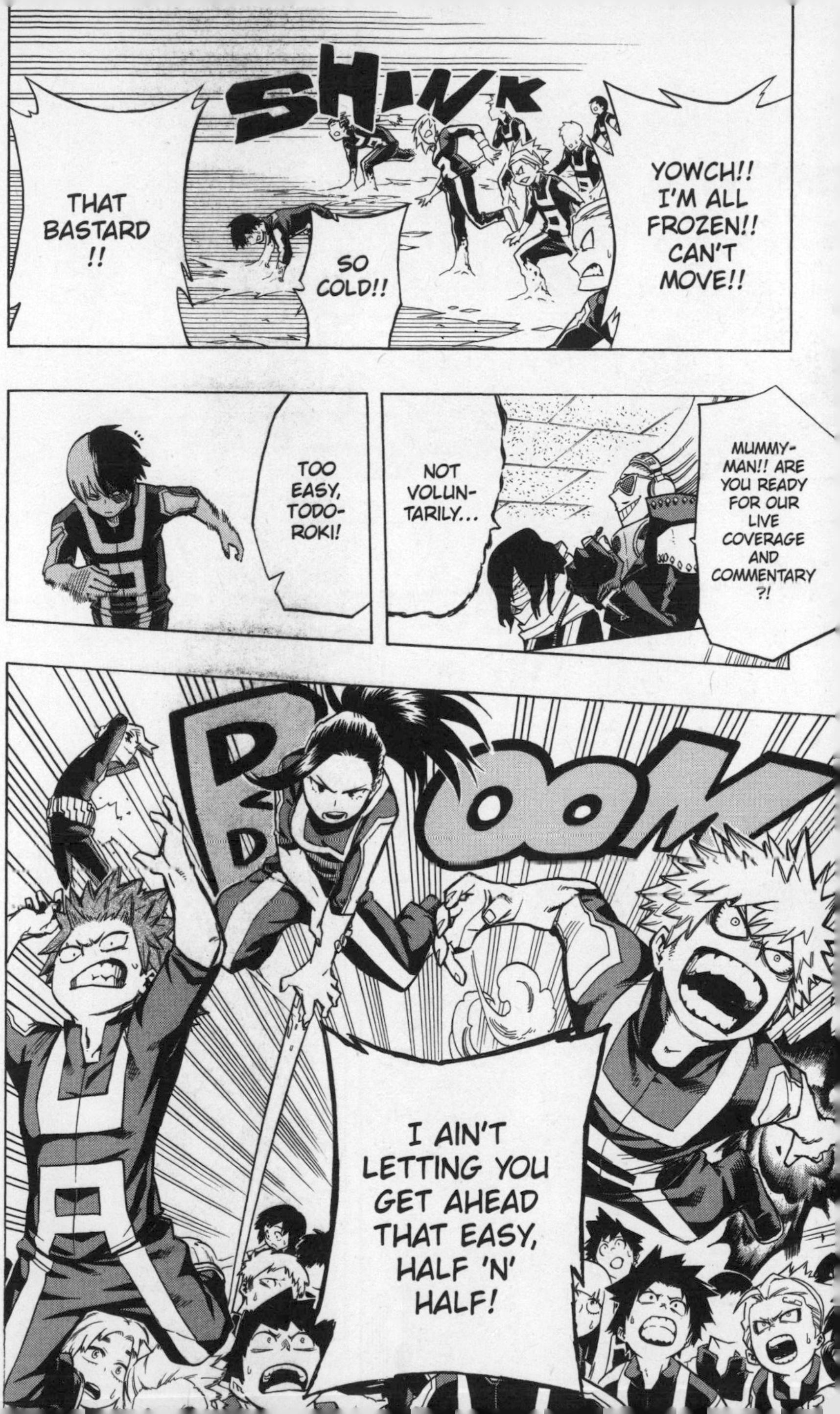
YOWCH!! I'M ALL FROZEN!! CAN'T MOVE!!
SO COLD!!
THAT BASTARD!!
MUMMY-MAN!! ARE YOU READY FOR OUR LIVE COVERAGE AND COMMENTARY?!
NOT VOLUNTARILY...
TOO EASY, TODOROKI!
I AIN'T LETTING YOU GET AHEAD THAT EASY, HALF 'N' HALF!

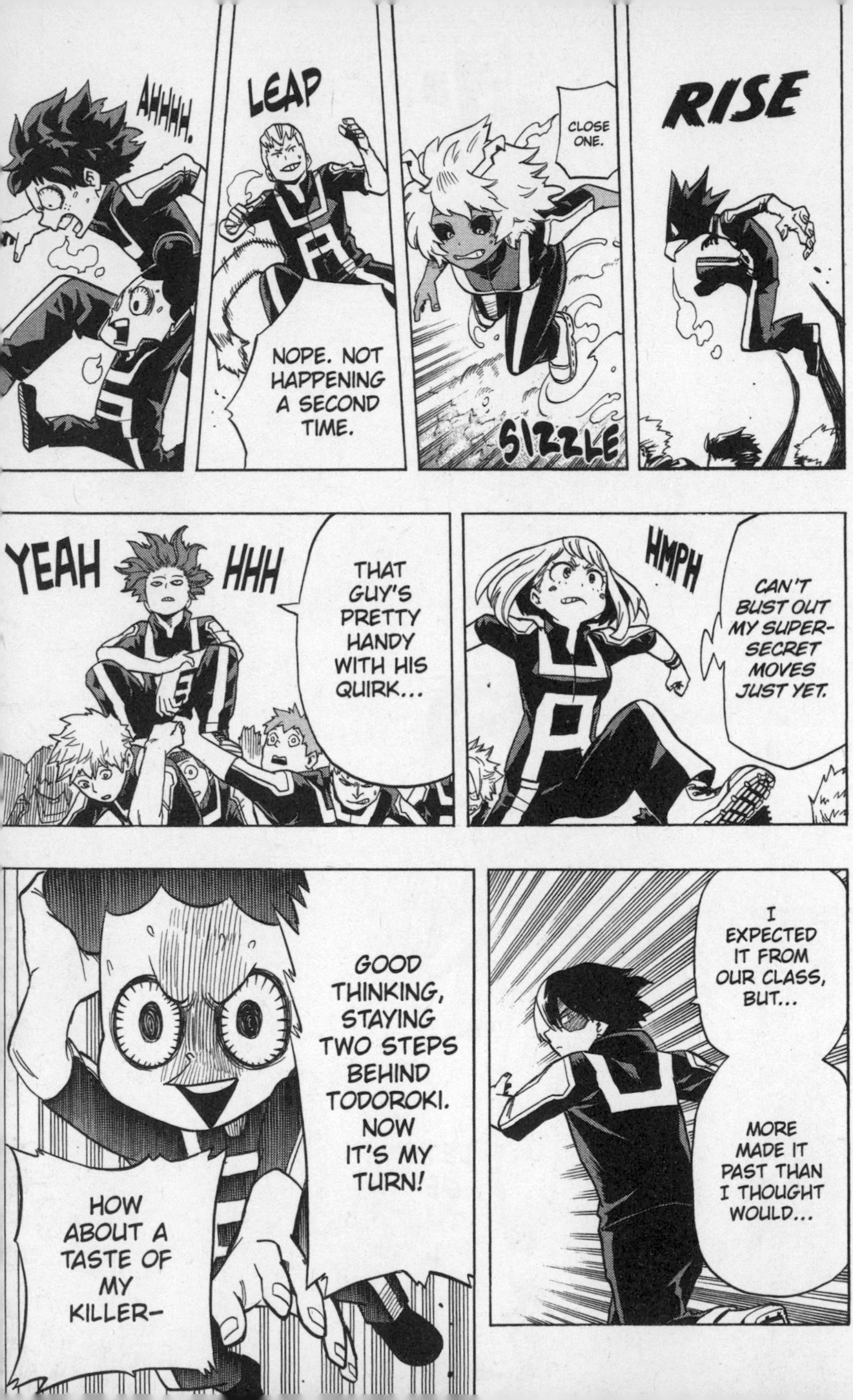
RISE
CLOSE ONE.
SIZZLE
LEAP
NOPE. NOT HAPPENING A SECOND TIME.
AHHHH.
HMPH
CAN'T BUST OUT MY SUPER-SECRET MOVES JUST YET.
YEAH
HHH
THAT GUY'S PRETTY HANDY WITH HIS QUIRK...
I EXPECTED IT FROM OUR CLASS, BUT...
MORE MADE IT PAST THAN I THOUGHT WOULD...
GOOD THINKING, STAYING TWO STEPS BEHIND TODOROKI. NOW IT'S MY TURN!
HOW ABOUT A TASTE OF MY KILLER-

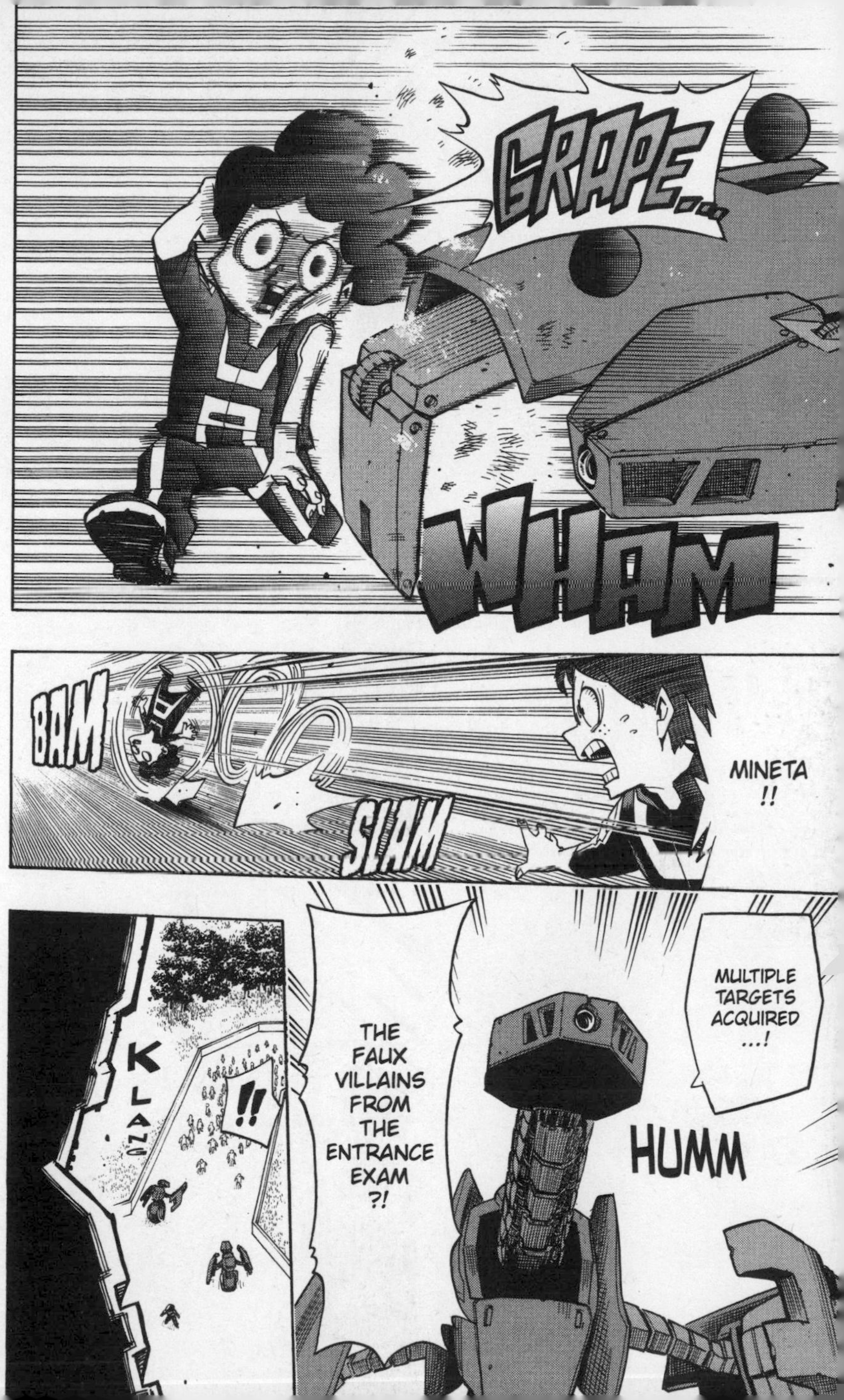
GRAPE...
WHAM
MINETA!!
SLAM
BAM
MULTIPLE TARGETS ACQUIRED...!
HUMM
THE FAUX VILLAINS FROM THE ENTRANCE EXAM?!
KLANG
!!

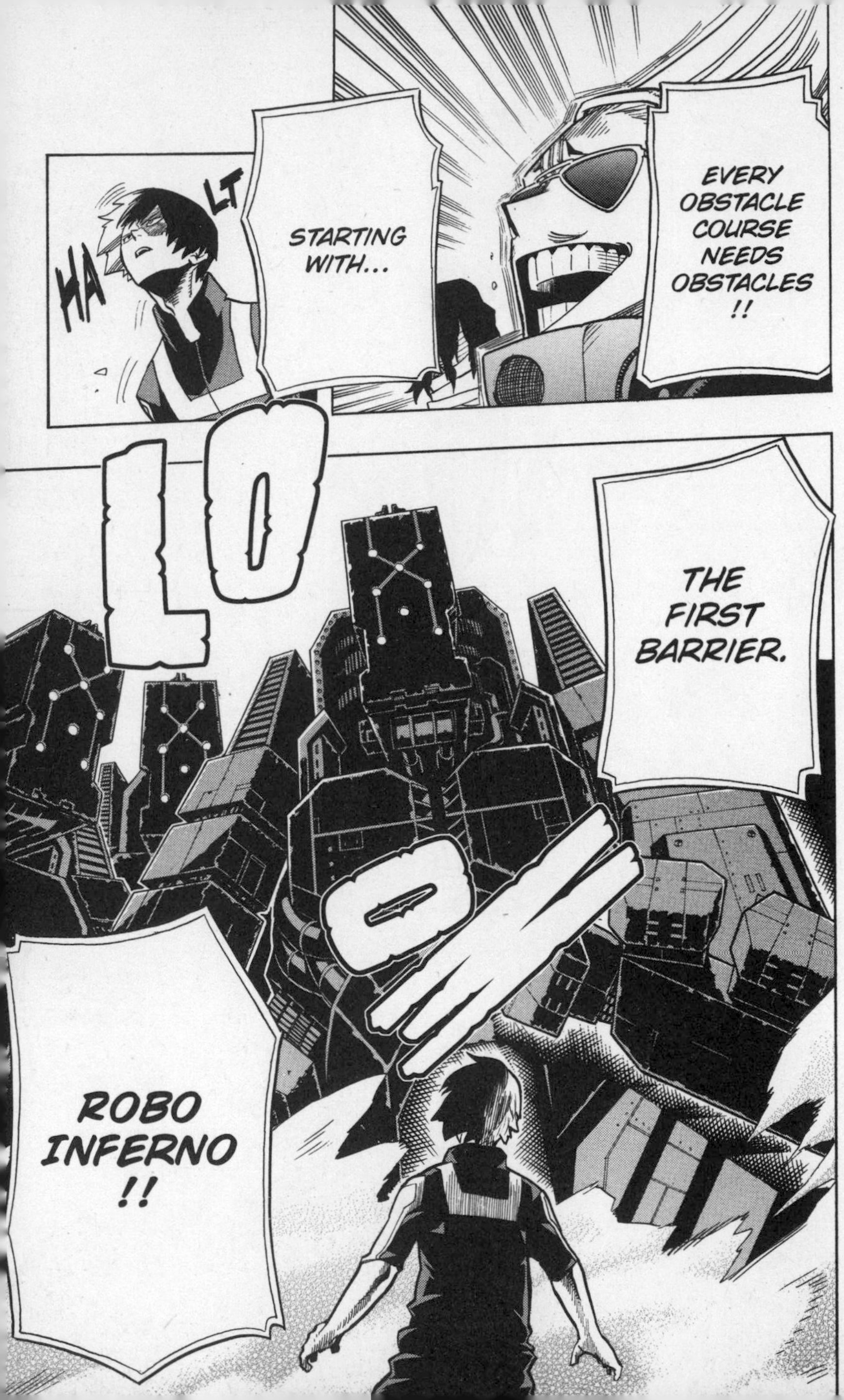
EVERY OBSTACLE COURSE NEEDS OBSTACLES !!
STARTING WITH...
HALT
THE FIRST BARRIER.
ROBO INFERNO !!

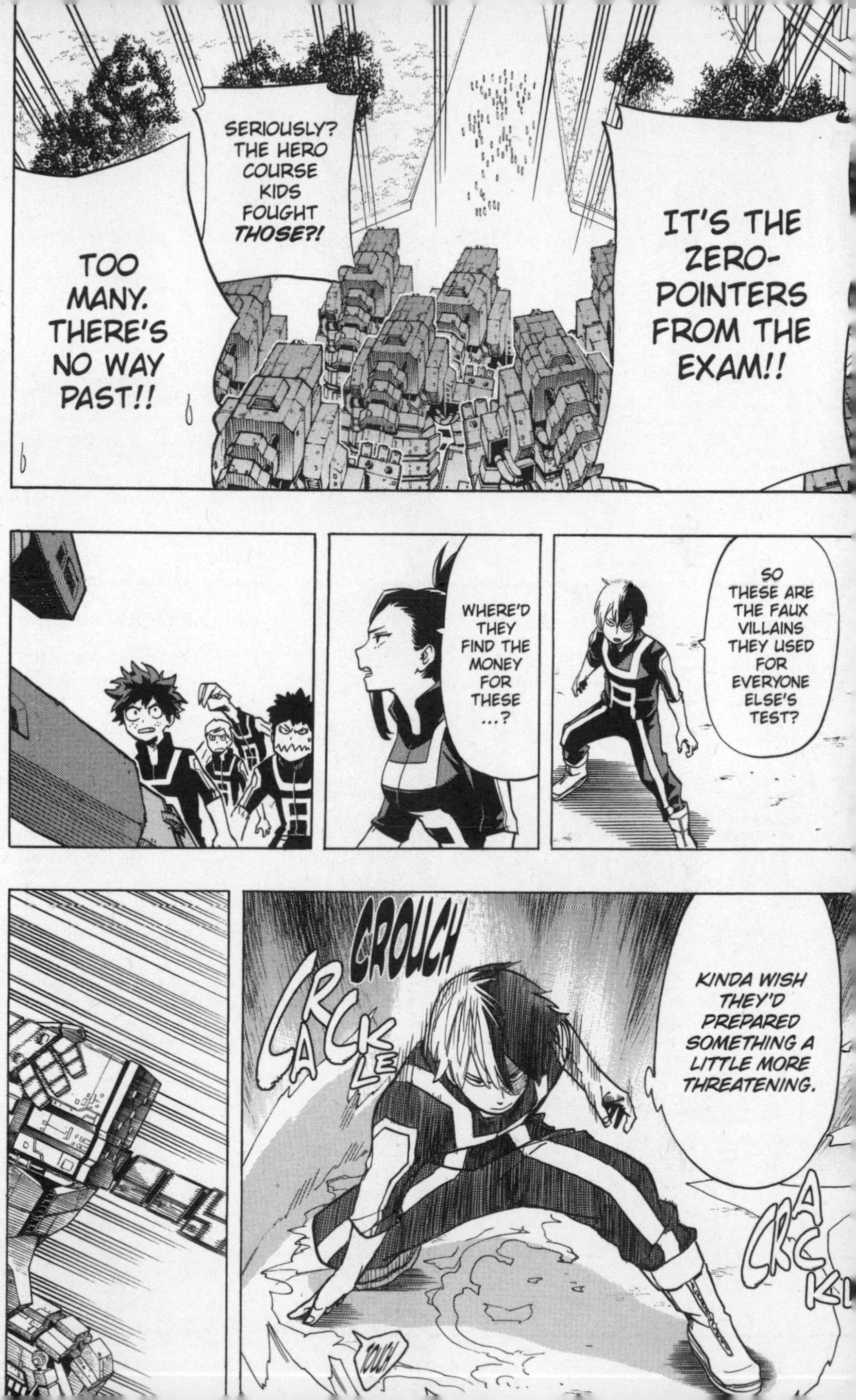
IT'S THE ZERO-POINTERS FROM THE EXAM!!
SERIOUSLY? THE HERO COURSE KIDS FOUGHT *THOSE?!*
TOO MANY. THERE'S NO WAY PAST!!
SO THESE ARE THE FAUX VILLAINS THEY USED FOR EVERYONE ELSE'S TEST?
WHERE'D THEY FIND THE MONEY FOR THESE ...?
KINDA WISH THEY'D PREPARED SOMETHING A LITTLE MORE THREATENING.
CROUCH
CRACKLE
CRACKL
TOUCH

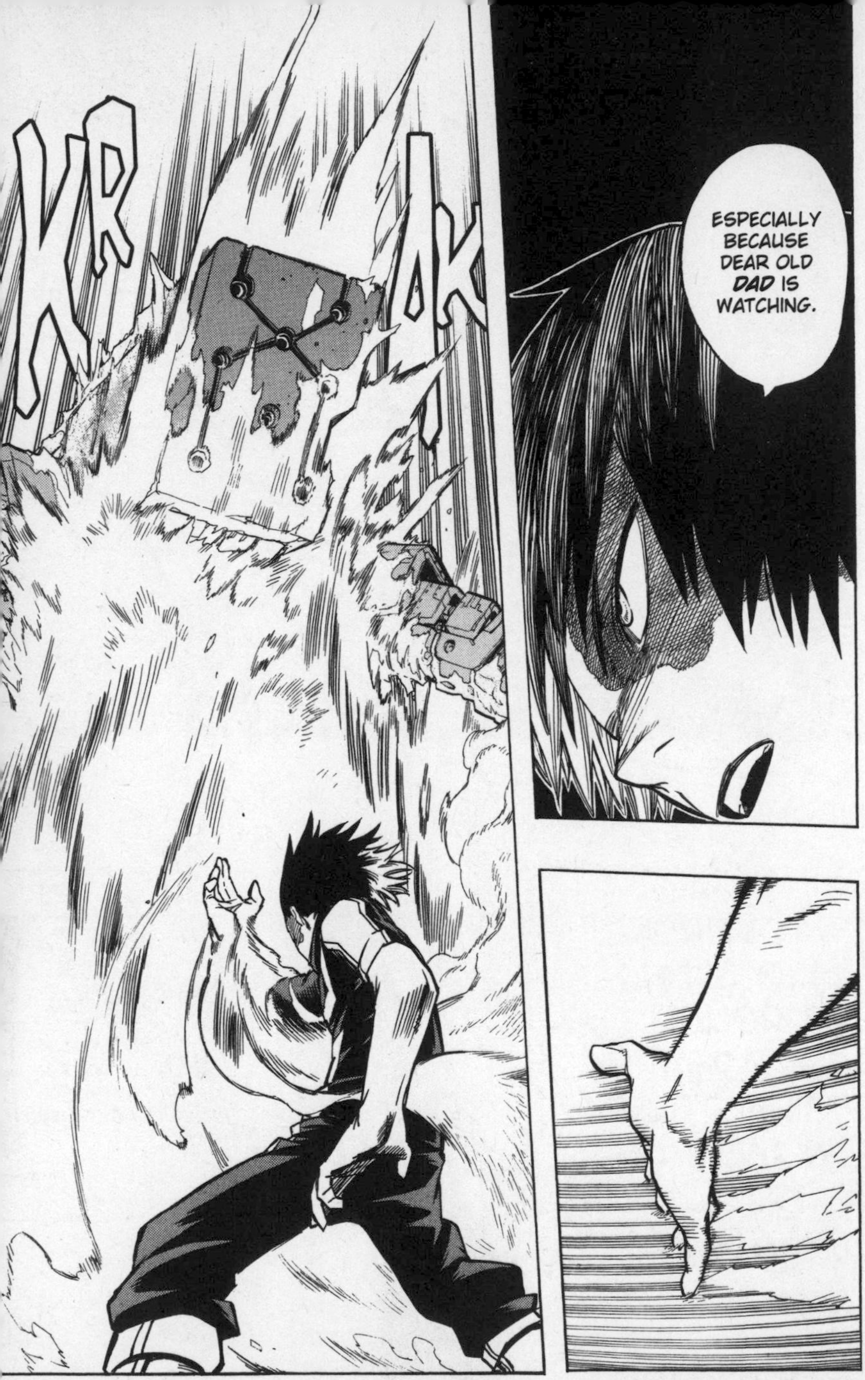
ESPECIALLY BECAUSE DEAR OLD *DAD* IS WATCHING.
KRAK

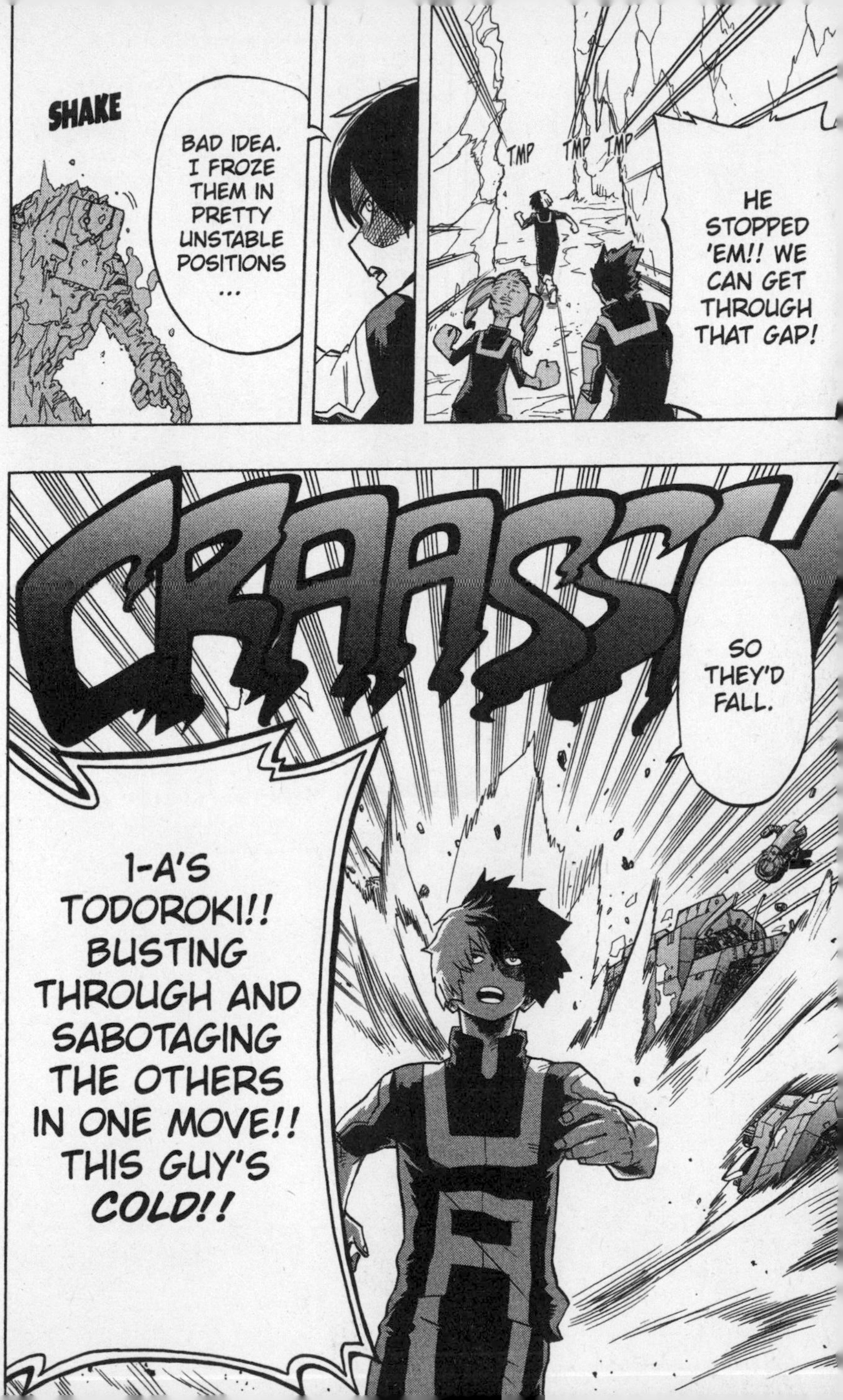
TMP TMP TMP
HE STOPPED 'EM!! WE CAN GET THROUGH THAT GAP!
BAD IDEA. I FROZE THEM IN PRETTY UNSTABLE POSITIONS ...
SHAKE
CRAASC
SO THEY'D FALL.
1-A'S TODOROKI!! BUSTING THROUGH AND SABOTAGING THE OTHERS IN ONE MOVE!! THIS GUY'S COLD!!

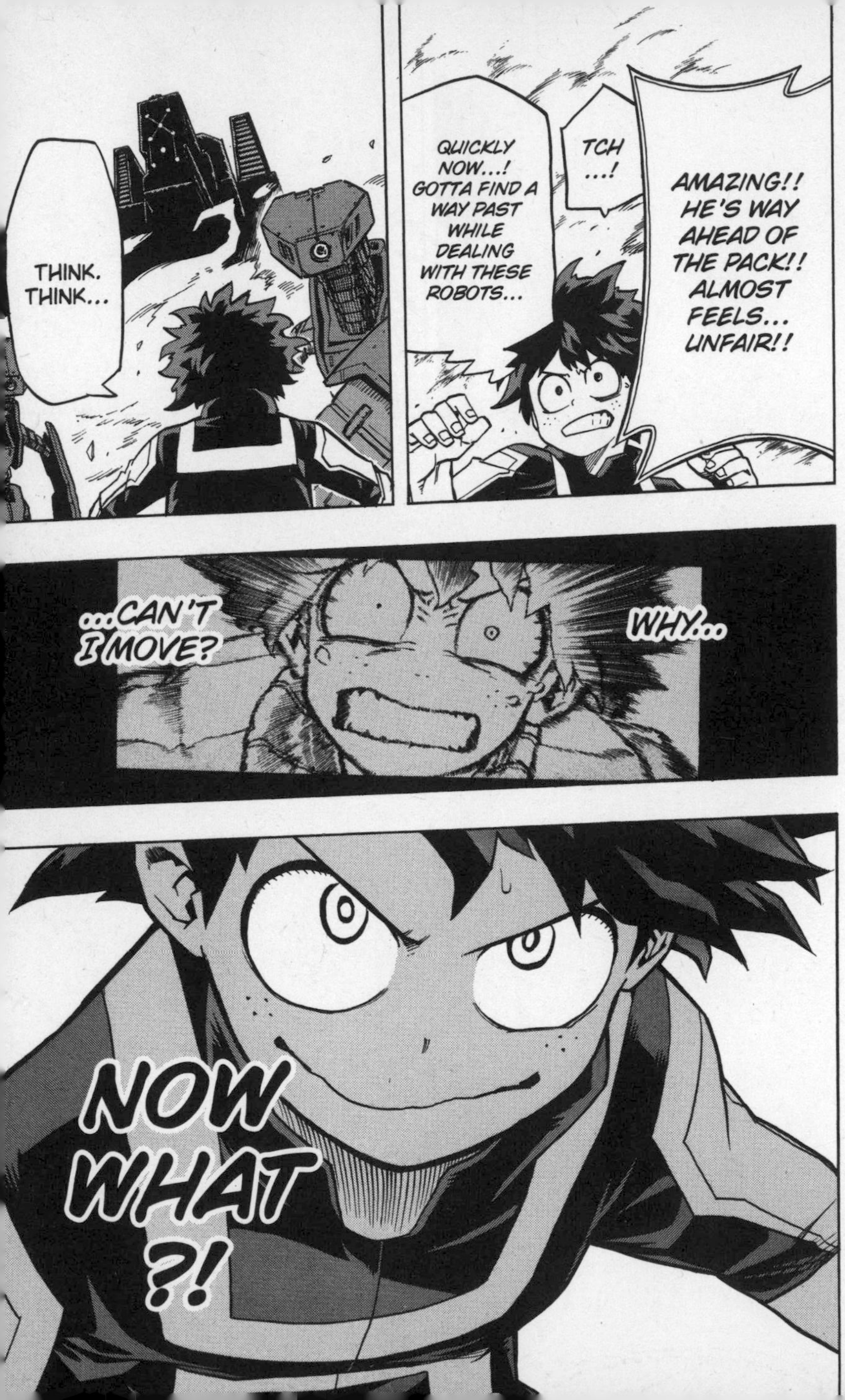
AMAZING!! HE'S WAY AHEAD OF THE PACK!! ALMOST FEELS... UNFAIR!!
TCH ...!
QUICKLY NOW...! GOTTA FIND A WAY PAST WHILE DEALING WITH THESE ROBOTS...
THINK. THINK...
WHY...
...CAN'T I MOVE?
NOW WHAT ?!

FUMIKAGE TOKOYAMI (15)

SUPRISINGLY CASUAL

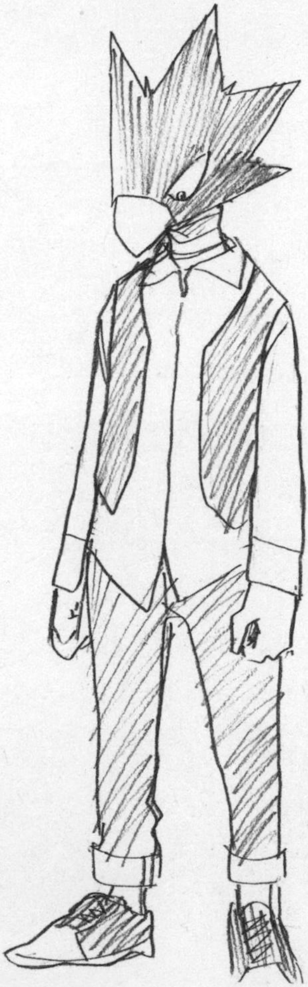

Birthday: 10/30
Height: 158 cm
Favorite Things: Dimly lit places, apples

BEHIND THE SCENES

I personally think this guy is cool beyond cool, but it's tough because he doesn't quite fit the rest of the world.

Compared to the others, I really struggle with him.

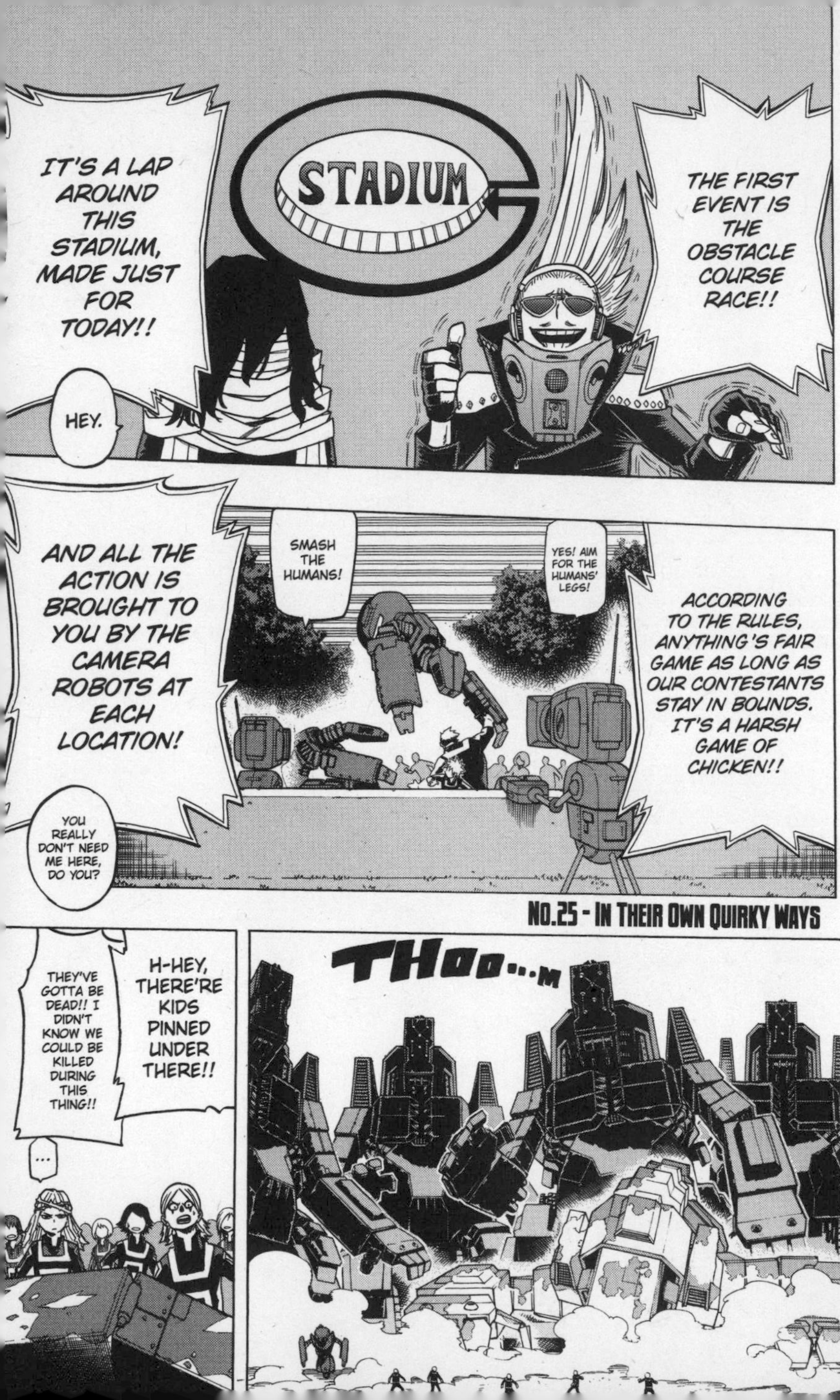
THE FIRST EVENT IS THE OBSTACLE COURSE RACE!!
STADIUM
IT'S A LAP AROUND THIS STADIUM, MADE JUST FOR TODAY!!
HEY.
ACCORDING TO THE RULES, ANYTHING'S FAIR GAME AS LONG AS OUR CONTESTANTS STAY IN BOUNDS. IT'S A HARSH GAME OF CHICKEN!!
YES! AIM FOR THE HUMANS' LEGS!
SMASH THE HUMANS!
AND ALL THE ACTION IS BROUGHT TO YOU BY THE CAMERA ROBOTS AT EACH LOCATION!
YOU REALLY DON'T NEED ME HERE, DO YOU?
NO.25 - IN THEIR OWN QUIRKY WAYS
THOO...M
H-HEY, THERE'RE KIDS PINNED UNDER THERE!!
THEY'VE GOTTA BE DEAD!! I DIDN'T KNOW WE COULD BE KILLED DURING THIS THING!!
...

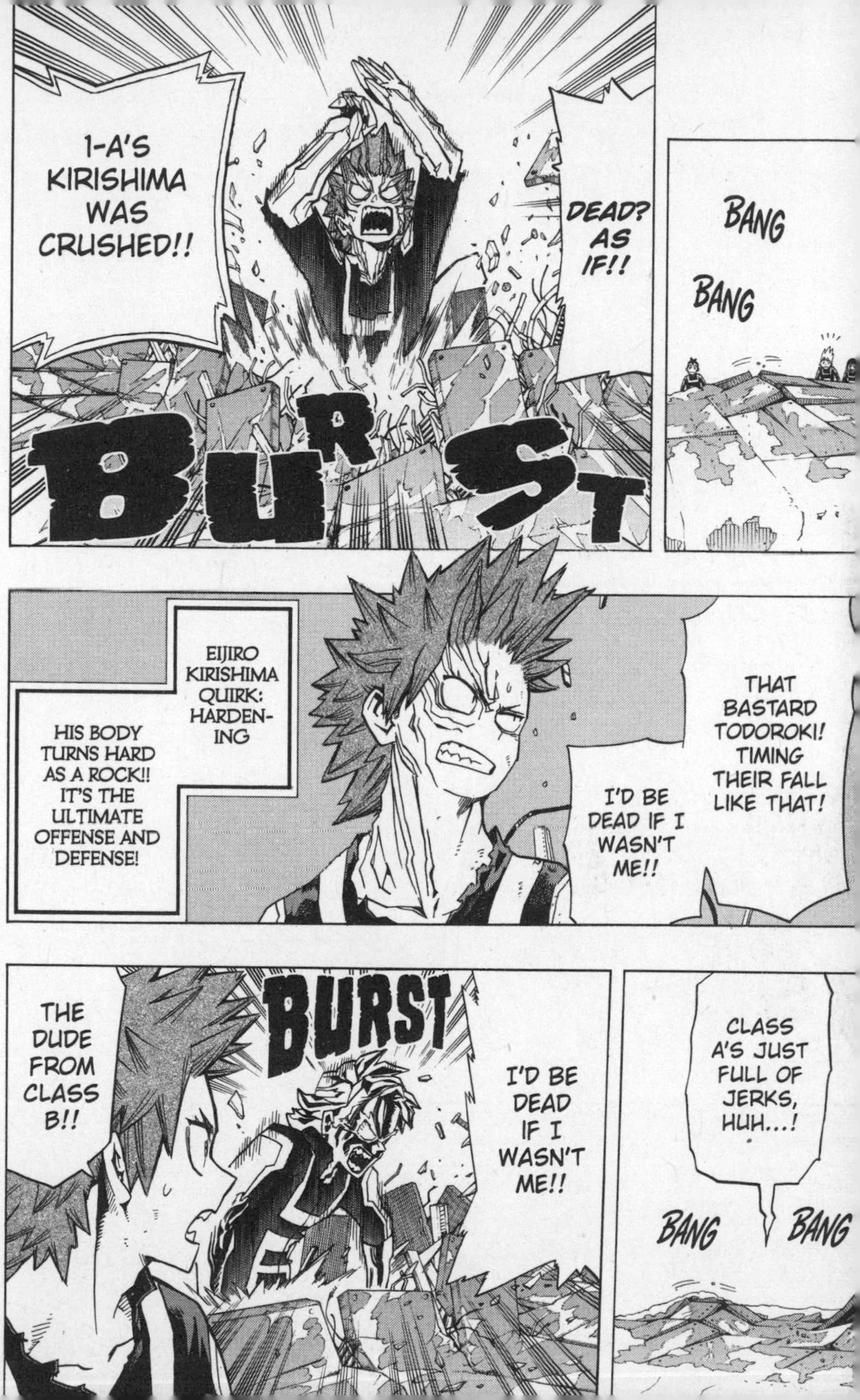
BANG
BANG
1-A'S KIRISHIMA WAS CRUSHED!!
DEAD? AS IF!!
BURST
THAT BASTARD TODOROKI! TIMING THEIR FALL LIKE THAT!
I'D BE DEAD IF I WASN'T ME!!
EIJIRO KIRISHIMA QUIRK: HARDEN-ING
HIS BODY TURNS HARD AS A ROCK!! IT'S THE ULTIMATE OFFENSE AND DEFENSE!
CLASS A'S JUST FULL OF JERKS, HUH...!
BANG
BANG
BURST
I'D BE DEAD IF I WASN'T ME!!
THE DUDE FROM CLASS B!!

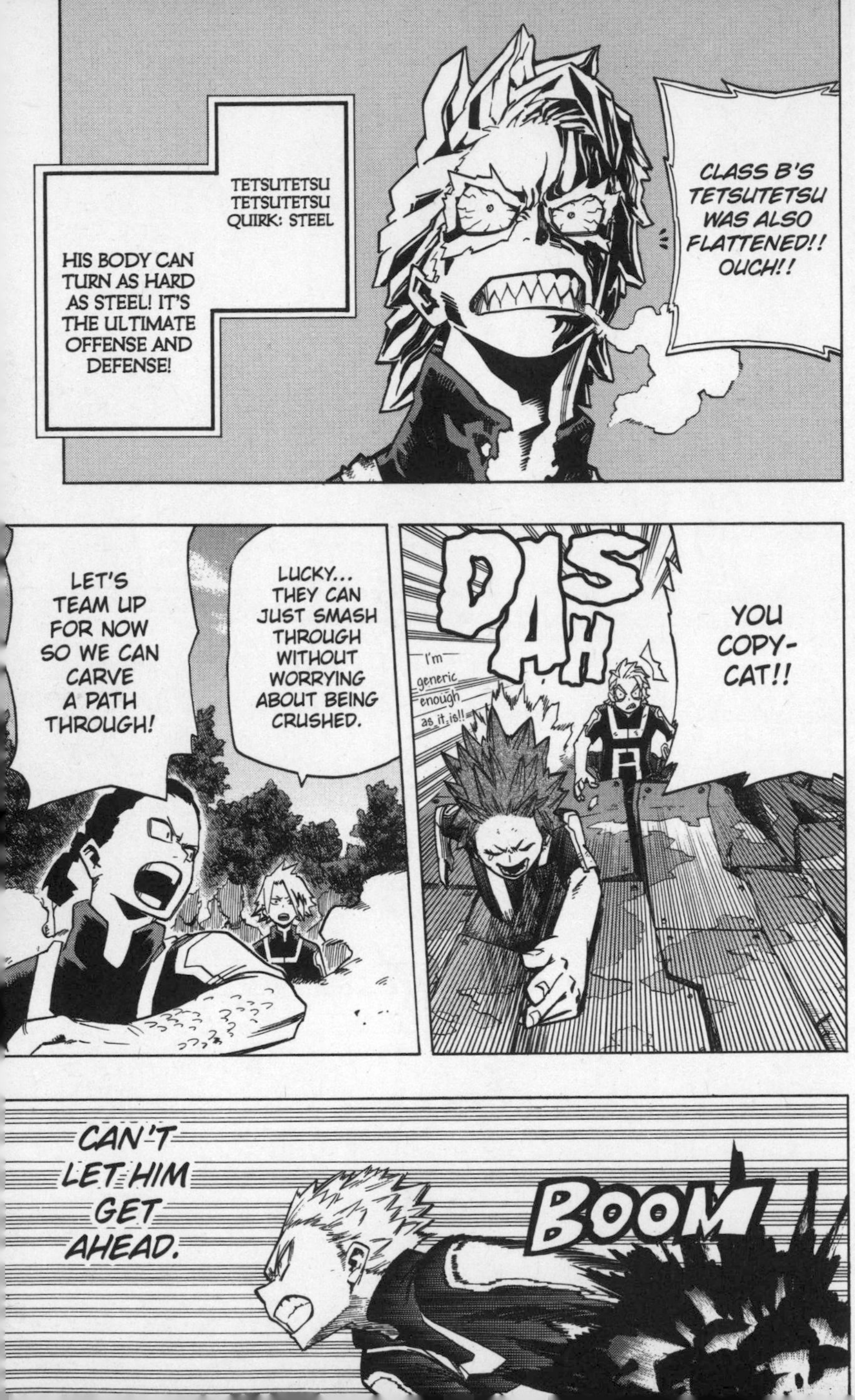
CLASS B'S TETSUTETSU WAS ALSO FLATTENED!! OUCH!!
TETSUTETSU TETSUTETSU QUIRK: STEEL
HIS BODY CAN TURN AS HARD AS STEEL! IT'S THE ULTIMATE OFFENSE AND DEFENSE!
YOU COPY-CAT!!
DASH
I'm generic enough as it is!!
LUCKY... THEY CAN JUST SMASH THROUGH WITHOUT WORRYING ABOUT BEING CRUSHED.
LET'S TEAM UP FOR NOW SO WE CAN CARVE A PATH THROUGH!
BOOM
CAN'T LET HIM GET AHEAD.

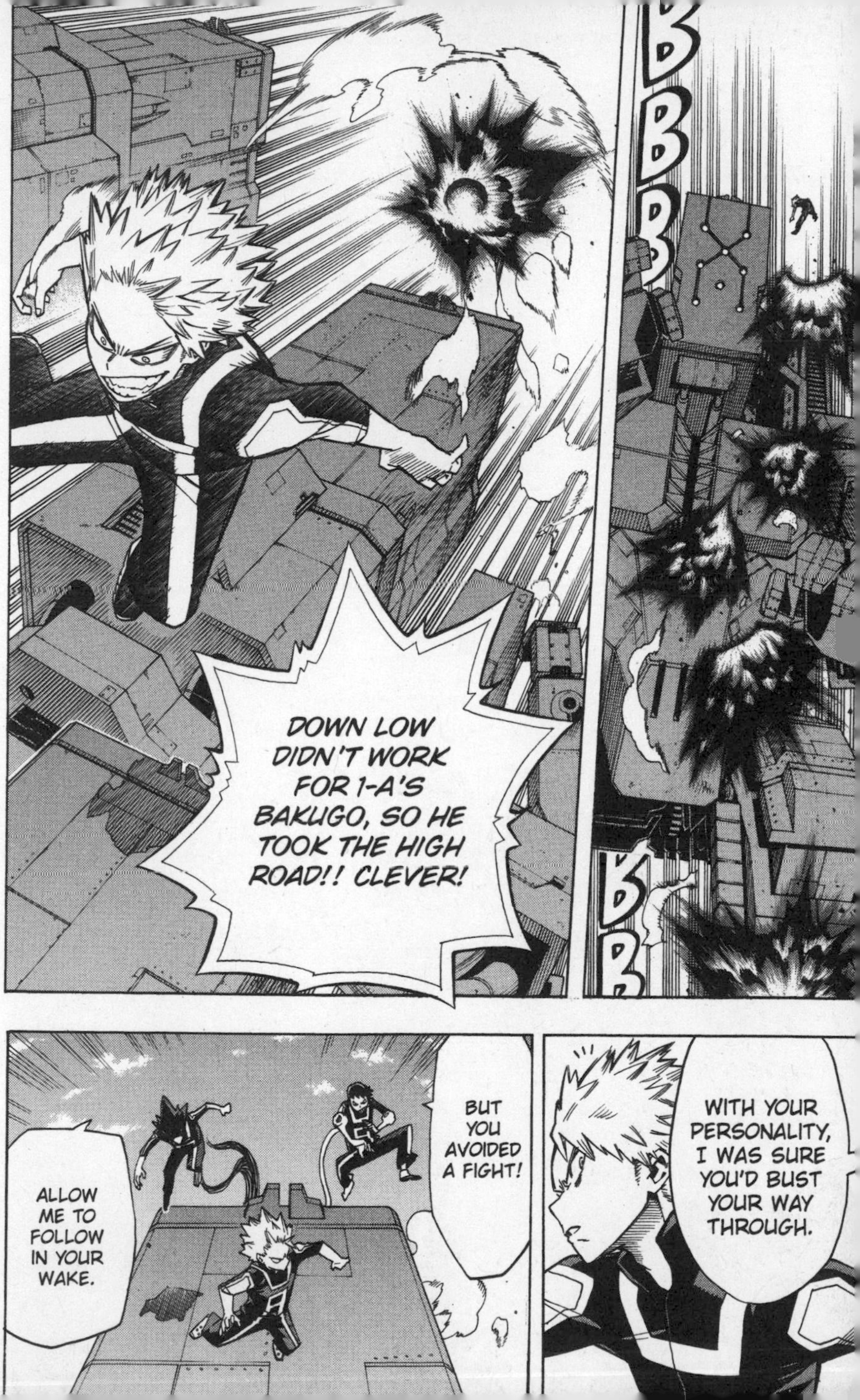
BBBB
DOWN LOW DIDN'T WORK FOR 1-A'S BAKUGO, SO HE TOOK THE HIGH ROAD!! CLEVER!
WITH YOUR PERSONALITY, I WAS SURE YOU'D BUST YOUR WAY THROUGH.
BUT YOU AVOIDED A FIGHT!
ALLOW ME TO FOLLOW IN YOUR WAKE.

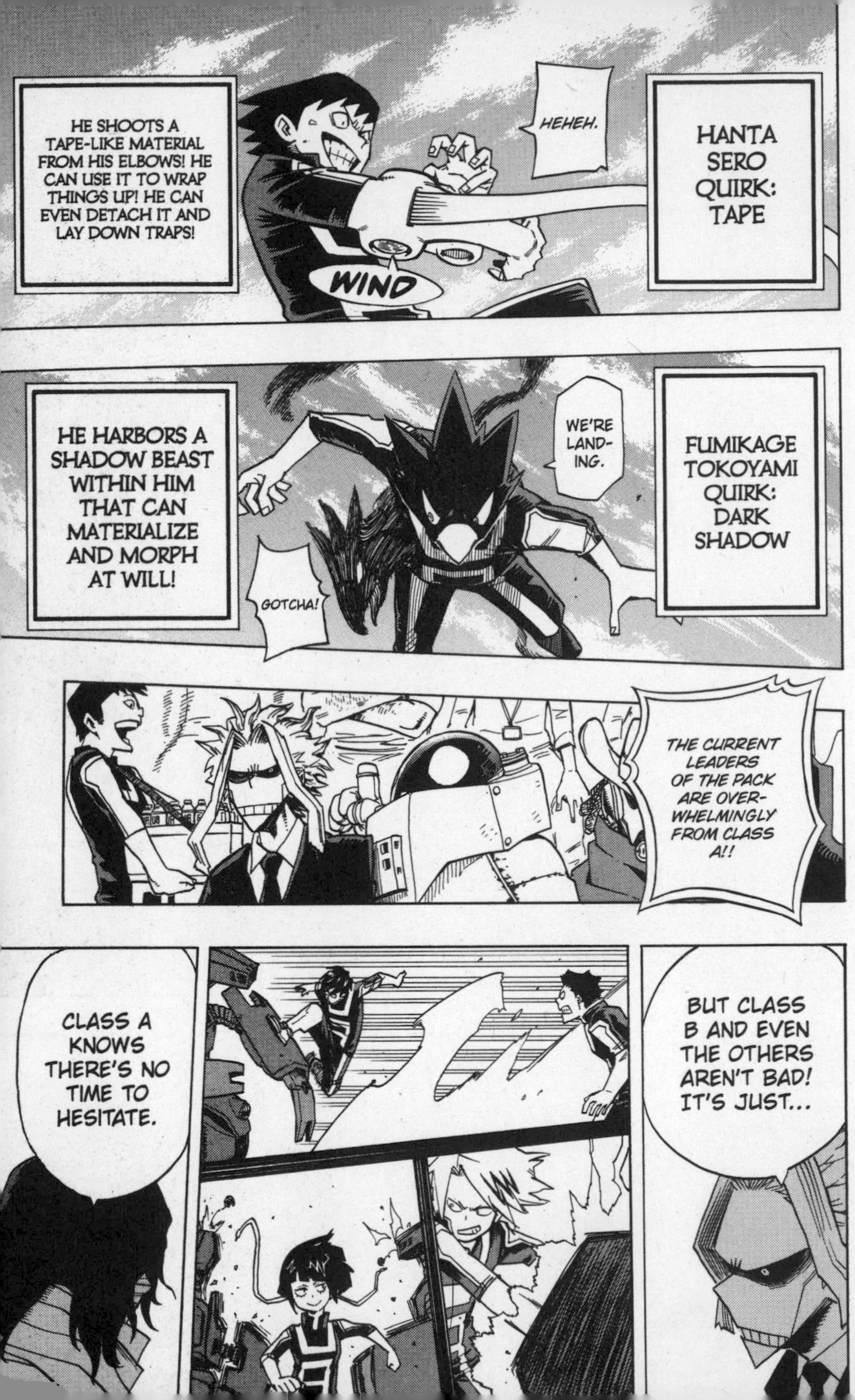
HANTA SERO QUIRK: TAPE
HEHEH.
HE SHOOTS A TAPE-LIKE MATERIAL FROM HIS ELBOWS! HE CAN USE IT TO WRAP THINGS UP! HE CAN EVEN DETACH IT AND LAY DOWN TRAPS!
WIND
FUMIKAGE TOKOYAMI QUIRK: DARK SHADOW
WE'RE LANDING.
HE HARBORS A SHADOW BEAST WITHIN HIM THAT CAN MATERIALIZE AND MORPH AT WILL!
GOTCHA!
THE CURRENT LEADERS OF THE PACK ARE OVERWHELMINGLY FROM CLASS A!!
BUT CLASS B AND EVEN THE OTHERS AREN'T BAD! IT'S JUST...
CLASS A KNOWS THERE'S NO TIME TO HESITATE.

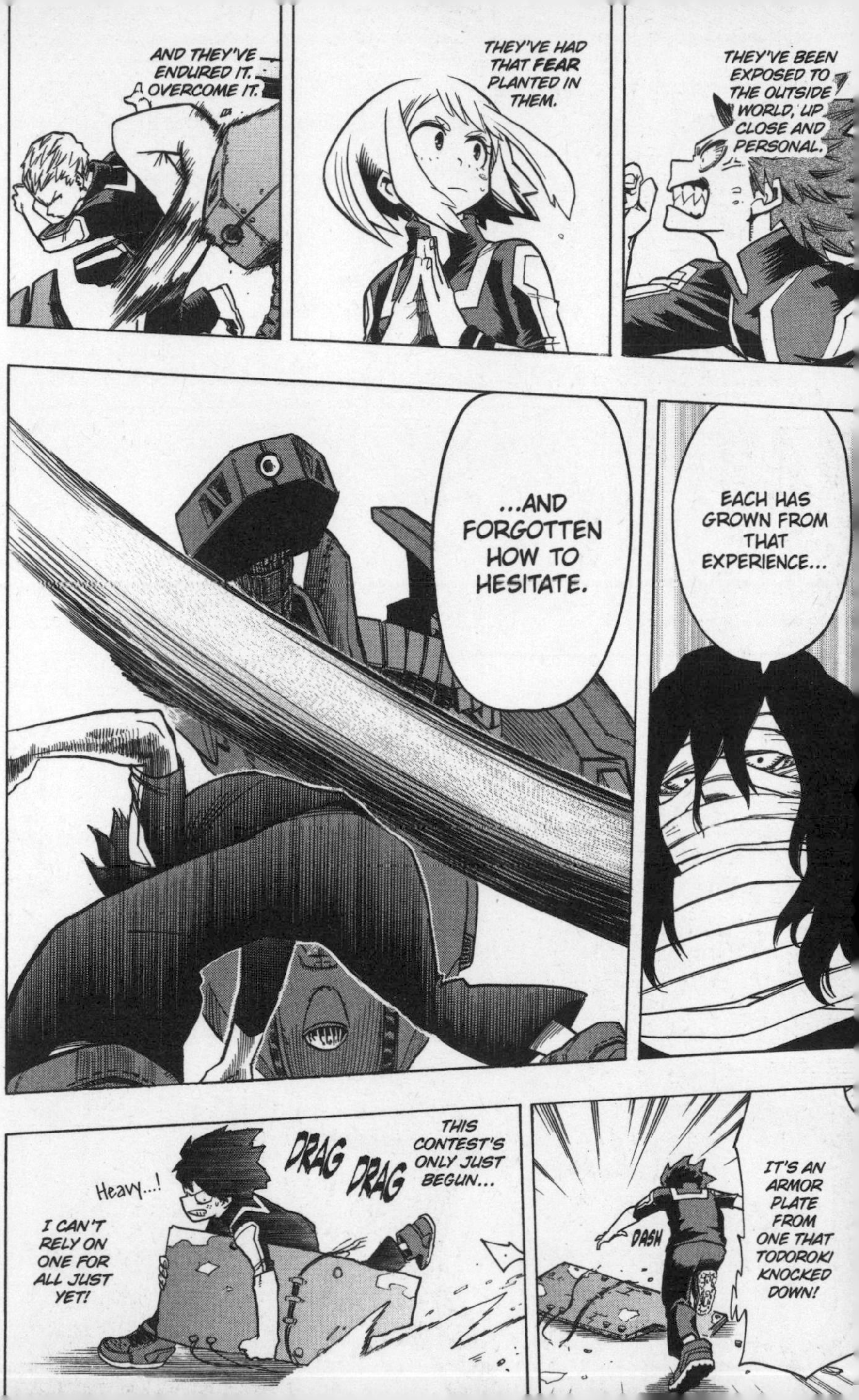
THEY'VE BEEN EXPOSED TO THE OUTSIDE WORLD, UP CLOSE AND PERSONAL.
THEY'VE HAD THAT FEAR PLANTED IN THEM.
AND THEY'VE ENDURED IT. OVERCOME IT.
EACH HAS GROWN FROM THAT EXPERIENCE...
...AND FORGOTTEN HOW TO HESITATE.
IT'S AN ARMOR PLATE FROM ONE THAT TODOROKI KNOCKED DOWN!
DASH
THIS CONTEST'S ONLY JUST BEGUN...
DRAG DRAG
Heavy...!
I CAN'T RELY ON ONE FOR ALL JUST YET!

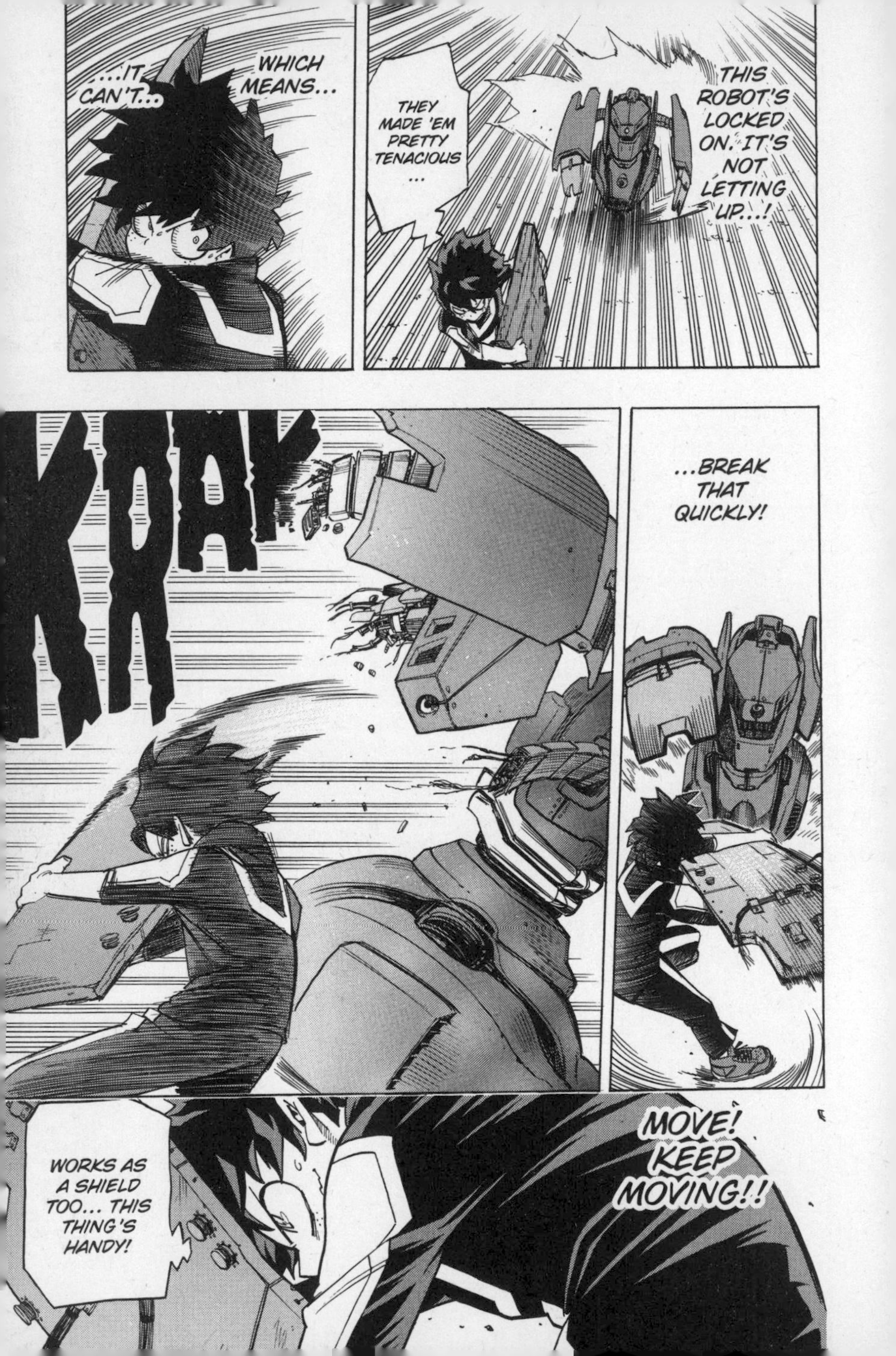
THIS ROBOT'S LOCKED ON. IT'S NOT LETTING UP...!
THEY MADE 'EM PRETTY TENACIOUS ...
WHICH MEANS...
...IT CAN'T...
...BREAK THAT QUICKLY!
KRAK
MOVE! KEEP MOVING!!
WORKS AS A SHIELD TOO... THIS THING'S HANDY!

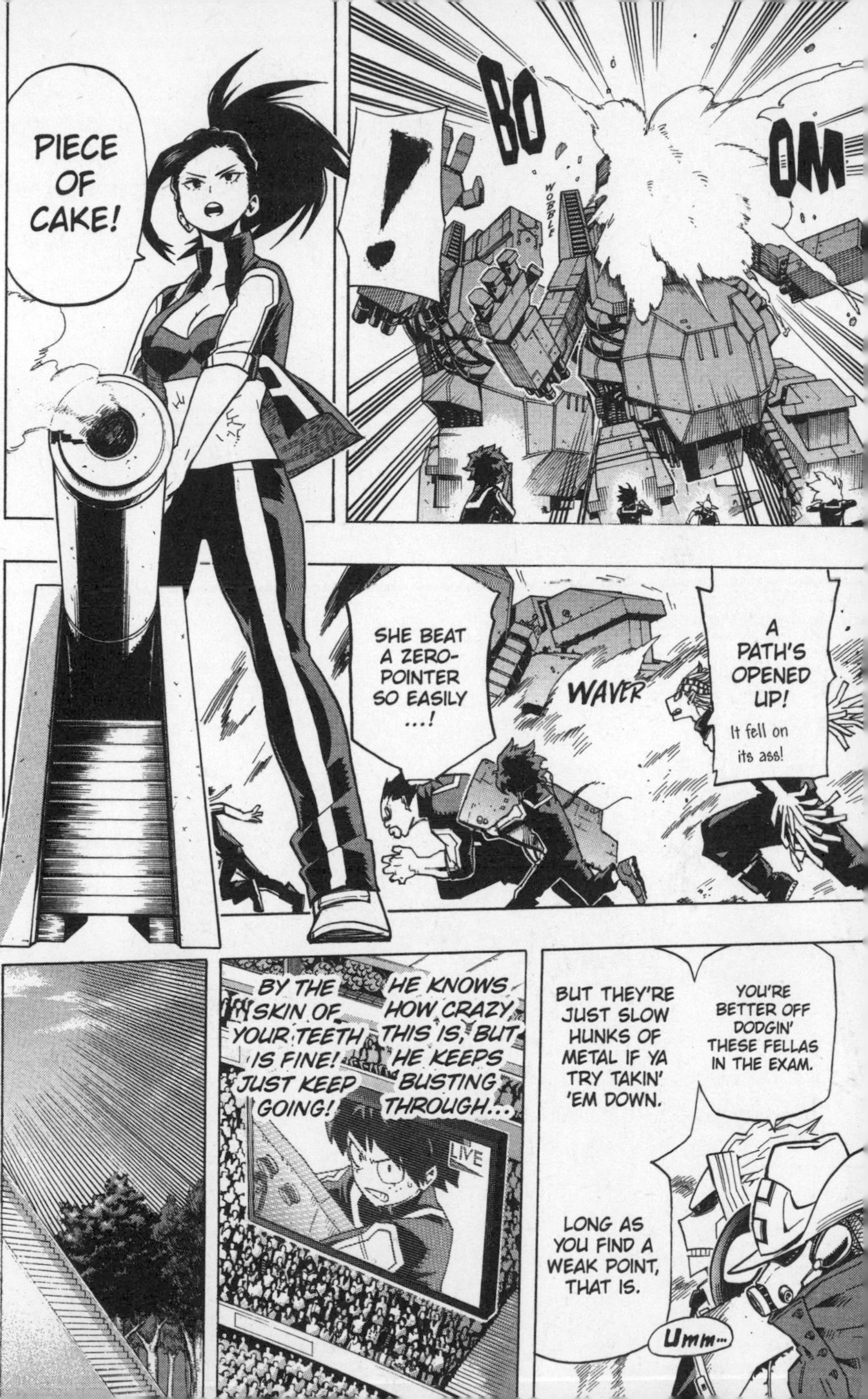
BO
OM
!
WOBBLE
A PATH'S OPENED UP!
It fell on its ass!
WAVER
SHE BEAT A ZERO-POINTER SO EASILY ...!
PIECE OF CAKE!
YOU'RE BETTER OFF DODGIN' THESE FELLAS IN THE EXAM.
BUT THEY'RE JUST SLOW HUNKS OF METAL IF YA TRY TAKIN' 'EM DOWN.
LONG AS YOU FIND A WEAK POINT, THAT IS.
Umm...
HE KNOWS HOW CRAZY THIS IS, BUT HE KEEPS BUSTING THROUGH...
BY THE SKIN OF YOUR TEETH IS FINE! JUST KEEP GOING!
LIVE

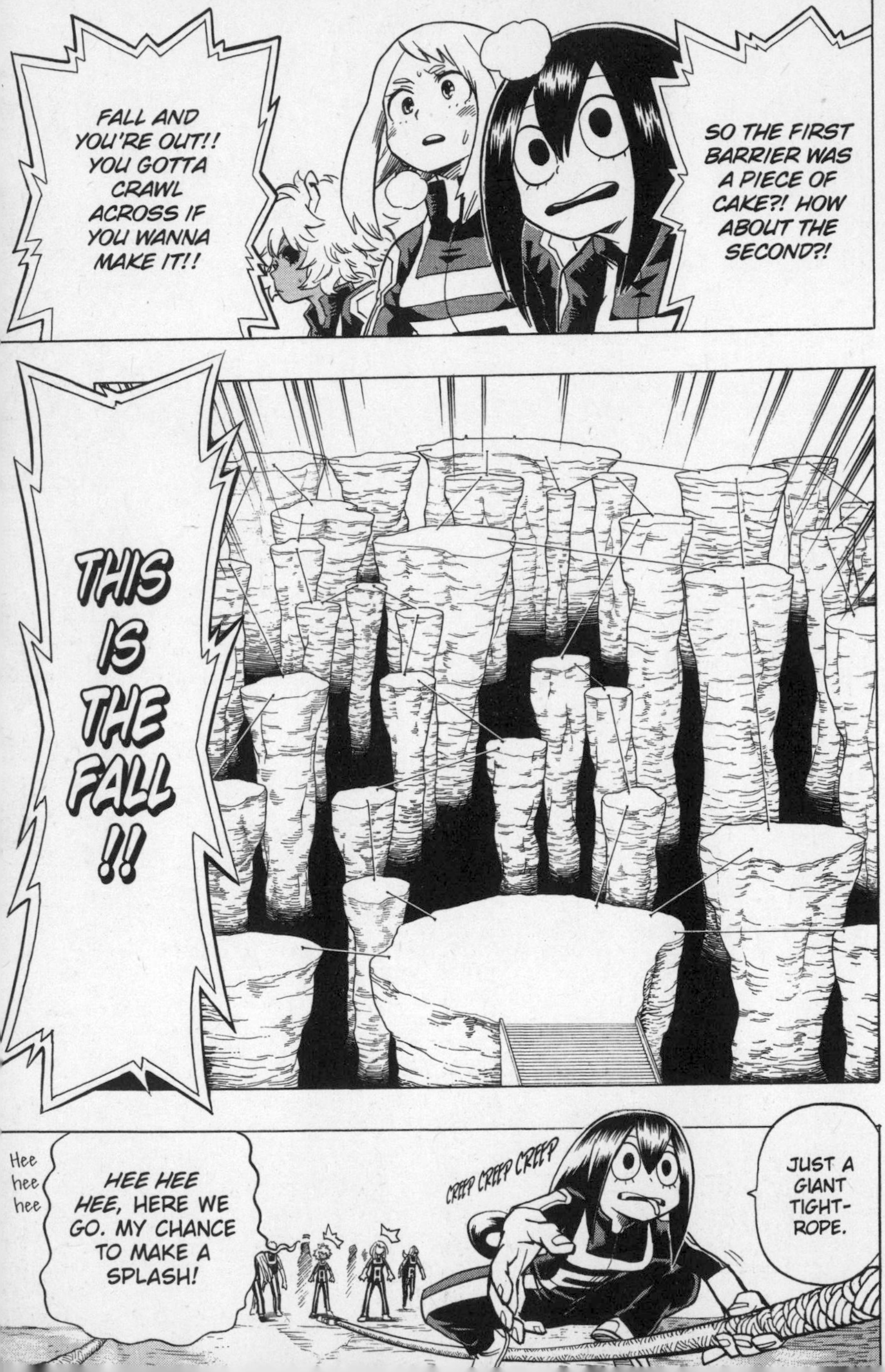
SO THE FIRST BARRIER WAS A PIECE OF CAKE?! HOW ABOUT THE SECOND?!
FALL AND YOU'RE OUT!! YOU GOTTA CRAWL ACROSS IF YOU WANNA MAKE IT!!
THIS IS THE FALL!!
JUST A GIANT TIGHT-ROPE.
CREEP CREEP CREEP
HEE HEE HEE, HERE WE GO. MY CHANCE TO MAKE A SPLASH!
Hee hee hee

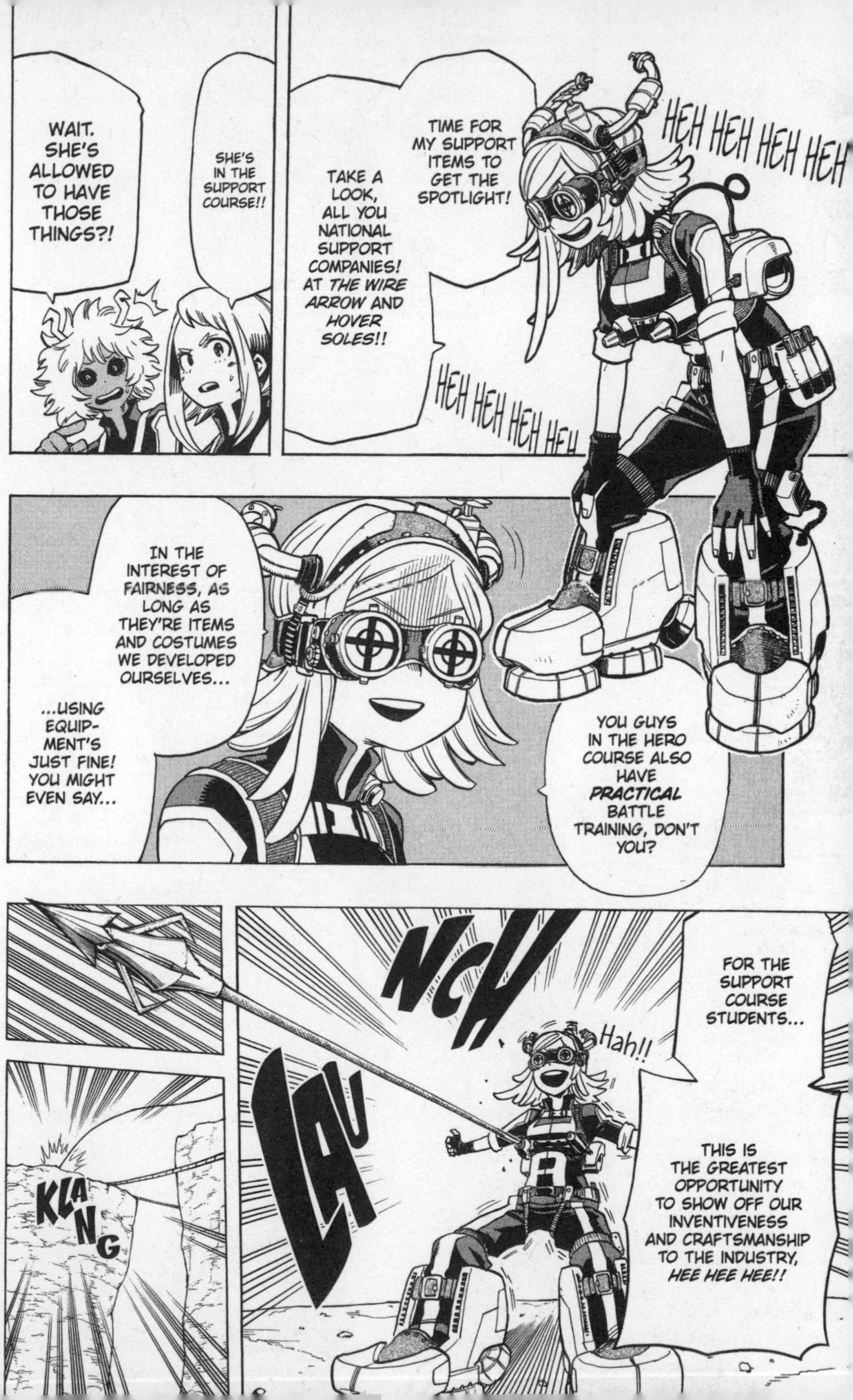
TIME FOR MY SUPPORT ITEMS TO GET THE SPOTLIGHT!
HEH HEH HEH HEH
TAKE A LOOK, ALL YOU NATIONAL SUPPORT COMPANIES! AT *THE WIRE ARROW* AND *HOVER SOLES*!!
HEH HEH HEH HEH
SHE'S IN THE SUPPORT COURSE!!
WAIT. SHE'S ALLOWED TO HAVE THOSE THINGS?!
YOU GUYS IN THE HERO COURSE ALSO HAVE ***PRACTICAL*** BATTLE TRAINING, DON'T YOU?
IN THE INTEREST OF FAIRNESS, AS LONG AS THEY'RE ITEMS AND COSTUMES WE DEVELOPED OURSELVES...
...USING EQUIPMENT'S JUST FINE! YOU MIGHT EVEN SAY...
FOR THE SUPPORT COURSE STUDENTS...
Hah!!
NCH
LAU
THIS IS THE GREATEST OPPORTUNITY TO SHOW OFF OUR INVENTIVENESS AND CRAFTSMANSHIP TO THE INDUSTRY, *HEE HEE HEE!!*
KLANG

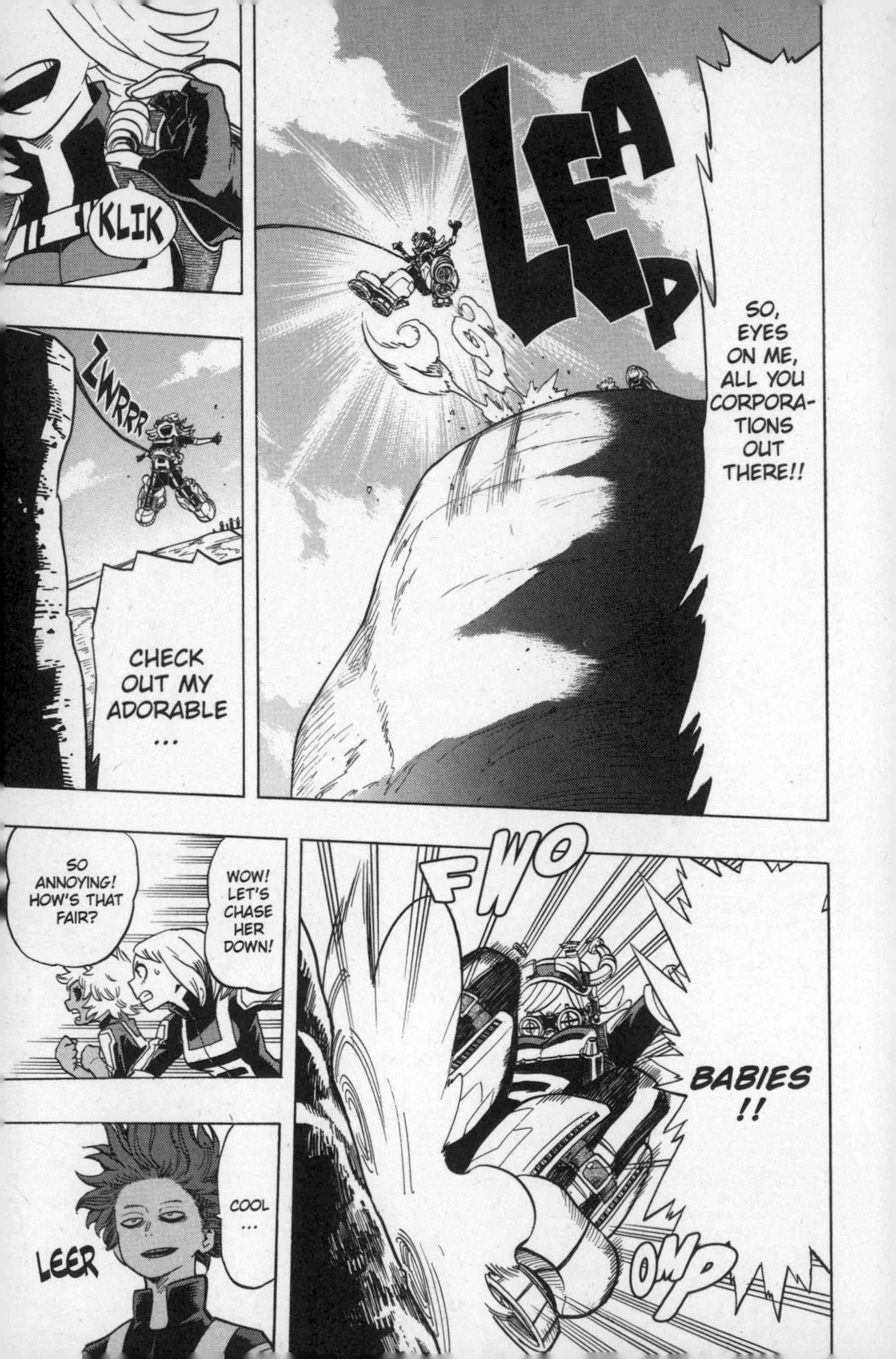
LEAP
SO, EYES ON ME, ALL YOU CORPORATIONS OUT THERE!!
KLIK
ZWRRR
CHECK OUT MY ADORABLE ...
FWO
BABIES !!
OMP
WOW! LET'S CHASE HER DOWN!
SO ANNOYING! HOW'S THAT FAIR?
COOL ...
LEER

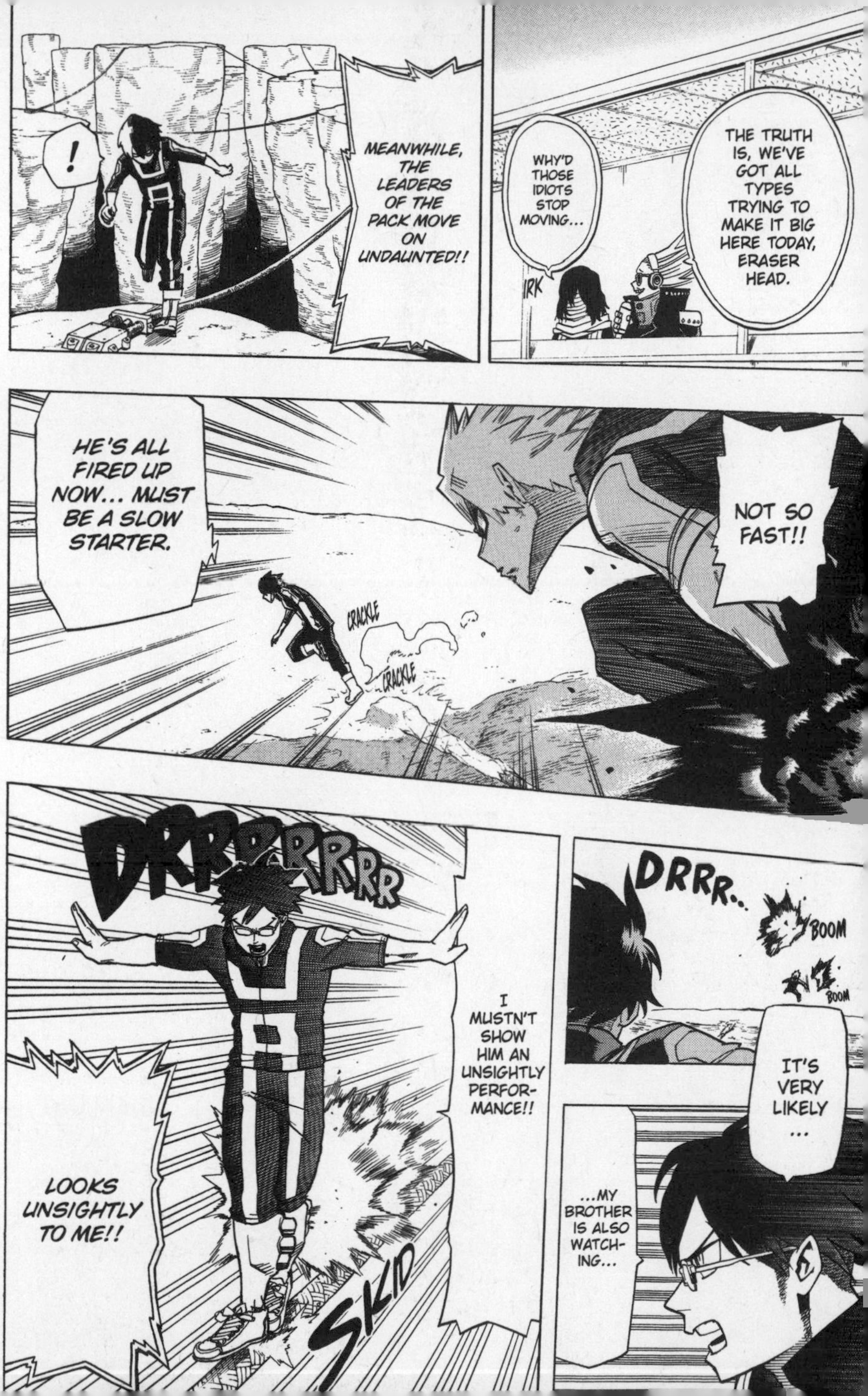
THE TRUTH IS, WE'VE GOT ALL TYPES TRYING TO MAKE IT BIG HERE TODAY, ERASER HEAD.
WHY'D THOSE IDIOTS STOP MOVING...
IRK
MEANWHILE, THE LEADERS OF THE PACK MOVE ON UNDAUNTED!!
!
NOT SO FAST!!
CRACKLE
CRACKLE
HE'S ALL FIRED UP NOW... MUST BE A SLOW STARTER.
DRRRR..
BOOM
BOOM
IT'S VERY LIKELY...
...MY BROTHER IS ALSO WATCHING...
DRRRRRRR
I MUSTN'T SHOW HIM AN UNSIGHTLY PERFORMANCE!!
LOOKS UNSIGHTLY TO ME!!
SKID

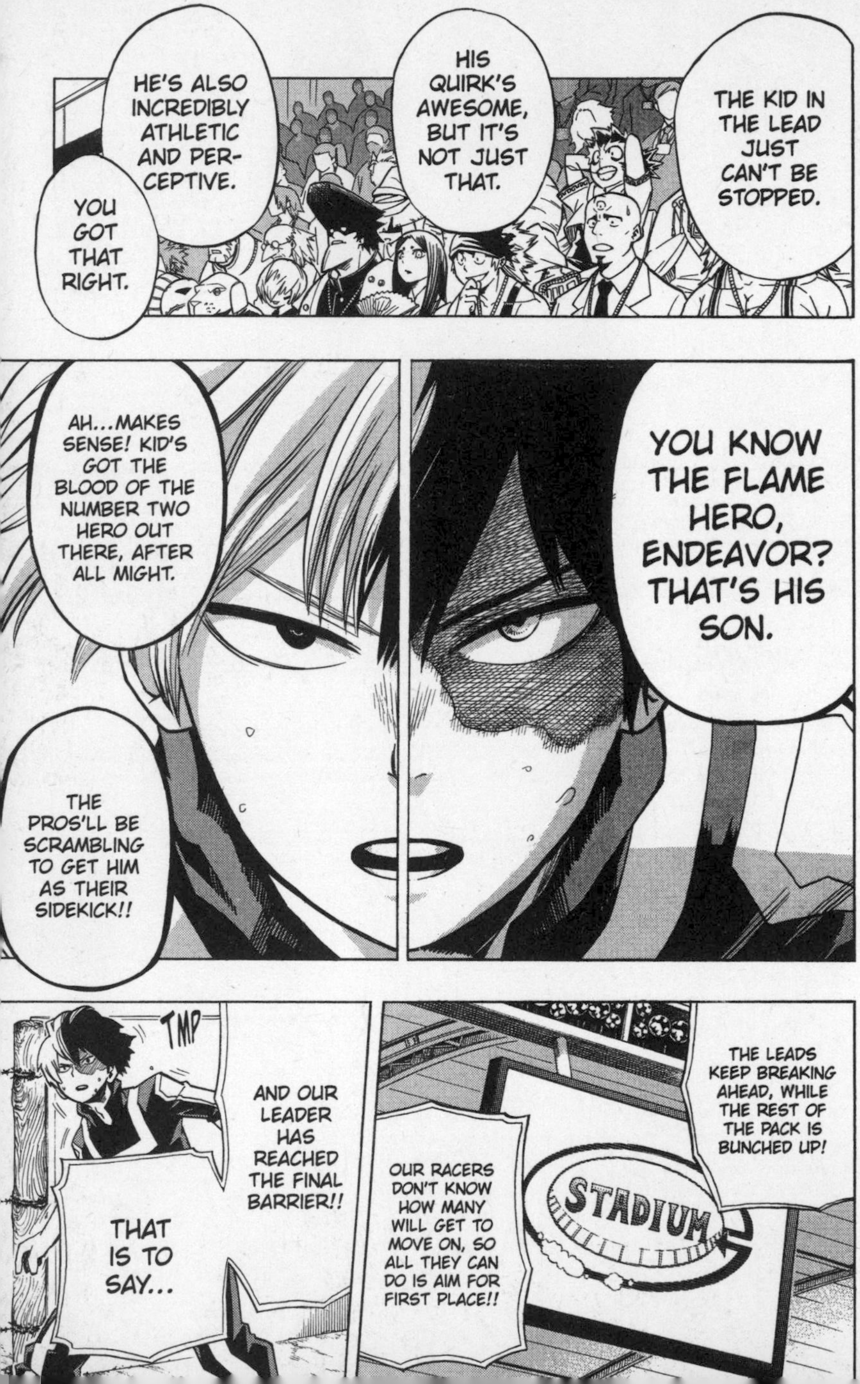
THE KID IN THE LEAD JUST CAN'T BE STOPPED.
HIS QUIRK'S AWESOME, BUT IT'S NOT JUST THAT.
HE'S ALSO INCREDIBLY ATHLETIC AND PER-CEPTIVE.
YOU GOT THAT RIGHT.
YOU KNOW THE FLAME HERO, ENDEAVOR? THAT'S HIS SON.
AH...MAKES SENSE! KID'S GOT THE BLOOD OF THE NUMBER TWO HERO OUT THERE, AFTER ALL MIGHT.
THE PROS'LL BE SCRAMBLING TO GET HIM AS THEIR SIDEKICK!!
THE LEADS KEEP BREAKING AHEAD, WHILE THE REST OF THE PACK IS BUNCHED UP!
STADIUM
OUR RACERS DON'T KNOW HOW MANY WILL GET TO MOVE ON, SO ALL THEY CAN DO IS AIM FOR FIRST PLACE!!
AND OUR LEADER HAS REACHED THE FINAL BARRIER!!
TMP
THAT IS TO SAY...

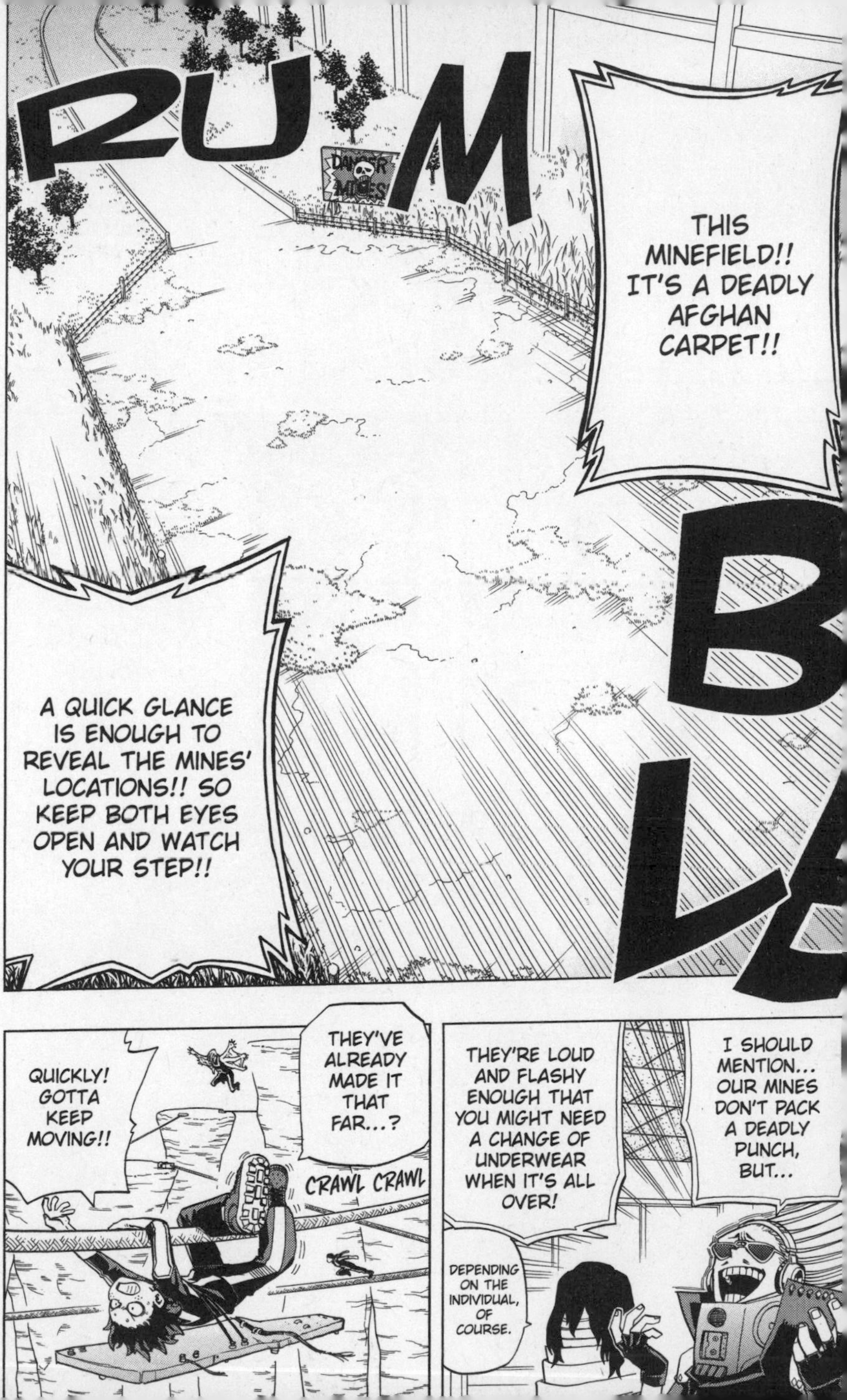

THIS MINEFIELD!! IT'S A DEADLY AFGHAN CARPET!!
RUM
A QUICK GLANCE IS ENOUGH TO REVEAL THE MINES' LOCATIONS!! SO KEEP BOTH EYES OPEN AND WATCH YOUR STEP!!
I SHOULD MENTION... OUR MINES DON'T PACK A DEADLY PUNCH, BUT...
THEY'RE LOUD AND FLASHY ENOUGH THAT YOU MIGHT NEED A CHANGE OF UNDERWEAR WHEN IT'S ALL OVER!
DEPENDING ON THE INDIVIDUAL, OF COURSE.
THEY'VE ALREADY MADE IT THAT FAR...?
QUICKLY! GOTTA KEEP MOVING!!
CRAWL CRAWL

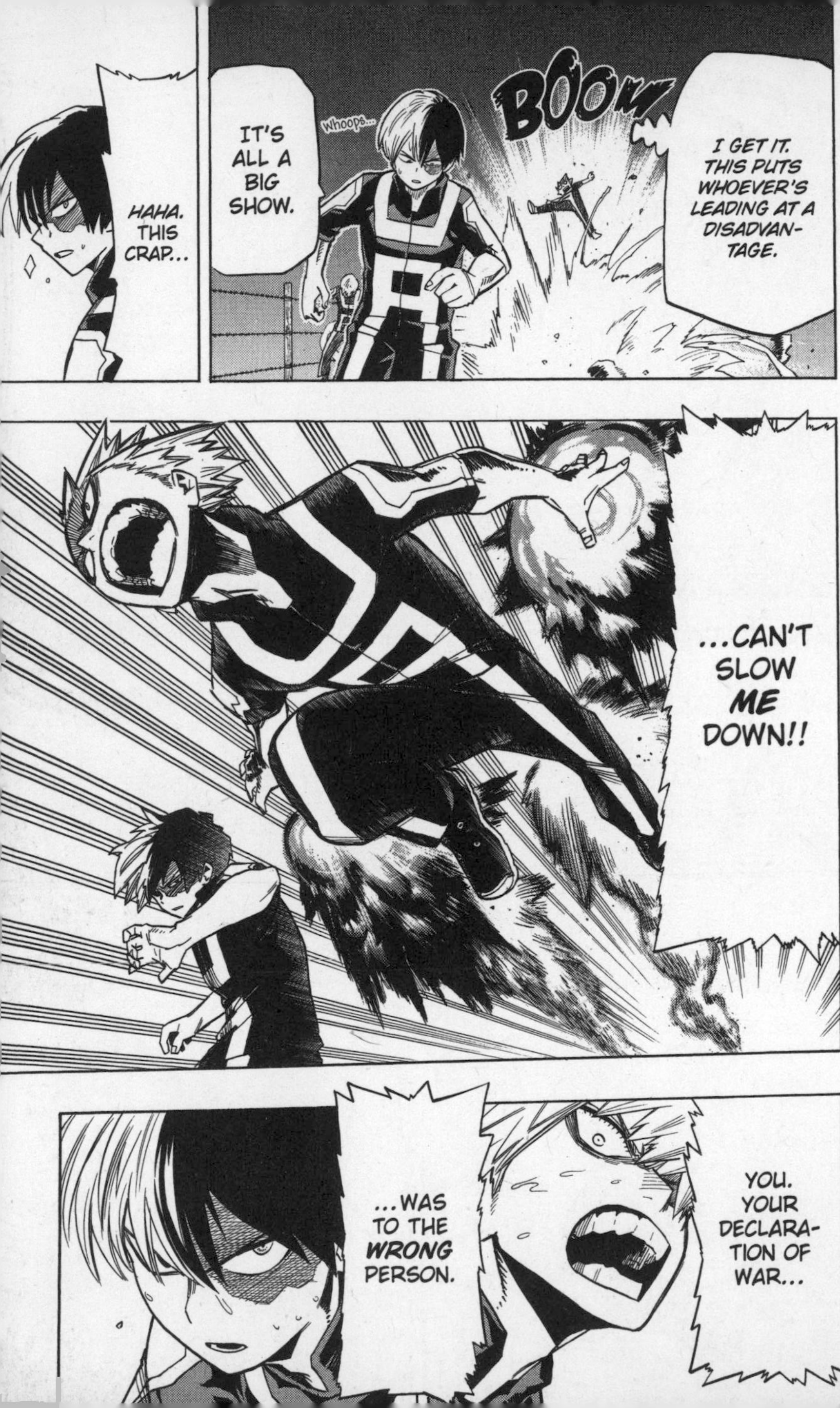
I GET IT. THIS PUTS WHOEVER'S LEADING AT A DISADVANTAGE.
BOOM
whoops...
IT'S ALL A BIG SHOW.
HAHA. THIS CRAP...
...CAN'T SLOW ME DOWN!!
YOU. YOUR DECLARATION OF WAR...
...WAS TO THE WRONG PERSON.

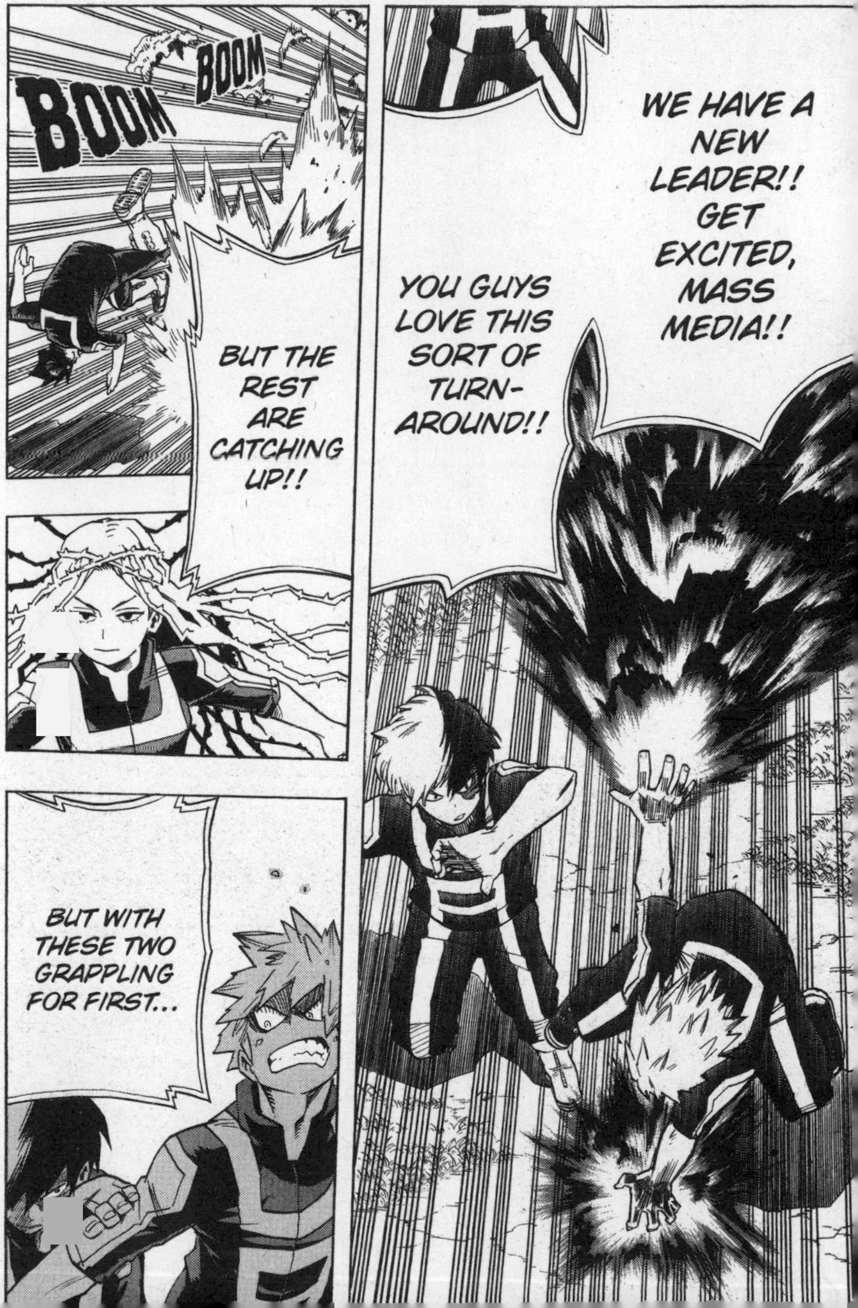
WE HAVE A NEW LEADER!! GET EXCITED, MASS MEDIA!!
YOU GUYS LOVE THIS SORT OF TURN-AROUND!!
BOOM
BOOM
BUT THE REST ARE CATCHING UP!!
BUT WITH THESE TWO GRAPPLING FOR FIRST...

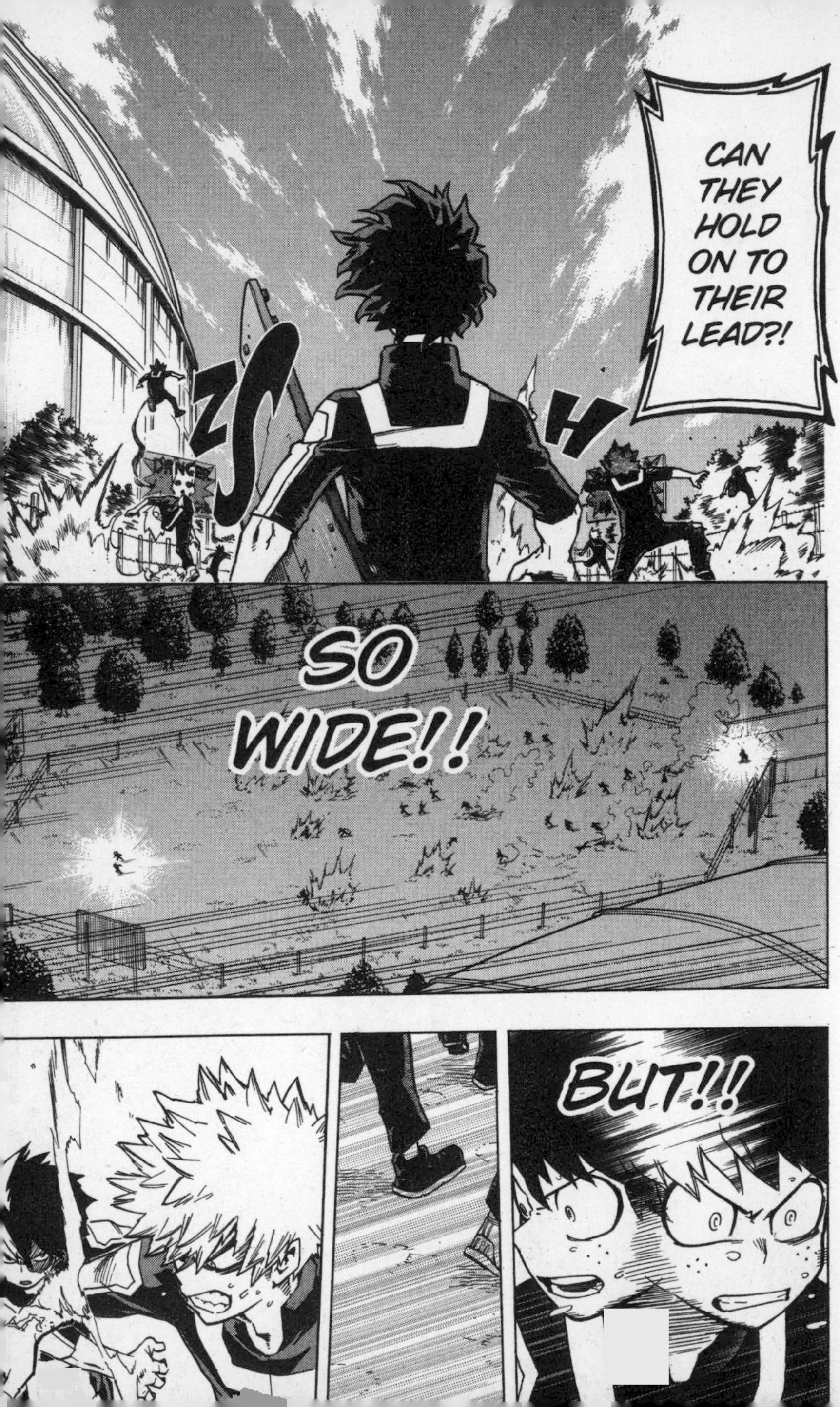
CAN THEY HOLD ON TO THEIR LEAD?!
DANGER
SO WIDE!!
BUT!!

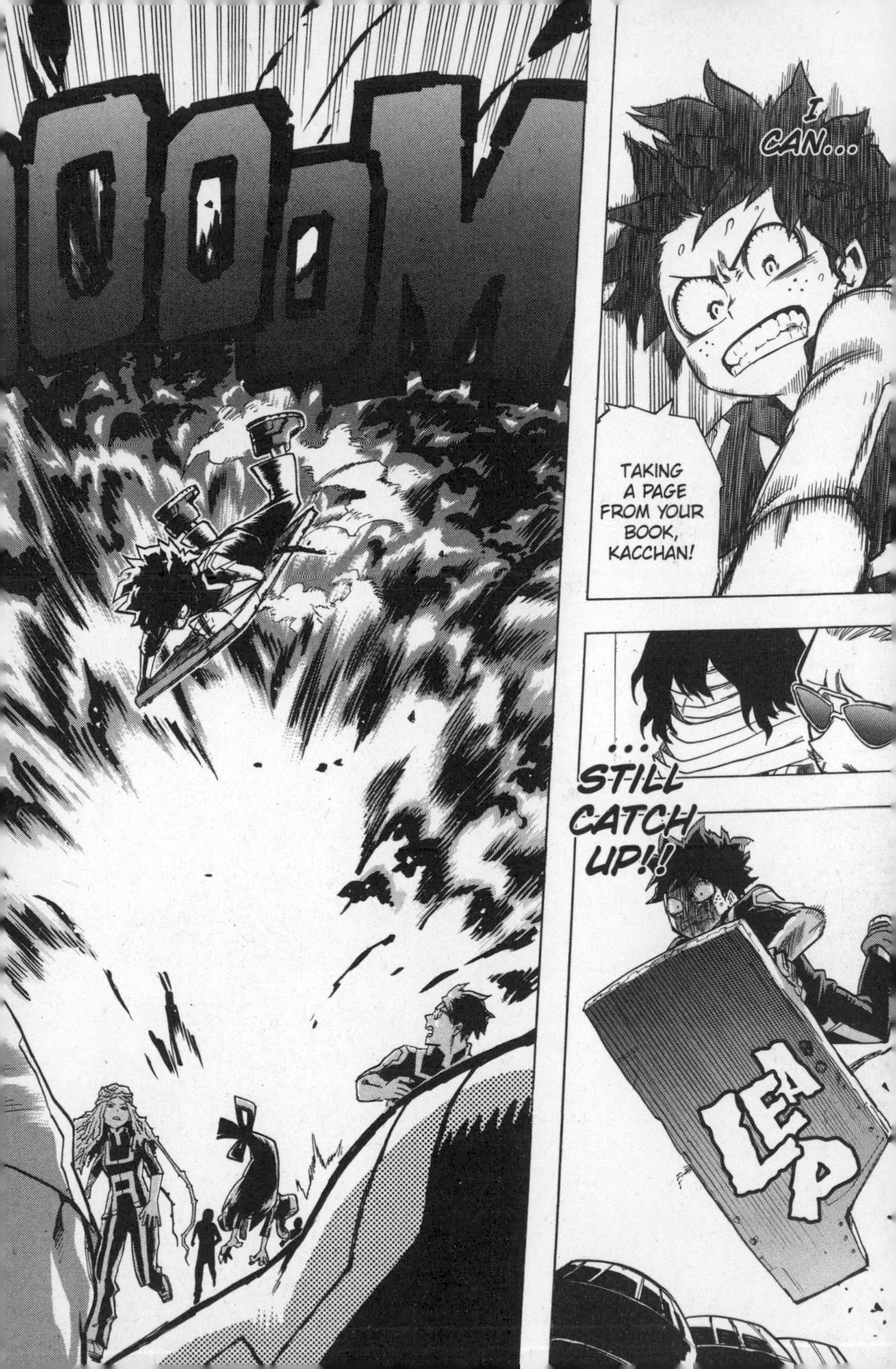
I CAN...
TAKING A PAGE FROM YOUR BOOK, KACCHAN!
...STILL CATCH UP!!
LEAP
OOOM

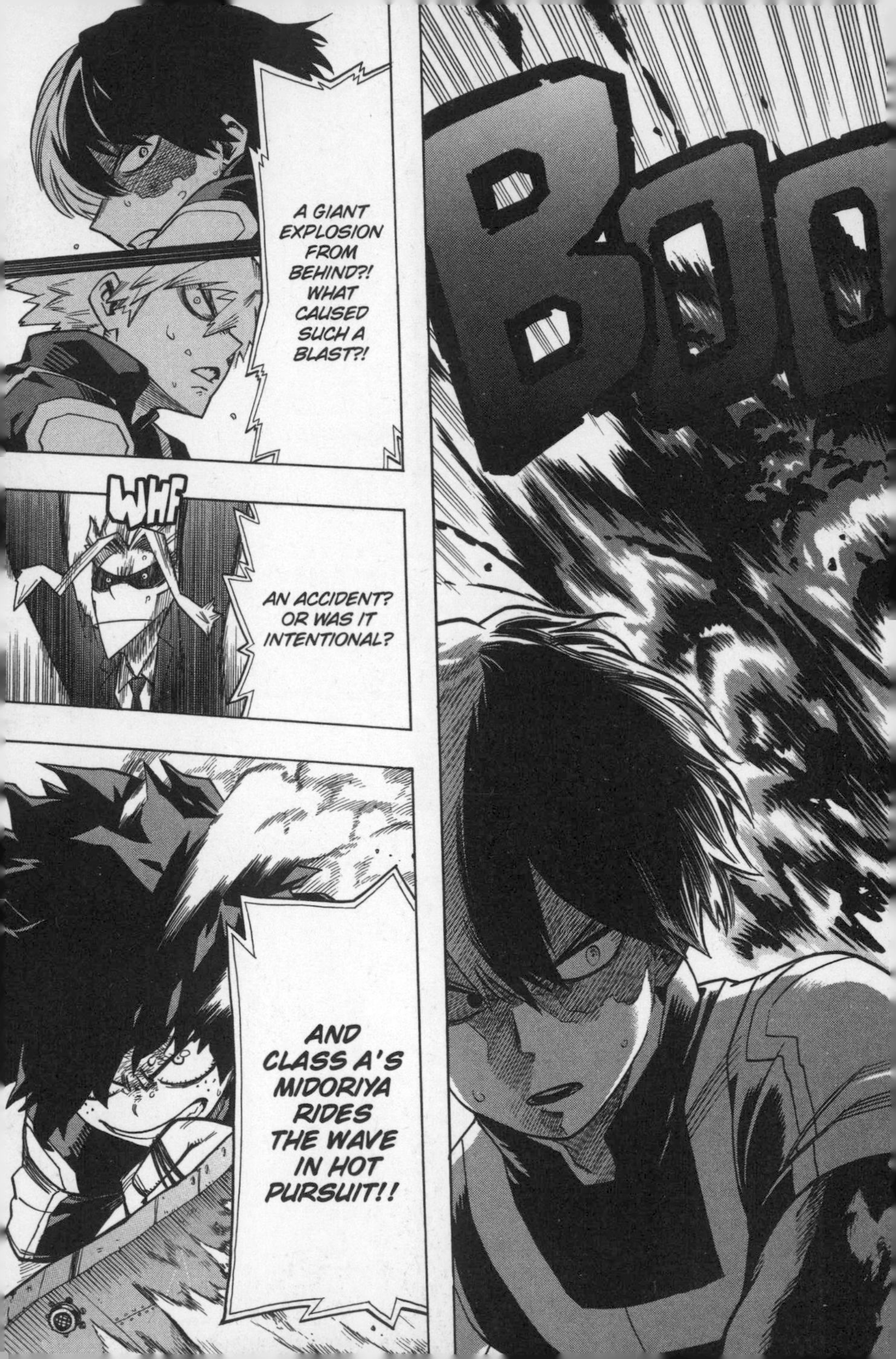
BOO
A GIANT EXPLOSION FROM BEHIND?! WHAT CAUSED SUCH A BLAST?!
WHF
AN ACCIDENT? OR WAS IT INTENTIONAL?
AND CLASS A'S MIDORIYA RIDES THE WAVE IN HOT PURSUIT!!

STREET CLOTHES

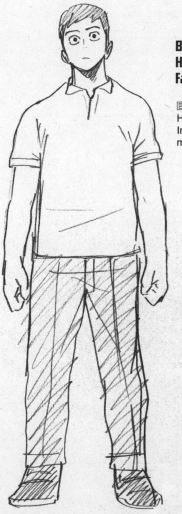

Birthday: 4/4
Height: 180 cm
Favorite Thing: Baseball

BEHIND THE SCENES
He's with the police.
In retrospect, I kind of wish I'd
made him more hard-boiled.

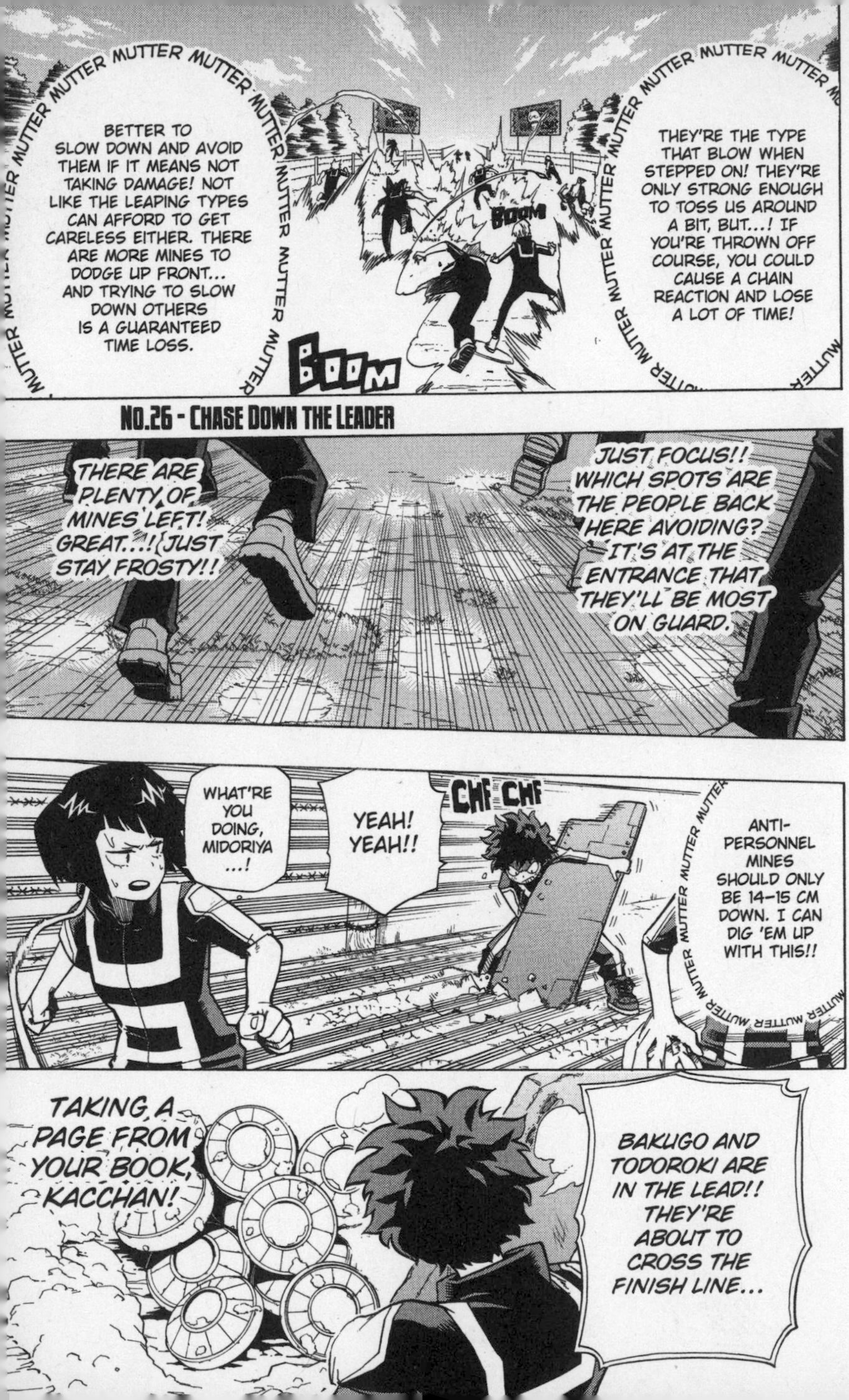
MUTTER MUTTER MUTTER MUTTER MUTTER
THEY'RE THE TYPE THAT BLOW WHEN STEPPED ON! THEY'RE ONLY STRONG ENOUGH TO TOSS US AROUND A BIT, BUT...! IF YOU'RE THROWN OFF COURSE, YOU COULD CAUSE A CHAIN REACTION AND LOSE A LOT OF TIME!
BOOM
MUTTER MUTTER MUTTER MUTTER MUTTER MUTTER
BETTER TO SLOW DOWN AND AVOID THEM IF IT MEANS NOT TAKING DAMAGE! NOT LIKE THE LEAPING TYPES CAN AFFORD TO GET CARELESS EITHER. THERE ARE MORE MINES TO DODGE UP FRONT... AND TRYING TO SLOW DOWN OTHERS IS A GUARANTEED TIME LOSS.
BOOM
No.26 - Chase Down the Leader
JUST FOCUS!! WHICH SPOTS ARE THE PEOPLE BACK HERE AVOIDING? IT'S AT THE ENTRANCE THAT THEY'LL BE MOST ON GUARD.
THERE ARE PLENTY OF MINES LEFT! GREAT...! JUST STAY FROSTY!!
MUTTER MUTTER MUTTER MUTTER
ANTI-PERSONNEL MINES SHOULD ONLY BE 14-15 CM DOWN. I CAN DIG 'EM UP WITH THIS!!
CHF CHF
YEAH! YEAH!!
WHAT'RE YOU DOING, MIDORIYA...!
BAKUGO AND TODOROKI ARE IN THE LEAD!! THEY'RE ABOUT TO CROSS THE FINISH LINE...
TAKING A PAGE FROM YOUR BOOK, KACCHAN!

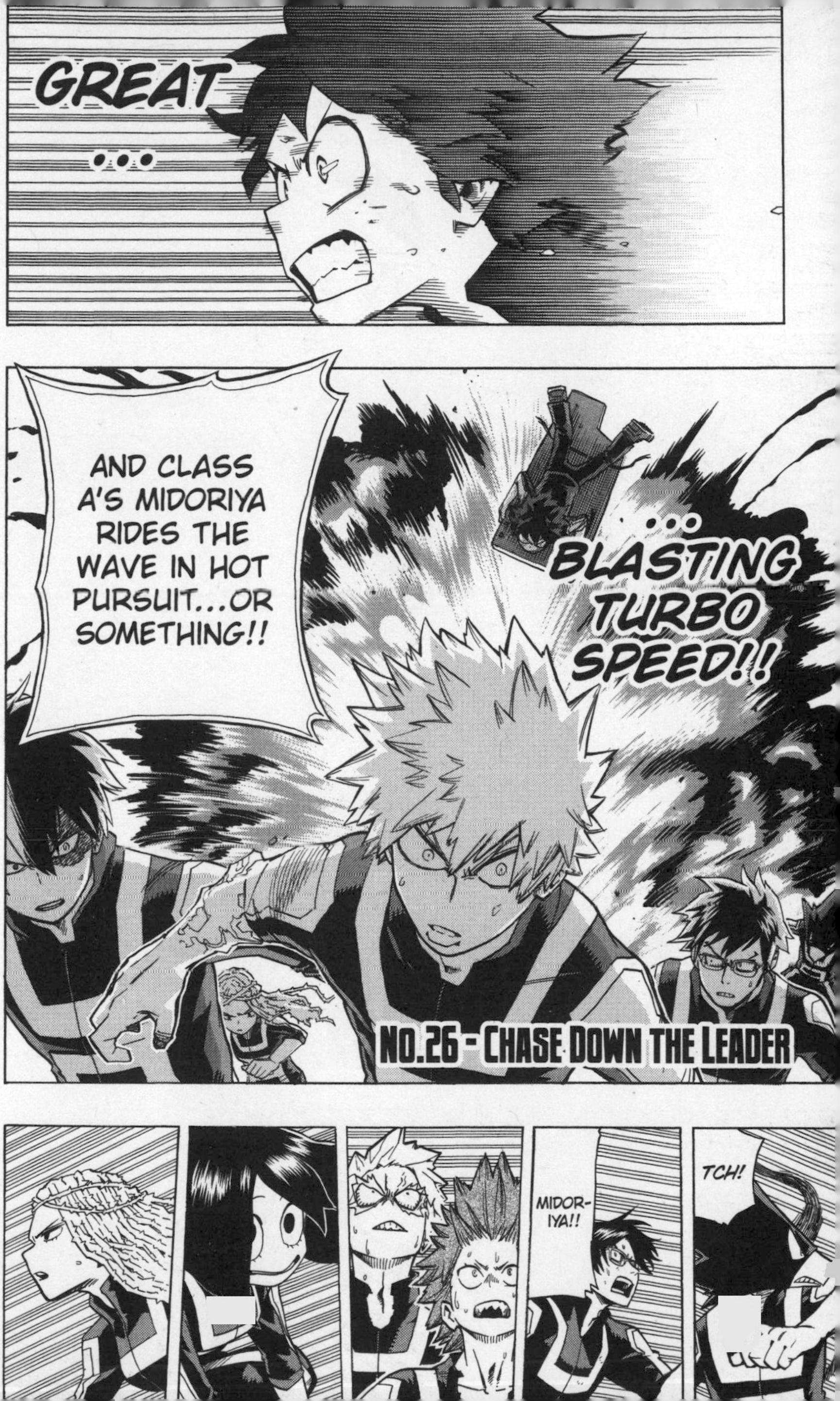
GREAT
...
...BLASTING TURBO SPEED!!
AND CLASS A'S MIDORIYA RIDES THE WAVE IN HOT PURSUIT...OR SOMETHING!!
No.26 - Chase Down the Leader
TCH!
MIDOR-IYA!!

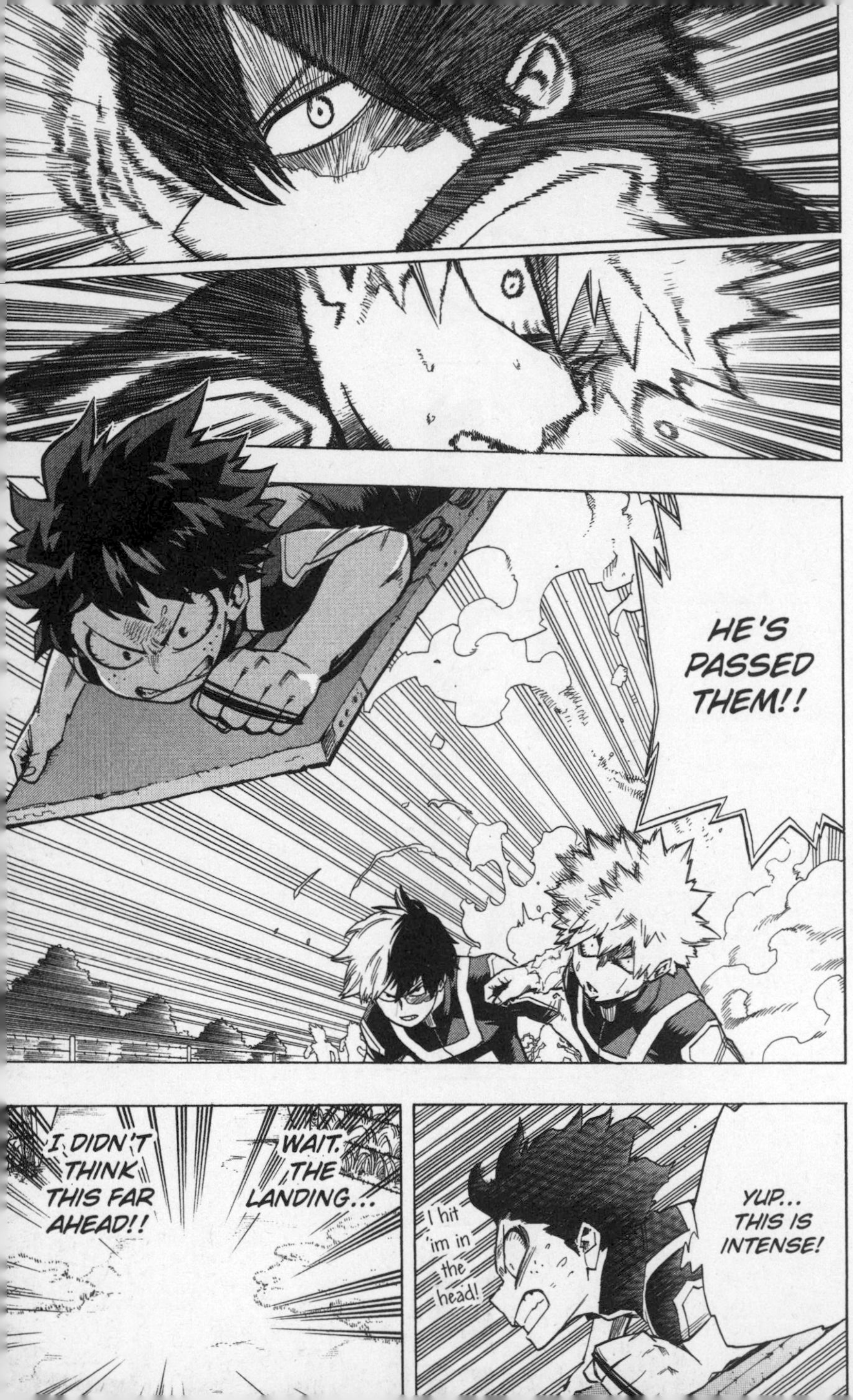
HE'S PASSED THEM!!
YUP... THIS IS INTENSE!
I hit 'im in the head!
WAIT. THE LANDING...
I DIDN'T THINK THIS FAR AHEAD!!

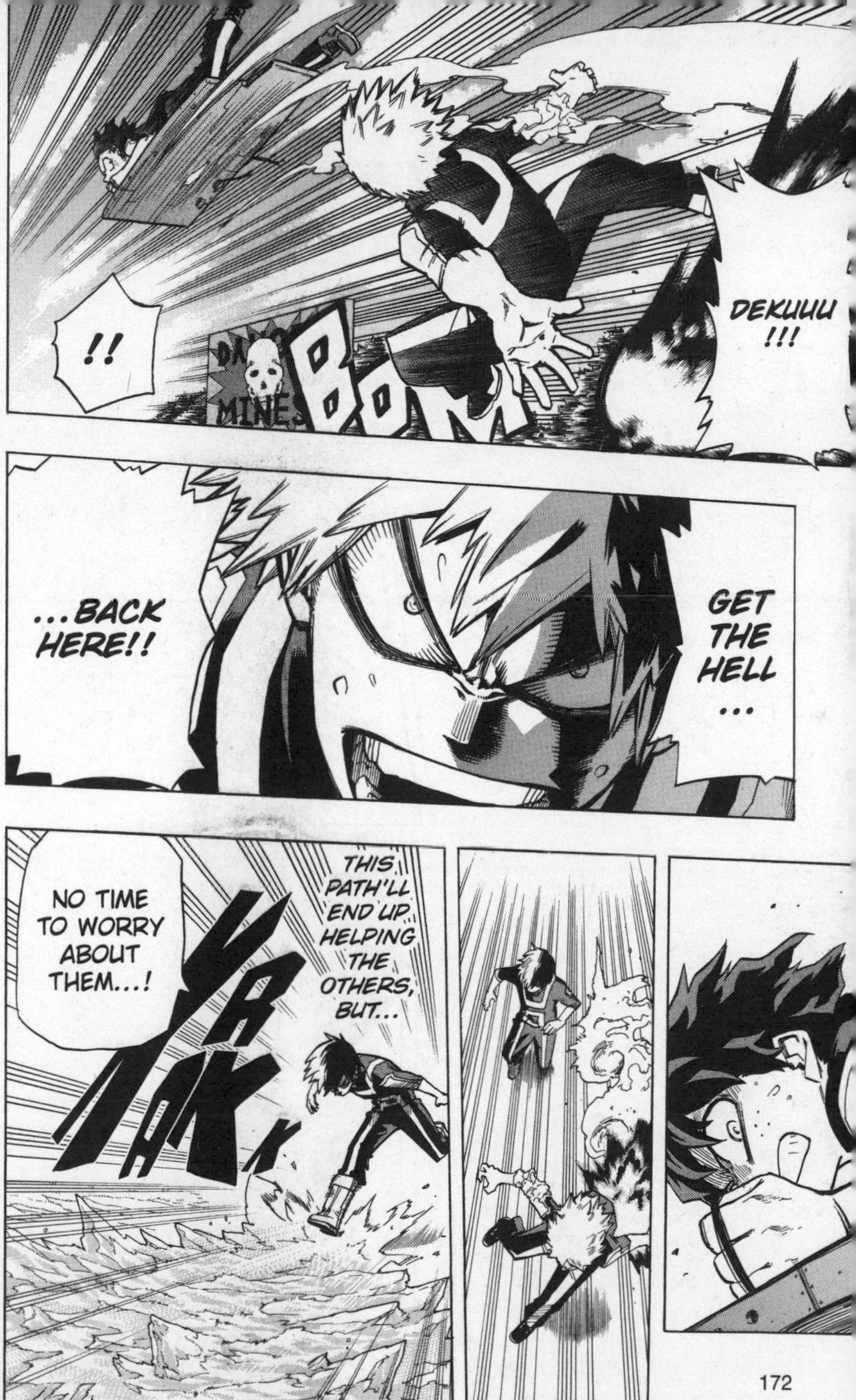
DEKUUU!!!
!!
BOOM
MINES
GET THE HELL...
...BACK HERE!!
THIS PATH'LL END UP HELPING THE OTHERS, BUT...
NO TIME TO WORRY ABOUT THEM...!

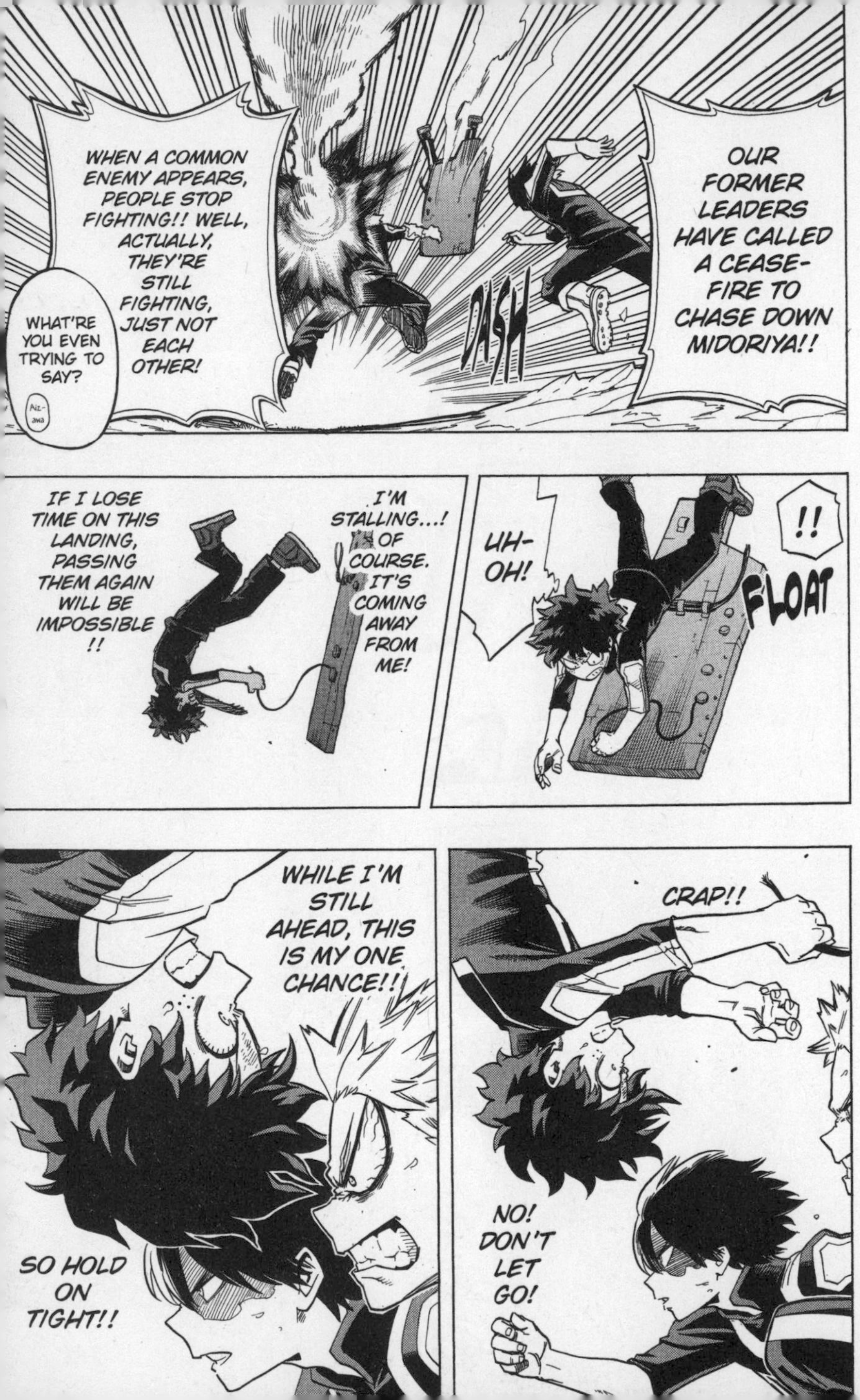
OUR FORMER LEADERS HAVE CALLED A CEASE-FIRE TO CHASE DOWN MIDORIYA!!
DASH
WHEN A COMMON ENEMY APPEARS, PEOPLE STOP FIGHTING!! WELL, ACTUALLY, THEY'RE STILL FIGHTING, JUST NOT EACH OTHER!
WHAT'RE YOU EVEN TRYING TO SAY?
Aiz-awa
!!
FLOAT
UH-OH!
I'M STALLING...! OF COURSE. IT'S COMING AWAY FROM ME!
IF I LOSE TIME ON THIS LANDING, PASSING THEM AGAIN WILL BE IMPOSSIBLE!!
CRAP!!
NO! DON'T LET GO!
WHILE I'M STILL AHEAD, THIS IS MY ONE CHANCE!!
SO HOLD ON TIGHT!!

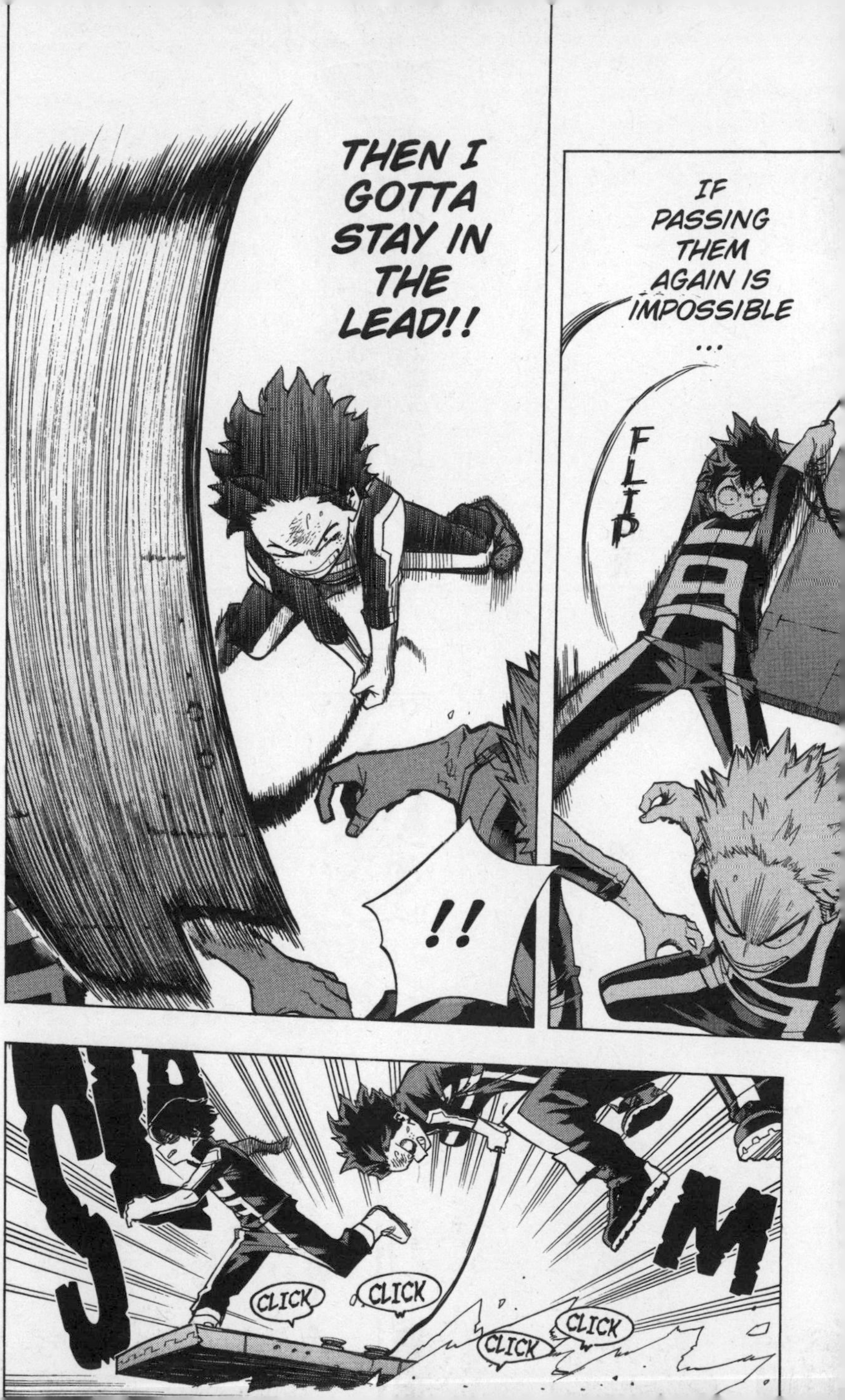
IF PASSING THEM AGAIN IS IMPOSSIBLE...
FLIP
THEN I GOTTA STAY IN THE LEAD!!
!!
SLAM
CLICK
CLICK
CLICK
CLICK

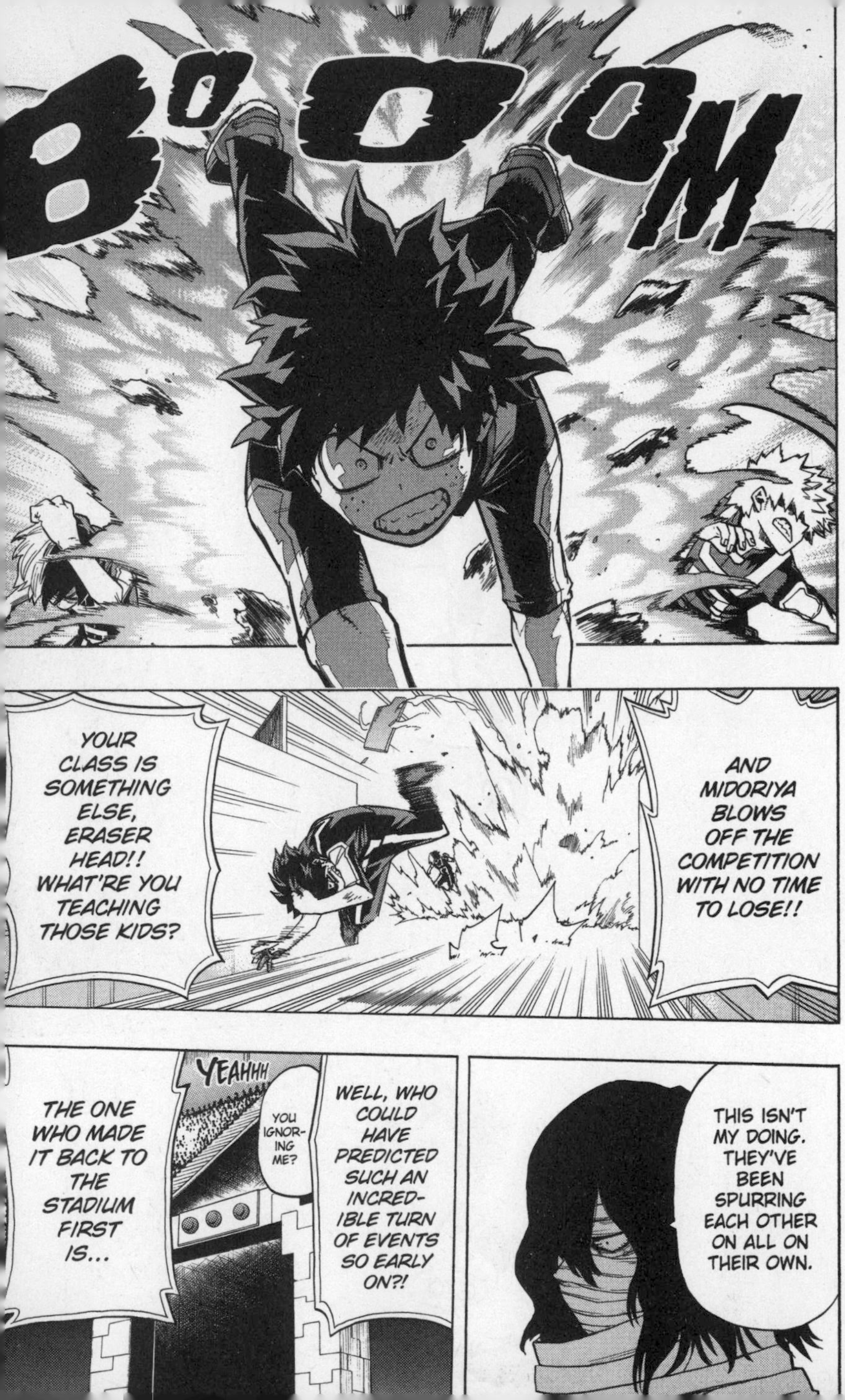
BOOOM
AND MIDORIYA BLOWS OFF THE COMPETITION WITH NO TIME TO LOSE!!
YOUR CLASS IS SOMETHING ELSE, ERASER HEAD!! WHAT'RE YOU TEACHING THOSE KIDS?
THIS ISN'T MY DOING. THEY'VE BEEN SPURRING EACH OTHER ON ALL ON THEIR OWN.
WELL, WHO COULD HAVE PREDICTED SUCH AN INCREDIBLE TURN OF EVENTS SO EARLY ON?!
YOU IGNORING ME?
YEAHHH
THE ONE WHO MADE IT BACK TO THE STADIUM FIRST IS...

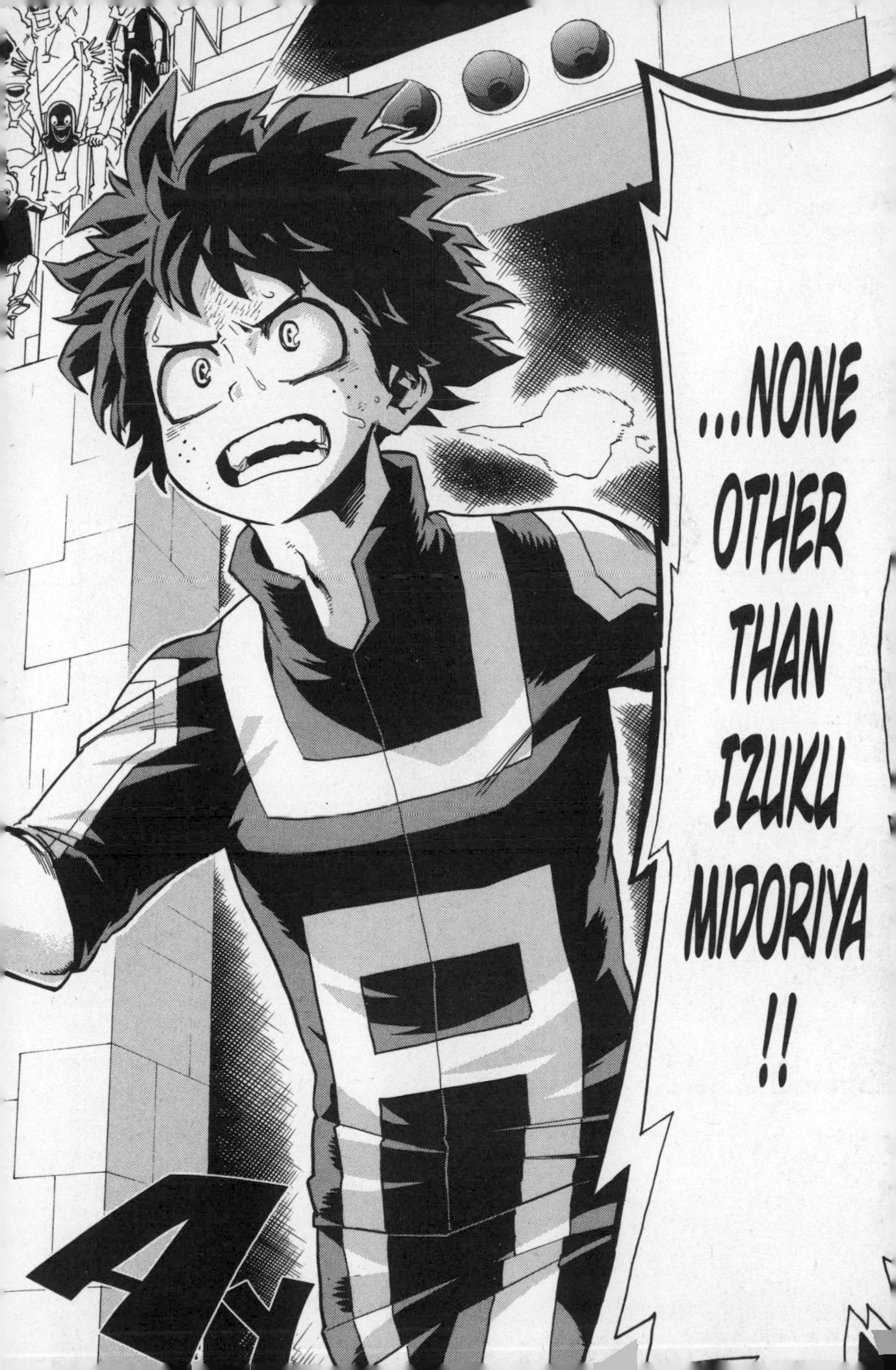
...NONE OTHER THAN IZUKU MIDORIYA !!

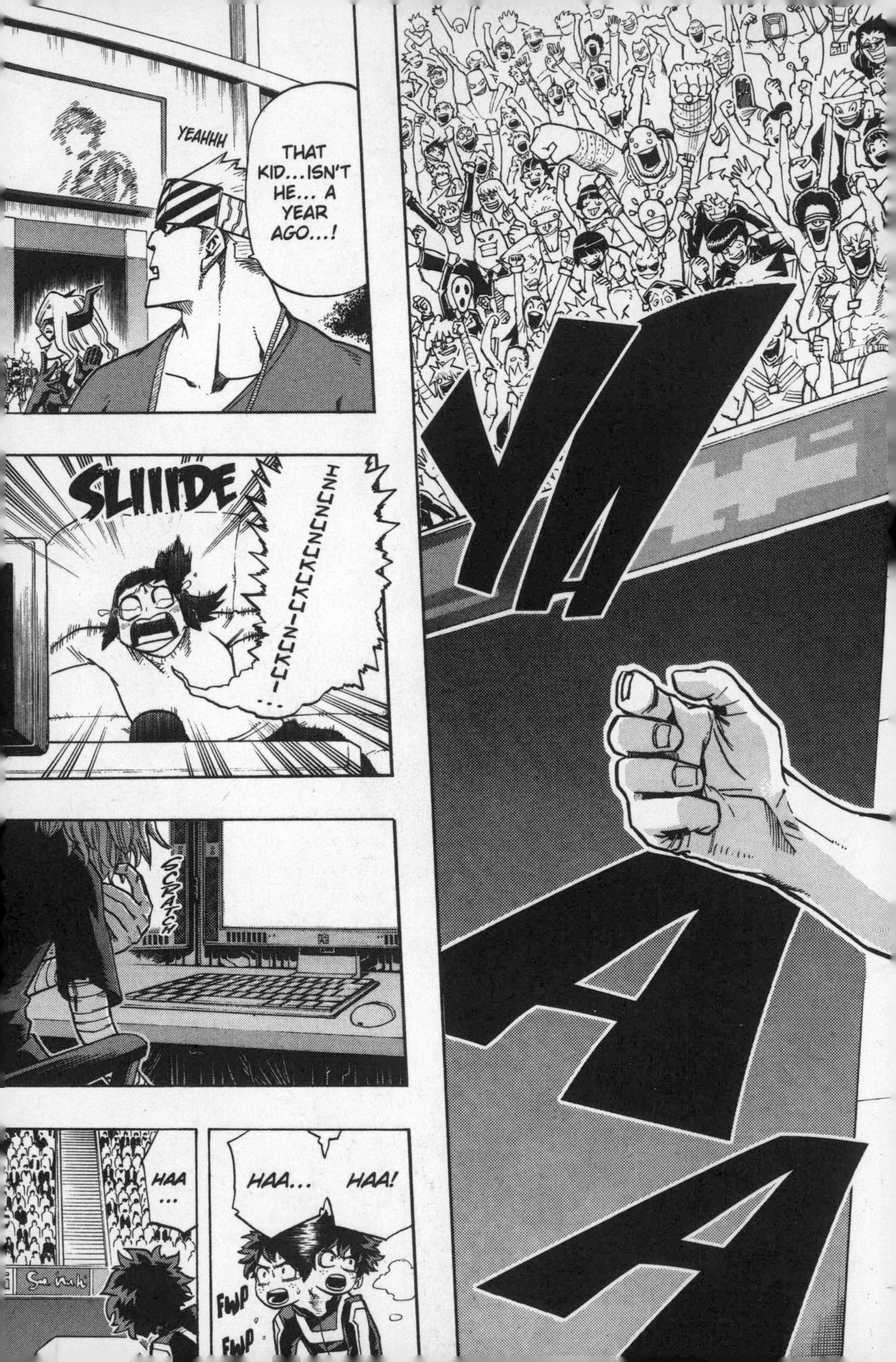
YAAA
YEAHHH
THAT KID...ISN'T HE... A YEAR AGO...!
SLIIIDE
IZUZUZUKUKUZU-KUZU-KU-...
SCRATCH
HAA... HAA!
FWP
FWP
HAA ...

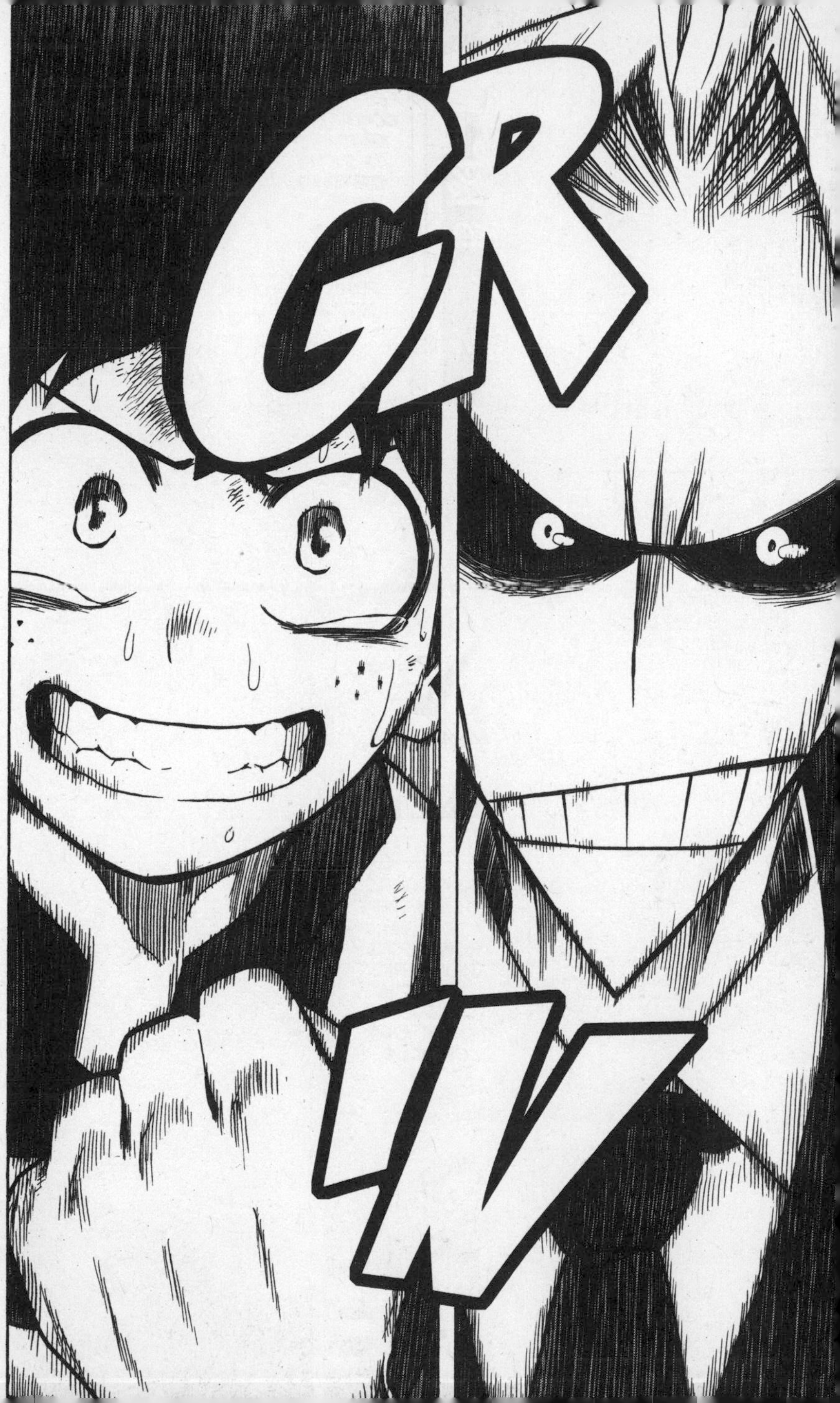
GRIN

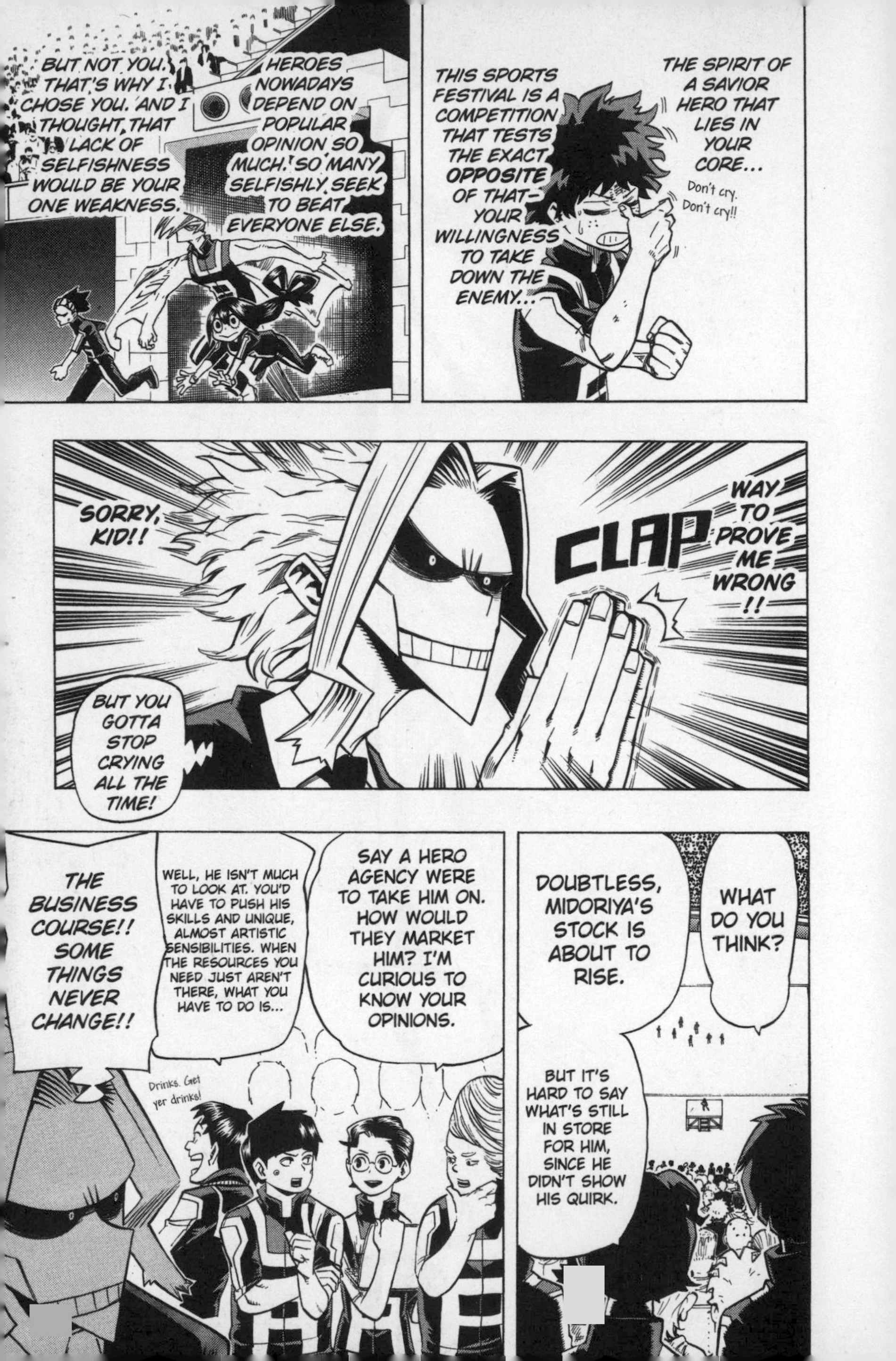
THE SPIRIT OF A SAVIOR HERO THAT LIES IN YOUR CORE...
Don't cry. Don't cry!!
THIS SPORTS FESTIVAL IS A COMPETITION THAT TESTS THE EXACT OPPOSITE OF THAT— YOUR WILLINGNESS TO TAKE DOWN THE ENEMY...
HEROES NOWADAYS DEPEND ON POPULAR OPINION SO MUCH. SO MANY SELFISHLY SEEK TO BEAT EVERYONE ELSE.
BUT NOT YOU. THAT'S WHY I CHOSE YOU. AND I THOUGHT THAT LACK OF SELFISHNESS WOULD BE YOUR ONE WEAKNESS.
WAY TO PROVE ME WRONG!!
CLAP
SORRY, KID!!
BUT YOU GOTTA STOP CRYING ALL THE TIME!
WHAT DO YOU THINK?
DOUBTLESS, MIDORIYA'S STOCK IS ABOUT TO RISE.
BUT IT'S HARD TO SAY WHAT'S STILL IN STORE FOR HIM, SINCE HE DIDN'T SHOW HIS QUIRK.
SAY A HERO AGENCY WERE TO TAKE HIM ON. HOW WOULD THEY MARKET HIM? I'M CURIOUS TO KNOW YOUR OPINIONS.
WELL, HE ISN'T MUCH TO LOOK AT. YOU'D HAVE TO PUSH HIS SKILLS AND UNIQUE, ALMOST ARTISTIC SENSIBILITIES. WHEN THE RESOURCES YOU NEED JUST AREN'T THERE, WHAT YOU HAVE TO DO IS...
THE BUSINESS COURSE!! SOME THINGS NEVER CHANGE!!
Drinks. Get yer drinks!

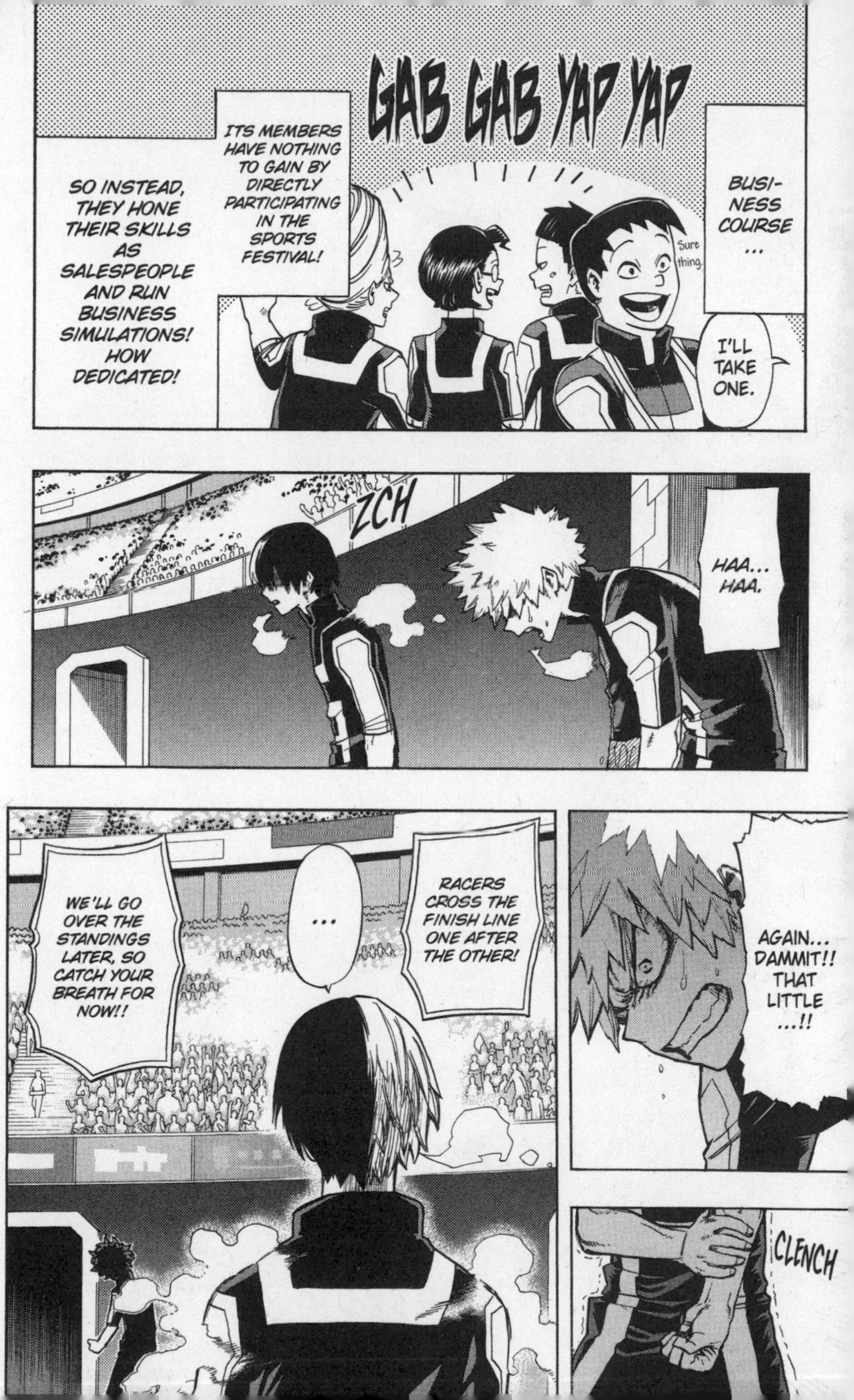
BUSI-NESS COURSE ...
Sure thing.
I'LL TAKE ONE.
GAB GAB YAP YAP
ITS MEMBERS HAVE NOTHING TO GAIN BY DIRECTLY PARTICIPATING IN THE SPORTS FESTIVAL!
SO INSTEAD, THEY HONE THEIR SKILLS AS SALESPEOPLE AND RUN BUSINESS SIMULATIONS! HOW DEDICATED!
HAA... HAA.
ZCH
AGAIN... DAMMIT!! THAT LITTLE ...!!
CLENCH
RACERS CROSS THE FINISH LINE ONE AFTER THE OTHER!
...
WE'LL GO OVER THE STANDINGS LATER, SO CATCH YOUR BREATH FOR NOW!!

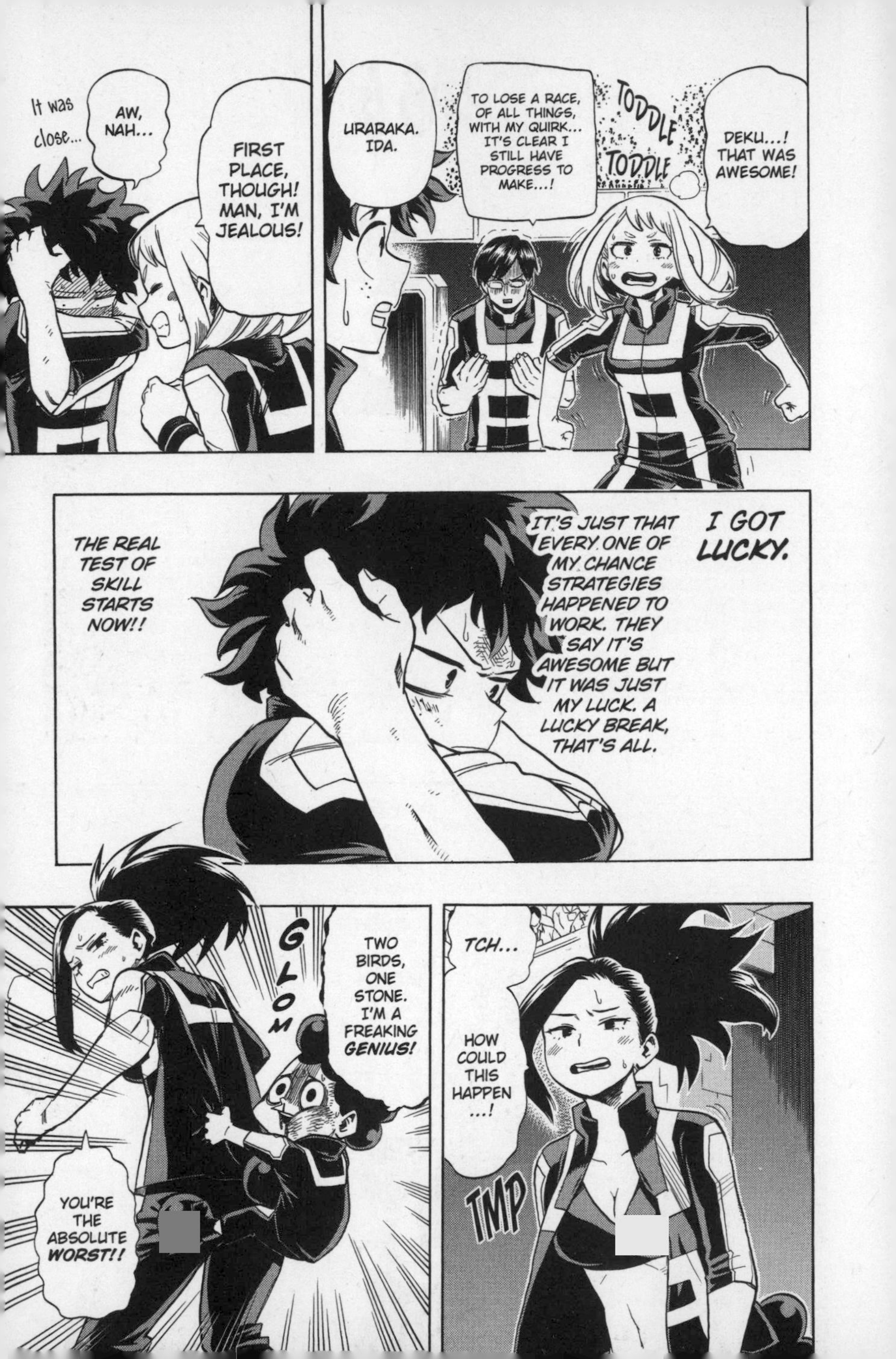
DEKU...! THAT WAS AWESOME!
TODDLE TODDLE
TO LOSE A RACE, OF ALL THINGS, WITH MY QUIRK... IT'S CLEAR I STILL HAVE PROGRESS TO MAKE...!
URARAKA. IDA.
FIRST PLACE, THOUGH! MAN, I'M JEALOUS!
AW, NAH...
It was close...
I GOT LUCKY.
IT'S JUST THAT EVERY ONE OF MY CHANCE STRATEGIES HAPPENED TO WORK. THEY SAY IT'S AWESOME BUT IT WAS JUST MY LUCK. A LUCKY BREAK, THAT'S ALL.
THE REAL TEST OF SKILL STARTS NOW!!
TCH...
HOW COULD THIS HAPPEN...!
TMP
TWO BIRDS, ONE STONE. I'M A FREAKING GENIUS!
GLOM
YOU'RE THE ABSOLUTE WORST!!

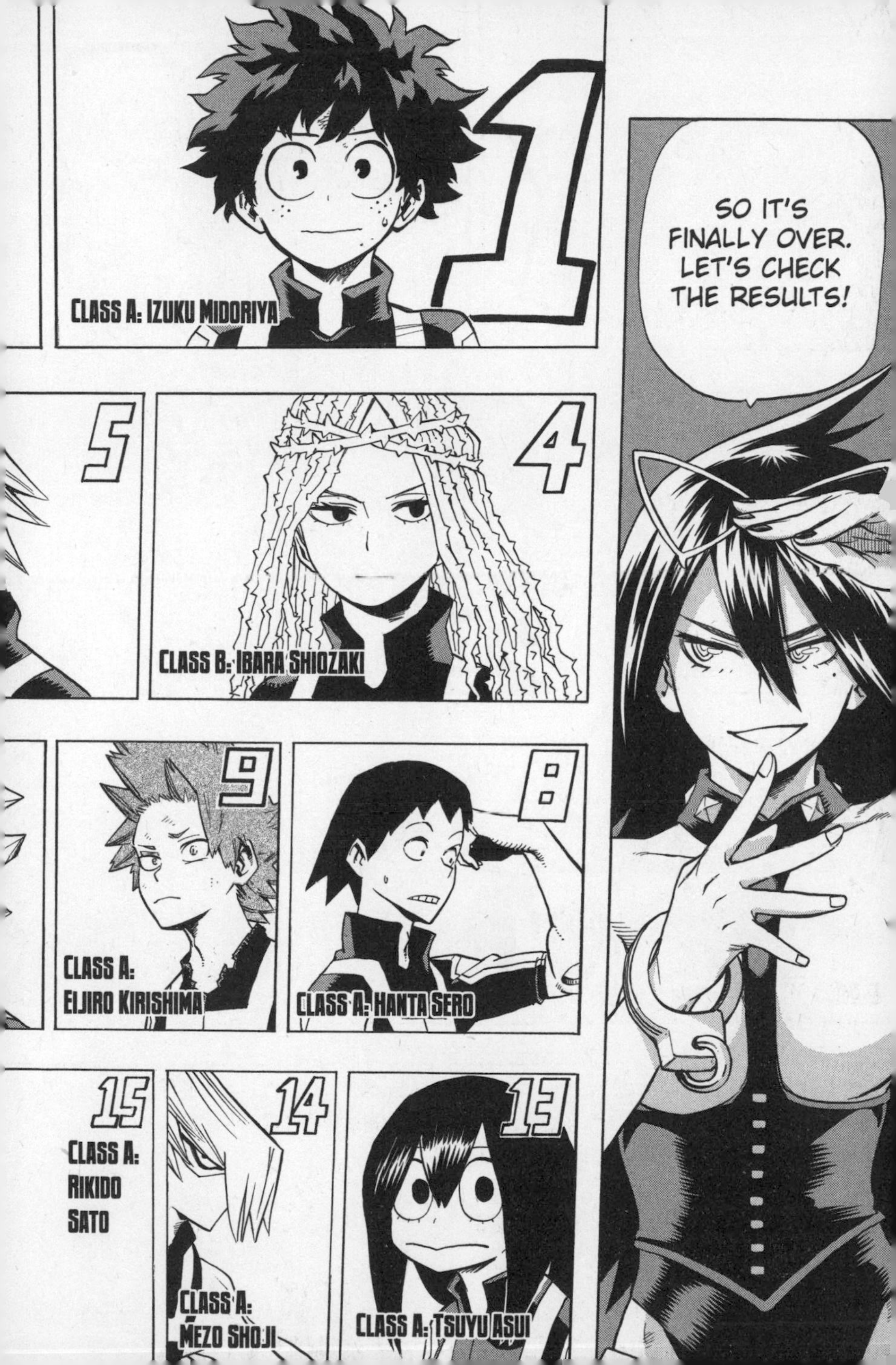
SO IT'S FINALLY OVER. LET'S CHECK THE RESULTS!
1
CLASS A: IZUKU MIDORIYA
4
CLASS B: IBARA SHIOZAKI
5
8
CLASS A: HANTA SERO
9
CLASS A: EIJIRO KIRISHIMA
13
CLASS A: TSUYU ASUI
14
CLASS A: MEZO SHOJI
15
CLASS A: RIKIDO SATO

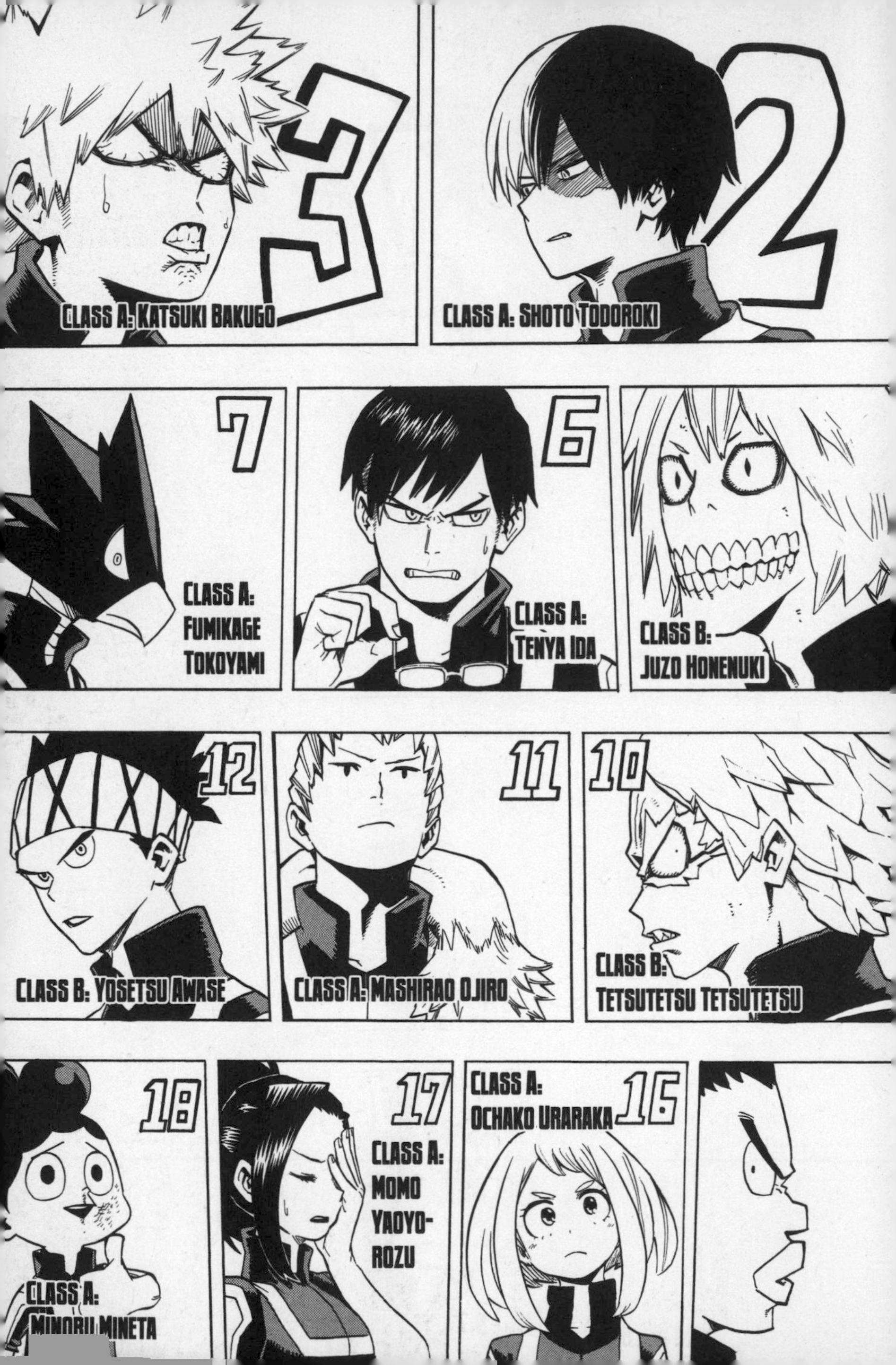
2
CLASS A: SHOTO TODOROKI
3
CLASS A: KATSUKI BAKUGO
CLASS B: JUZO HONENUKI
6
CLASS A: TENYA IDA
7
CLASS A: FUMIKAGE TOKOYAMI
10
CLASS B: TETSUTETSU TETSUTETSU
11
CLASS A: MASHIRAO OJIRO
12
CLASS B: YOSETSU AWASE
CLASS A: OCHAKO URARAKA
16
17
CLASS A: MOMO YAOYO-ROZU
18
CLASS A: MINORU MINETA

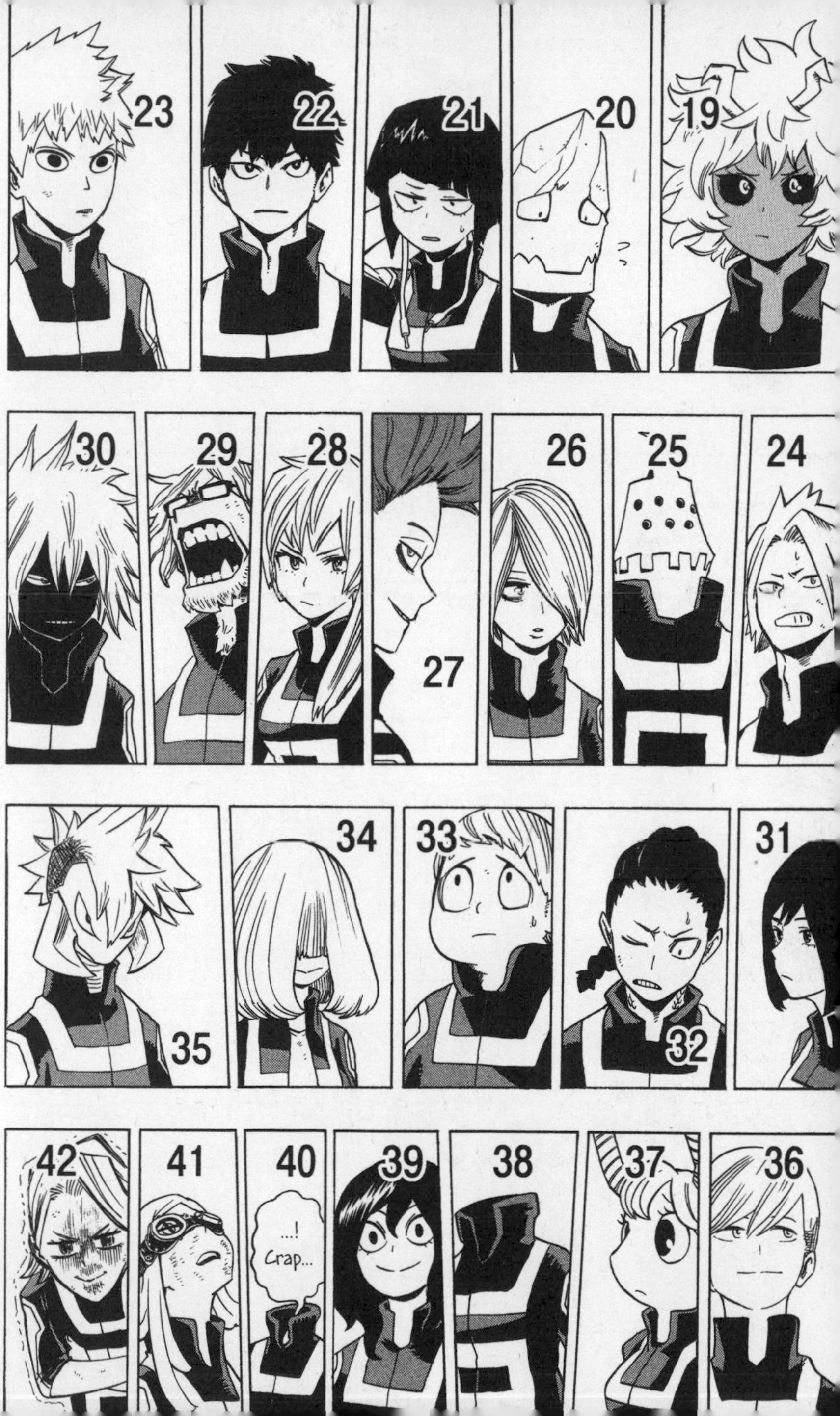

19
20
21
22
23
24
25
26
27
28
29
30
31
32
33
34
35
36
37
38
39
40
...! Crap...
41
42

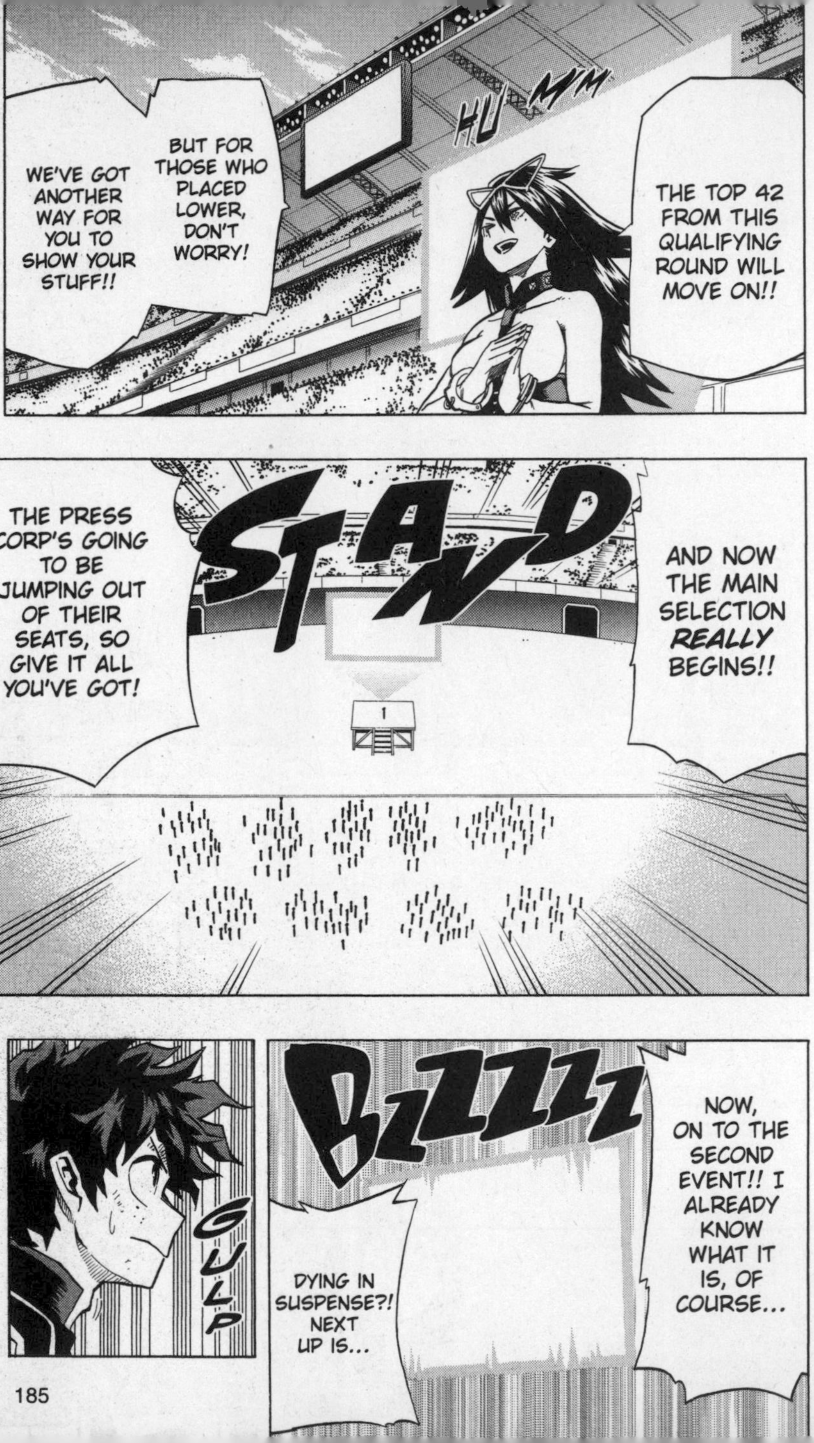
THE TOP 42 FROM THIS QUALIFYING ROUND WILL MOVE ON!!
HUMMM
BUT FOR THOSE WHO PLACED LOWER, DON'T WORRY!
WE'VE GOT ANOTHER WAY FOR YOU TO SHOW YOUR STUFF!!
AND NOW THE MAIN SELECTION *REALLY* BEGINS!!
STAND
THE PRESS CORP'S GOING TO BE JUMPING OUT OF THEIR SEATS, SO GIVE IT ALL YOU'VE GOT!
1
BZZZZ
NOW, ON TO THE SECOND EVENT!! I ALREADY KNOW WHAT IT IS, OF COURSE...
DYING IN SUSPENSE?! NEXT UP IS...
GULP

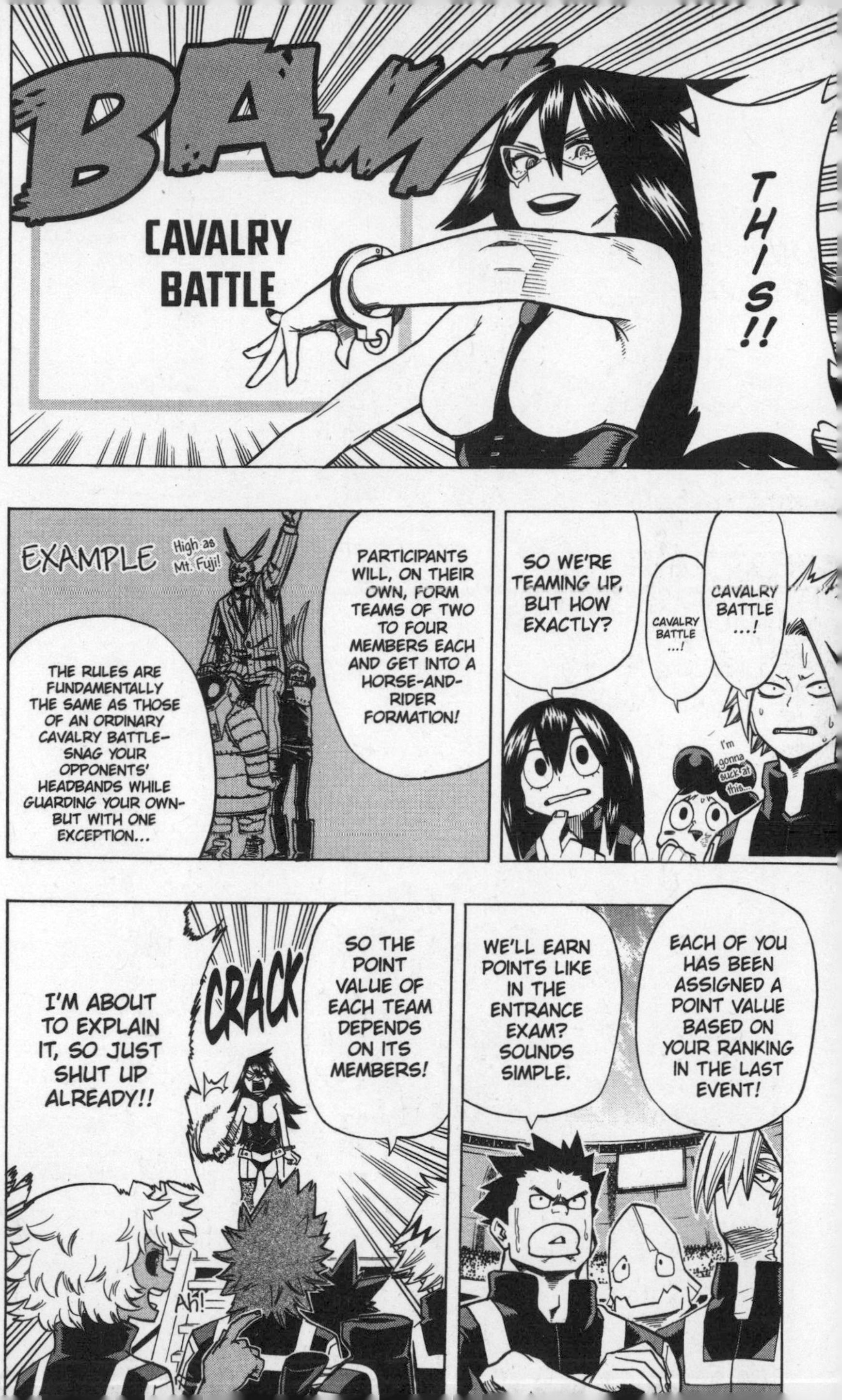
THIS!!
BAM
CAVALRY BATTLE
CAVALRY BATTLE ...!
CAVALRY BATTLE ...!
SO WE'RE TEAMING UP, BUT HOW EXACTLY?
I'm gonna suck at this...
PARTICIPANTS WILL, ON THEIR OWN, FORM TEAMS OF TWO TO FOUR MEMBERS EACH AND GET INTO A HORSE-AND-RIDER FORMATION!
EXAMPLE
High as Mt. Fuji!
THE RULES ARE FUNDAMENTALLY THE SAME AS THOSE OF AN ORDINARY CAVALRY BATTLE-SNAG YOUR OPPONENTS' HEADBANDS WHILE GUARDING YOUR OWN-BUT WITH ONE EXCEPTION...
EACH OF YOU HAS BEEN ASSIGNED A POINT VALUE BASED ON YOUR RANKING IN THE LAST EVENT!
WE'LL EARN POINTS LIKE IN THE ENTRANCE EXAM? SOUNDS SIMPLE.
SO THE POINT VALUE OF EACH TEAM DEPENDS ON ITS MEMBERS!
CRACK
I'M ABOUT TO EXPLAIN IT, SO JUST SHUT UP ALREADY!!
Ah!

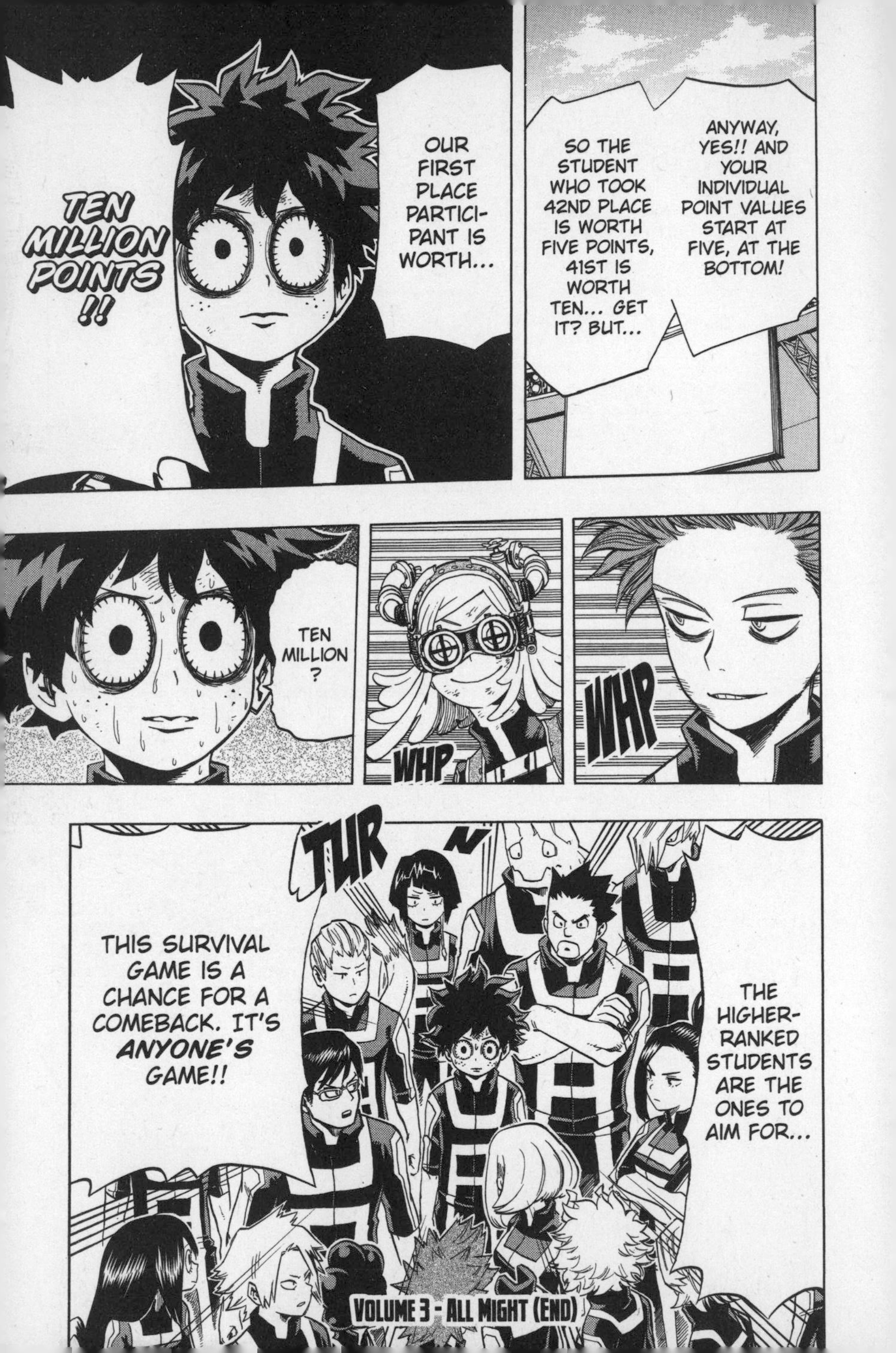
ANYWAY, YES!! AND YOUR INDIVIDUAL POINT VALUES START AT FIVE, AT THE BOTTOM!
SO THE STUDENT WHO TOOK 42ND PLACE IS WORTH FIVE POINTS, 41ST IS WORTH TEN... GET IT? BUT...
OUR FIRST PLACE PARTICI-PANT IS WORTH...
TEN MILLION POINTS!!
WHP
WHP
TEN MILLION?
TURN
THE HIGHER-RANKED STUDENTS ARE THE ONES TO AIM FOR...
THIS SURVIVAL GAME IS A CHANCE FOR A COMEBACK. IT'S *ANYONE'S* GAME!!
VOLUME 3 - ALL MIGHT (END)

BONUS CHAPTER 1

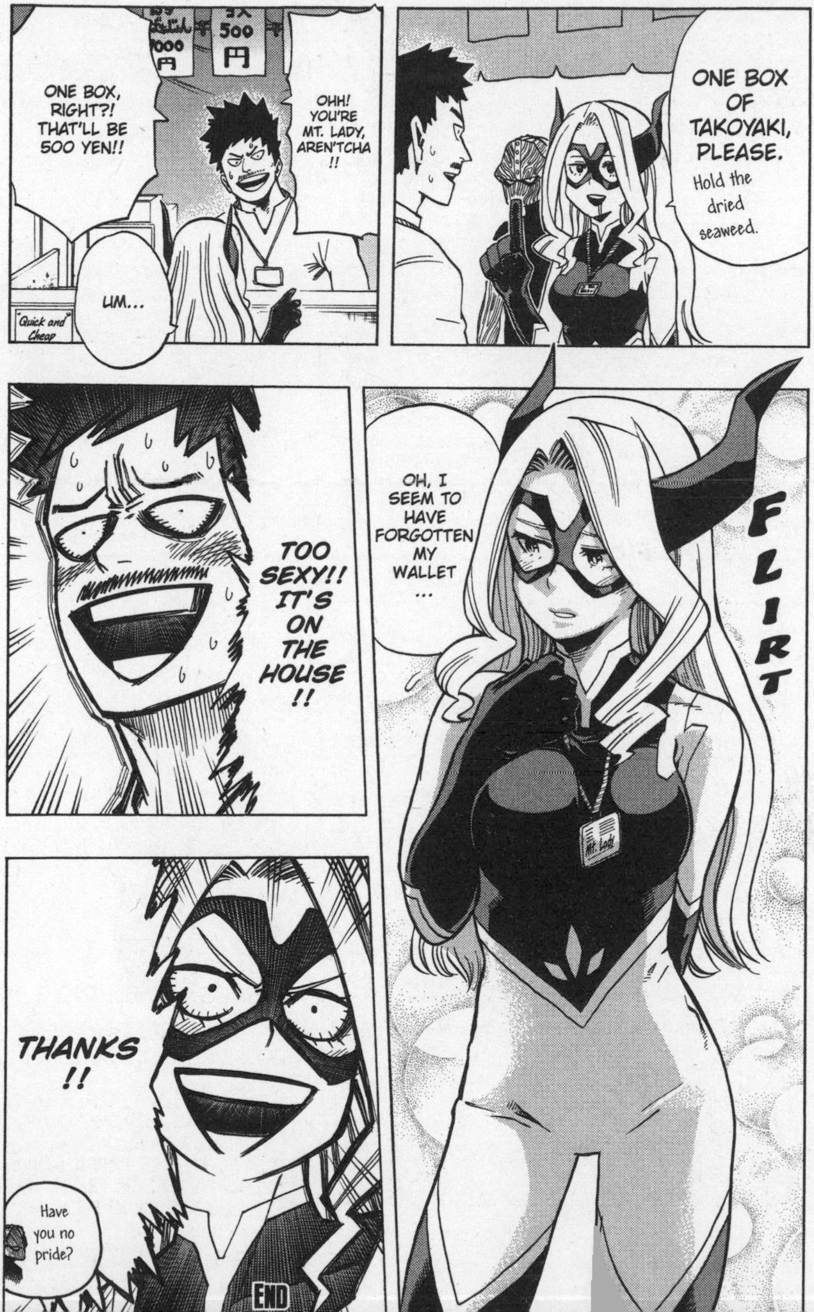
ONE BOX OF TAKOYAKI, PLEASE.
Hold the dried seaweed.
OHH! YOU'RE MT. LADY, AREN'TCHA!!
ONE BOX, RIGHT?! THAT'LL BE 500 YEN!!
UM...
"Quick and" Cheap
FLIRT
OH, I SEEM TO HAVE FORGOTTEN MY WALLET ...
TOO SEXY!! IT'S ON THE HOUSE!!
THANKS!!
Have you no pride?
END

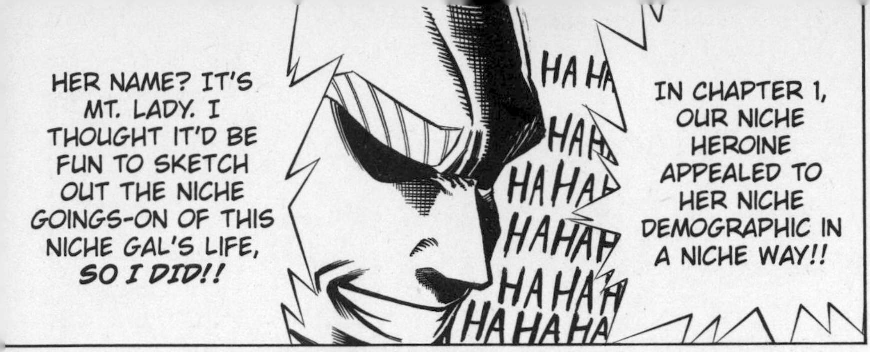
IN CHAPTER 1, OUR NICHE HEROINE APPEALED TO HER NICHE DEMOGRAPHIC IN A NICHE WAY!!
HA HA HA HA HA HA HA HA HA HA HA HA HA HA HA HA HA HA
HER NAME? IT'S MT. LADY. I THOUGHT IT'D BE FUN TO SKETCH OUT THE NICHE GOINGS-ON OF THIS NICHE GAL'S LIFE, SO I DID!!

BONUS CHAPTER 2

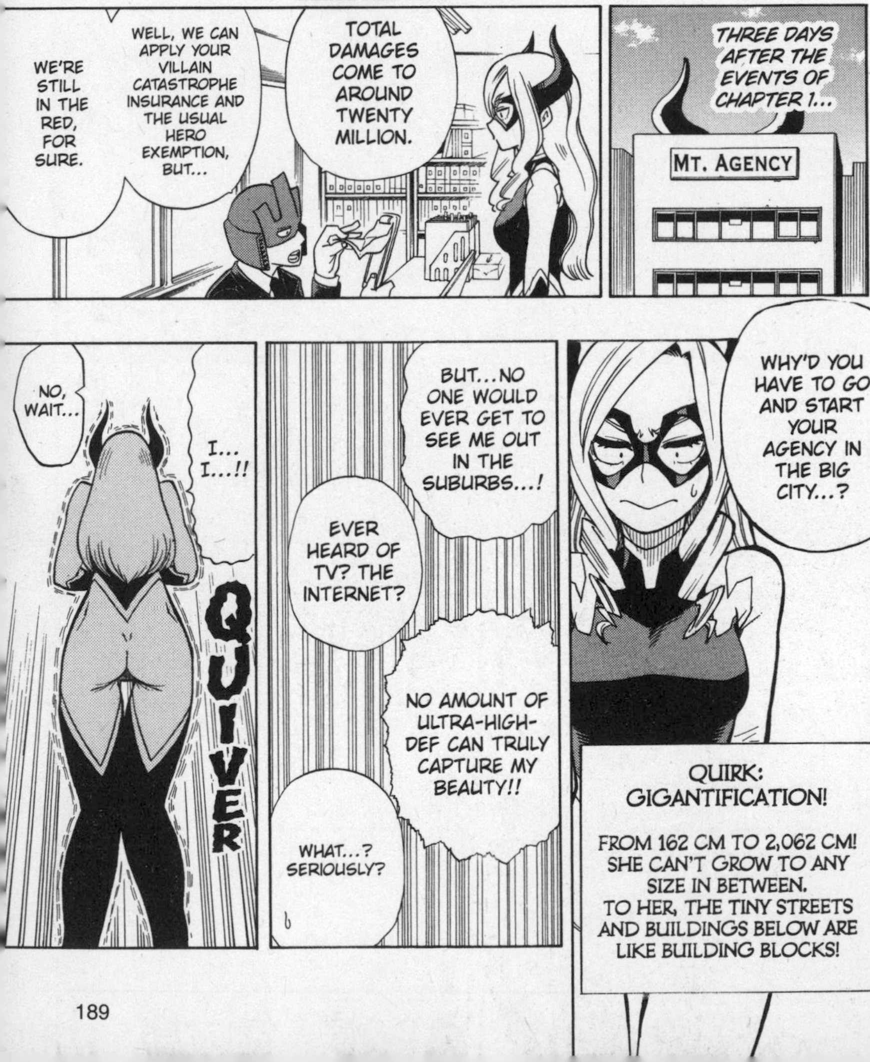
THREE DAYS AFTER THE EVENTS OF CHAPTER 1...
MT. AGENCY
TOTAL DAMAGES COME TO AROUND TWENTY MILLION.
WELL, WE CAN APPLY YOUR VILLAIN CATASTROPHE INSURANCE AND THE USUAL HERO EXEMPTION, BUT...
WE'RE STILL IN THE RED, FOR SURE.
WHY'D YOU HAVE TO GO AND START YOUR AGENCY IN THE BIG CITY...?
QUIRK: GIGANTIFICATION!
FROM 162 CM TO 2,062 CM! SHE CAN'T GROW TO ANY SIZE IN BETWEEN. TO HER, THE TINY STREETS AND BUILDINGS BELOW ARE LIKE BUILDING BLOCKS!
BUT...NO ONE WOULD EVER GET TO SEE ME OUT IN THE SUBURBS...!
EVER HEARD OF TV? THE INTERNET?
NO AMOUNT OF ULTRA-HIGH-DEF CAN TRULY CAPTURE MY BEAUTY!!
WHAT...? SERIOUSLY?
I... I...!!
NO, WAIT...
QUIVER

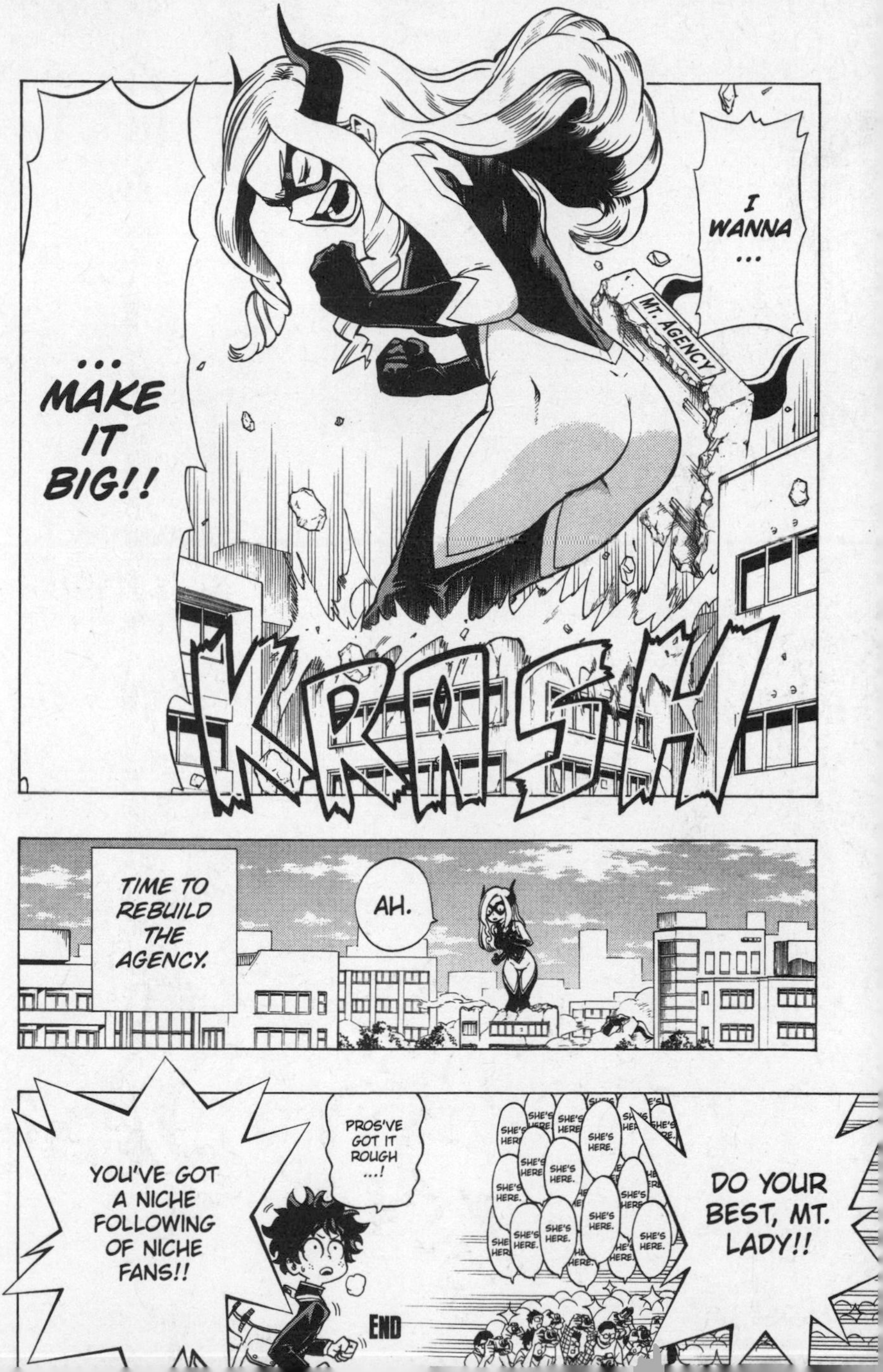
I WANNA ...
MT. AGENCY
... MAKE IT BIG!!
KRASH
AH.
TIME TO REBUILD THE AGENCY.
DO YOUR BEST, MT. LADY!!
SHE'S HERE.
PROS'VE GOT IT ROUGH ...!
YOU'VE GOT A NICHE FOLLOWING OF NICHE FANS!!
END

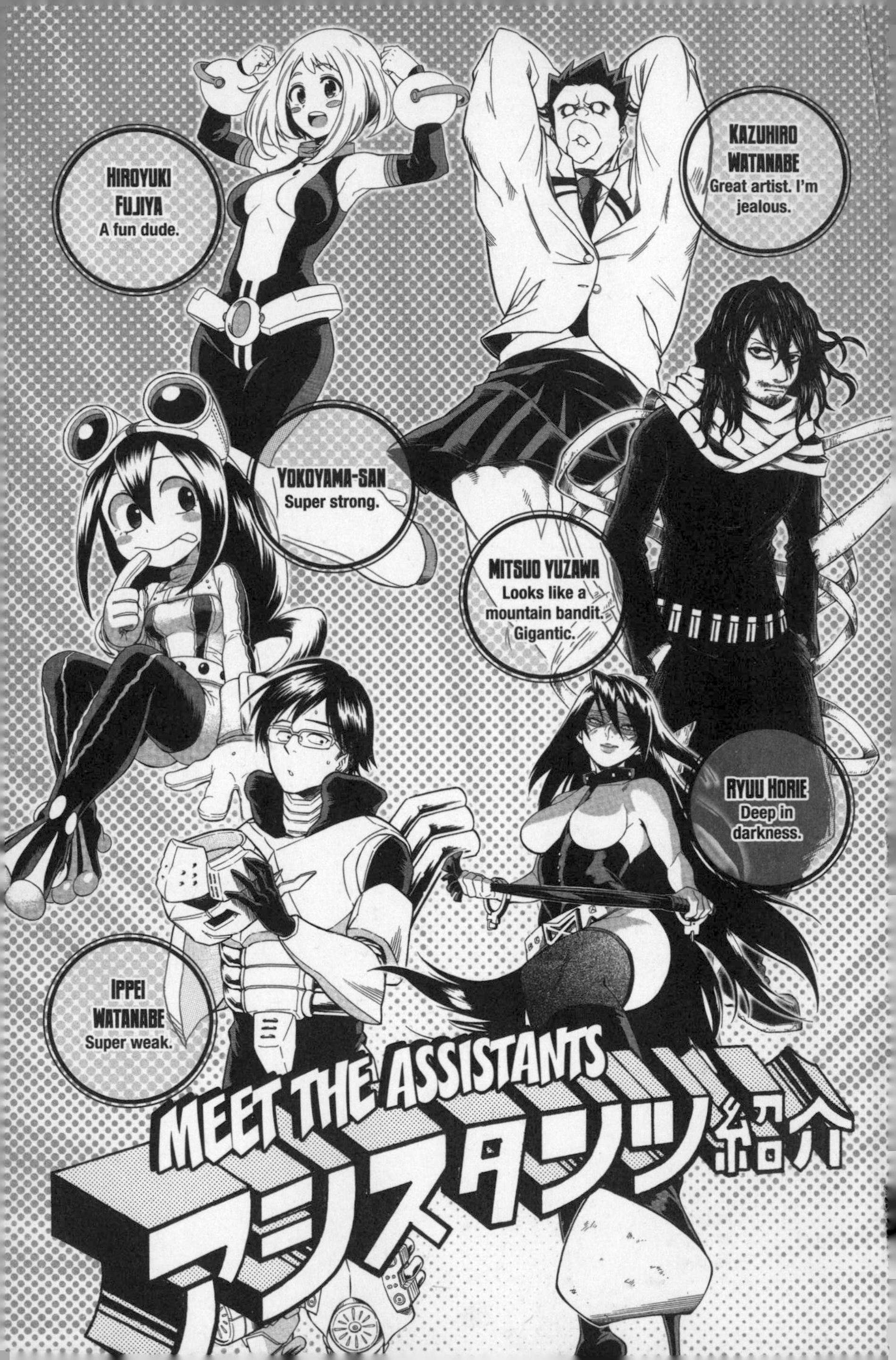

KAZUHIRO WATANABE
Great artist. I'm jealous.
HIROYUKI FUJIYA
A fun dude.
YOKOYAMA-SAN
Super strong.
MITSUO YUZAWA
Looks like a mountain bandit. Gigantic.
RYUU HORIE
Deep in darkness.
IPPEI WATANABE
Super weak.
MEET THE ASSISTANTS
アシスタンツ紹介

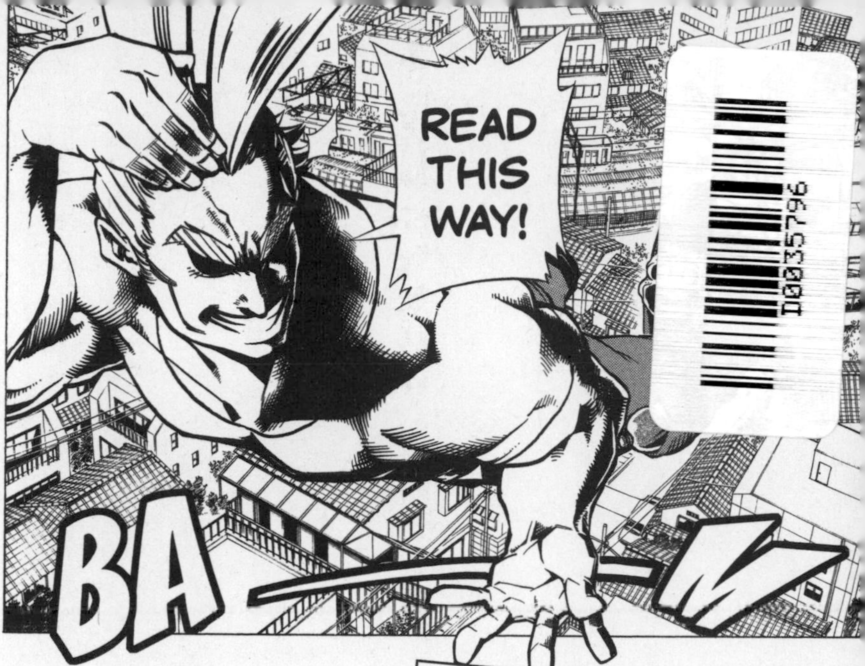
READ THIS WAY!
BA-M

MY HERO ACADEMIA

reads from right to left, starting in the upper-right corner. Japanese is read from right to left, meaning that action, sound effects and word-balloon order are completely reversed from English order.

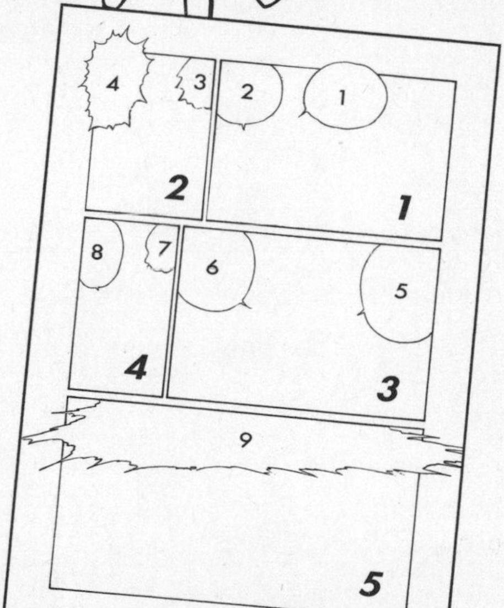
1
2
3
4
5
6
7
8
9
1
2
3
4
5
142